OUR "REG READERS RAVE!

"**G**od bless the *Bathroom Reader*. A lavatory without it is like a Pinto without a bumper: You could use it, but who'd want to?"

—Gregory H., New Jersey

"I love your books! I have lost count of the prizes I have won on radio stations, drawings, and other contests. When I was pregnant, I actually looked forward to those trips to the can, because I knew that you guys would be there to greet me. My husband sometimes thought I got stuck!! Keep up the good work!!!"

—Jen G., Ohio

"You guys write the funniest, most informative books I've ever read! All my friends love the crazy facts and funny stories! Thank you so much for providing the world with something great to do when you're in the loo!"

—Nathaniel Y., Pennsylvania

"I received *Uncle John's All-Purpose Extra Strength Bathroom Reader* for my birthday. I love the book and can't stop reading it. I got it because I always spend a lot of time in the bathroom, never really reading much, just doing a lot of thinking, so my parents decided that it would be a good gift. And for once, they were right. In one month I have learned more than in 12 years at school! Thanks and keep up the good work!"

—Jon P., Pennsylvania

"This book is very useful for people who were not born in America. I got so many information that I needed to know but had no one to ask."

—Seung Sun J., South Korea

"Keep on publishing. I need them. Can't live without them. Help me. I need more. Arggghhhhh..."

—Dan F., California

"It all started with the Bathroom Reader 2000 Desktop Calendar, I couldn't help but skip ahead. Then it was all down the drain from there. I bought the 12th and 13th editions and I'm currently awaiting your next installment. Your articles are great for those with a short attention span like myself."
—*Keith S., Massachusetts*

"Everyone here at Tehachapi, Level 2 Yard, Dorm 2, loves your *Bathroom Readers*."
—*The men at the California Correctional Institution, Tehachapi*

"This past Father's Day I purchased *Uncle John's Great Big Bathroom Reader* for my husband. I can tell he enjoys it very much from the laughter coming from the bathroom in the middle of the night. Last week a local radio station held a contest. The question was, "In the movie *Lords of Flatbush*, how was Sylvester Stallone paid?" My husband remembered reading "25 T-shirts" in your *Bathroom Reader*. He won tickets to go see the Beach Boys in concert, complete with backstage passes! I couldn't believe he won. And all because I bought him a *Bathroom Reader*."
—*Bob and Gloria S., Pennsylvania*

"Just got back from my brother's cottage on Big Hawk Lake near Dorset, Ontario. He had a copy in his bathroom. Once I picked it up it was constantly with me over the next five days, both in and out of the bathroom. Just got home last night and miss the *Bathroom Reader* already. Good thing you included your Web address which led me where I am right now. Can't wait to pick up my own copy."
—*Tony H., Ontario*

"Congratulations on a superb dynasty of reading material and good luck on future editions. Many a leg has been numbed due to the absorbing nature of your Encyclopedia Commodica."
—*Mac J., Virginia*

"To you, dear Uncle John, I place full credit for everything I know."
—*Lauren F., New Jersey*

Uncle John's

Supremely Satisfying Bathroom Reader

The Bathroom Readers' Institute

Bathroom Readers' Press
Ashland, Oregon

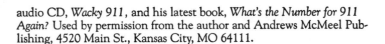

THANK YOU!

The Bathroom Readers' Institute sincerely thanks the people whose advice and assistance made this book possible.

Gordon Javna
John Javna
John Dollison
Jennifer & Zipper
Jeff Altemus
Jay Newman
Sharilyn Hovind
Michael Brunsfeld
Janet Spencer
Dylan Drake
Selene Foster
Eric Stahlman
Erin Keenan
Kim Weimer
Sharon Freed
Lori Larson
Sam Javna
Gideon Javna
Jeff Cheek
Taylor Clark
Jonathan Lee F.
Howard Richler
Matt Marchese
Abby McGowen
Maggie Javna

Allen Orso
Mike Nicita
Georgine Lidell
Bernadette Bailie
Paul Stanley
Randy Apa
Barb Porshe
Paula Leith
JJWPR Gunnels
Samuel Hartstein
David Hartstein
Mustard Press
Project A
Ricky Meatball
Sarah Cribb
Independent Printing Co.
Digital Image Graphics
Bill Zurynetz
Briana Bergman
Andrea Freewater
Liz Stahlman
Thomas Crapper
Porter
Marley & Catie Pratt
Hi to Dee and Kellar!

*　　*　　*

"Truth is stranger than fiction—fiction has to make sense." **—Leo Rosten**

Hiya Sophie! Hiya Jessie!

CONTENTS

NOTE
Because the BRI understands your reading needs, we've
divided the contents by length as well as subject.
Short—a quick read
Medium—2 to 3 pages
Long—for those extended visits, when something
a little more involved is required
*Extended—for those leg-numbing experiences

INTRODUCTION

Greetings once again from the Bathroom Readers' Institute and welcome to the 14th edition of *Uncle John's Bathroom Reader*. We've just finished putting it together and we think this one could be our best ever. It's always hard for us to keep perspective, so we'll let you be the judge.

We like to think that our main goal is to tell stories—about the origins of everyday things; about the histories of people and events forgotten; about topics most of us never even realized had stories. In any edition of the *Bathroom Reader* that's what you'll find and this one is no different.

Here's some of what we've included...

• The fascinating history of photography, the explosive story of volcanoes, and how chocolate evolved from bitter to sweet.

• This season we've focused on the origin of football. Even if you're not a sports fan, you'll love reading the story behind it.

• We have two new categories: A few articles on women inventors turned into a whole section about some of the most amazing women you've never heard of. Then there's a section on Canadiana. To our loyal readers from the Great White North—bet you don't know the history of the Royal Canadian Mounted Police. (It's on page 254.)

•Another first: "Unkle John's Greatest Bloopers," a few of the (gasp!) mistakes we've made over the past 14 years. Hey, we love bloopers, even our own.

• Join the Party! Relive the birth of the two-party system in the United States. It's an enlightening story of idealism versus human nature and the struggle to stand up for what you believe in. This was slated for our next edition, but we were feeling patriotic, so at the last minute we decided to include it.

• For the past three years, we've been promising you the history of the bra, and with this edition we're finally fulfilling our promise.

Finally... Jennifer keeps reminding me to mention the website, mention the website, mention the website. "Jennifer," I keep saying. "None of this shameless promotion(*www.bathroomreader.com*) in the Introduction. If our readers want to find us on the Internet (*www.bathroomreader.com*), they just have to find us on their own."

Oh... one more thing.

Last October, on a plane from L.A. to Newark, a young man and his mother were sitting next to me. We struck up a conversation and pretty soon I was spouting trivia (I can't help it). During a lull in the repartee, the young man said to me, "Hey, have you ever read *Uncle John's Bathroom Readers*? I've got them all." I was speechless (for a moment). All of them? It made me feel great to know that the work we put into these books brings pleasure to so many people. So to all our readers, we just want to say thanks, friends.

Now, as the sun sets here in Ashland, Oregon, remember...

"It's a weird world out there, so keep on flushin'."

And, as always,

Go with the Flow!

Uncle John and the BRI Staff

P.S. Did we mention our website: *www.bathroomreader.com*

YOU'RE MY INSPIRATION

*It's fascinating to see that some of our favorite songs were
inspired by real people. Here are a few examples.*

THE GIRL FROM IPANEMA. In 1962 two Brazillian
songwriters named Antonio Carlos Jobim and Vinicius de
Moraes were sitting in a bar near Ipanema beach. When a
particularly striking woman named Heloisa Pinheiro sashayed past
on her way to the beach, both men let out an "Ahhhhhh." They
did that every day when she walked by. And they wrote a song
about her—"The Girl From Ipanema." It became a huge hit that
put the bossa nova style of Brazillian music on the map.

WONDERFUL TONIGHT. Clapton wrote this song about his
wife, Patti Boyd Harrison. Don't let the title fool you—he intended the song "as an ironic and slightly exasperated comment on the
amount of time she took getting ready to go out."

PEGGY SUE. The song by Buddy Holly and the Crickets was
originally called "Cindy Lou"...until Crickets drummer Jerry
Allison asked Holly to rename it so that he could impress his
girlfriend Peggy Sue Rackham. It worked—Peggy Sue and Jerry
eloped a year later, prompting Holly to follow up with "Peggy
Sue Got Married." She recently appeared in a *Hot Rod* magazine
layout alongside Buddy Holly's Chevy Impala.

MY SHARONA. In 1978 Doug Fieger met a 17-year-old high
school senior named Sharona Alperin. He fell in love; she didn't.
He pursued her for more than a year, writing "My Sharona," an
ode to his sexual frustration. Four months after the song was written, Sharona finally came around. She and Fieger got engaged...
but never married. Feiger's group, The Knack, made the song a
#1 hit in 1979. Today Sharona sells Beverly Hills real estate—and
isn't above letting her upscale customers know she is the inspiration for the song.

Martin Van Buren was the first U.S. president actually born in the United States.

COURT TRANSQUIPS

*We're back with one of our regular features. Check
out this real-life exchange—it was actually said
in court, and recorded word for word.*

Clerk: "Please repeat after me: 'I swear by Almighty God…'"

Witness: "I swear by Almighty God."

Clerk: "That the evidence that I give…"

Witness: "That's right."

Clerk: "Repeat it."

Witness: "Repeat it."

Clerk: "No! Repeat what I said."

Witness: "What you said when?"

Clerk: "That the evidence that I give…"

Witness: "That the evidence that I give."

Clerk: "Shall be the truth and…"

Witness: "It will, and nothing but the truth!"

Clerk: "Please, just repeat after me: 'Shall be the truth and…'"

Witness: "I'm not a scholar, you know."

Clerk: "We can appreciate that. Just repeat after me: 'Shall be the truth and…'"

Witness: "Shall be the truth and."

Clerk: "Say: 'Nothing…'"

Witness: "Okay." (Witness remains silent.)

Clerk: "No! Don't say nothing. Say: 'Nothing but the truth…'"

Witness: "Yes."

Clerk: "Can't you say: 'Nothing but the truth?'"

Witness: "Yes."

Clerk: "Well? Do so."

Witness: "You're confusing me."

Clerk: "Just say: 'Nothing but the truth.'"

Witness: "Is that all?"

Clerk: "Yes."

Witness: "Okay. I understand."

Clerk: "Then say it."

Witness: "What?"

Clerk: "Nothing but the truth…"

Witness: "But I do! That's just it."

Clerk: "You must say: 'Nothing but the truth.'"

Witness: "I WILL say nothing but the truth!"

Clerk: "Please, just repeat these four words: 'Nothing.' 'But.' 'The.' 'Truth.'"

Witness: "What? You mean, like, now?"

Clerk: "Yes! Now. Please. Just say those four words."

Witness: "Nothing. But. The. Truth."

Clerk: "Thank you."

Witness: "I'm just not a scholar."

When the ground temperature is below freezing, it can't hail.

FOUNDING FATHERS

You already know the names. Here's who they belong to.

JOYCE C. HALL

Background: Hall started out selling picture postcards from a shoe box, but soon realized that greeting cards with envelopes would be more profitable.

Famous Name: He started a new company, Hallmark Cards, a play on his name and the word for quality, and in 1916 produced his first card. But the innovation that made Hallmark so successful had little to do with the cards themselves—it was their display cases. Previously, cards were purchased by asking a clerk to choose an appropriate one. Hall introduced display cases featuring rows of cards that the customer could browse through. When he died in 1982, the company he founded in a shoebox was worth $1.5 billion.

ORVILLE GIBSON

Background: In 1881 Gibson got a job working in a shoe store in Kalamazoo, Michigan, but in his spare time, he built musical instruments from wood.

Famous Name: The instruments were so popular that he quit the shoe store, and in 1902 he incorporated the Gibson Mandolin and Guitar Company. Gibson died in 1918, two years before a Gibson employee invented a microphone that would fit inside the guitar, creating a prototype of the electric guitar.

BENJAMIN FRANKLIN GOODRICH

Background: Goodrich was a surgeon in the Union Army, but when the bloody Civil War ended, he gave up medicine. In 1870 he bought the failing Hudson River Rubber Company and moved it from New York to Akron, Ohio, where it thrived.

Famous Name: In Akron, he produced his first actual product, a fire hose. The company went on to invent vinyl, synthetic rubber, and the first tubeless automobile tire, but not before changing its name to the B.F. Goodrich Company.

DAVID PACKARD

Background: David Packard was an engineer with the General Electric Company. In 1938 he moved to California, where he renewed a friendship with William Hewlett. The two went into the electronics business, making oscillators that were smaller, cheaper, and better than anything else on the market.

Famous Name: Working from a small garage in Palo Alto, the Hewlett-Packard company earned $1,000 that first year. Today the garage is a state landmark: "The Birthplace of Silicon Valley." Packard died in 1996 leaving an estate worth billions.

RICHARD WARREN SEARS

Background: In 1886 Richard Sears managed a railroad office in rural Minnesota. As station agent, he had the opportunity to buy an unclaimed shipment of gold watches. He quickly sold them all...then ordered more. He sold those, too, then took his $5,000 in profits and moved to Chicago.

Famous Name: Sears advertised for a watchmaker; the ad was answered by Alva Curtis Roebuck. Within two years they were partners, selling their wares via a mail-order catalog under the name...Sears, Roebuck & Co.

PAUL ORFALEA

Background: After graduating from the University of California at Santa Barbara, Orfalea opened a small copy shop next to a taco stand in nearby Isla Vista, starting with a single copy machine.

Famous Name: Business was brisk. He soon expanded the store, then branched out to the rest of California, and then all over the country. And all the stores bore his name, the nickname he got in college because of his curly red hair...Kinko's.

JAMES BEAUREGARD BEAM

Background: Beam was running the distillery founded by his great-grandfather, Jacob Beam, until 1920, when the Volstead Act made the sale of alcoholic beverages illegal and he had to close the place down.

Famous Name: When Prohibition was repealed in 1933, he celebrated by building a new distillery and introducing a new bourbon, which he named for himself...Jim Beam.

A bird's eyes, unlike human eyes, keep everything in focus at all times.

OOPS!

Everyone enjoys reading about someone else's blunders.
So go ahead and feel superior for a few minutes.

CHUTE!

"Twenty-year-old Mie Larsen was enjoying a Sunday tennis match with her boyfriend in Guildford, Surrey, when a British Army parachutist accidentally landed on her and knocked out her teeth. Parachutist Sgt. Gary Bird of the Royal Artillery display team was supposed to land a quarter of a mile away. 'I was in the middle of a game when I suddenly heard somebody shout, "Watch out!"' said Larsen. 'I saw this man coming straight at me, feet first, at high speed.' She tried to run out of the way but became trapped in the net, and Sergeant Bird landed on her back. Larsen, who suffered a fractured wrist, cuts, and bruises in addition to the broken teeth, plans to sue the Ministry of Defense."

—**"The Edge,"** *The Oregonian*

PU-U-USH

BIRCHINGTON, England—"A 31-year-old woman had to be rescued by firemen after getting stuck in a dog flap. She and a friend were coming back from a late-night party and stopped at a friend's house where the pair were supposed to be dog-sitting. After discovering that the house keys were lost, she attempted to get in the house via the doggie door. She managed to squeeze the top half of her body through the opening, but her bottom half proved to be more tricky.

"According to Officer Dave Coker, 'We tried pushing on her backside and pulling her by the thighs but we couldn't budge her. In the end we had to take out the complete plastic frame and cut her free.' After the rescue, the woman explained she was desperate to get into the house because the dogs inside were barking loudly."

—*Bizarre News*

DRIVE, HE SAID

LITTLETON, Colo.—"Mamileti Lakshmihart put himself in 'double jeopardy' after he backed his truck into the same patrol

---

The average car has 15,000 parts.

car that had pulled him over. After being given a warning, the 36-year-old became confused when he went to pull away and put his truck into reverse. The vehicle jerked backward and smashed the front of the patrol car, doing more than $1,000 in damage. Lakshmihart received a summons for careless driving."

—*Bizarre News*

FINDERS KEEPERS

NEW YORK—"The money came from all over—Italy, France, Turkey—intended for a United Nations environmental fund. But the $700,000 ended up in the account of a Brooklyn woman, who quit her job and spent much of the extra money before the bank noticed the error and froze the account.

"Now Susan Madakor, 40, a single mother who lives in public housing, is fighting to get the money back. She went to court last week to ask a judge to grant her the money instead of the U.N.

"The windfall showed up as 13 wire transfers from various countries between February and October 1998. Chase Manhattan Bank said the foreign governments used an account number with one incorrect digit. Madakor quit her $23,000-a-year job at a textile company and bought a laundry business for $100,000, set up a college fund for her 10-year-old son, paid off $30,000 in credit card debt, furnished a new apartment, and leased a van. She was negotiating to buy a liquor store when Chase discovered the mistake."

—*Anchorage Daily News*

"BUT I HAVE A LICENSE"

KALAMAZOO, Mich.—"Frank S. is the proud owner of a 1958 Edsel Corsair. However, this automobile's most unique feature, the push-button transmission, is also its most dangerous. Frank was about to take his dog, Buddy, to the store with him when he got out of the car to get something from the house. As he walked around the car, the dog stood up against the dashboard and hit the push button, putting the car in drive and pinning Frank's legs between the bumper and garage door. He was trapped for 20 minutes until his wife came home and heard him yelling for help. Amazingly, Frank suffered only bruising on both legs. The dog is no longer allowed in the car."

—*Bizarre News*

A stack of one trillion new dollar bills would be 69,000 miles high.

PELE'S CURSE

Thinking of visiting Hawaii? Make sure that photos and memories are all you take home with you. Pele's watching...

BETWEEN A ROCK AND A HARD PLACE

Thousands of tourists visit Hawaii's scenic Volcanoes National Park every year, and every year a little bit of the park leaves with them. Many visitors can't resist taking a few of the park's unique lava rocks or a handful of dark black sand as a reminder of their visit to the island. No harm done, right?

Try telling that to Timothy Murray, one of many who have suffered terrible luck since taking home a memento from the park. "My life literally fell apart," says Murray, 32, who naively scooped black sand into a pop bottle during a 1997 trip.

Upon returning home to Florida, Murray's luck took a sharp turn for the worse: He lost his job. His fiancée dumped him without warning. He began hitting the bottle. His pet died. FBI agents—who had received a tip from someone *in Hawaii*—arrested him for a minor computer copyright infringement violation. "The FBI agents said they never arrest people for what I did," says Murray. "They told me, 'You really must have pissed someone off.' After some research, I figured out who it was."

It was Pele.

LEGEND HAS IT...

Here's the legend: Of all the deities in Hawaiian lore, the most well known—and most feared—is Pele, the fiery-tempered volcano goddess who Hawaiians believe created their islands. Pele is the daughter of the Earth goddess Haumea. According to myth, Pele spent most of her youth learning to make and control fire. But she was wild and the sea goddess, Namaka, was the one who had to put out her mistakes. Haumea knew that Namaka would hunt Pele down and punish her, so she sent Pele to find a secluded home, where she could make as much fire as she pleased without disturbing anyone. Pele chose Hawaii—then only a tiny atoll—which she made to rise out of the sea in a storm of volcanic activity. But Namaka tracked Pele down and confronted her. Fire and water

Q: What was the first tropical storm named after a male? A: Bud.

clashed in a violent brawl. Namaka got the upper hand and banished Pele to Hawaii's volcanoes forever.

The hot-tempered goddess jealously guards her domain and takes out her anger at Namaka on the hapless humans who dare cross her. Hawaiians say that before every major eruption, Pele appears as a withered old woman walking along remote back roads. Those who pass her by find their homes destroyed by hot magma. However, those who offer her a ride find that a river of molten lava has stopped inches from their property. Many park visitors have reported meeting an old woman who asks for a cigarette, lights it with a snap of her fingers, and then vanishes mysteriously. Though Pele may like to tease humans playfully at times, she is dead serious about one thing: don't steal her property, or else.

HAWAIIAN PUNCH

The stories of Pele's revenge on the tourists who make off with her rocks are many. Since pinching a few rocks, Denver business owner Larry Bell has needed emergency heart surgery, had his marriage nearly fall apart, seen his daughter plagued by mysterious heath problems, and had to relocate his business. One Los Angeles lava thief who was building a house watched helplessly as her basement floor caved in, her interior walls bent peculiarly, a worker drove a nail through his wrist, and her father-in-law fell off the roof and broke several ribs—all in the weeks following her return from the park.

According to such "victims," Pele in her wrath has made cars break down, brought down stock prices, torn Achilles tendons, and even steered lawnmowers over toes.

HOMEWARD BOUND

Can this horrible luck be reversed? Every day, shipments of contraband lava rocks, shells, and even old shoes filled with sand are delivered anonymously to the post offices and park stations around Volcanoes National Park. The packages come from all over the world, sometimes containing debris taken from the park decades earlier. Some former visitors are so terrified of Pele's curse that they return to the park in person just to make sure that their rocks are put back in the exact spot they were taken from. One letter contained a single grain of sand, which the writer found in the cuff of a pair of pants he had worn while walking on the beach. In another letter, addressed to "Queen Pele, Hawaii," the writer's plea was simple: "Oh, please stop punishing me!"

ROAD TO RECOVERY

Most park rangers insist that there is no curse of Pele, that it's only natural that a small percentage of the many people who go through the park every year will suffer some misfortune after leaving. The rangers claim that the practice of returning rocks is culturally insensitive and a waste of their time.

But there's no fooling Timothy Murray. "You may have your doubts about Pele," he says. "But let me tell you, when these things happen, you are willing to be on your knees in front of anyone or anything. Since I sent the sand back, I've started getting my life back. That's all I know." Murray's message to future park visitors: Beware Pele's wrath. Leave the rocks alone.

*   *   *

AMAZING LUCK

In 1829, four days out of Sydney, Australia, a heavy storm struck the vessel *Mermaid*, and drove it into a reef. All 22 on board jumped ship and swam to a large rock. After three days of waiting, another ship, the *Swiftsure*, found and rescued them. Five days later another storm struck. The *Swiftsure* was swept into a ridge and wrecked. Both crews escaped and waited for rescue on some nearby rocks. They were soon picked up by the schooner *Governor Ready*, which caught fire three hours later. Once again they abandoned ship, this time in lifeboats. Along came the cutter *Comet*, which had been blown off course by a storm. The crew of the *Comet* loaded the crews and passengers of all three vessels on board. Five days later a storm snapped the *Comet's* mast, ripped her sails, and ruined her rudder. The *Comet's* crew loaded into the longboat, leaving the passengers to cling to floating bits of wreckage. After 18 hours passed the mail boat *Jupiter* came along and rescued everyone, only to hit a reef and sink two days later. Fortunately, the passenger vessel *City of Leeds* was nearby and picked up everyone, finally delivering them back to Sydney. The doomed voyage sank five ships, but incredibly not a single life was lost.

A New Yorker could eat out every night of their life and never eat at the same restaurant twice.

LET ME WRITE SIGN— I SPEAK ENGLISH GOOD

When signs in a foreign country are in English, any combination of words is possible. Here are some real-life examples.

On the grass in a Paris park: "Please do not be a dog."

Outside a Hong Kong dress shop: "Ladies have fits upstairs."

A sign posted in Germany's Black Forest: "It is strictly forbidden on our Black Forest camping site that people of different gender, for instance men and women, live together in one tent unless they are married with each other for that purpose."

At a Belgrade hotel: "Restauroom open daily."

Outside an Athens shop: "Park one hour. Later dick dock goes the money clock."

In a Rome hotel room: "Please dial 7 to retrieve your auto from the garbage."

In menu in Nepal: "Complimentary glass wine or bear."

In a Paris guidebook: "To call a broad from France, first dial 00, then the country's code and then your number."

In a Tokyo rental car: "When passenger of foot heave in sight, tootle the horn. Trumpet him melodiously at first, but if he still obstacles your passage then tootle him with vigor."

Detour sign in Japan: "Stop: Drive Sideways"

At a Seoul hotel desk: "Choose twin bed or marriage size; we regret no King Kong size."

In a Chinese menu: "Cold Shredded Children and Sea Blubber in Spicy Sauce"

On packaging for a kitchen knife in Korea: "Warning: Keep out of children."

On an Italian train: "Water not potatoble."

Good start: A one-day-old antelope can run 23 mph.

WORD ORIGINS

Ever wonder where these words come from?
Here are the interesting stories behind them.

MAYDAY

Meaning: A distress signal

Origin: "Mayday!—the international radio distress signal—has nothing to do with the first of May. It represents the pronunciation of the French *m'aider*, 'help me,' or the latter part of the phrase *venez m'aider*, 'come help me.'" (From *Word Mysteries & Histories*, by the editors of The American Heritage Dictionaries)

CASTLE

Meaning: A large building, usually of the medieval period, fortified as a stronghold

Origin: "*Castle* was one of the earliest words adopted by the British from their Norman conquerors. Originally hailing from the Latin *castellum* (diminutive of *castrum*, 'fort'), it reminds us that Old English also acquired *castrum*, still present in such place-names as Doncaster and Winchester. From Old French's *chastel* (a version of *castel*) came the word *château* (circumflex accent marking the lost 's')." (From *The Secret Lives of Words*, by Paul West)

CARTEL

Meaning: A combination of businesses formed to regulate prices, or of political interest groups in order to promote a particular cause or legislation

Origin: "The word comes from the Italian *cartello*. In the 16th century it meant a written challenge to a duel. In the 17th century it came to mean an agreement between warring nations concerning the exchange of prisoners of war. In the 20th century it acquired its meaning of an association of producers who seek to obtain monopoly advantages for their members.

"Today the term refers chiefly to international associations seeking to control a world market by setting prices, restricting production, or allocating sales territories among their members." (From *Fighting Words*, by Christine Ammer)

Men of few words: 20 of the first 30 U.S. presidents did not have middle names.

GARGANTUAN

Meaning: Gigantic, colossal

Origin: "The legend of a giant named *Gargantua* had existed in French folklore for at least a century before François Rabelais wrote his masterpiece, *Gargantua and Pantagruel*, in 1532. Just before the giantess Gargamelle gave birth to Gargantua she consumed sixteen large casks, two barrels, and six jugs full of tripe. Emerging from his mother's left ear, he proceeded to cry, 'Give me a drink! a drink! a drink!' Given the enormous size of Gargantua and everything that surrounds him, it is no wonder that from his name the adjective was formed." (From *Inventing English: The Imaginative Origins of Everyday Expressions*, by Dale Corey)

SLOGAN

Meaning: A short, memorable phrase

Origin: "All slogans, whether they be catchy advertising phrases or the rallying cries of political parties, are direct descendants of Gaelic battle cries. The word itself derives from the *sluagh-ghairm* (the battle cry of the Gaels). Gaelic soldiers repeated these cries, usually the name of their clan or clan leader, in unison as they advanced against an enemy. Over the years the word came to describe any catchy phrase inducing people to support a cause or a commercial product." (From *The Facts on File Encyclopedia of Word and Phrase Origins*, by Robert Hendrickson)

MIGRAINE

Meaning: A severe recurring headache

Origin: "Migraine had its beginning as a word in the Greco-Latin parts *hemi-*, 'half,' and *cranium*, 'skull,' which is descriptive of the violent headache that attacks one-half of the head." (From *Word Origins*, by Wilfred Funk)

PALACE

Meaning: An official residence of royalty or a high dignitary

Origin: "The word comes through Old French from the Latin *Palatium*, the name of the Palatine hill in Rome, where the house of the emperor (Augustus) was situated." (From *The Oxford Dictionary of Phrase and Fable*)

Ukulele means "jumping flea" in Hawaiian.

FAMOUS FOR 15 MINUTES

Here's proof that Andy Warhol was right when he said that "in the future, everyone will be famous for 15 minutes."

THE STAR: Steven Thoburn, a greengrocer in Sunderland, England

THE HEADLINE: *In for a Penny, In for a Pound: Brits Chip in to Help Greengrocer Fight the System—The Metric System*

WHAT HAPPENED: In July 2001, a woman walked into Thoburn's market stall and asked for a pound of bananas, so Thoburn sold her a pound of bananas. Not long afterward, his stall was raided by agents of the Sunderland city council, who charged him with refusing to convert from pounds and ounces to the metric system as required by the European Union. He was later convicted of two counts of violating the Weights and Measures Act of 1985 and sentenced to six months' probation.

By that point the court costs had climbed to more than £75,000. The Sunderland council promised not to sue for court costs unless Thoburn appealed his conviction and lost. Fearing bankruptcy, he agreed to give up the fight.

THE AFTERMATH: Thoburn's case resonated with British citizens who feared losing their autonomy—not to mention their their traditional pints of ale, pints of milk, and even the country mile— to unelected bureaucrats in the European Union. Supporters raised more than £100,000 for a defense fund, prompting Thoburn to resume his appeal. At last report, he's still fighting his conviction. "All I did was sell a pound of bananas to a woman who asked for a pound of bananas," he says. "What's wrong with that?"

THE STAR: Lisa Gebhart, a 25-year-old fundraiser for the Democratic Party

THE HEADLINE: *Pushy White House Intern Proves a Picture is Worth a Thousand Words and Then Some*

WHAT HAPPENED: In 1996 Gebhart went to a fundraiser for

then-President Bill Clinton. She wanted to shake hands with the president, so she made her way up to the front of the rope line just as he was approaching. "I was all beaming," she says, "just ten feet away from him. Then someone pushed me from behind, trying to get in there, very rude....I had seen Monica Lewinsky around, but I didn't know her. She couldn't wait to get to Clinton." Lewinsky got a hug; all Gebhart got was a handshake.

When news of Clinton's affair with Lewinsky broke in 1998, footage of the 1996 hug, with a smiling Gebhart standing next to Lewinsky, became one of the most famous images of the Clinton presidency.

THE AFTERMATH: By the time the scandal broke, Gebhart had met a Welshman named Dean Longhurst over the Internet and was communicating with him by e-mail. Longhurst asked what Gebhart looked like. "I e-mailed him, 'Watch the news.'"

"When I saw her in real life," Longhurst told reporters in April 2001, "I thought she was even more beautiful." The two eventually met, fell in love, and got married.

THE STAR: Clint Hallam, a 48-year-old New Zealand man who lost his right hand in an "industrial accident"

THE HEADLINE: *Man Takes Hands-Off Approach to Hands-On Surgery; Still, You've Got to Hand It to Doctors for Trying*

WHAT HAPPENED: Hallam made medical history in September 1998 when a team of microsurgeons in Lyons, France, successfully attached the right forearm of a dead Frenchman to his right arm, replacing the forearm he claimed to have lost in an industrial accident a few years earlier. It was the world's first successful hand transplant. Bonus: Because the surgery was so experimental, the surgery and a lifetime supply of anti-rejection drugs were provided free.

Hallam qualified for the groundbreaking surgery following months of interviews and psychological testing. He was evaluated to determine not just whether he was emotionally capable of living with another man's hand attached to his body, but also whether he was likely to stick to the rigorous physical and drug regimens necessary to prevent his body from rejecting the forearm.

But the battery of tests failed to reveal that Hallam was lying about his "industrial job accident"—he was actually an ex-con and

The diamond is the only gem composed of a single element (carbon).

lost the limb in a chainsaw accident he suffered while serving time for fraud. He also turned out to be spectacularly unsuited for the surgery.

Hallam's new hand progressed to the point that he could write with it, hold a fork, and feel temperatures and pain. But then he went off his anti-rejection drugs and stopped coming in for checkups.

THE AFTERMATH: Hallam's body rejected his hand, and on February 2, 2001, he had to have it surgically removed. (The second surgery wasn't free: Hallum had to pay $4,000.) Says Dr. Nadey Hakim, "We gave him the chance of a lifetime and he ruined it."

THE STAR: "Two-Ton" Tony Galento, a saloon bouncer and professional boxer who lived in Orange, New Jersey, in the late 1930s

THE HEADLINE: *Two-Ton Tony Flattens the Champ*

WHAT HAPPENED: Two-Ton Tony wasn't much of a boxer; at 5'9", 240 pounds with a shape like a beer barrel, about all he was good at was throwing clumsy—but powerful—left hooks. His training technique consisted of sitting in the bar of New York's Plaza Hotel with his girlfriend and consuming huge quantities of beer, pasta, and cigars while his sparring partners jogged the footpaths of Central Park without him. "Why should I pay dem punks all dat money," he explained, "and then go out and run in the rain myself?"

His brush with the big time came in 1939, when he was inexplicably signed to fight Joe Louis in a championship bout at Yankee Stadium. "I'll moider da bum," Two-Ton Tony predicted. Needless to say, Louis was as shocked as everybody else when Two-Ton Tony clocked him with a haymaker early in the fight and laid him out flat on the canvas. The blow turned out to be little more than a wakeup call, however: Louis quickly made it back to his feet and proceeded to beat Two-Ton Tony so savagely that frightened ringsiders begged the referee to stop the fight, which he finally did in the fourth round. It took 23 stitches to close the cuts on Galento's face and healing his wounded pride took even more effort. For years afterward he blamed the referee for ending the fight "just when tings was goin' my way."

THE AFTERMATH: Two-Ton Tony fought 114 fights between 1929 and 1944 and won 82 of them. In 1947, by then up to 275 pounds, he turned to professional wrestling. His fans had not forgotten him—he sold out his first wrestling fight, and more than 2,000 people had to be turned away. He died in 1979.

The first person to wear silk stockings: England's Queen Elizabeth I. They were a gift.

VIVA VIDAL

Wry observations from Gore Vidal, one of America's greatest authors and most savvy satirists.

"A good deed never goes unpunished."

"Since no one can ever know for certain whether or not his own view of life is the correct one, it is absolutely impossible for him to know if someone else's is the wrong one."

"Half of the American people never read a newspaper. Half never voted for president. One hopes it is the same half."

"'I just sort of drifted into it.' That's almost always the explanation for everything."

"Before the cards that one is dealt by life are the cards that fate has dealt. One's family."

"Any American who is prepared to run for president should automatically be disqualified from ever doing so."

"There is no such thing as a true account of anything."

"There is no human problem which could not be solved if people would simply do as I advise."

"It is not enough to succeed. Others must fail."

"I have found that there is no attitude so bizarre that one will not encounter it sooner or later if one travels far enough."

"A narcissist is someone better looking than you are."

"Most lives are spent putting on and taking off masks."

"Those who have not undergone minor disasters are being held in reserve for something major."

"I have always found men quite fathomable. They look entirely to their own interest."

"One's neighbor is always the enemy. That is the nature of things."

FLUBBED HEADLINES

*These are 100% honest-to-goodness headlines. Can
you figure out what they were trying to say?*

Raleigh, N.C., Lays
Down Law: Two Pigs Per
Household

*DR. TACKETT GIVES
TALK ON MOON*

**CHOU REMAINS
CREMATED**

Mauling by Bear Leaves
Woman Grateful for Life

PLO INVITED TO RAID DEBATES

*Louisiana Governor Defends
His Wife, Gift from Korean*

ROBBER HOLDS UP
ALBERT'S HOSIERY

***New housing for elderly not
yet dead***

SILENT TEAMSTER GETS
CRUEL PUNISHMENT:
LAWYER

Greeks Fine Hookers

Council spits on shade tree
appointment

***FEDERAL AGENTS RAID GUN
SHOP, FIND WEAPONS***

TUNA BITING OFF
WASHINGTON COAST

*Connie Tied, Nude Policeman
Testifies*

Shouting match ends teacher's
hearing

DEATH ROW INMATE SEEKS
DIVORCE

*MAN GOES BERSERK IN
CAR SALESROOM, MANY
VOLVOS HURT*

TOXIC DIAPERS FOUND
IN WASH.

**Policeman Shot in Basque
Area**

CITY OUTLAWS GIVING OUT
PHONE NUMBERS, ADDRESSES
OF POLICE

**MEN PICKY ABOUT
NOSES**

Yellow snow studied to test
nutrition

***Hand Waves Goodbye to
County Board***

Body search reveals $4,000
in crack

**County Wants Money for
Taking Dump**

April Slated as Child Abuse Month

Lady luck? One in four compulsive gamblers are women.

AND THE WIENER IS...

How do you feel about wieners? They look silly and have a funny name...but they're loved by millions. This collection of wiener facts and quotes is from BRI stalwart Jess Brallier.

• "Some people don't salivate when they walk by a hot dog stand and smell that great symbol of American cuisine, bursting with grease and salt. But they are a very, very small group."
—*The New York Times*

• Known as "The Animal," Ed Krachie is America's wiener-eating champion. His best? 22.5 wieners—including buns—in 12 minutes.

• The favorite meal of acclaimed actress Marlene Dietrich was hot dogs and champagne.

• Wieners are an economical buy. With virtually no weight loss during preparation, a pound of wieners yields a pound of edible food.

• Lucky dog: In May 2000, Larry Ross stopped for a hot dog at Mr. K's Party Shoppe in Utica, Mich. He had a $100 bill, and bought lotto tickets with the change. One ticket was a $181.5 million winner.

• "Grilling wieners—or even sauteing them in a pan—makes them look nicer."
—**Julia Child**

• In 1970, at Camp David, the presidential retreat, wieners were served to Great Britain's Prince Charles and Princess Anne.

• NASA included the hot dog as a regular menu item on its Apollo moon flights, Skylab missions, and the space shuttle.

• More hot dogs—2 million a year—are sold at Chicago's O'Hare International Airport than at any other single location in the world.

• The U.S. Department of Agriculture "officially recognizes" the following as legitimate names for the hot dog: 1) wiener, 2) frankfurter, 3) frank, 4) furter, 5) hot dog.

• Randomly slash a hot dog as it heats, and it'll curl into funny shapes.

Holy cow! An average dairy cow produces four times her body weight in manure each year.

LUCKY FINDS

*Ever found something really valuable? It's one of the
best feelings in the world. Here's an installment
of a regular* Bathroom Reader *feature.*

THE TRIP OF A LIFETIME

The Find: Taxi driver

Where He Was Found: In his taxicab, near Brighton in Southern England

The Story: In August 2001, Colin Bagshaw, 39, and his girlfriend hailed a cab and climbed in for a ride across town. In the cab, Bagshaw's girlfriend happened to look at the driver's identification badge and saw that his name was *Barry* Bagshaw—the driver was Colin's father, whom he hadn't seen since 1966. His parents' marriage had broken up while his father was serving in the army in Hong Kong; since then Colin had always assumed that his father was dead. He wasn't dead—in fact, in recent years he had been living just a few blocks from his son without realizing it. It's a good thing they found each other when they did, because Colin was about to move away. "The blood just drained out of me when he said 'I'm your son,'" Barry Bagshaw, 61, told the BBC. "I didn't recognize him."

FOWL PLAY

The Find: A piece of paper stuffed into a leather-bound datebook from 1964

Where It Was Found: In a box of old books in Shelbyville, Kentucky

The Story: Homeowners Tommy and Cherry Settle found the datebook while looking through boxes in their basement. Inside the datebook they found a recipe for fried chicken, one that called for 11 herbs and spices—a number that immediately clicked with the Settles, because their home was once owned by Kentucky Fried Chicken founder Colonel Harland Sanders. The Settles believe the recipe may be a copy of Colonel Sanders's "Original Recipe," a carefully guarded trade secret and the foundation upon which the $20 billion fast-food chain is built. Only a handful of

KFC employees know the recipe, and each of them is sworn to secrecy. When the company subcontracts out the recipe to other manufacturers, they always use at least two companies, so that no one else knows the complete recipe.

So is the Settles' find the genuine article? The Settles think so, because when they asked KFC about it, the chain filed a lawsuit to force them to hand the recipe over. "They didn't say anything," Cherry Settle says, "They just sent this court document." Estimated "value," priceless. If the recipe ever gets out, KFC is powerless to stop anyone else from using it.

LOST AND FOUND

The Find: A gold and sapphire ring

Where It Was Found: Stuck to the bottom of a shoe

The Story: In 1999 Katie Smith of Harrow, England, lost the ring, which was valued at $45, somewhere in her apartment. She looked for it and then gave it up for lost when she couldn't find it. Then in September 1999, she and her boyfriend Dave Gould went on a 10,000-mile trip around the world. They hiked along the banks of the Nile; they hiked across a desert; they hiked up a mountain in Costa Rica. Then they went back home to England. While Dave was cleaning off the mud that had accumulated during the trip, he found the ring…stuck to the sole of his hiking shoe. "It's a miracle it stayed in one piece after the pounding it took," Smith told reporters. "I never thought I'd see it again."

SUNKEN TREASURE

The Find: Bottles of beer—lots of bottles of beer

Where It Was Found: At the bottom of a river in Australia

The Story: On Easter weekend 2001, the driver of a beer truck lost control of his rig when a tire blew out as he was driving along the Tweed River in New South Wales. When the truck crashed, an estimated 24,000 bottles of beer ended up in the river. But they didn't stay there long: according to news reports, "several hundred people, some fully clad in scuba gear, spent the Easter weekend diving for the beer and loading up their cars, with one person reported to have recovered 400 bottles alone."

There's a producing oil well beneath the Oklahoma State capitol building.

ALIENS STRUTTED AROUND IN MY WIFE'S PANTYHOSE

Some people consider the Weekly World News *a low-brow tabloid. Uncle John calls it one of America's best satire magazines. They have important news stories, too...like this one repinted from the April 1997 edition. AND IT COULD BE TRUE.*

SPACE INVADERS

"CHICAGO—In one of the most frightening and bizarre alien encounters ever recorded, a man was paralyzed by a ray gun, then forced to watch as a trio of E.T.s rummaged through his wife's lingerie drawer—and tried everything on!

"Carl Keaston, 41, says he was helpless to stop the grotesque space creatures, who gleefully modeled his wife Karen's intimate apparel, cooing in delight as they strutted around his bedroom and preened in front of a mirror.

"'I tried to scream, but I couldn't get my mouth to work,' Keaston recalled. 'I had to lie in bed, watching as those things put on my wife's bras and pantyhose—even the teddy I'd given her on Valentine's Day. It was sickening.'

"Keaston, a machinist described by neighbors as a 'normal guy,' says the bewildering episode took place on April 8, when his wife was out of town visiting her mother.

"'I was lying in bed watching some golf on TV when all of a sudden the reception got fuzzy,' Keaston told reporters. 'I got up and tried to adjust the set—then the whole house shook as if something heavy had landed on the roof.'

IT AIN'T SANTA CLAUS

"Moments later, Keaston claims, three pale, slightly built creatures entered the bedroom. When he confronted them, he says, one pointed a cylindrical object at him.

"'A blue light came out and I felt my body go numb,' he said. 'I fell back on the bed.'

Number of women who believe they've been abducted by aliens: 13,528....

"As he watched in disbelief, the aliens explored the room, chattering excitedly, and stopped at the dresser. Then the strange intruders pulled open his wife's lingerie drawer.

"'When I saw them pawing my wife's panties with those long spindly fingers of theirs, I wanted to slug them,' he says. 'Then, when they put them on, I almost threw up.'

"After an ordeal that lasted about 20 minutes, Keaston says the aliens left, taking with them only two items—a black thong and a pair of pantyhose.

"While initially skeptical, UFO investigators are now taking the odd tale very seriously.

"'At first this sounded like an instance of sleep paralysis. This happens when you have a vivid dream and somehow become aware that your body is immobile,' said one UFO expert who's probing the case.

"'However, we've found physical evidence to support Mr. Keaston's story: Some of the underwear left behind is radioactive.'"

*   *   *

STUDENT BLOOPERS

Excerpts from real student essays and quiz answers:

• On April 14, 1865, Lincoln went to the theater and got shot in his seat by one of the actors in a moving picture show. The believed assassinator was John Wilkes Booth, a supposedly insane actor. This ruined Booth's career.

• George Washington married Martha Curtis and in due time became the Father of Our Country. The Constitution of the United States was adopted to secure domestic hostility. Under the Constitution the people enjoyed the right to keep bare arms.

• One of the causes of the Revolutionary Wars was the English put tacks in their tea.

• Writing at the same time as Shakespeare was Miquel Cervantes. He wrote *Donkey Hote*. The next great author was John Milton. Milton wrote *Paradise Lost*. Then his wife died and he wrote *Paradise Regained*.

IT'S ABOUT TIME

It flows like a river, it flies when you're having fun,
and it waits for no man ... but what do we really
know about time? Read on to find out.

WHO INVENTED DAYLIGHT SAVING TIME?
Ben Franklin did. In 1784 he wrote an essay suggesting that setting clocks ahead in the spring and behind in the fall would be a wise idea because it would save expensive candles. But the idea wasn't taken seriously until 1907 when a British builder named William Willett was riding through the countryside early one morning and noticed that in spite of the full daylight, all the cottages' curtains were still drawn. It was a waste of daylight, he thought, and he wrote a pamphlet advocating that the nation set its clocks ahead by 20-minute increments on each of the four Sundays in April, and set them back on the four Sundays in October. A bill introduced in Parliament in 1909 was roundly ridiculed, but the advent of World War I brought a dire need to conserve coal, so the British Summer Time Act was passed in 1916. It set the time ahead one hour in the spring and back one hour in the fall.

The United States followed suit and enacted Daylight Saving Time in 1918 to conserve fuel for the war effort, but the measure was so unpopular that it was repealed in 1919. It was reinstated during World War II, again to conserve fuel, but when the war ended, some localities opted to continue observing it and some didn't. And those that did couldn't agree on when to set their clocks forward and back. On a single 35-mile stretch of highway between West Virginia and Ohio, for example, a traveler could pass through no less than seven time changes. Confusion reigned.

Bus Stop

The transportation industry, led by the Greyhound Bus Company, lobbied hard to remedy the situation, and finally in 1966 Congress passed the Uniform Time Act. The law didn't make Daylight Saving Time mandatory, but said that individual states needed to observe it or not on a uniform basis.

Daylight Saving Time is now observed in about 70 countries around the world.

In 1992 Barbie came out with her own exercise video.

Note: It's singular, not plural—it's Daylight Saving, not Daylight Savings. Why? We're saving daylight. According to the Department of Transportation, the United States saves about 1% of its energy every day DST is in effect. Maybe that makes it worth the effort for Americans to change three billion timepieces twice a year.

WHY ARE THERE 24 HOURS IN A DAY?

The standard started with the ancient Sumerians, who also invented the first known system of writing. Their mathematical system was based on the number 12; just as ours is based on the number 10. The Sumerians, it is surmised, counted not the 10 digits of the hands, but the 12 segments of the 4 fingers on each hand. Twelve was considered a magical number because it is the lowest number with the greatest number of divisors—it is easily split into half or thirds or quarters or sixths, whereas 10 can only be cut in half or into fifths.

Their systems of weights, measures, and money were all based on 12, and so was their system of time. It was the Sumerians who first divided the day into 12 parts, with each segment equal to 2 of our hours. Later, the Egyptians modified the system by dividing the day into 24 segments. And in case you were wondering, the Babylonians are responsible for our current system of having 60 minutes in an hour and 60 seconds in a minute.

WHY ARE THERE TIME ZONES?

You can thank the railroads for this one. Before the transcontinental railroads, there were no time zones. Noon in any city was whenever the sun reached the meridian of that particular place. Time actually varied by one minute for every 13 miles traveled, and cities only a few hundred miles apart had times that were different, which made scheduling trains very difficult. For example, when it was noon in Chicago, it was 12:31 in Pittsburgh, 12:17 in Toledo, 11:50 in St. Louis, and 11:27 in Omaha. At one time, U.S. railroads had nearly 300 different time zones. This lack of consistency wasn't just inconvenient, it was dangerous. The possibility of train wrecks increased dramatically by the conflicting schedules. Something had to be done—not locally—but on a global basis.

By 1847 Great Britain had a unified time system, which meant they had a single time zone across the entire country. That was

---

Dogs of War: Versatility Ltd. of Dorset, England, manufactures bulletproof vests for dogs.

fine for the small island nation. But it wasn't as easy in North America—the United States and Canada cover some 60 degrees of longitude.

In 1872 the Time-Table Convention was founded in St. Louis to look for a solution. Charles Dowd, a school principal from New York, recommended that the U.S. set up standard time zones, and brought his idea to Congress. Most lawmakers agreed with the idea, but were afraid it would upset their constituents, so the bill was stalled on the House floor for more than a decade.

STANDARD SANFORD

It wasn't until Sir Sanford Fleming, a well-respected Canadian Railroad engineer, brought a specific solution to Washington that the idea began to take hold. His idea: because there are 24 hours in a day, divide the Earth's 360 degrees by 24, which will create 24 equal time zones separated by 15 degrees.

In 1882 the Standard Time system was finally adopted, officially dividing the United States into four time zones—Eastern, Central, Mountain, and Pacific. At noon on Sunday, November 18, 1883— a day that became known as "the day with two noons"—the railroads set their clocks to this system.

On October 13, 1884, leaders from 25 nations gathered at the International Meridian Conference in Washington, D.C., divided the world into 24 time zones, with Greenwich, England, chosen to be the "prime meridian". The day would begin there and time would change by one hour for each 15 degrees traveled from that point.

Slowly but surely the rest of the world adapted to the new time zones. Some applauded it, others rejected it—but because the railroads were *the* primary means of transportation and shipping at the time, people had little choice.

Still, it wasn't until 1918 that Congress got around to making the Standard Time Act a matter of law—a law made, coincidentally, in conjunction with passing the first Daylight Saving Time Act.

*   *   *

"We must not allow the clock and the calendar to blind us to the fact that each moment of life is a miracle and mystery."

—*H. G. Wells*

Tall tale: 25% of American men are now six feet or taller, compared to only 4% in 1900.

FIRST LADY FIRSTS

Mrs. Uncle John insists that women don't read in the bathroom—and we might believe her... if we didn't get so many letters from women who do. In their honor, here's a bit of forgotten political history.

First Lady: Lucy Ware Webb Hayes, wife of Rutherford B. Hayes
Notable First: The first First Lady to be called a First Lady
Background: From Martha Washington through Julie Grant, presidential wives did not have a title. In 1876, newspaper writer Mary Clemmer Ames first referred to Mrs. Hayes, wife of the 19th president, as "the First Lady" in her column, "Woman's Letter from Washington."

First Lady: Frances Folsom Cleveland, wife of Grover Cleveland
Notable First: The first First Lady to be married in the White House
Background: Frances Folsom was only 21 when she married 49-year-old President Cleveland on June 2, 1886. It was the first nuptial ceremony held in the White House for a presidential couple. Mrs. Cleveland was the nation's youngest First Lady. She was also the first First Lady to give birth to a child in the White House, when her daughter Esther was born in 1893.

First Lady: Letitia Christian Tyler, first wife of John Tyler
Notable First: The first First Lady to die in the White House
Background: John Tyler became president when President William Henry Harrison died 30 days after being sworn in. Letitia Tyler had suffered a paralytic stroke several years earlier, so her duties as First Lady were actually assigned to her daughter-in-law, Priscilla Cooper Tyler. After a lengthy illness, probably tuberculosis, Letitia died in September 1842.

First Lady: Jacqueline Bouvier Kennedy, wife of John F. Kennedy
Notable First: The first (and only) First Lady to receive an Emmy Award
Background: To prod Congress into passing a bill giving permanent

---

Marlene Dietrich's beauty secret: to emphasize her

museum status to the White House, she conducted a tour of the mansion for television, which earned her a Special Emmy.

First Lady: Helen Herron Taft, wife of William H. Taft
Notable First: The first First Lady to decree that no bald-headed waiter or butler could serve in the White House
Background: Feeling the previous occupants of the White House were too informal and lacked dignity, Helen Taft, wife of the 27th president, thought this rule would create a favorable impression for guests. (Not to be confused with Lou Henry Hoover, wife of the 31st president, who insisted that all butlers, waiters, and footmen must be exactly five feet, eight inches tall.)

First Lady: Eliza McCardle Johnson, wife of Andrew Johnson
Notable First: The first First Lady to teach her husband to read and write (before he was president)
Background: President Andrew Johnson was born into poverty. Apprenticed to a tailor at a young age, he never spent a single day in school in his entire life. In 1827, the 19-year-old tailor married 16-year-old Eliza McCardle. Every night, after supper, Mrs. Johnson taught her husband how to read and write.

First Lady: Patricia Ryan Nixon, wife of Richard M. Nixon
Notable First: The first First Lady to visit an overseas combat zone
Background: "Visit" may be a slight overstatement. During the Nixons' 1969 trip to South Vietnam, Pat Nixon flew over the troops in an open helicopter.

First Lady: Florence Kling Harding, wife of Warren G. Harding
Notable First: The first First Lady to vote
Background: Women were granted the right to vote in August of 1920—perfect timing for Florence Harding, a strong supporter of Women's Suffrage. A couple of months later she cast her first ballot (presumably) for her husband Warren, who won the election by a landslide.

high cheekbones, she had her upper molars removed.

MOW 'EM DOWN

*You'd be surprised how many times lawnmowers find their way
into the news for one reason or another. Here's just a few
of the "clippings" that we've collected over the years.*

OBI-LAWN KENOBI
In 2000 the German garden equipment maker Wolf-
Garten introduced a prototype of the first mower in the
world that cuts grass using lasers instead of blades. Called the Zero,
the mower uses a computer-guided array of four powerful lasers
capable of cutting grass to an accuracy of one millimeter. And that's
only the beginning—a stream of air then mixes the zapped blades
with fertilizer before dumping them back on the lawn. The mower
comes complete with a leather seat, CD player, and even Internet
access. Estimated retail price when the commercial model hits the
market in 2002: $30,000.

A MORE NATURAL APPROACH

Scientists at Australian National University prefer a more low-
tech approach: They've introduced the Rolling Rabbit Run, the
world's first lawnmower powered entirely by rabbits. Constructed
from bicycle wheels, chicken wire, and buckets, the device is basically a cylindrical rabbit cage that rolls around on the lawn as the
rabbits eat the grass and fertilize it "naturally." Perfecting the
mower took a little longer than expected because scientists could-
n't get the rabbits to roll cage on their own. They finally solved
the problem by replacing the original pair of rabbits—one male,
one female—with two males, after discovering that the male and
the female kept stopping to mate.

LAWN JOCKEY

In 1997, 12-year-old Ryan Tripp of Beaver, Utah, hopped onto his
dad's riding lawnmower and set out for Washington, D.C., more
than 3,000 miles away. He made the trip (with his parents' permission) to raise money for a four-month-old girl in his town who
needed a liver transplant. Ryan arrived in Washington 42 days
later, shattering the record for the world's longest trip on a lawn-

---

Why isn't iron added to milk? Iron-fortified milk turns coffee green.

mower. Still, not everything went according to plan: Tripp had hoped to mow the White House lawn upon his arrival, but he couldn't get permission and had to settle for mowing a patch of grass at the U.S. Capitol. Bonus: He got to skip five weeks of school.

THE LAWN ARM OF THE LAW

• In 1992 author Stephen King sued to have his name removed from *Stephen King's Lawnmower Man*, a film based on his short story by the same name. King's suit alleged that the movie bore no resemblance to his original story—the tale of a man who "cuts his lawn by eating it, and is ultimately swallowed by a lawnmower."

• In December 1999 Sacramento, California, police were called to the residence of one Francis Karnes, 39, after neighbors report-ed hearing shots fired. They arrived several minutes later. Sure enough, Karnes had indeed fired off a few shots—at his lawnmow-er, after it refused to start. He was arrested and charged with reck-less endangerment; no word on whether the mower survived the assault.

• In March 1995, an unidentified 54-year-old Norwegian man was convicted of drunken driving—on a lawnmower—near the town of Haugesund. According to newspaper reports, police did not notice anything erratic about the man's driving, they just administered an alcohol test as part of a random spot-check of "motorists." The test revealed that the man had consumed the equivalent of three beers, well over the legal limit in Norway. He was convicted of driving under the influence, fined $795, and sentenced to 24 days in jail. But a court later suspended the sentence after concluding that "the lawnmower's top speed of 6 mph was too slow to be dan-gerous."

• On a Saturday morning in July 1996, Rickey Worthley of Bel-ton, Missouri, woke up his 17-year-old son Michael at 6 a.m. and told him to mow the lawn. When Michael told his father that 6 a.m. was too early to mow the lawn and that he wanted to sleep a few hours longer, Worthley dragged the mower into Michael's room, fired it up, and started mowing the carpet. Michael called the cops on pop; they arrested Worthley and charged him with assault. Injured party: the carpet.

Armadillos can walk underwater in order to cross rivers.

FIRSTS

Ever wonder where the first movie theater opened? Or when the lawn mower was invented? Here are the stories of when and how several things we take for granted came were created, from The Book of Firsts, *by Patrick Robertson.*

THE FIRST MOVIE THEATER

Date: June 26, 1896

Background: The first permanent movie theater was the 400-seat Vitascope Hall in New Orleans. Admission was 10 cents. Patrons were allowed to look in the projection room and see the Edison Vitascope projector for another 10 cents. Most of the films shown there were short scenic items, including the first English film to be released in America, Robert Paul's *Waves Off Dover.* A major attraction was the film *May Irwin Kiss,* which introduced sex to the American screen.

THE FIRST CHRISTMAS TREE WITH ELECTRIC LIGHTS

Date: December 1882

Background: The first electrically illuminated Christmas tree was installed in the New York City home of Edward H. Johnson, an associate of Thomas Edison. The first commercially produced Christmas tree lamps were manufactured in nine-socket sets by the Edison General Electric Co. in 1901. Each socket took a miniature 2-candlepower carbon-filament lamp operating on 32 volts.

THE FIRST DEPARTMENT STORE

Date: 1848

Background: Alexander Turney Stewart opened the Marble Dry Goods Palace on Broadway in New York City. Stewart had been a schoolmaster in Ireland before he emigrated in 1823 and set up his own business. At the time of its erection the Marble Dry Goods Palace was the largest shop in the world, extending the whole length of a city block. By 1876, the year of his death, Stewart's company had annual sales of $70 million, and his personal fortune was estimated at $80 million. He was never known to have given away any of his vast wealth.

CAMERA OBSCURA

Uncle John has an interesting chicken-and-egg question for you: What came first, the camera or the film? If you think they were invented at about the same time, this story will surprise you.

PICTURE THIS

The ancient principle of the camera is child's play. Hard to believe? Here's a simple experiment you can try at home: Cover the windows of a room with black construction paper or aluminum foil until absolutely no light is let in. Turn out the lights. Then poke a tiny hole in the paper or foil, so that a single pinprick of light enters the room and strikes the wall opposite the windows. What do you see?

If you do it just right, when the light enters the "dark room" (*camera obscura* in Latin) and hits the wall, it will form a faint upside-down image of the view outside the window. This simple phenomenon is the basis upon which the science of photography is built.

One of the first people to make note of such an image was a Chinese scholar Mo Ti, who lived in the fifth century B.C. In the 10th century A.D., Arab physicist Alhazen discovered that the smaller he made the hole, the sharper the image came into focus. If the hole was tiny enough, the image became very clear.

THROUGH THE LOOKING GLASS

Reproducing the image created by a camera obscura was easy: you simply held a piece of paper up against the wall, so that the image landed on the paper, then traced it. The camera obscura became a useful scientific tool. Scientists built special "dark rooms" for the sole purpose of studying the sky, eclipses, changes in the seasons, and other natural events. The tracings made with the aid of the camera obscuras were so detailed and accurate that by the 1500s, people were using them to paint portraits, landscapes, and other scenes.

In 1568 a professor at the University of Padua named Daniello Barbaro discovered that replacing the primitive pinhole with a glass lens brought the camera obscura image into a brighter and sharper focus.

Ice covers about 15% of the Earth's land mass.

In the 17th century, scientists and artists developed portable camera obscuras that allowed them to study objects in the field. Early versions were essentially lightproof tents with lenses sewn into the walls. Later versions were two-foot-long wooden boxes that projected an image onto a piece of frosted glass built into the lid. The user could then trace the image by placing a piece of paper over the glass.

PUTTING THINGS IN PERSPECTIVE

The images created by these early single-lens camera obscuras were circular in shape, with distortion along the edges. In the 1700s, a complex multilens system was introduced that corrected the distortion, and the camera obscura became as common a part of the painter's art as brushes and paint.

Artists weren't the only ones putting the camera to use—explorers took them on expeditions all over the world so that they could record the wonders they encountered. In the process, the boxes literally changed the way people saw the world.

IMAGE PROBLEMS

For all of these improvements, there was still no way to *capture* the camera obscura's image other than by manually tracing it. There it was, tantalizingly projected onto a wall or a pane of frosted glass. You could look at it, you could reach out and touch it. But capturing the actaul image was as impossible as capturing one's own shadow. It would remain so for another 75 years...until the invention of film.

So which came first, the camera or the film? The camera—by centuries.

For part II of the "History of Photography," turn to page 107.

For part II of the "History of Photography," turn to page 107.

*   *   *

THE TIMES THEY ARE A-CHANGIN'

The state of Arizona does not follow Daylight Saving Time, with the exception of the Navajo Reservation, which does—except for the Hopi Partitioned Land which lies inside the Navajo Reservation, which doesn't.

HOY, HOY

*Professor Howard Richler, etymologist and BRI
member, sent us this explanation of why we say
what we say every time the phone rings...Hello?*

BACKGROUND
The common English word of greeting dates back to the
14th century. Some sources say *hello* descends from the Old
German *hala*, a form of "to fetch." Others believe the word to be a
derivative of the Middle French *hola*, meaning "hey there." Still
another theory claims *hello* is a derivative of the cry *au loup* used
by Norman English hunters when they spotted a wolf.

Today, "Hello" is the most common telephone greeting in the
United States. But Alexander Graham Bell, inventor of the telephone, actually preferred the term "Ahoy." In fact, the first telephone operators in New Haven, Connecticut, greeted callers with
"Ahoy! Ahoy!" The problem was that although "Ahoy" was sea-
worthy, it didn't resonate with landlubbers in Peoria.

WHO IS SPEAKING?

Expressions such as "Are you there?"—one of the first telephone
salutations—were too long, and "Good day" and "Good morning"
could be confusing in a continent with so many time zones.
American phone companies hunted for a new word to politely
and neutrally initiate telephone conversations. Enter "Hello."

By the late 1890s, only 10 years after Bell's invention went into
commercial use, Hello was a clear victor over "Ahoy." It was in
such common use that telephone operators were called "hello
girls." But Bell didn't like it. On January 12, 1914, he wrote in a
letter that he had "never used the exclamation hello in connection with the telephone. My call is, and always has been "hoy,
hoy." He spent the rest of his life lobbying for the adoption of
"Hoy" or "Ahoy."

Why did Bell disdain the use of "Hello"? Because he didn't
think of it. Who did? Bell's rival, Thomas Edison. Edison thought
"Hoy, hoy" was silly and is generally credited with introducing
"Hello" as an alternative telephone greeting.

America's most popular candy bar? Snickers.

WHAT THE #!&%?

Here are the origins of several symbols we use in everyday life.

? QUESTION MARK

Origin: When early scholars wrote in Latin, they would place the word *questio*—meaning "question"—at the end of a sentence to indicate a query. To conserve valuable space, writing it was soon shortened to *qo*, which caused another problem—readers might mistake it for the ending of a word. So, they squashed the letters into a symbol: a lowercase *q* on top of an *o*. Over time the *o* shrank to a dot and the *q* to a squiggle, giving us our current question mark.

! EXCLAMATION POINT

Origin: Like the question mark, the exclamation point was invented by stacking letters. The mark comes from the Latin word *io*, meaning "exclamation of joy." Written vertically, with the *i* above the *o*, it forms the exclamation point we use today.

= EQUAL SIGN

Origin: Invented by English mathematician Robert Recorde in 1557, with this rationale: "I will sette as I doe often in woorke use, a paire of paralleles, or Gemowe [i.e., twin] lines of one length, thus: =====, bicause noe 2 thynges, can be more equalle." His equal signs were about five times as long as the current ones, and it took more than a century for his sign to be accepted over its rival: a strange curly symbol invented by Descartes.

& AMPERSAND

Origin: This symbol is a stylized *et*, Latin for "and." Although it was invented by the Roman scribe Marcus Tullius Tiro in the first century B.C., it didn't get its strange name until centuries later. In the early 1800s, schoolchildren learned this symbol as the 27th letter of the alphabet: X, Y, Z, &. But the symbol had no name. So, they ended their ABCs with "and, per se, and", meaning "&, which means 'and.'" This phrase was slurred into one garbled word that eventually caught on with everyone: *ampersand*.

In 1790 there were 66 slaves for every 100 Europeans in the state of Virginia.

OCTOTHORP

Origin: The odd name for this ancient sign for numbering derives from *thorpe*, the Old Norse word for a village or farm that is often seen in British placenames. The symbol was originally used in map-making, representing a village surrounded by eight fields, so it was named the *octothorp*.

$ DOLLAR SIGN

Origin: When the U.S. government began issuing its own money in 1794, it used the common world currency: the *peso*—also called the Spanish *dollar*. The first American silver dollars were identical to Spanish pesos in weight and value, so they took the same written abbreviation: Ps. That evolved into a P with an s written right on top of it, and when people began to omit the circular part of the p, the sign simply became an S with a vertical line through it.

QQ OLYMPIC RINGS

Origin: Designed in 1913 by Baron Pierre de Coubertin, the five rings represent the five regions of the world that participated in the Olympics: Africa, the Americas, Asia, Europe, and Oceania. While the individual rings do not symbolize any single continent, the five colors—red, blue, green, yellow, and black—were chosen because at least one of them is found on the flag of every nation. The plain white background is symbolic of peace.

"THE SYMBOL"

Origin: Okay, so we're running out of symbols, but this is a great pop culture story: In 1993, Prince's dissatisfaction with his record label, Warner Bros., finally reached its peak. Despite his superstar status and his $100 million contract, the Purple One didn't feel he had enough creative control over his music. So "in protest," Prince announced that Prince would never perform for Warner Bros. again—this unpronounceable symbol would instead.

The symbol for the Artist Formerly Known as Prince combined three ancient symbols: the male symbol, the female symbol, and the alchemy symbol for soapstone, which was supposed to reflect his artistic genius. Prince retired the symbol when his contract with Warner Bros. ran out in 2000. Today, he is again Prince.

Clue originally meant "ball of twine." That's why you "unravel" clues to solve a mystery.

CLASSIC HOAXES

The BRI library is full of books on hoaxes. We love them. It's amazing how many times people have pulled off clever scams... and gotten away with it. Here are a few of our favorites.

THE MYSTERIOUS CHICKEN OF THE APOCALYPSE

Background: In a small village near Leeds, England, in 1806, a hen laid an egg that had the words "Christ is Coming," inscribed in black on its surface. The hen's owner, a woman named Mary Bateman, explained that God had come to her in a vision and told her that the hen would lay a total of 14 such eggs, at which point the world would be destroyed in the apocalypse. Only the holy would survive to live with Christ in heaven; everyone else was condemned to burn in hell.

But there was some good news: God had given Bateman special slips of paper sealed with the inscription "J.C." Anyone possessing one of these slips would be automatically admitted into heaven... and Mary Bateman was willing to part with the papers for a shilling apiece.

"Great numbers visited the spot, and examined these wondrous eggs, convinced that the day of judgement was near at hand," Charles Mackay writes in *Extraordinary Popular Delusions and the Madness of Crowds*. "The believers suddenly became religious, prayed violently, and flattered themselves that they repented them of their evil courses." By the time the 14th and final egg was about to be laid, more than 1,000 people had coughed up a shilling to be admitted into heaven.

Exposed: A doctor who was skeptical of the story traveled to Leeds to investigate the eggs in person. When he discovered that the messages had been written on them with corrosive ink, he informed the local authorities, who raided the tavern where the chicken was being kept... just as Mary Bateman was cruelly shoving an inscribed egg into the hen to "lay" later that day.

Batemen was sent to jail but was soon released. No longer able to make a living in the prophecy business, she became an abortionist, which was illegal, and for which she was later hanged.

THE AMITYVILLE HORROR

Background: In 1974 a man named Ronald DeFeo murdered his parents and four siblings as they slept in their home in Amityville, New York. He was convicted of the crimes and sentenced to six consecutive life sentences in prison.

The "murder house" was later sold for a song to a struggling couple named George and Kathy Lutz, who moved in a week before Christmas in 1975. Twenty-eight days later, they moved out, claiming the house was haunted—and that the evil spirits that had driven them away probably also caused DeFeo to murder his entire family. Their story inspired the 1977 bestselling book *The Amityville Horror*, and the hit film that premiered in 1979.

Exposed: In 1979 Ronald DeFeo's defense attorney William Weber filed a lawsuit against the Lutzes, accusing them of fraud and breach of contract, claiming that they reneged on an agreement to collaborate with Weber on the book. So where did the haunted house story come from? In an interview with the Associated Press, Weber admitted that he and the Lutzes had "concocted the horror story scam over many bottles of wine."

SOBER SUE

Background: One afternoon in 1908, the managers of Hammerstein's Victoria Theater on Broadway marched a woman onstage during intermission and offered $1,000 to anyone in the audience who could make the woman—introduced as "Sober Sue"—laugh. When no one in the audience succeeded in getting Sober Sue to even crack a smile, the theater managers upped the ante by inviting New York's top comedians to try.

Over the next several weeks, just about every headlining comedian in New York City performed their best material in front of Sober Sue, hoping to benefit from the publicity if they were first to get her to laugh. Everyone failed, but Sober Sue became one of Broadway's top theater attractions.

Exposed: It wasn't until after she left town that Sober Sue's secret finally leaked out: Her facial muscles were paralyzed—she couldn't have laughed even if she had wanted to. The Victoria Theater had cooked up the "contest" to trick New York's most famous—and most expensive—comedians into performing their routines for free.

RANDOM SCIENCE TRIVIA

Some fascinating facts about the world around us.

If you could tap the energy released by an average-sized hurricane, it would be enough to satisfy all U.S. energy needs for six months.

In any given year, about 26,000 meteorites land on the Earth's surface, the vast majority dropping into the oceans. Only seven people in recorded history have been hit by one.

When glass breaks, the cracks travel faster than 3,000 mph.

Gold is so rare that all of the pure gold produced in the last 500 years would fit inside a 50-foot cube.

At least 100,000 separate chemical reactions occur in the human brain every second.

About 70% of Earth is covered with water, yet just 1% of it is drinkable.

Sound travels through steel 15 times faster than it travels through air.

To escape the Earth's gravitational pull, a spacecraft has to move faster than seven miles per second—a speed that would take you from New York to Philadelphia in under 20 seconds.

Rain contains vitamin B12.

According to a University of Michigan study, men are six times more likely to be struck by lightning than women are.

If you could capture a comet's entire 10,000-mile vapor trail in a container, the condensed vapor would occupy less than one cubic inch of space.

Earth travels through space at 66,600 miles per hour— eight times faster than the speed of a bullet.

THE BIRTH OF THE DISHWASHER

We mentioned Josephine Cochrane briefly in our fourth Bathroom Reader, but we've wanted to tell the whole story for years. Thanks to her, most of us don't have to suffer through "dishpan hands."

DISH-RESPECT

What really is the mother of invention? When it comes to the invention of the dishwasher, necessity had nothing to do with it. It was chipped china.

Josephine Cochrane was a wealthy socialite from Shelbyville, Illinois. She gave a lot of dinner parties and was very proud of her china, which had been in the family since the 17th century. But her servants weren't particularly careful with the priceless dishes as they washed them after each party. Pieces were chipped; pieces were cracked; pieces were broken. Cochrane felt that the only way to protect her treasures was to wash them herself...but she hated the job.

Why should a rich 44-year-old woman be doing this menial job? Why wasn't there a machine that would wash the dishes for her? Well, there was—sort of. The first dishwasher was patented in 1850 by Joel Houghton. It was a wooden machine that splashed water on dishes when a hand-turned wheel was rotated. It didn't work very well, so Cochrane decided to invent a better one.

TO THE DRAWING BOARD

First, she set up a workshop in her woodshed. She measured her dishes, and designed wire racks to hold them. She placed the racks inside a wheel, then laid the wheel inside a tub. The wheel turned while hot soapy water squirted up from the bottom of the tub, falling down on the dishes. Then clean hot water squirted up to rinse them. And finally, the dishes air-dried. It worked.

But while she was busy working on the dishwasher, her ailing husband died. Mrs. Cochrane was left with little money and a lot of debt. Now she needed to follow through on this invention not for convenience, but out of necessity. She needed to earn a living.

Cochrane patented her design in 1886. A Chicago machine

firm manufactured them for her while she managed the company and marketed the product.

Although Cochrane's wealthy friends immediately ordered the "Cochrane Dishwasher" for their own kitchens, the home model did not sell well. Few homes had electricity in those days. Water heaters were rare. Most available water was hard and did not create suds well. And the price tag of $150 was huge—equivalent to about $4,500 today. Furthermore, many housewives felt that there was nothing wrong with wahing dishes by hand—it was a relaxing way to end the day.

Cochrane tried changing her sales pitch to point out that the water in her dishwashing machines was hotter than human hands could stand, resulting in germ-free dishes. But it didn't matter: Her strongest potential market was not private homes, it was industry.

SUCCESS!

Cochrane got her big break when she exhibited her dishwasher at the World's Columbian Expo of 1893 in Chicago. Against heavy competition from around the world, her dishwasher received first prize for "best mechanical construction for durability and adaptation to a particular line of work." And she sold dishwashers to many of the restaurants and other establishments catering to the large crowds at the Expo. Hotels, restaurants, boardinghouses, and hospitals immediately saw the advantage of being able to wash, scald, rinse, and dry dozens of dishes of all shapes and sizes in minutes. One of the concessionaires sent her this glowing tribute: "Your machine washed without delay soiled dishes left by eight relays of a thousand soldiers each, completing each lot within 30 minutes."

Cochrane continued to improve her product, designing models with revolving washing systems, a centrifugal pump, and a hose for draining into a sink. She ignored the clergy (who claimed the dishwasher was immoral because it denied women the labor to which God had called them) and the servants (who claimed it would put them out of business). The company kept growing, pushed by Josephine Cochrane's energy and ambition until her death at age 74 in 1913. By the 1950s, the world finally caught up with Cochrane. Dishwashers became commonplace in ordinary homes... using the same design principles she had invented 70 years before.

LUNAR BASEBALL

It gives us great comfort to know that scientists are hard at work...figuring out what it would be like to play baseball on the moon. From Think Tank: If Baseball Expands to the Moon, Be Sure to Back Up Those Fences, *by Bruce Weber.*

SPACE CASE?

It isn't, perhaps, the most pragmatic of disciplines, but Peter Brancazio probably has it all to himself. A lot of people have applied the laws of physics to sports, Mr. Brancazio among them. He's the guy who demonstrated that Michael Jordan's vaunted hang time was only eight-tenths of a second, and that a rising fastball doesn't really rise. (It just doesn't fall as quickly as the batter expects.)

But because he taught astronomy in the physics department of Brooklyn College (he is now retired), Mr. Brancazio, 62, asserts with pride that he is uniquely qualified for his current specialty. That would be the physics of *lunar* sports, which probes the scientific issues that would be involved should, for example, George Steinbrenner contemplate moving the Yankees from the Bronx to outer space.

"About 10 years ago, there was talk about returning to the moon," Mr. Brancazio said. "I taught astronomy, and I'm a sports fan, and I wondered what it would be like to play all sorts of sports on the moon."

His lecture on the subject, delivered at the City University of New York, was initially composed for a science fiction convention. But he eventually discovered its uses as a teaching tool.

"There are things you take for granted in sports that affect the field of play, like the Earth's gravity and its atmosphere," he said.

LUNARDOME

There's no air on the moon, of course. This means all athletes would have to wear unwieldy spacesuits, and how interesting would that be to play or watch? Mr. Brancazio, who brings a measure of earthly practicality to his calculations, concluded that lunar sports must be conducted indoors, in pressurized, domed arenas

---

Jay North, star of TV's *Dennis the Menace*, was also the voice of Bam-Bam Rubble.

where air—and air resistance—would be the same as it is on Earth.

Lunar gravity, about a sixth of what it is here, would remain a significant factor indoors, rendering certain sports impossible. Tennis is out; you couldn't hit a ball with enough topspin to keep it on the court. And basketball is out; the baskets would have to be 60 feet high. On the other hand, diving and gymnastics would be more balletic.

Mr. Brancazio's primary focus, however, was baseball; he's the kind of Brooklyn Dodger fan who still winces when you say Ralph Branca, and he seems hopeful if not serious when he envisions future recreational possibilities on a populated moon base. An understanding of how the game would change, he said, begins with the difference between mass and weight. The former is a measurement of an object's resistance to being accelerated; the latter measures the force of gravity on an object. Given equal air resistance on Earth and in a lunar stadium, the mass—of a person, say, or a ball—remains constant; its weight on the moon, however, is one-sixth of its weight on Earth.

So you couldn't run any faster on the moon than you can here (you would have to develop a kind of low-lying, hopping stride, however, so you didn't launch yourself into the air with every push off the ball of your foot); and you couldn't throw a ball any faster, either.

"The bat will feel lighter when you pick it up," Mr. Brancazio said, because it doesn't weigh as much. "But swinging it"—its mass doesn't change—"isn't any easier."

FLY BALL

Is this an advantage for hitters or pitchers? Well, that depends on how you spin it—the ball, that is. The rotation on a ball is a force that works in conjunction with air resistance and gravity to create a total force that determines the path of a ball. Curve balls, sliders, and sinkers—which are all thrown with a degree of overspin and break downward—would be less effective on the moon because the break is not as enhanced by a lesser gravitational pull. A ball thrown with enough backspin, however, would be something no major leaguer has ever seen—a rising fastball that isn't merely an illusion.

The distance between the pitcher's mound to the plate is 60 feet, 6 inches, and on Earth, over that span, gravity causes a thrown ball to drop about 3 feet, Mr. Brancazio said. A backspin of, say, 1,800 rotations per minute can reduce that drop by a foot and a half.

"But on the moon the ball rises if the spin is greater than 600 rpm's," he said, "because the lift force it produces is greater than the weight of the ball."

PLAY BALL

Of course, if the batter does manage to hit the ball, a whole other set of these physical forces, come into play. The ball will travel farther, and over an unfamiliar arc; one scenario outlined by Mr. Brancazio shows that a fly ball struck with enough backspin will rise and do a loop-de-loop before proceeding into the outfield. More generally, Mr. Brancazio said, consider a batted ball that rises at an angle of 40 degrees, travels 385 feet—a deep drive if not a home run—and stays aloft for 5 seconds on Earth. On the moon the same ball will go 890 feet and stay in the air for 21.1 seconds.

"This raises interesting questions," Mr. Brancazio said. "Where do you put the fences? And where do you position the outfielders? They can't run any faster, but the ball will stay in the air long enough for them to possibly make a play. So you'll have a situation where the batter can hit the ball, circle the bases and go into the dugout and watch to see if he's scored."

*　　*　　*

HE TAKES ALL THE CREDIT

"Robert Meier of Tampa, Florida, was accused of marrying his comatose girlfriend, Constance Sewell, hours before she died, then running up $20,000 on her credit cards. He told police he knew it was wrong, but the woman's dog told him to do it. However, the investigator who searched the apartment said, 'The dog was in the garage and didn't say anything.'"

—Strange Days #2

The Arctic is classified as a desert...annual precipitation is less than 4 inches a year.

WILL'S WISECRACKS

Thoughts and observations from political humorist Will Durst.

"[George W. Bush] said there was no room in the Republican Party for racists. Boy, I knew there were a lot of them; I didn't think all the slots were full."

"The federal government announced it was worried about the long-term effects of medical marijuana on the terminally ill."

"In America, we'll give you the shirt off our back, as long as there's the off chance we can trap you in a blind alley and strip you naked."

"Colleges are banning alcohol on campus, sending the message to kids, 'If you want to drink, get a car.'"

"Guns don't kill people. It's those darn bullets that put the holes in that the blood leaks out of way too quick."

"If you're not confused, you're not paying attention."

"I hate the outdoors. To me the outdoors is where the car is."

"Hillary Clinton made a hundred thousand on a thousand-dollar investment. Forget the New York senatorship—put her in charge of Social Security!"

"Patrick Buchanan doesn't believe in evolution and some say he is his own best argument."

"Racism is so stupid. There's more than enough reasons to dislike people on an individual basis."

"I'm all in favor of billionaires running for president instead of politicians. That way we eliminate the middlemen."

"Jesse Ventura refereed a WCW event and caused an outcry. The wrestlers were afraid the appearance of a politician would cheapen the sport."

"To me, Las Vegas is America, because there's money everywhere, and none of it is yours."

"If God has cable, we are the 24-hour doofus network."

The game Simon Says was originally called Do This, Do That.

Q & A:
ASK THE EXPERTS

Kids always ask their parents questions like "Why is the sky blue?"
Uncle John asks the experts. Here are some of their answers.

JUST BLOW IT OFF
Q: *How does blowing on food cool it off?*
A: "When you see steam rising from hot food, it's because heat is coming out. The steam acts like a blanket that helps keep the heat in. The faster you blow the blanket of steam away, the faster the heat can leave the food, and the faster the food cools down." (From *Why Does Popcorn Pop?*, by Catherine Ripley)

PERCHANCE TO DREAM
Q: *Do insects sleep?*
A: "Let's put it this way. They get quiet and curl up and look like they're sleeping. But what's really going on inside those molecule-sized brains nobody knows.

"The one sure way to know if an animal is sleeping is to hook it up to a machine that measures electrical patterns in the brain. That's how we know that birds and mammals—animals like dogs, cats, cows, and pigs—actually sleep. The problem with bugs is they don't have enough brains to hook the wires to. So we don't really know what they're doing." (From *Know It All!*, by Ed Zotti)

GOOD HORSE SENSE
Q: *How much is one horsepower?*
A: "Although it was originally intended to be measured as the average rate at which a horse does work, one horsepower has now been standardized to equal exactly 550 foot-pounds of work per second, or 746 watts of power.

"Speaking of watts, they're named after James Watt, the Scottish engineer who invented an improved steam engine and then created the term *horsepower*. He needed some way to convince potential customers that his engine could outperform the horse. By devising a system of measurement based on the power of a horse, customers could easily compare the work potential of his engine versus that of the beast." (From *Everything You Pretend to Know and Are Afraid Someone Will Ask*, by Lynette Padwa)

SKY WRITING

Q: *Why do migrating ducks and geese fly in V formation?*

A: "Scientists aren't really sure why this behavior occurs. Some believe that each bird in the V receives lift from the bird in front of it. (Lift, an upward draft created by air currents rushing over and under the wing, is also what gets airplanes off the ground.) By staying in close V formation, each bird, except the leader, may get enough of a lift that it can fly longer with less effort.

"It may also be that the V formation helps birds avoid midair collisions, because each bird knows its position and can see the other members of the flock." (From *101 Questions and Answers About Backyard Wildlife*, by Ann Squire)

EYE DON'T THINK SO

Q: *Will TV cause eye damage?*

A: "Although the contrast between a bright screen and a dark room will temporarily tire the eyes, there is no long-term eye damage. According to Dr. Theodore Lawwill, of the American Academy of Ophthalmology, 'children like to be as close to the action as possible and would climb into the TV if they could.' Nevertheless, young children are able to focus sharply on objects as close as a few centimeters away from their eyes.'

"Dr. William Beckner, of the National Council on Radiation Protection, also dispels the notion that TV causes radiation damage: 'No matter how close you sit to the set, X-rays just aren't a problem.'" (From *The Odd Body: Mysteries of Our Weird and Wonderful Bodies Explained*, by Dr. Stephen Juan)

TREASURE TROVE

Q: *How much gold does the United States store in Fort Knox?*

A: "The U.S. Bullion Depository at Fort Knox contains approximately 315 million troy ounces of gold. At the official government price of $42.222 per troy ounce, the gold in the vault is worth $13 billion. At a market price of $300 an ounce, the gold would be worth $94.5 billion." (From *Do Fish Drink Water?*, by Bill McLain)

Queen Elizabeth II was *Time* magazine's "Man of the Year" for 1952.

TEST YOUR EGG I.Q.

How well do you know your yolks from your whites? Are you an egghead...or an empty shell? Take our quiz and find out.

1. Without breaking it open, how can you tell if an egg is fresh?
a) Carefully feel the shell—if it has soft spots, the egg is rotten.
b) Hold the egg up your ear and shake it. If you hear the yolk sloshing around inside, the egg is still fresh. A silent egg is a rotten egg.
c) Drop the egg in a glass of water. If it sinks to the bottom and lays on its side, it's fresh. If it sinks to the bottom and "stands" on one end, it's old but probably still edible. If it floats, it's rotten.

2. Which part of the egg is known as the "chalazae"?
a) The protective coating on the outside of the shell.
b) The membrane separating the yolk from the white.
c) The thin strands of egg white that connect the yolk to the shell.

3. What's the difference between Grade A and Grade AA eggs?
a) Grade AA eggs contain twice as much vitamin A, because the hens get a diet of fortified chicken feed.
b) Grade AA eggs have plumper yolks and thicker whites.
c) Grade AA hens, also known as "yearlings" or "freshmen" hens, are younger and healthier than the hens that lay Grade A eggs.

4. What's the best way to store an egg in the refrigerator?
a) With the tapered end pointing up.
b) With the tapered end pointing down.
c) Neither—eggs keep best when they're lying on their side.

5. Without breaking it open, how can you tell if an egg is cooked?
a) Spin it on a flat surface—raw eggs wobble; cooked ones don't.
b) Hold it up to a bright light—eggshells that have been cooked for seven minutes or longer are slightly transparent.
c) Carefully examine the shell—it's physically impossible to boil an egg without cracking the shell in at least one place.

Answers on page 507.

Monkey see, monkey do: Americans eat 12 billion bananas a year.

CHI MARKS THE SPOT

Ever heard of a chiasmus? Here's a clue:
Never let a fool kiss you or a kiss fool you.

GRAMMAR LESSON
Chiasmus is one of those parts of speech you didn't know even had a name. What is it? It's a figure of speech in which the order of the words in the first of two parallel clauses is reversed in the second, which gives it extra power or wit. Here are some examples:

"Ask not what your country can do for you; ask what you can do for your country." —John F. Kennedy

"It's not the men in my life; it's the life in my men." —Mae West

Get the idea? Chiasmus (pronounced kye-AZ-muss) is named after the Greek letter chi (x), and indicates a crisscross arrangement of phrases. Here are some more examples:

"Pleasure's a sin, and sometimes sin's a pleasure." —Lord Byron

"The value of marriage is not that adults produce children, but that children produce adults." —Peter De Vries

CHIAMUS CLASSICS
Certain chiasmuses, such as "All for one and one for all," and the shortened Cicero quote "Eat to live, not live to eat" are also word palindromes—where the words, when repeated in reverse order, read identically.

Chiasmuses appear to reveal hidden truths and are popular in Biblical writing:

"Whoever sheds the blood of man; by man shall his blood be shed." —Genesis 9:6

"There is no fear in love; but perfect love casteth out fear."
—1 John 4:18

"Many that are first shall be last; and the last shall be first."
—Matthew 19:30

Red blood cells live for 4 months. In that time they make 75,000 trips to the lungs and back.

The two lines can express contradictory sentiments, as in the French proverb "Love makes time pass; time makes love pass"— the first line is romantic, the second line strips away this romance. Ernest Hemingway was fond of asking people which of these two statements they preferred: "Man can be destroyed but not defeated," or "Man can be defeated but not destroyed."

MODERN WORDPLAY

A chiasmus can also be implied. Oscar Wilde was a master at this type of ironic wordplay. Some of his classics: "Work is the curse of the drinking class" and "The English have a miraculous power of turning wine into water."

Other implied chiasmus quips include Mae West's lines "A hard man is good to find" and "A waist is a terrible thing to mind," Groucho Marx's "Time wounds all heels," and Kermit the frog's observation that "Time's fun when you're having flies." A hangover has been described as "the wrath of grapes," and a critic who provided a harsh opening night review was said to have "stoned the first cast."

Had enough? The elements need not even be whole words; parts of words will suffice. There's Randy Hanzlick's song lyric, "I'd rather have a *bottle* in *front* of me than have a *frontal* lo*botomy*," and the Edwardian toast "Here's *champagne* for our *real* friends and *real pain* for our *sham* friends."

Finally, consider the chiasmus contest held by *The Washington Post* some years ago. The winning entry read:

Bill Clinton before: "I don't know how I can make this any clearer."

Bill Clinton after: "I don't know how I can clear this with my Maker."

*　　*　　*

GETTING THE LEAD OUT

Plumbing pipe was originally made from wood or earthenware. Eventually lead was used. The Latin word for "lead" is *plumbum* from which we get the word "plumber."

Marlon Brando owns a remote controlled whoopie cushion.

A (BAD) NIGHT AT THE OPERA

One of Uncle John's favorite movies is the Marx Brothers'
classic A Night at the Opera. *The Marx brothers perform some*
unbelievable—and hilarious—antics on opening night...but
are they so far-fetched? Here are some real-life examples
of what can happen at the opera. Honk-honk!

CARMEN GET IT

A performance of *Carmen* was being staged in a bull ring
in Mexico City. The singer playing the part of Don José
had a long wait between acts 3 and 4, so he decided to dash out
for a beer in a local tavern. No sooner had he entered than he was
arrested by a couple of cops who saw his scruffy costume, thought
he was a bum, and dragged him off to jail. When he insisted he
was a tenor singing in the opera, they accused him of being drunk.
He could only convince them...by singing. (They let him go.)

DUMB GIOVANNI

In 1958 Cesare Siepi was playing the part of Don Giovanni in the
Vienna State Opera. The script called for him to descend into
Hell using a stagelift. So Cesare said good-bye to the world, and
stepped into the netherworld. But the lift got stuck halfway down,
leaving his head and shoulders visible to the audience. Stage tech-
nicians brought the lift back up and tried to lower it again, but it
got stuck a second time and was raised back to stage level. Cesare
sang in Italian, "Oh my God, how wonderful—Hell is full!"

NOISE POLLUTION

When *The Wreckers* opened in England in 1901, King Edward VII
to came to the opening. Conductor Sir Thomas Beecham later
asked the king's private secretary if the king had liked the music.
"I don't know," was the reply. "But you were sitting right next to
him—surely he must have said something!" "Oh, yes—he did. He
woke up three-quarters of the way through and said, 'That's the
fourth time that infernal noise has roused me!'"

What were they thinking? In 1915 someone made a silent movie version of the opera *Carmen.*

JUST LIKE LEMMINGS

In the opera *Tosca*, two soldiers are to execute the character Cavaradossi while the heroine, Tosca, watches in horror. Prior to the performance in San Francisco in 1961, the director had too little time to instruct the firing squad. He told them, "When I cue you, march on stage, wait until the officer lowers his sword, then shoot." When they asked how to exit the stage, he said, "Exit with the principal characters." The soldiers marched on stage and were amazed to see two people against the execution wall: Tosca and Cavaradossi. They hadn't been told which one to shoot—so when the officer dropped his sword, they had to choose—and they shot Tosca. Wrong. Cavaradossi dropped dead 20 yards away, while the person they had just shot ran over to him weeping and wailing in Italian. Tosca then climbed to the top of the castle battlement to commit suicide. The firing squad, having been instructed to exit with the principal characters, followed her, leaping to their deaths as the curtains closed.

DEADPAN PERFORMANCE

In 1849 *Charles VI* premiered in Paris. At the beginning of the aria called "Oh God, Kill Him!", a member of the opera company fell dead. The next night at the same point in the production, a member of the audience died. When the orchestra leader fell dead at the third performance, Napoléon III banned the opera for good.

SLAPSTICK OOPERA

In 1960 the diva playing the role of Donna Elvira was singing in *Don Giovanni* in New York was to make her entrance in a sedan chair carried by two porters, then step out and begin singing. Unfortunately, she weighed a lot and the two porters struggled with the sedan chair. The porter in front set his burden down to get a better grip, which threw all the weight on the porter in the rear, who in turn threw the chair forward. The violent rocking of the chair caused the soprano inside to fall forward into a somersault, where she promptly got stuck. The porters couldn't see inside the sedan chair, had no idea what had happened, and carried her onstage like that. There was nothing for her to do except sing upside down from the chair. When they carried her offstage at the end of the song, an axe was needed to extricate her from the chair. Her first act upon regaining her freedom was to slap the two porters.

The saguaro cactus can grow 4 stories tall, weigh 10 tons, and live 200 years.

UNCLE JOHN'S LIST OF SIXES

Uncle John's sixth sense tells him you're going to like this page.

Nobel Prize Categories
Peace, Chemistry, Physics, Physiology & Medicine, Literature, Economics

Wives of Henry VIII
Katherine of Aragon, Ann Boleyn, Jane Seymour, Anne of Cleves, Catherine Howard, Catherine Parr

Rodeo Contests
Saddle bronco riding, Bareback riding, Calf roping, Bull riding, Steer wrestling, Team roping

Parts of the Circulatory System
Heart, Arteries, Arterioles, Capillaries, Venules, Veins

Enemies of Mankind (Hinduism)
Lust, Angst, Envy, Avarice, Spiritual ignorance, Pride

Categories of Dog Breeds
Working, Sporting, Hounds, Terriers, Nonsporting, Toy

Layers of the Earth
Crust, Upper mantle, Lower mantle, Outer core, Transition region, Inner core

Foreign Places Named for U.S. Presidents
Cape Washington, Antarctica; Monrovia, Liberia; Lincoln Island, South China Sea; Cleveland, Brazil; Mount Eisenhower, Alberta, Canada; Avenue de President Kennedy, Paris

Branches of the U.S. Armed Forces
Army, Navy, Air Force, Marines, National Guard, Coast Guard

Elements (Buddhism)
Earth, Water, Fire, Wind, Space, Consciousness

Grades of Meat
Prime, Choice, Good, Standard, Commercial, Utility

Sinister Six (Spider-Man's Arch Enemies)
Kraven the Hunter, Dr. Octopus, Mystero, Vulture, Electro, Sandman

Hockey Positions
Center, Left wing, Right wing, Left defense, Right defense, Goalie

D'oh! 40% of car-theft victims left their keys in the ignition.

BATHROOM FENG SHUI

Is it Eastern wisdom or mumbo-jumbo? Whatever else it is, Feng Shui
is a popular method of interior design, based around the harmonious
flow of "ch'i"—the ever-present life force. Naturally we figured
there must be feng shui for our favorite room, and we found
it in this excerpt from Feng Shui, *by Derek Walters.*

ANCIENT WISDOM
A complex blend of common sense, fine aesthetics, and
mystical philosophy, *Feng Shui* is a traditional Chinese
technique which aims to ensure that all things are in harmony
with their surroundings. Its application ranges from the planning
of entire cities to the placing of a single flower in a vase, from the
orientation of high-rise office blocks to the interior furnishing of a
humble studio apartment. What Westerners might refer to as the
"feel" of a place—good or bad—the Chinese call *Feng Shui*. Having
the correct *Feng Shui* in the home is said to enhance happiness and
prosperity.

The term *Feng Shui*, literally translated, means "Wind and
Water"; these are regarded as being akin to the flow of vital ener-
gies, called *ch'i* (meaning breath, air, or current), through which
Feng Shui operates.

BATHROOM DYNAMICS

As might be expected, the bathroom is associated with the element
Water, which belongs to the North direction. As a consequence,
the Northern side of the house will be the most suitable location for
it. The purpose of the bathroom is to cleanse the body, externally
and internally; and for this reason, the *ch'i* should be encouraged to
flow through quickly and not allowed to settle or stagnate. According to Chinese tradition, elaborate bathrooms, which inhibit the
flow of *ch'i*, should therefore be avoided.

No matter how small the bathroom, according to *Feng Shui*
principles, there should be a window leading to the outside. This
is not merely for ventilation. Despite the fact that modern fans can
adequately keep the air fresh—possibly even more efficiently than
natural ventilation—if the bathroom does not have one exterior
wall, it follows that the room is situated in the core of the building,

a feature which is highly undesirable. In traditional Chinese houses, the central area was an enclosed courtyard, which had an almost sacred function. Not even trees were allowed to occupy the center, and it would be considered extremely disagreeable to have the bathroom there. If, however, the bathroom is centrally placed, it should be abundantly mirrored, if possible on each wall.

KITCHEN-NYET

An old rule of *Feng Shui*, echoed by many Western designers, is that the kitchen should not be next to the bathroom. But such a regulation is often impracticable; the position of these rooms are determined by the access to a main water supply and drainage. If the kitchen and the bathroom are likely to be close to each other, there should be a passage, storeroom, or cupboard between them. If it is absolutely impossible to avoid the two rooms being adjacent, then the kitchen wall which backs up to the bathroom must *not* be the one which houses the stove, and preferably should be opposite it. Putting the bathroom above the kitchen (a common Western practice) is considered extremely bad *Feng Shui* because waste will flow past a vital area.

Despite the convenience of an en suite bathroom, this is not favorable according to the principles of *Feng Shui*. The objection is to the presence of water in close proximity to the sleeper. Therefore, it is advisable to separate the bathroom from the bedroom either with an intervening corridor, a built-in wardrobe, or adequate insulation. In essence, the bedroom should be the last call of the *ch'i* through the house. *Ch'i* should enter softly, and leave just as quietly.

PIPE DREAMS

Water should not be seen flowing away; thus, waste pipes, overflows, and drains should be covered or concealed. Many Chinese bathrooms, instead of having baths or showers, have floor-mounted sinks and scoops with which water is poured over the body. This method of bathing conserves water. Interestingly, although there is no shortage of water in Southeast Asia, wasting water infers financial waste. (In Chinese, *Shui*—"water"—is slang for "money.")

A final note: Unless the bathroom has several windows, open space should not be obscured by potted plants. They obstruct the flow of the *ch'i*, creating unhealthy stagnant areas.

Plants, like people, run fevers when they're sick.

STRANGE LAWSUITS

These days, it seems that people will sue each other over practically anything. Here are a few real-life examples of unusual legal battles.

THE PLAINTIFF: Teri Smith Tyler

THE DEFENDANTS: Jimmy Carter, Bill Clinton, Ross Perot, IBM, American Cyanamid, BCCI, David Rockefeller, and NASA

THE LAWSUIT: Tyler claimed to be a cyborg (part human, part robot) receiving telepathic instructions from "Proteus." According to the $5.6 billion lawsuit, she claimed the defendants had a secret plan to breed and enslave millions of black women.

THE VERDICT: Not guilty. Said the judge, "If this Court cannot order dismissal of *this* complaint...no district court can ever dismiss *any* complaint."

THE PLAINTIFF: Oreste Lodi

THE DEFENDANT: Oreste Lodi

THE LAWSUIT: Lodi, the defendant, was beneficiary to a trust fund. Lodi, the plaintiff, claimed he was tired of the defendant controlling his estate. So Lodi sued himself, asking the court to revoke his birth certificate so that he, Lodi, the plaintiff, could take control of his money away from Lodi, the defendant, and get sole possession of the trust.

THE VERDICT: Case dismissed. The decision, the court said, was eminently fair: "Although it is true that, as plaintiff, he loses, it is equally true that, as defendant, he wins!"

THE PLAINTIFF: Freshman Jason Wilkins

THE DEFENDANT: University of Idaho

THE LAWSUIT: Wilkins "mooned" some friends from his third-floor dorm window. But as he leaned his naked butt against the glass, he fell through and plummeted to the ground below, suffering a broken vertebra and severe cuts and bruises over his entire body. Humiliated, Wilkins sued the university for failing to warn students about "the dangerous nature of windows."

THE VERDICT: Not guilty. Wilkins suffered additional injury—

If there are 10 books on a bookshelf, they can be arranged in 3,628,800 different ways.

to his ego—when the local newspaper revealed the fact that he "was not intoxicated" at the time of the accident.

THE PLAINTIFFS: Ivan Jordan, Kaziah Hancock, and Cindy Stewart, three former members of The True and Living Church of Jesus Christ of Saints of the Last Days
THE DEFENDANT: Jim Harmston, self-proclaimed prophet
THE LAWSUIT: The three claimed that they had turned over all of their money and possessions to Harmston. Value: $264,390. In return, Harmston promised them a face-to-face meeting with Jesus Christ and did not deliver. Papers filed with the court said that Harmston took advantage of their "deepest spiritual needs."
THE VERDICT: Unknown.

THE PLAINTIFF: Robert Kropinski
THE DEFENDANT: Maharishi International University
THE LAWSUIT: Kropinski sued because, after 11 years at MIU, he still had not achieved "the perfect state of life" that was promised. Nor had he learned how to reverse the aging process or how to fly, which were also promised. He had only learned to "hop with his legs folded."
THE VERDICT: The jury agreed that the university had misled Kropinski and awarded him $137,890.

*　　*　　*

IN HOT PURSUIT

Selma Troyanoski, 53, an elected member of the board of supervisors of Portage County, Wisconsin, was charged with attempting to obstruct an officer in Lake Geneva, Wisconsin. The incident began when Troyanoski pulled into a rest stop for a nap. When an investigating officer saw her slumped over and tried to investigate, she suddenly sped off, leading police on a chase at speeds of up to 110 mph.

Officers finally cornered Troyanoski in a residential neighborhood. When she refused to exit the vehicle, they smashed her car window and opened the door to pull her out. That was when they discovered she wasn't wearing pants or underwear. She had fled the cops out of embarrassment. Troyanoski explained that she prefers to drive without pants or underwear on long trips because she "gets very sweaty." She faces up to three years in prison.

An astronaut can reach the moon in less time than it took a...

REVENGE!

Revenge, Uncle John is fond of saying, is a dish best served cold...with a side salad and French rolls.

ALL SHOOK UP

Victims: Red and Sonny West, members of Elvis Presley's "Memphis Mafia," and Dave Hebler, his bodyguard

What Happened: In July 1976, Vernon Presley fired all three men, possibly to cut costs, possibly because Elvis was growing paranoid.

Revenge: They wrote *Elvis: What Happened?*, a devastating exposé that shattered the King's public image by revealing for the first time the lurid and bizarre details of his private life, including his temper tantrums, drug habit, and sex life. Two weeks after it was published in 1977, Elvis died, leaving conspiracy theorists to speculate that the book drove him to suicide.

HELLO?

Victim: Almon Brown Strowger, a Kansas City undertaker

What Happened: In the late 1880s, a friend of Strowger's passed away. He expected to get the funeral business, but the call never came. He blamed the local switchboard operator, whom he suspected of steering calls to her husband—a rival undertaker.

Revenge: Strowger invented the world's first automatic telephone exchange (and later the first dial telephone), making it possible for people to dial directly, without the help of an operator.

WHERE THE STREETS HAVE HIS NAME

Victim: Cripple Creek, Colorado

What Happened: *Collier's* magazine commissioned writer and gourmet Julian Street to write a travel article about Cripple Creek, Colorado. When he arrived in town, Street happened to stroll down Myers Avenue and strike up a conversation with a red-headed woman named Madame Leo, who informed him that he was in the heart of the town's red-light district. Street described his conversation with the bawdy lady at length in his article. Cripple Creek's town fathers were humiliated.

Revenge: They changed the name of Myers Ave. to Julian Street.

MOUNT PELÉE

What's worse than a volcanic eruption in your town? A volcanic eruption in your town on Election Day. Here's one of the strangest events in the history of Western democracy.

E LECTION DAY POLITICS
One of the worst volcanic disasters in history was caused not by the eruption...but by politics.

Mount Pelée, on the island of Martinique in the Caribbean Sea, began smoking and shaking in late April 1902. The people of St. Pierre, the town at the base of the volcano, remembered that the volcano had rumbled years earlier, but since it had quieted down and was seemingly dormant, they weren't too concerned... at first.

But when scalding mud flows began pouring down the mountain and ashes fell faster than they could be swept away, many changed their minds and thought the town should be evacuated. As it happened, the city's elections were only a few days away. The mayor and the governor of the island were concerned about the growing popularity of a radical political party that stood for equal rights for all races and threatened the white supremacy of the island.

Mayor Fouche and Governor Mouttet refused to allow anything to delay the election even a single day. The editor of the paper was on their side and published articles by fictional "volcano experts" who had supposedly examined the situation and said there was no danger.

BLOWBACK

Soon the volcano became more violent. A giant mudslide wiped out the sugar mill on the edge of town, taking the factory workers with it, and a huge seismic wave spawned by undersea earthquakes wiped out the entire seafront district. People began packing to leave, but found the roads out of town blocked by soldiers sent by the governor. He was determined to prevent anyone from leaving before the election.

The people went to the local church and begged the bishop to intervene on their behalf, but he refused to go against the wishes of the state. At dawn on election day, Mount Pelée exploded. A colossal cloud of super-heated gasses, ash, and rock blew out of a notch in the crater, directly at the town four miles away, at a rate of 100 mph. Within three minutes, the entire population—including the mayor, governor, bishop, and newspaper editor—was dead. Even ships anchored offshore were set ablaze, killing crew members and passengers.

Only two people in the town survived. A black prisoner condemned to death for murdering a white man was to have been hanged that day, but the governor had granted him clemency in the hopes that it would give him some of the black vote. The prisoner was being held in an underground cell with one small window facing away from the volcano. He was horribly burned, but survived and later toured with the Barnum and Bailey Circus as a sideshow attraction.

The only other survivor was the town cobbler, a religious fanatic who had been hiding in his cellar, praying, when the mountain erupted. He, too, was terribly burned, and some reports say that he never regained his sanity after coming out of his cellar to find every single one of the townfolk—30,000 people in all—dead.

* * *

RIDICULOUS POLITICAL WORDS

- **Flugie:** A rule that helps only the rule maker.
- **Bloviate:** To speechify pompously.
- **Speechify:** To deliver a speech in a tedious way.
- **Roorback:** An invented rumor intended to smear an opponent.
- **Bafflegab:** Intentionally confusing jargon.
- **Gobbledygook:** Nonsensical explanation, bafflegab.
- **Snollygoster:** A politician who puts politics ahead of principle.
- **Boondoggle:** Wasteful or crooked government-funded project.
- **Mugwump:** A political maverick.

When you soft-pedal something, you are referring to the piano pedal used to mute the tone.

UNCLE JOHN'S STALL OF FAME

Here are some creative ways that people have gotten involved with bathrooms, toilets, toilet paper, etc.

Honoree: Lam Sai Wing of Hong Kong
Notable Achievement: Building a pot of gold
True Story: When Lam Sai Wing was growing up in communist China, he dreamed of someday being rich. He eventually moved to Hong Kong and opened a jewelry store called 3-D Gold and by 2001 had the money to build the toilet of his dreams...out of gold. And he had enough money left over to build an entire bathroom of gold—wash basins, toilet brushes, toilet paper holders, towel holders, mirror frames, doors, even bathroom tiles. He topped it all off with a ceiling encrusted with precious gems. Total cost: $4.9 million, which Lam offsets by charging admission to the bathroom. Peeking into the restroom costs $4; to use the facilities, you have to spend at least $138 in the store.

Honoree: Greg Kotis, an inspired playwright
Notable Achievement: Writing a musical about urinals...and actually making it onto Broadway
True Story: Trying to live in Paris on $4 a day, Kotis slept on park benches and often had to choose between eating and using the city's pay urinals. One rainy afternoon while making such a choice (he chose food), a thought occurred to him: What if a single evil corporation—the Urine Good Company—controlled all of the pay urinals in a city?

"I just stood there maybe fifteen minutes. In the rain. Thinking it out," he says. Inspired, he wrote a play called *Urinetown, The Musical*. After a sold-out off-Broadway run, it opened on the Great White Way in September 2001. Highlight: A song called "It's a Privilege to Pee."

Honoree: Carl Rennie Davis, a pub owner in Stourbridge, England

---

Elvis had a pet monkey named Scatter.

Notable Achievement: Converting his men's room urinals into an electronic arcade game...of sorts

True Story: Davis installed paddle wheels in the drainpipes of his men's room urinals; then he hooked each one up to a row of vertical lights. How many lights flash depends on how long—and how "strong"—a person uses the urinal. Customers can compete to see who can light the most lights, and because extra rows of lights are mounted over the bar, ladies in the pub can follow the action.

Honoree: The Kimberly-Clark company

Notable Achievement: Building a better toilet paper roll

True Story: How can you improve on a classic? Kimberly-Clark took out the cardboard tube and made it a solid block of toilet paper. Now it's "coreless"! Here's the good news: The new roll has twice as much paper, so you change it half as often. Now, the bad news: It requires a special kind of dispenser and you can't have one—so far, they're strictly for commercial use in offices and restaurants. Maybe someday...

Honoree: Bob Ernst, a playwright and high school drama teacher in San Francisco

Notable Achievement: Writing and producing the only play ever staged in a bathroom

True Story: Ernst, 56, wrote a one-act play called *The John*, about a man named Alvin who meets Death in a theater men's room during an intermission of "King Lear." He staged the play in a men's room in the basement of the Maritime Hall in San Francisco, which he booked for $100 a day. Ernst, who plays both Alvin and Death, performed in front of 20 spectators who sat on folding chairs wedged into the space between the second and fourth stalls.

Why write a play that takes place in a bathroom? "Death can happen anywhere, anytime," Ernst says. "Elvis died in a john, you know. One minute you're here, the next you're gone. That's the way it is."

INCREDIBLE ANIMAL FACTS

Sit. Fetch. Roll over. Even more interesting than watching animals perform tricks we teach them, is watching what they do naturally. This list of truly amazing facts about animals was compiled by BRI staffer Taylor Clark.

• The world's longest earthworms—found only in a small corner of Australia—can grow to as long as 12 feet and as thick as a soda can.

• Ancient Romans trained elephants to perform on a tightrope.

• Squids have the largest eyes in nature—up to 16 inches across.

• Australia's mallee bird can tell temperature with its tongue, accurate to within two degrees.

• Potbellied sloths sleep 20 hours a day and are in danger of extinction because mating takes too much energy.

• Most kangaroo rats never drink water.

• The chamois—a goatlike mountain antelope—can balance on a point of rock the size of a quarter.

• Robins become drunk after eating holly berries and often fall off power lines.

• Octopus eyes resemble human eyes—the U.S. Air Force once taught an octopus to "read" by distinguishing letterlike shapes.

• A woodpecker's beak moves at a speed of 100 mph.

• By using air currents to keep it aloft, an albatross may fly up to 87,000 mi. on a single feeding trip without ever touching the ground. That's more than three times around the Earth.

• Polar bears are so perfectly insulated from the cold that they spend most of their time trying to cool down.

• Whales can communicate with each other from over 3,000 miles away (but the message takes over an hour to get there).

• Domesticated elephants have learned to stuff mud into the cowbells around their necks before sneaking out at night to steal bananas.

• A mouse has more bones than a human.

In 1977 New York hunters killed 83,204 deer...and 7 fellow hunters.

THEY TOOK THE PLUNGE

In 1886 a man named Carl Graham rode a barrel through the rapids below Niagara Falls, starting a craze of riding the rapids in barrels. Soon, people started looking for a bigger challenge—riding the falls.

OVER A BARREL

There are three individual falls at Niagara. At American Falls, 300 tons of water drop 180 feet per second and boulders as big as houses litter the base. No one has ever survived a trip over it. Luna Falls, only 90 feet wide, is too small to ride. At Horseshoe Falls, 2,700 tons of water pass over every second. Rocks cannot withstand the constant onslaught of water, boulders are pulverized. But there is a deep plunge pool at the bottom, making it the only fall that can be ridden.

DAREDEVILS

Here are the people who have dared to go over Niagara Falls in a barrel:

• **Annie Edson Taylor** (1901). The first person ever to go over Niagara in a barrel, this widowed, unemployed schoolteacher was 63 years old when she did it. She used an oak wine barrel padded with cushions. After the plunge, she spent 17 minutes bobbing around before assistants pulled her ashore. Emerging dazed but unhurt, she said, "No one ought ever do that again." She was incoherent for several days afterward.

• **Bobby Leach** (1911). This circus stuntman went over the falls in a steel barrel and survived. Fifteen years later, while on tour with his famous barrel in New Zealand, Leach slipped on an orange peel and fell. He broke his leg, which later had to be amputated, leading to gangrene, which killed him.

• **Charles Stephens** (1920). A 58-year-old barber, he had a fair reputation as a high-dive and parachute artist, but thought a trip over Niagara Falls would make him really famous. He attached a 100-pound anvil to the bottom of his barrel for ballast and then got in and strapped his feet to the anvil. He surrounded himself with pillows and inserted his arms into two straps bolted inside the barrel. The force of the plunge caused the bottom to drop out of the barrel. The anvil, together with Mr. Stephens, sank to the bot-

---

Apples and oranges: Apples ripen after being picked. Oranges don't.

tom. The only part of the barrel recovered was a stave with an arm strap attached to it; Stephens' right arm was still threaded through the strap. A tattoo on the arm read, "Forget me not, Annie." Annie was his wife and mother of his 11 children.

- **Jean Lussier** (1928). Lussier made the trip not in a barrel but in a six-foot rubber ball lined with rubber tubes. After bobbing about at the bottom of the falls for an hour, he was pulled to shore and emerged unharmed in front of an audience of more than 100,000. Afterward he sold small souvenir pieces of the inner tubes for 50 cents each. When he ran out of authentic pieces, he peddled rubber purchased from a nearby tire store.

- **George Strathakis** (1930). This 46-year-old Greek chef went over to generate publicity for his book, *The Mysterious Veil of Humanity Through the Ages*. His airtight barrel was trapped behind the falls for over 14 hours before rescuers could retrieve it; by then it was out of air. Only his pet turtle, Sonny Boy, taken along for good luck, survived.

- **William "Red" Hill, Jr.** (1951). Hill, 38, should have known better: his father was a boatman who retrieved the bodies of suicide victims from the waters below the falls. Hill didn't use a barrel, he used "The Thing"—made of 13 inner tubes, a fish net, and canvas straps. Thousands of people watched as "The Thing" became trapped under the falling water. Finally a few inner tubes emerged from the mist. His mangled body turned up the next day.

- **Nathan Boya** (1961). He made the trip in a steel sphere covered by six layers of rubber, which he called the "Plunge-o-Sphere." He emerged unhurt to find the police waiting for him. He was fined $100—the minimum sentence for violating the Niagara Parks Act.

- **Karel Soucek** (1984). The first Canadian to survive the plunge. His barrel had liquid foam insulation, two eye holes, and a snorkel. The fall took 3.2 seconds but left Soucek trapped in dangerous waters for 45 minutes before being pulled free. Fortunately, he suffered only minor injuries. Six months later, he recreated the spectacle at the Houston Astrodome in front of 45,000 spectators. His barrel was hoisted to the top of the dome by a crane and released into a water tank, 10 feet in diameter and 10 feet deep. But the barrel missed—it hit the edge of the water tank and killed him.

- **Steven Trotter** (1985). This Rhode Island bartender went over

---

On average, a sheep trained to turn the lights on and off will leave them on 82% of the time.

the falls in two plastic pickle barrels wrapped in inner tubes. At the age of 22, he became the youngest person ever to make the trip. He was fined $5,000 for the stunt, but he more than made up for that with his talk show fees. On the 10th anniversary of the stunt, he returned with a woman named Lori Martin and they became the first coed couple to go over together.

• **Dave Munday** (1985). Munday has dared the falls four times to date. In 1985 a police officer saw him and immediately radioed Hydro-Control to cut the water flow, which stopped the barrel. Later that year he made the trip successfully in an aluminum barrel. In 1990 his barrel got stuck at the very brink of the falls, but in 1993 he succeeded again, this time in a converted diving bell, and at age 56, became the first person to go over the falls twice.

• **Peter DeBernardi and Geoffrey Petkovich** (1989). Canadian residents of Niagara Falls, they were the first people to go over the falls as a team, face to face in the same ten-foot steel barrel. Both men survived, suffering only minor injuries. Petkovich, who had been drinking, emerged wearing only a necktie and cowboy boots. They were arrested by the Niagara Parks Police.

• **Jessie Sharp** (1990). 28-year-old Sharp rode the falls in a kayak. His plan was to gather so much momentum that he would avoid the thundering water and land in the pools at the bottom, then ride the rapids downstream to Lewiston, New York—where he had dinner reservations. He didn't wear a life jacket or a helmet—he wanted his face to show clearly on the videotape his friends were shooting. Minutes after he entered the water above the falls, police ordered the hydroelectric dam to shut the water flow, intending to stop him. It didn't stop him, but it slowed him down. He dropped over the falls like a sack of bricks. His kayak was recovered, but his body was never found.

• **Robert Overacker** (1995). The 39-year-old Overacker was attracted to thrill sports. He wanted a career as a stuntman and thought performing the ultimate stunt would provide him with good publicity. He went over the falls on a jet ski, wearing a self-inflating life vest, a crash helmet, and a wet suit. A rocket-propelled parachute was supposed to be deployed at the brink of the falls—but it failed to inflate. His body was recovered by the tour boat *Maid of the Mist*.

Fate of the only parking meter in Owyhee County, Idaho: An irate motorist shot it in 1979.

THEY WENT THATAWAY

*We're not just fascinated by the way famous people
lived, we're fascinated by the way they die, too.
Here are a few stories from our BRI files.*

MARY TODD LINCOLN

Claim to Fame: Widow of President Abraham Lincoln

How She Died: In bed with "Mr. Lincoln."

Postmortem: Mrs. Lincoln's life was filled with tragedy: Her son Tad died from tuberculosis in 1850 when he was only 3; her son Willie died of typhoid fever in 1862 when he was 11; her husband was assassinated in 1865; and her 18-year-old son Thomas died in 1871. Only one of her children, Robert Lincoln, survived into adulthood.

Mary Lincoln never recovered from the shock of her husband's death, and her son Thomas' death sent her completely over the edge. She suffered from hallucinations and by 1875 was so disturbed that she attempted suicide. Robert had her committed to an asylum that very night.

Four months later, she was released and sent to live with her sister in Illinois, and in June 1876, a jury ruled that she had regained her sanity. In 1879 Mrs. Lincoln's health began to deteriorate. By now reclusive and nearly blind, she spent most of the last 18 months of her life locked in her bedroom, where she slept on one side of the bed because she was convinced that her husband was sleeping on the other side. She died on July 16, 1882, at the age of 63, after suffering a stroke.

JOHN DENVER

Claim to Fame: A singer and songwriter, Denver shot to fame in the 1970s with hits like "Rocky Mountain High" and "Take Me Home, Country Road."

How He Died: He crashed his own airplane.

Postmortem: Denver was a lifelong aviation buff and an experi-

---

Broccoli was first introduced to the U.S. in the 1920s.

enced pilot. He learned to fly from his father, an ex-Air Force pilot who made his living training pilots to fly Lear Jets.

Denver had just bought an aerobatic plane known as a Long-EZ shortly before the crash and was still getting used to flying it. According to the report released by the National Transportation Safety Board, he needed an extra seatback cushion for his feet to reach the foot pedals, but when he used the cushion he had trouble reaching the fuel tank selector handle located behind his left shoulder. The NTSB speculates that he took off without enough fuel. When one of his tanks ran dry and the engine lost power, Denver accidentally stepped on the right rudder pedal while reaching over his left shoulder with his right arm to switch to the other fuel tank, and crashed the plane into the sea.

Final Irony: Denver's first big success came in 1967, when he wrote the Peter, Paul, and Mary hit "Leaving on a Jet Plane."

L. RON HUBBARD

Claim to Fame: Science-fiction writer and founder of the Church of Scientology

How He Died: No one knows for sure.

Postmortem: Hubbard founded his church in 1952. The larger it grew and the more money it collected from followers, the more controversial it became. A British court condemned Scientology as "immoral, socially obnoxious, corrupt, sinister and dangerous;" a Los Angeles court denounced it as "schizophrenic and paranoid."

Hubbard had a lot of enemies in law-enforcement agencies in the U.S....the IRS suspected him of skimming millions in church funds. For a time he avoided prosecutors by sailing around the Mediterranean, and from 1976 to 1979 he lived in hiding in small desert towns in Southern California. Then in 1980 he vanished. He didn't resurface until January 25, 1986, when someone called a funeral home in San Luis Obispo, California, and instructed them to pick up a body from a ranch about 20 miles north of town. The corpse was identified as Lafayette Ronald Hubbard.

The FBI's fingerprint files confirmed that the man really was Hubbard. The official cause of death: a cerebral hemorrhage. But a "certificate of religious belief" filed on behalf of Hubbard prevented the coroner from conducting an autopsy, so we'll never really know.

How did grocers get their name? They sold goods by the gross.

CURE FOR WHAT AILS YE

The medical profession pooh-poohs folk remedies, but who knows? Just because the cure involves fish skins or live frogs, that doesn't make it wrong, does it? Read on for some of Uncle John's favorite folk remedies.

To cure a cold, tie fish skin to your feet.

To cure mosquito bites, rub them with vinegar, oil, butter, onion, garlic, or lemon peel and then blow on them.

To get rid of freckles, rub a live frog over your face.

To cure earaches, plug the ears with a shelled snail or a slice of warm bacon. Another cure: Pour some pig's milk, warm oil, or sap from a male ash tree on them.

Drinking red pepper tea or putting dry pepper in your stockings will cure the chills.

In order to get rid of warts, put a piece of silver and some stones in a little sack and leave it on a road—the person who picks up the sack will take on the warts.

Another way to be rid of warts: steal a piece of steak and bury it where three roads cross.

You can cure throat illnesses by rubbing the soles of your feet with an unguent made of garlic cooked in lard, but some prefer spitting in a frog's mouth.

A general medicinal drink: kerosene with sugar.

Passing a child under the belly of a horse three times can cure the child's cough.

Insomniacs should rub their temples with cat fat or eat chicken feet with cooked milkweed. Or they can smoke a mixture of black tobacco, toad powder, and honey.

Pierced ears are said to cure eye trouble.

For an upset stomach, dip a comb in holy water, then leave it in a pot of wine. The comb must stay on the person's belly for 24 hours. This person must then drink a mouthful of the wine and throw away the rest.

Chew slowly: Choking on food is the seventh leading cause of death in America.

THE HISTORY OF FOOTBALL, PART I

*If you're a fan of Monday Night Football, you may not realize
that football was invented by college students long before
the pros came along. Here's Part I. Hut, hut, hike!*

CLASS WARFARE

In 1827 the sophomores of Harvard University challenged the freshmen class to a game of "ball," to be played on the first Monday of the new academic year. The freshmen accepted.

That first game was a pretty informal affair; they just kicked around an inflated pig's bladder—a *pigskin*. There were few rules and there was no limit to how many people could play on each team so the *entire* freshman class played the *entire* sophomore class, minus anyone who chickened out. The young gentlemen—many of whom were very drunk—must have had a good time, because the freshman-sophomore ball game became an annual Harvard tradition.

...A very violent Harvard tradition: "The game consisted of kicking, pushing, slugging, and getting angry," Allison Danzig writes in *The History of American Football*. "Anyone who felt like joining in and getting his shins barked, his eyes blacked or his teeth knocked out, was free to do so." The sophomores had an advantage, because as returning students they could recognize their teammates on the field; the incoming freshmen could not.

Some years the game erupted into a full-blown riot, and even when it didn't it was still pretty rough; game day became known as "Bloody Monday." The 1860 Bloody Monday game was *so* bloody, in fact, that the university banned football altogether.

PREHISTORIC FOOTBALL

Games involving teams of people kicking and throwing a ball toward opposing goals have probably been around for as long as there have been things to kick; no one knows for sure when the first football-type game was played or who played in it. Different football games are believed to have appeared independently of one

---

13% of adults say "the last day of summer" is the "occasion they dread the most."

another in cultures all over the world. In China, for example, people were kicking around balls stuffed with human hair as far back as 300 B.C.

ENGLISH FOOTBALL

The ancient Greeks played a game called *Harpaston* on a rectangular field marked off with goal lines. When the Romans conquered Greece in 146 B.C. they picked up the game, renamed it *Harpastum*, and spread it all over the Roman Empire, including England and Ireland. (Tradition has it that the first English game, or *melee*, was played "with the head of an enemy Dane.")

By the 12th century, many neighboring towns or parishes in the British Isles played an annual football game against one another on Shrove Tuesday, the British equivalent of Mardi Gras, as a sort of last, violent hurrah before the start of Lent on Ash Wednesday.

An inflated pig's bladder or some other kind of ball was brought out to whatever served as the traditional starting point of the game: the town square, marketplace, or a field between the two towns. A local dignitary threw the ball into the crowd of hundreds or in some cases thousands of participating townspeople, who immediately surged toward it. As the quickest, strongest participants muscled their way toward the center of the action, the people at the periphery grabbed on for dear life, pushing, pulling, punching, and kicking each other as they tried to somehow steer the brawling mass of humanity toward the goal.

FREE-FOR-ALL

There were no rules or referees and no restrictions on how the ball could be kicked, carried, or thrown. Some matches restricted participation to young men only; others allowed women and children as well. Most games lasted for hours on end, with the action ending only when it became too dark to play (unless people decided to play in the dark).

"Broken shins, broken heads, torn coats, and lost hats are among the minor accidents of this fearful contest," one chronicler wrote of the annual Shrove Tuesday game between the St. Peter and All Saints parishes in the town of Derby, England, in 1795. "And it frequently happens that persons fall, fainting and bleeding beneath the feet of the surrounding mob. ... Still the crowd is encouraged by respectable persons...urging on the players with shouts, and even handing refreshment to those who are exhausted."

US AGAINST THEM

Shrove Tuesday matches and other annual games proved to be an effective means for neighboring towns to settle scores that had arisen since the year before. It was the element of revenge, perhaps more than any other, that allowed football to survive, Stephen Fox writes in *Big Leagues*:

> Football came down the centuries less as recreation than as an expression of durable animosities between longstanding rivals. The essential point was to smite the enemy, not to play the game. Football by itself was too rough and risky to attract many players without the extra, emboldening goad supplied by smoldering feuds and hatreds.

Playing football proved such a compelling distraction that it even got in the way of other more traditional forms of violence: In 1389 King Richard II tried to ban the game, claiming that it threatened the kingdom's defenses by interfering with archery practice. He failed, as did every other monarch who tried to ban football.

CINDERELLA STORY

By the early 1800s, traditional Shrove Tuesday football games had faded into history, replaced by similar grudge-match games between rival English secondary schools. The game they played was similar to modern-day "English football," or soccer, a kicking game that did not allow touching or running with the ball. The game remained virtually unchanged until 1823, when someone broke the rules at the now-famous Rugby school. William Web Ellis happened to get the ball just as the clock began to strike five. The rules stipulated that all games ended on the final stroke of five, but Ellis was too far away from the goal to have a shot at scoring. With only seconds left, he picked up the ball and ran across the goal line, just as the clock struck five.

Carrying the ball was against the rules, but it was also fun. And as the Rugby students quickly realized, so was tackling the ball carrier. "Rugby rules" football soon began to emerge as a separate sport. Rugby even developed its own egg-shaped ball, which was easier to carry under the arm than the traditional round ball.

FOOTBALL IN AMERICA

Rugby enthusiasts brought the new game with them to the far reaches of the British empire, but in the United States it was still virtually unknown. By the early 1800s, many eastern universities were starting to invent their homegrown versions of football, with each college making up its own set of rules. As with Harvard, many of these games were blood-sport rituals that allowed students to bond with their own classmates against men of other classes. Princeton played a game called "ballown" as early as 1820, and Yale began playing a rowdy form of soccer in 1851.

Because each university's game was different, the schools did not play each other until 1869, when Rutgers and nearby Princeton University both adopted the soccer rules of the London Football Association and played what historians consider to be the country's first intercollegiate football game. (Rutgers won, 6–4.)

Columbia and Yale started playing Rutgers and Princeton in 1870; and in 1871, Harvard lifted their ban on football, but they played their own version, known as "the Boston Game." Unlike the soccer played at other universities, the Boston Game was more than just a kicking game. A player could pick up the ball whenever he wanted and pass it to his teammates; he was even allowed to run with it.

CANADIAN IMPORT

In 1874 the rugby team at Canada's McGill University challenged Harvard to a series of three games of football. On May 14, the two schools played the Boston Game. Harvard won, 3–0. The next day, they played rugby, which meant that tackling was allowed, and *carrying* the ball across the goal line and touching the ground with it—making a "touchdown"—was scored just like a kicked goal.

Switching from the Boston Game to rugby wasn't easy for the Harvard team, since no one on the team had ever even seen rugby played before. The game ended in a 0–0 tie, but the Harvard team enjoyed rugby so much that when they made a trip to Montreal later that year to play the third game, they played rugby again. This time they beat McGill 3–0, and were so taken with the new game that they abandoned the Boston Game and switched to rugby.

GETTING THE BALL ROLLING

In 1875 Yale decided to try rugby and challenged Harvard to a game. The game retained much of its rugby character, with a few concessions to Yale's rules thrown in for good measure: Touchdowns, for example, had no value, but gave the scoring team a chance to kick a goal.

A record crowd of 2,000 spectators showed up to watch the game that day, and Yale lost, 0–4. That didn't matter—the crowds were huge and the Yale players had fun. They switched to rugby in 1876.

Two Princeton students watching in the stands that afternoon enjoyed the Harvard-Yale game so much that they convinced the Princeton student body to change over to rugby and to invite representatives from Harvard, Yale, and Columbia to form an Intercollegiate Football Association to draw up a uniform set of rules.

THE THIRD MAN

Another person watching from the stands at that first Harvard-Yale game was a 16-year-old named Walter Camp, who would enter Yale the following year. Camp was thrilled by what he'd seen on the playing field, and as he left the game that day he made two promises to himself: 1) the next time, Yale would win, and 2) he would be on the team.

Camp got everything he wanted—he made the team and Yale beat Harvard, 1–0. And he got a lot more than that: He went on to play halfback for Yale (1877–1882), then coached the team (1888–1892), winning 67 games and losing only two. He also served on every collegiate football rules committee from 1878 until his death in 1925, and was so instrumental in guiding and shaping the new game that was beginning to evolve out of rugby that sports historians consider him the father of American football.

Ready to move the ball downfield? Turn to page 155
for Part II of the The History of Football.

so that when he drove down dirt roads he would leave a trail of "TM"s.

BOX-OFFICE BLOOPERS

We all love bloopers. Here are a bunch of movie mistakes to look for in popular films. You can find more in a book called Roman Soldiers Don't Wear Watches: 333 Film Flubs, *by Bill Givens.*

Movie: *Terminator 2: Judgment Day* (1991)
Scene: As Arnold Schwarzenegger's cyborg character heads toward a bar, he passes a parked car.
Blooper: Arnie's cranial read-out says the car he's scanning is a Plymouth sedan. It's actually a Ford.

Movie: *Forrest Gump* (1994)
Scene: In a sequence set around 1970, someone is shown reading a copy of *USA Today*.
Blooper: The newspaper wasn't created until 1982.

Movie: *Camelot* (1967)
Scene: King Arthur (Richard Harris) expounds on the joys of his mythical kingdom.
Blooper: The 6th-century king has a 20th-century Band-Aid on the back of his neck.

Movie: *Wayne's World* (1992)
Scene: Wayne and Garth are filming their cable access show.
Blooper: The exterior shot of the house show it's night. Look out the window of the interior shot: it's daytime.

Movie: *The Invisible Man* (1933)
Scene: Claude Rains, in the title role, strips completely naked and uses his invisibility to elude police.
Blooper: The police track his footprints in the snow. But check out the footprints—they're made by feet wearing shoes.

Movie: *Field of Dreams* (1989)
Scene: Shoeless Joe Jackson is shown batting right-handed.
Blooper: The real Shoeless Joe was left-handed.

Before appearing in *The Exorcist*, Linda Blair starred in a mustard commercial on TV.

Movie: *The Wizard of Oz* (1939)
Scene: Before the Wicked Witch of the West sends her flying monkeys to capture Dorothy and friends in the Haunted Forest, she tells the head monkey that she has "sent a little insect on ahead to take the fight out of them." What does she mean by that? She's referring to a song-and-dance sequence featuring "The Jitterbug," a bug that causes its victims to dance wildly until they are exhausted.
Blooper: The sequence was cut from the film before its release.

Movie: *Face-Off* (1997)
Scene: The hero (John Travolta) learns that a bomb is about to go off somewhere. But where? He's got six days to pry the information from the villain. We then see the bomb—it shows 216 hours.
Blooper: Do the math: 216 hours equals *nine* days. Did someone forget to tell us we've gone to 36-hour days?

Movie: *Entrapment* (1999)
Scene: Catherine Zeta-Jones's character says she needs 10 seconds to download computer files that will steal billions of dollars from an international bank. She states further that after 11:00 p.m. her computer will steal 1/10th of a second every minute, totaling ten seconds by midnight.
Blooper: More Hollywood math: One-tenth of a second per minute for 60 minutes equals only six seconds…four shy of the required ten.

Movie: *The Story of Robin Hood* (1952)
Scene: In one scene, Maid Marian (played by Joan Rice) wears a dress with a zipper in the back.
Blooper: Did they have zippers in the 12th century?

Movie: *Wild Wild West* (1999)
Scene: After thwarting the plans of the evil Loveless (Kenneth Branagh), Jim West (Will Smith) and Artemus Gordon (Kevin Kline) ride off into the sunset heading back to Washington, D.C.
Blooper: A romantic notion, but impossible: Washington is in the east and the sun sets in the west.

The average American worker has held 8 different jobs by the age of 40.

NEVER SAY NEVER

A few pearls of wisdom from 599 Things You Should Never Do, *edited by Ed Morrow.*

"Never send a man to do a horse's job."
—**Mr. Ed**

"Never lose your cigar cutter in your pocket."
—**Martha Stewart**

Never offend people with style when you can offend them with substance.
—**Sam Brown**

"Never bet on baseball."
—**Pete Rose**

"Never grow a wishbone where your backbone ought to be."
—**Clementine Paddleford**

"Never buy a case until you've tried at least one bottle."
—**Frank J. Paul**

"Never try to use a cat's claw for a toothpick."
—**Randy Glasbergen**

"Never tell a lie till the truth doesn't fit."
—**American Adage**

"Never run away from a gun. Bullets can travel faster than you can."
—**Wild Bill Hickock**

"Never do anything and you'll never make any mistakes."
—**Anonymous**

"Never argue with the bouncer."
—**Ken Cruickshank**

"Never do wrong...when people are looking."
—**Mark Twain**

"Never appeal to a man's 'better nature'—he may not have one."
—**Robert A. Heinlein**

"Never say you know a man until you have divided an inheritance with him."
—**Johann Kaspar Lavater**

"Never try to tell everything you know. It may take too short a time."
—**Norman Ford**

ERROL FLYNN'S LAST STAND

In the second Bathroom Reader, *we had a look at the accusation that Errol Flynn was a Nazi spy during World War II (not true). Here's the story of how he tried to revive his fading career by starring in a screen version of* William Tell *in 1953.*

LUCKY BREAK

In 1935 the British film actor Robert Donat fell ill and had to drop out of the starring role in the Warner Bros. swashbuckler *Captain Blood*, prompting Jack Warner to offer the part to another actor, George Brent. Brent tried out for the role but was rejected: he looked too silly in the period costumes for audiences to take him seriously. So Warner offered the job to a nobody—26-year-old Errol Flynn, a struggling actor who had had only tiny roles in a few Hollywood films.

"I didn't know if he could act," Warner remembered in 1973, "but he was handsomer than hell and radiated charm. So I hired him."

RISE AND FALL

Overnight, *Captain Blood* turned Flynn into the biggest action hero in Hollywood, and he built a reputation with films like *Charge of the Light Brigade* (1936), *The Adventures of Robin Hood* (1938), and *The Sea Hawk* (1940).

If anything, Flynn's private life was even more "adventurous" than his on-screen life. He was a hard-drinking, brawling womanizer with a fondness for underage girls, something that caught up with him in 1942 when he was brought up on statutory rape charges involving two teenagers. He was acquitted, but the humiliation of the experience reportedly broke his spirit.

Flynn was further demoralized when a bad heart kept him out of World War II. Years of heavy drinking began to catch up with him, eroding his good looks and sabotaging his box-office appeal. What little clout he had left in Hollywood was destroyed by his erratic behavior on the set and his inability to control his drinking.

Star of *Son of Captain Blood*, the sequel to *Captain Blood?* Flynn's son, Sean Flynn.

WILLIAM TELL

By the early 1950s, Flynn's career was on the ropes and he was nearly out of money. He was desperate to make a comeback and in his hour of need, turned to the genre that had made him a star nearly 20 years before: the swashbuckler.

This time Flynn hoped that starring in a film version of *William Tell*, the legendary Swiss archer, would bring him back from the dead. But alcoholism and a recent bout of hepatitis scared serious investors away, so Flynn was forced to raise funds in Europe, where he finally cobbled together $150,000 from the Italian government and $50,000 from one Count Fossataro, a former police chief of Venice. It wasn't nearly enough money, so Flynn put $500,000, virtually all that remained of his fortune, on the line to get things moving.

Most of the money went toward constructing an entire Alpine village next to Mont Blanc in Italy; with the funds that were left, he was only able to film for two weeks, producing about 30 minutes' worth of footage.

ONE LAST CHANCE

Desperate, Flynn packed up his 30 minutes of film and brought it to the Venice Film Festival, where he hoped screenings of it would attract new backers. But once again, his health got in the way. "Suffering from dysentery and diarrhea," Harry Waldman writes in *Scenes Unseen*, Flynn "was more preoccupied with finding a bathroom at short notice than making polite conversation."

Flynn's frequent pit stops doomed his attempts to find financing, so one evening he pulled the only stunt he could think of that might get him some money—he staged a fall in his hotel and faked paralysis, in the hopes of winning a large insurance settlement from the hotel. The ruse backfired—all it did was illustrate just how troubled the star of *William Tell* was, ruining what little chance was left of getting a backer.

The film was dead, Flynn had lost his savings, and his career never did recover. He spent his final years playing the only roles that still came naturally to him—drunks—and died at the age of 50 in 1959. His 30 minutes of *William Tell* footage has been lost; about all that survives is the Alpine village itself, which today is a popular tourist attraction.

AMERICA'S MONEY LAUNDRESS

*When the folks behind Mrs. Butterworth's syrup came up with
the name, they probably had no idea they were naming their
product after a colonial counterfeiter...but they were.*

DESIGNING WOMAN
Mary Peck Butterworth was the daughter of an innkeeper
and the wife of a carpenter in Colonial Massachusetts. In
the early 1700s, she was raising seven children and her family desperately needed more money. Some women would have taken up
sewing—Mary Butterworth became a counterfeiter. With a little
bit of work and some experimentation, she invented a method of
counterfeiting that not only produced passable bills but also left
no incriminating evidence of the crime.

Here's how she did it: First she placed a piece of damp,
starched muslin on top of the bill she wanted to copy. Then she
ran a hot iron over the cloth, which caused the material to pick
up a light impression of the printing from the bill. Then she
ironed the muslin hard enough to transfer the pattern to a blank
piece of paper in order to produce the counterfeit bill. Finally, she
used a quill pen to outline the writing on the bill and touch it up.
The incriminating evidence—the used piece of muslin—was then
burned.

COLONIAL COUNTERFEIT RING

Butterworth set up a veritable cottage industry. Three of her
brothers and a sister-in-law helped manufacture the money. The
bills were then fenced for half their face value. Over a period of
seven years, the Butterworth gang made and sold over £1,000
worth of bogus bills—roughly equivalent to $130,000 today—
without sophisticated technology and without being detected.

In 1715 the £5 note had to be recalled because there was a
flood of phony bills in circulation. At the same time, authorities
eyed with suspicion the large house Butterworth and her husband
had just built, but they couldn't prove anything.

When used to make ethyl alcohol, an acre of potatoes will produce enough fuel to fill 25 cars.

EXPOSED

Then in 1723, one of Butterworth's carpenters traveled to Newport, Rhode Island, to witness the mass hanging of 26 pirates. There he met three young girls. Treating them to dinner and drinks, he paid for the party with one of the many counterfeit bills he had in his wallet, but was caught by the innkeeper. After he was arrested, he quickly revealed the details of the counterfeit operation.

Mary Butterworth was imprisoned, but with no counterfeiting plates in evidence, she was promptly released. No one knows whether she gave up counterfeiting after that. Regardless, she died in 1775 at the age of 89, a respected member of the community...as far as anyone knows.

* * *

NUDES IN THE NEWS

• Vincent Bethell, 28, was thrown out of a British courtroom in August 2000 after he appeared in the nude to answer charges of disorderly behavior. Bethel, a nude activist, had been arrested while walking naked through the streets of London and vows to remain naked until England's anti-nudity laws are repealed.

• Female members of Nigeria's ruling People's Democratic Party threatened to march naked through Lagos if the party's "lack of respect" for female members continues. "We are prepared to protest by walking the streets naked and camping in our nudity in front of Commodore Bode George's house for seven days," said protest organizer Alhaja Ali-Balogun. Displays of nudity by older women, seen as "mothers of the nation" in Nigeria, are considered taboo.

• Anti-logging activist Dona Nieto, who calls herself La Tigresa, has hit upon a novel way of getting lumberjacks to listen to her campaign to preserve ancient redwoods: she removes her top and recites "Goddess-based, nude Buddhist guerrilla poetry" while the loggers ogle her chest. "They stop their chainsaws and they stop their trucks and they pay attention," she says. "I've changed some of these guys' lives."

What do the inventors of Coke, Pepsi, and Dr. Pepper have in common?

JUST PLANE WEIRD

Planning a plane trip in the near future? Don't read this! Fold over the corner of the page and save it for another day. We warned you.

SMOKING FLIGHT

On November 19, 2000, a drunken passenger on an American Airlines flight from Tokyo to Seattle locked himself into a restroom about an hour into the flight and lit up a cigarette. Not a good idea—American Airline flights are nonsmoking. When the man refused repeated requests to extinguish his cigarettes and come out of the restroom, the plane returned to Tokyo, where he was removed from the flight and reprimanded by airport police. He later made a written apology to American Airlines and promised "never to do it again." Too late: According to news reports, American Airlines sued him "for losses caused by his bad behavior."

NUT CASE

In April 2001, Cathay Pacific Airlines fired pilot Scott Munro. Reason for dismissal: He threw nuts at the company's chief executive after running into him at a bar. "He was dismissed for throwing things at me," CEO David Turnbull told the *South China Morning Post*. "We have to operate a disciplined company, and you do not throw things at the chief executive."

THE LATE MR. KOTIADIS

On November 21, 2000, a Greek businessman named Nikita Kotiadis was arrested at Athens airport after phoning in a bomb threat on his own flight. Reason: Kotiadis was running late, and he wanted to delay the flight from taking off until he could get to the airport. He might have gotten away with it if he'd placed the call himself. But he had his secretary call, and she identified him by name before putting him on the line. Kotiadis made his threat and then raced for the airport, where he was arrested on the spot. He was later sentenced to seven months in prison for "obstructing transportation."

They were all Civil War veterans.

THE NAKED TRUTH

On March 11, 2001, police boarded an Olympic Airways flight to Paris and arrested 23-year-old Jeremy Benjamin Mauri after he stripped naked during the safety demonstration. As they removed him from the plane, Mauri offered this bizarre explanation: "I did it for a joke; I'm impotent."

YOUR TAX DOLLARS AT WORK

In June 2001 a British company called Roke Manor Research announced that it had found a way to detect and track America's "invisible" stealth bombers. Their secret weapon: cell phones—when a stealth bomber flies over an area with cellular phone coverage, the aircraft disrupts the cellular signals in such a way that it's possible to calculate its location to within 30 feet using a laptop computer and a Global Positioning Satellite navigation system.

"We just use the normal phone calls that are flying about in the ether," says Roke Manor's spokesperson Peter Lloyd. "The front of the stealth plane cannot be detected by conventional radar, but its bottom surface reflects very well. It's remarkable that a stealth system that cost $158 billion to develop is beaten by mobile phone technology."

BAG LADY

An 83-year-old grandmother on an American Airlines flight from Miami, Florida to Bogota, Colombia was taken into custody after she made a bomb threat while the plane was taxiing for takeoff. An official with American said that Beatriz Escobar De Rodriguez, a native of Colombia, made the threat after she tried to board the plane with a carry-on bag that was too big to fit in the overhead compartment or under her seat. When told it would have to be checked and placed in the cargo bay of the plane, she replied, "Did you see the bomb in my suitcase?" What she meant is unknown, but it didn't matter—she said the "B-word." The plane returned to the gate; grandma was arrested and thrown in jail. "Her penalty depends on the judge," a court spokesman told reporters. "She might end up in jail."

DO YOU SPEAK CANADIAN?

Here's an article that was sent to us by Canadian professor Howard Richler. Of course we know that a country the size of Canada has many different regional dialects...but it still made us laugh.

SPEAKING CANADIAN

So you think there's no such thing as Canadian English, eh? Then tell me what this means:

The beerslinger posted a sign warning that hosers with Molson muscles, rubbies, and sh*t-disturbers would not be welcome. No sirree. Folks were drinking bloody Caesars and brown cows at the booze can. Heck, even the Gravol was free.

Translation for the non-Canadian reader: A "beerslinger" is an informal term for a bartender; a "hoser" means a lout; a "rubby" refers to a derelict alcoholic known to mix rubbing alcohol with what he is imbibing; "Molson muscles" is a term for a beer-belly; "brown cow" and "bloody Caesar" are names for two cocktails in Canada; a "booze can" is a term for an illegal bar usually in someone's home; a "sh*t-disturber" refers to one who likes to create trouble; and "Gravol" is the Canadian proprietary name of an anti-nausea medication.

Here are some more Canadianisms:

All-dressed: Food served with all the optional garnishes

Cuffy: Cigarette butt

Browned off: Fed up or disheartened

Two-four: A case of beer

First Peoples: The politically correct term for Canadian Indians

Bazoo: Old rusted car

Fuddle duddle: A euphemism for "go to hell"

Keener: Eager beaver

Steamie: A steamed hot dog

Gitch: Underwear

Howdy, neighbor: 36% of the Great Lakes lie within Canadian territory.

The Can: Canada

Schmuck: Verb meaning "to flatten," as in, "He got schmucked on the road"

Bite moose: Go away

Garburator: A garbage disposal unit

Anglophone: An English-language speaker

Francophone: A French-language speaker

Allophone: Immigrant who speaks neither English nor French

Wobbly pop: Alcohol

Keep yer stick on the ice: Pay attention

Skookum: Big and powerful (a west coast term derived from Chinook jargon)

And let's not forget unique French-Canadian English phraseology, such as "Throw me down the stairs my shoes," or "Throw the horse over the fence some hay."

So, all you hosers from Beantown, the Big Easy, and La La Land, before you visit your neighbors to the north in T.O. (Toronto, Ontario) or up island in B.C. (British Columbia), remember that you don't have a monopoly on the English language. And although the Canadian national persona is extremely polite, don't forget that ice hockey is the national pastime and "drop the gloves," a hockey term for "prepare to fight," is also part of Canadian English.

*   *   *

A POLITICIAN IS BORN

In 1946 the following ad appeared in several southern California newspapers: "Wanted: Congressman candidate with no previous political experience to defeat a man who has represented the district in the House for 10 years. Any young man, resident of district, preferably a veteran, fair education, may apply for the job." The ad had been placed by the Republican party. A man who answered the ad was awarded the job and did in fact defeat incumbent Jerry Voorhis after a dirty campaign. The man who kicked off his political career by replying to a want ad...Richard M. Nixon.

FAMILIAR PHRASES

Here are the origins to some common phrases.

WIN HANDS DOWN
Meaning: To win by an enormous margin.
Origin: If a racehorse jockey is so far ahead of the competition that there is no danger he will be passed again, he can drop the reins—and his hands—and let the horse finish the race without spurring it on.

BAKER'S DOZEN
Meaning: Thirteen—one more than a dozen.
Origin: In the Middle Ages, bakers who sold loaves of bread that were lighter than the legal weight were subjected to harsh penalties. To prevent being accused of cheating on the weight, bakers would often give away an extra loaf with every dozen.

CLEAN AS A WHISTLE
Meaning: Exceptionally clean or smooth.
Origin: This phrase appeared at the beginning of the 19th century, describing the whistling noise made as a sword tears through the air to decapitate a victim cleanly, in a single stroke.

LOADED FOR BEAR
Meaning: Prepared for any contingency.
Origin: American pioneers traveling alone through the woods, needed to be prepared for anything if they wanted to return intact. They carried guns powerful enough to bring down any dangerous predator they happened to meet, especially the fiercest and most territorial creature in the land—the bear.

BET YOUR BOTTOM DOLLAR
Meaning: It's a sure thing; to bet everything you have.
Origin: Just as they do today, 19th-century poker players would keep their betting chips—or "dollars"—in high stacks at the table, taking from the top when betting. When a hand was so good that a

A single, isolated heart cell will "beat" for as long as it has a fresh supply of blood.

player wanted to wager the entire stack, they would pick up or push the stack by the bottom chip—literally betting with their bottom dollar.

TO FIGHT FIRE WITH FIRE

Meaning: To respond in like manner; a desperate measure.

Origin: In order to extinguish huge prairie and forest fires in the early West, desperate American settlers would sometimes set fire to a strip of land in the path of the advancing fire and then extinguish it, leaving a barren strip with nothing for the approaching fire to feed on. Although effective, this tactic was—and still is—extremely dangerous, as the backfire itself can get out of control.

TO GET ONE'S GOAT

Meaning: To aggravate.

Origin: Hyperactive racehorses were often given goats as stablemates because their presence tended to have a calming effect on the horses. After the horse became attached to the goat, it got very upset when its companion disappeared—making it run poorly on the track. In the 19th century, when a devious gambler wanted a horse to lose, he would get the horse's goat and take it away the night before the race, thus agitating the horse.

IN THE NICK OF TIME

Meaning: Without a second to spare.

Origin: Even into the 18th century, some businessmen still kept track of transactions and time by carving notches—or nicks—on a "tally stick." Someone arriving just before the next nick was carved would arrive in time to save the next day's interest—in the nick of time.

MAKE MONEY HAND OVER FIST

Meaning: Rapid success in a business venture.

Origin: Sailors through the ages have used the same hand-over-hand motion when climbing up ropes, hauling in nets, and hoisting sails. The best seamen were those who could do this action the fastest. In the 19th century, Americans adapted the expression "hand over fist"—describing one hand clenching a rope and the other deftly moving above it—to suggest quickness and success.

In case you've forgotten: *E Pluribus Unum* means "from many, one."

WHAT'S THE NUMBER FOR 911?

Here are some of our favorite transcripts of 911 calls. Believe it or not, they are all true.

Dispatcher: "Nine-one-one. What's your emergency?"
Caller: "I heard what sounded like gunshots coming from the brown house on the corner here."
Dispatcher: "Do you have an address."
Caller: "No, I'm wearing a blouse and slacks. Why?"

Dispatcher: "Nine-one-one. What's your emergency?"
Caller: "Someone broke into my house and took a bite out of my ham-and-cheese sandwich."
Dispatcher: "Excuse me?"
Caller: "I made a ham-and-cheese sandwich and left it on the kitchen table, and when I came back from the bathroom, someone had taken a bite out of it."
Dispatcher: "Was anything else taken?"
Caller: "No. But this has happened to me before, and I'm sick and tired of it."

Dispatcher: "Nine-one-one."
Caller: "Hi, is this the police?"
Dispatcher: "This is 911. Do you need police assistance?"
Caller: "Well, I don't know who to call. Can you tell me how to cook a turkey? I've never cooked one before."

Dispatcher: "Nine-one-one. Fire or emergency?"
Caller: "Fire, I guess."
Dispatcher: "How can I help you, sir?"
Caller: "I was wondering... does the Fire Department put snow chains on their trucks?"
Dispatcher: "Yes, sir. Do you have an emergency?"
Caller: "Well, I've spent the last four hours trying to put these darn chains on my tires and...well...do you think the Fire Department could come over and help me?"
Dispatcher: "Help you what?"
Caller: "Help me get these damn chains on my car!"

The average American worker receives 201 phone, paper, and e-mail messages per day.

BAD MEDICINE

*Most of us take modern medical science for granted. MRIs, pain
relievers, and the polio vaccine may not seem like a big deal today, but
if you look back a couple hundred years, it may change your mind.*

MALPRACTICE
These days you can easily find dozens of effective remedies at the local pharmacy to treat anything from a sore
toe to scalp itch. So it's hard to imagine that less than 200 years
ago, a person complaining to a trusted physician about a simple
ailment was likely to undergo barbaric treatment that included
draining of the blood, blistering of the skin, and induced vomiting.

In the 1800s, doctors were scarce and ill-trained. There were
no regulations concerning the education of physicians. With just a
little booklearning or information passed down by a family member, almost anyone could set up shop and call himself a doctor.
There were no antibiotics, no X-rays, no vaccines, and none of
the diagnostic tools we now take for granted.

Surgery was often performed by barbers. Not only did they give
haircuts and shaves, but they also extracted teeth, lanced boils,
and bled patients. In fact, the colors of the familiar barber's pole
are derived from the practice of bloodletting: red for blood, and
white for bandages. The pole itself was sometimes grasped by the
patient in order to make his veins stand out and make the bloodletting easier. In the end, the patient was as likely to die from the
treatment as from the illness.

KING OF PAIN

People of the 19th century accepted pain as an inevitable part of
life. The aches and pains we associate with a long day of work or a
touch of the flu couldn't be quelled by popping an aspirin—that
wonder drug wasn't introduced until 1899. The common rationale
was that pain was a punishment from God, and to endure it was
good for the soul.

There were no anesthetics either. Until the 1840s all surgeries
were performed without it. For this reason, not to mention the

real possibility of death from blood loss, surgeons had to be quick. Records show that during the Battle of Bordello, Dominique Jean Larrey (1766–1842), a surgeon in Napoléon's army, performed 200 amputations in the first 24 hours. Even at that speed, the mortality rate was almost 100% due to shock or infection. Septicemia, or blood poisoning, was an ever-present danger. Surgeons traveled from dissection room to operating room, never once changing their coats or washing their hands.

HUMOROUS—BUT NOT FUNNY

Most physicians of the 1800s still subscribed to the ancient Greek belief that the body was made up of four "humors" corresponding to the four elements of the Earth: yellow bile (air), black bile (water), phlegm (Earth), and blood (fire). The Greeks believed that a lack or excess of these humors caused all illnesses, and had to be treated accordingly. If a doctor suspected a buildup of bad blood, the patient would be "cured" by the cutting and draining of the offensive liquid. There are even records of primitive transfusions using sheep's or cow's blood.

Dr. Benjamin Rush (1745–1813), a signer of the Declaration of Independence, humanitarian, and renowned physician, was a noted believer in "humor" therapy. To maintain balance among the humors, Rush prescribed a horrifying course of bloodletting, blistering, and swinging of the body, a treatment in which the patient would be strapped into a chair, suspended from the ceiling by a rope, and swung violently back and forth to induce vomiting. Once patients vomited, they were brought down and the treatment was considered a success.

QUICK, CALL ME A QUACK

In the 1820s and 1830s, people had little faith in "scientific" medicine, due no doubt to treatments that were painful and usually produced no results other than infection or death. A new movement of treating illnesses with old folk remedies grew out of the public's fear and distrust of doctors. The medical profession called it *quackery*. The word is thought to originate either from the phrase "quicksilver doctor," which refers to the use of highly poisonous mercury as a cure, or from *kwaksalver*, an early Dutch term meaning "someone who prattles about the efficacy of his remedies."

Either way, quacks promised quick results and easy answers without evidence to support their claims. They sold cure-all elixirs—such as Lydia Pinkham's Vegetable Compound, which was 80% vegetable extracts and 20% alcohol—and patent medicines laced with cocaine, opium, and caffeine. Morphine-based mixtures were even sold in the Sears catalog. Patients often felt better after taking a swig (or several swigs), but these patent medicines didn't cure anything.

SCIENCE IS GOLDEN

What changed? In 1865 Dr. Joseph Lister noted that almost half of patients with amputations were dying. The main cause: post-operative sepsis infections, or sepsis for short. He blamed it on unsanitary conditions, comparing the smell of an operating room to a city sewer. Inspired by Louis Pasteur's theory that decay was caused by living organisms in the air, which on entering matter made it ferment, Lister made the connection with sepsis. He had also heard that carbolic acid was being used to treat sewage, so he began using it to clean wounds and sterilize instruments.

In 1846 Scottish surgeon Dr. Robert Liston (1794–1847) introduced the use of ether as an anesthetic, making it possible for doctors to operate on patients with less pain.

Other advances included the invention of the clinical thermometer, stethoscope, and hypodermic needle, the development of anthrax, rabies, and smallpox vaccines in the 19th century; and the discovery of penicillin in the early 20th century.

When technology started catching up with advances in medicine, X-rays, the incandescent light, and even the invention of the telephone changed things dramatically for both patient and surgeon. But was it the end of quackery? Not by a long shot.

To read about Modern Quackery, go to page 300.

To read about Modern Quackery, go to page 300.

*   *   *

Sweet Dreams. According to Betty Bethards in *The Dream Book: Symbols for Self-Understanding*, "toilet dreams" have to do with how well the dreamer is "flushing out negativity and wastes," including letting go of unneeded thoughts and experiences and releasing the past so as to live fully in the present.

Number one health complaint Americans report to their doctors: insomnia.

POLI-TALKS

Politicians aren't getting much respect these days—but then, it sounds like they don't deserve much, either.

"The more we remove penalties for being a bum, the more bumism is going to blossom."
Sen. Jesse Helms (R-NC), on welfare

"We didn't send you to Washington to make intelligent decisions. We sent you to represent us."
—Kent York, a Texas pastor, to Rep. Bill Sarpalius (D-TX)

"President Clinton had a bill, e-i-e-i-o. And in that bill was lots of pork, e-i-e-i-o."
—Sen. Alfonse D'Amato (R-NY)

"I have orders to be awakened at any time in the case of a national emergency, even if I'm in a cabinet meeting."
—Ronald Reagan

"The present system may be flawed, but that's not to say that we in Congress can't make it worse."
—Rep. E. Clay Shaw, Jr. (R-FL)

"Is the country still here?"
—Calvin Coolidge, waking from a nap

"We've killed health care; now we've got to make sure our fingerprints aren't on it."
—Sen. Bob Packwood (R-OR), in 1994, on the GOP blocking Clinton's health-care reforms

"Ambiguously definitive—or is it definitively ambiguous?"
—Sen. Bill Bradley, on being unclear about his presidential ambitions

"It's no exaggeration to say that the undecideds could go one way or another."
—George H. W. Bush

"We didn't get the pay raise—why work?"
—Bob Dole, in 1989, on the slow pace of Senate activity

"Welcome to President Clinton, Mrs. Clinton, and my fellow astronauts."
—Al Gore, 1998

When George Washington was president, there were about 350 federal employees.

JUMP ROPE RHYMES

Remember those long summer days when you were a kid…jumping rope and making up rhymes? Here are some great old jump rope rhymes found in Zickary Zan, Childhood Folklore, *by Jack and Olivia Solomon.*

Bubble Gum

Bubble gum, bubble gum,
Chew and blow.
Bubble gum, bubble gum,
Scrape your toe.
Bubble gum, bubble gum,
Tastes so sweet,
Get that bubble gum off your feet.

Alligator Purse

Mother, Mother, I am ill,
Send for the doctor to give me a pill.
In came the doctor,
In came the nurse,
In came the lady with the alligator purse.

Hot Dog

My mother is a butcher;
My father cuts the meat.
I'm a little hot dog Running down the street.
How many hot dogs did I sell?

Mary Mack

Mary Mack, dressed in black
Silver gold buttons down her back.
Ask her ma for fifteen cents
To see the elephant jump the fence.
He jumped so high he touched the sky
And won't come back
Until the Fourth of July.

K-i-s-s-i-n-g

(John) and (Karen) sitting in a tree
K-i-s-s-i-n-g.
First comes love, then comes marriage,
Then comes (Karen) with a baby carriage.
How many babies did she have?

Rooms for Rent

Rooms for rent,
Inquire within,
When I move out,
Let (Ann) move in.

Margie

Margie drank some marmalade,
Margie drank some pop,
Margie drank some other things
That made her stomach flop;
Whoops went the marmalade,
Whoops went the pop,
Whoops went the other things
That made her stomach flop.

How Many Years?

Apple, peach, pumpkin pie.
How many years before I die?
One, two, three, etc.

Dressed in Green

Cinderella, dressed in green,
Went upstairs to eat ice cream.
How many spoonfuls did she eat?

Americans use 4.8 billion gallons of water flushing toilets each day.

THE WORLD'S FIRST PHOTOGRAPH

In part one of our story (page 45), we told you about the camera
obscura, the drawing tool that eventually evolved into the modern
camera. In this installment, we introduce you to some
of the people who played a role in inventing film.

SPIRITS IN THE MATERIAL WORLD

In 1674 an alchemist named Christoph Adolph Balduin performed a chemistry experiment that he hoped would help him isolate the mysterious natural force he called the *Weltgeist,* or "universal spirit." He dissolved some chalk (calcium carbonate) in nitric acid to create a sludgy substance that would easily absorb moisture from the atmosphere. Balduin believed that if he could distill the moisture from the sludge, he would capture the universal spirit in pure form.

Needless to say, Balduin didn't know much about chemistry (not many 17th-century alchemists did), because when he distilled the sludge, all he got was water. But he noticed that when he heated the dried-out crud that was left over, it glowed in the dark. He named this mysterious substance *phosphorus,* Greek for "bringer of light," (today it's called calcium nitrate).

What did this have to do with photography? Nothing...until a German anatomy professor named Johann Heinrich Schulze tried to repeat Balduin's experiment in 1727. By chance he used nitric acid that contained traces of silver. He left the chalk-acid mixture out in the sun; by the time he came back to it, it had turned a deep purple.

MESSAGE IN A BOTTLE

Schulze wasn't the first person to observe that substances containing silver salts turn dark when exposed to the sun. But it had always been assumed that it was the heat that caused the reaction. Schulze suspected that light was to blame and came up with an experiment to test his theory: He cut a stencil of some words on a piece of paper. He put the stencil on the side of a glass bottle and

---

Seeing is believing: Even a blind chameleon will change its color to match its surroundings.

covered the rest of the glass with dark material. He filled the bottle with the chalk dissolved in nitric acid and left it out in the sun, to see if the sunlight would "write" the stenciled words onto the material.

"It was not long," he wrote later, "before the sun's rays, where they hit the glass through the cut-out parts of the paper, wrote each word on the chalk precipitate so exactly and distinctly that many who were curious about the experiment took occasion to attribute the thing to some sort of trick." In a nod to Balduin, Schulze called the material *scotophorus*, or "bringer of darkness."

Schulze didn't understand why the substance turned dark, but today we do: When light strikes photosensitive silver crystals, some of the atoms of silver separate out from the compound. Exactly how many atoms separate depends on how much light strikes the material. With enough light, however, the silver will become visible to the naked eye, and the material becomes dark. This is the chemical principle upon which all film photography would be based.

Schulze couldn't figure out how to control the reaction—the silver salts darkened every time they were exposed to light, obliterating whatever writing or image had been created. As far as he could tell, the material had no use, but it was still interesting, and as word of his discovery spread, scientists all over Europe repeated the experiment.

PAPERWORK

One man who learned of Schulze's experiment was Thomas Wedgwood, son of the legendary English potter Josiah Wedgwood. Wedgwood thought he could use the process to make duplicates of artwork for his pottery.

He started out by soaking pieces of paper in a solution of silver nitrate to make them photosensitive (sensitive to light). He then laid his sketches on top of these materials and put them out in the sun. The sunlight would shine through the sketch where the paper was blank, but would be blocked where there was ink, creating a reverse, or "negative," image of the original sketch. The experiment worked. Wedgwood became the first person in history to transfer an image onto photosensitive paper.

Wedgwood might have become the father of photography, but his health was so poor that he had to abandon his research before

---

he could reach his next goal: recording the image created by a camera obscura. And like Schulze, he died without figuring out how to arrest the photosensitive reaction so that his images would be made permanent. Even when viewed by candlelight, it was just a matter of time before they disappeared into darkness forever.

FIXING THE PROBLEM

The next major contributor to the chemistry of photography was a 19th-century French physicist named Joseph-Nicéphore Niepce.

Niepce was looking for a way to copy artwork automatically, to avoid having to pay artists to do it. He repeated the experiments of Schulze and Wedgwood and searched for chemicals that would give him positive images, but finally, after years of failed experiments, gave up on chemicals that change color and started looking for chemicals that harden when exposed to light. That's when his luck began to change.

Having worked as a printer, Niepce was familiar with "bitumen of Judea," an asphalt compound dating back to the Egyptians and commonly used by lithographers. He knew that when bitumen of Judea was exposed to sunlight, it hardened to the point that solvents would no longer dissolve it. So he smeared a metal printing plate with the stuff, placed an ink drawing on top of the plate, and left them both out in the sun. Just as he expected, the sunlight passed through the blank paper, striking the bitumen of Judea underneath and causing it to harden.

But where the sunlight was blocked by the ink, the bitumen of Judea remained soft and could be washed away with solvents. The result was a perfect copy of the original drawing. Niepce named the process *heliography*, after *helios*, the Greek word for "sun," and *graphos*, "writing."

THE NEXT LEVEL

Taking his discovery to the next step, one sunny morning in 1827, Niepce smeared some bitumen of Judea onto a printing plate and put it inside a camera obscura. Then he pointed the camera obscura out of an upstairs window of his country home and left it there for most of the day. In the process, he took what historians consider to be the world's first true photograph.

For part III of our history of photography, turn to page 180.

For part III of our history of photography, turn to page 180.

Distance that a silver-spotted skipper caterpillar can propel its own fecies: 5 feet.

THE HOUSE CALL OF A LIFETIME

*Every collector has a Holy Grail that they hope find at a yard sale,
or a flea market someday. Baseball card collectors dream of finding
an original Honus Wagner; book collectors hope to spot a copy
of Edgar Allen Poe's* The Tamerlane *gathering dust on a
bookstore shelf. Here's the story of an amateur antique
collector found what he was looking for.*

THE PERFECT STORM

One winter in the early 1980s, a two-day snowstorm knocked out telephone service to much of the village of East Hampton, New York. One of the people sent out into the snow to restore service was cable repairman Morgan MacWhinnie.

MacWhinnie was just finishing repairing an underground cable when an old man wearing slippers and a bathrobe came out of a run-down clapboard house and asked him to check the phones inside. MacWhinnie wanted to move on to his next repair call, but he decided it would be quicker to humor the old man than it would be to argue with him. So he went into the house.

DIAMONDS IN THE ROUGH

The old man turned out to be a pack rat: he had old aluminum TV dinner trays stacked to the ceiling in the kitchen, and mountains of trash in other parts of the dark, dusty house. MacWhinnie checked the extension in the kitchen; it had a dial tone. Then the old man insisted that he check the extension in the bedroom, too. MacWhinnie wanted to leave, but the old man was insistent, so he let the man show him the way to the upstairs room.

As MacWhinnie made his way through the cluttered dining room, he was surprised to see what appeared to be an antique tea table and a matching bonnet-top highboy chest of drawers poking out of the dust and debris. Then, after he checked the extension in the bedroom (it was fine) and prepared to leave, he saw a matching drop-leaf dining table next to the front door.

All dogs except the Chow have a pink tongue. The Chow's tongue is blue-black.

NEWPORT STYLE

As it turns out, MacWhinnie's hobby was collecting antiques. He knew a lot about 18th-century American furniture and he was almost certain the pieces were valuable. In fact, he suspected they were made in Newport, Rhode Island, in the 1780s, the period considered the golden age of the Newport style. If he was right, the furniture was worth a lot of money, but he had no way of knowing for sure.

The old man told MacWhinnie that the furniture belonged to his landlady, a woman named Caroline Tillinghast. MacWhinnie called her and told her he thought he pieces were valuable and asked if she'd consider selling them. She said no—the house was a rental property and she needed the furniture for the tenants. MacWhinnie let the matter drop, but he never forgot what he saw that day.

SECOND TRY

Ten years later, MacWhinnie happened to tell his story to an antiques dealer named Leigh Keno. (Does the name sound familiar? He and his twin brother Leslie appear regularly on the PBS TV series *Antiques Roadshow*.) When he heard MacWhinnie's story, Keno thought the pieces must be reproductions but agreed that they were worth a look just in case, so they called Tillinghast to see if she would let them come over and examine the furniture. Yes, she told them, and now was a good time, because the old man had recently passed away and she was having the house cleaned for new tenants.

THE REAL DEAL

MacWhinnie was right—the pieces were genuine. They turned out to be the work of John Goddard, considered the most talented cabinetmaker of the period. Finally, nearly a decade after MacWhinnie had asked her the first time, Tillinghast agreed to put the antiques up for sale. She believed they were worth "in excess of $25,000"—and she was right. A few weeks, later Keno brokered the sale to a collector for $1 million. As for MacWhinnie, he and Keno split the hefty commission 50–50.

THE SECRET HITLER FILE

There's nothing funny about Hitler, but he is endlessly fascinating. Since Congress passed the Nazi War Crimes Disclosure Act in 1998, almost 3 million classified files have been opened to the public—including a 1942 secret profile of Adolf Hitler compiled by the OSS. Here are some excerpts.

PERSONAL APPEARANCE

• "Hitler never allows anyone to see him while he is naked or bathing. He refuses to use colognes or scents of any sort on his body.

• "No matter how warm he feels, Hitler will never take off his coat in public.

• "In 1923, Nazi press secretary Dr. Sedgwick tried to convince Hitler to get rid of his trademark mustache or grow it normally. Hitler answered: 'Do not worry about my mustache. If it is not the fashion now, it will be later because I wear it!'"

SOCIAL BEHAVIOR

• "While dining with others, Hitler will allow the conversation to linger on general topics, but after a couple of hours he will inevitably begin one of his many monologues. These speeches are flawless from start to finish because he rehearses them any time he gets a moment.

• "His favorite topics include: 'When I was a soldier,' 'When I was in Vienna,' 'When I was in prison,' and 'When I was the leader in the early days of the party.'

• "If Hitler begins speaking about Wagner and the opera, no one dares interrupt him. He will often sermonize on this topic until his audience falls asleep.

PERSONAL HABITS

• "Hitler has no interest in sports or games of any kind and never exercised, except for an occasional walk.

• "He paces frequently inside rooms, always to the same tune that he whistles to himself and always diagonally across the room, from corner to corner.

- "He always rides in an open car for parades regardless of the weather, and expects the same of his entire staff, telling them: 'We are not bourgeois, but soldiers.'

- "Hitler's handwriting is impeccable. When famous psychologist Carl Jung saw Hitler's handwriting in 1937, he remarked: 'Behind this handwriting I recognize the typical characteristics of a man with essentially feminine instincts.'"

ENTERTAINMENT

- "Hitler loves the circus. He takes real pleasure in the idea that underpaid performers are risking their lives to please him.

- "He went to the circus on several occasions in 1933 and sent extremely expensive chocolates and flowers to the female performers. Hitler even remembered their names and would worry about them and their families in the event of an accident.

- "He isn't interested in wild animal acts, unless there is a woman in danger.

- "Nearly every night Hitler will see a movie in his private theatre, mainly foreign films that are banned to the German public. He loves comedies and will often laugh merrily at Jewish comedians. Hitler even liked a few Jewish singers, but after hearing them he would remark that it was too bad he or she wasn't an Aryan.

- "Hitler's staff secretly made films for him of the torture and execution of political prisoners, which he very much enjoyed viewing. His executive assistants also secure pornographic pictures and movies for him.

- "He loves newsreels—especially when he is in them.

- "He adores gypsy music, Wagner's operas, and especially American college football marches and alma maters.

- "To excite the masses, he also uses American College football-style music during his speeches." His rallying cry—'Sieg Heil!'—was even modeled after the cheering techniques used by American football cheerleaders.

FAMOUS LAST WORDS

If you had to pick some last words, what would they be?

"Turn up the lights. I don't want to go home in the dark."
—**O. Henry,** *writer*

"I've got a terrible headache."
—**Franklin D. Roosevelt**

"That was the best ice cream soda I ever tasted."
—**Lou Costello**

"Tell my mother that I died for my country. I thought I did it for the best. Useless! Useless!"
—**John Wilkes Booth**

"I want that fifty bucks you owe me and I want it now!"
—**Carl "Alfalfa" Switzer,** *shot in a bar by a drunk*

"I'm a broken machine, but I'm ready."
—**Woodrow Wilson**

"Who's there?"
—**Billy the Kid,** *before being shot by Pat Garrett*

"Mozart!"
—**Gustav Mahler,** *Austrian composer*

"Bury me among my people. I do not wish to rise among pale faces."
—**Red Jacket,** *Chief of the Seneca*

"Turn your back to me, please Henry. I am so sick now. The police are getting many complaints. Look out I want that G-note. Look out for Jimmy Valentine, for he's a friend of mine. Come on, come on, Jim. OK, OK, I am all through. I can't do another thing. Look out for mamma. Look out for her. Police, mamma, Helen, please take me out. I will settle the incident. Come on, open the soak duckets; the chimney sweeps. Talk to the sword. Shut up, you got a big mouth! Please help me to get up. Henry! Max! Come over here. French Canadian bean soup. I want to pay. Let them leave me alone."
—**Dutch Schultz,** *Chicago gangster*

"Don't worry, be happy."
—**Meher Baba,** *Indian guru*

Nut jobs: The U.S. military specifications for fruitcake are 18 pages long.

BEHIND THE HITS

Ever wonder what inspired some of your favorite songs?
Here are a few inside stories about popular tunes.

The Artist: Screamin' Jay Hawkins
The Song: "I Put a Spell on You" (1956)
The Story: Hawkins's signature tune was originally intended as a ballad, but it came out as the haunted howling of a jilted lover. Listeners may have guessed (correctly) that the singer had been drinking when he laid down the vocals, and according to Hawkins, "Every member of the band was drunk." Even the recording engineer and the A&R man, Arnold Maxin, were plastered. It was Maxin who effectively changed the song from a torch song to a frenzied rant by supplying the band with several cases of Italian Swiss Colony Muscatel. "We partied and we partied," Jay recalled, "and somewhere along the road I blanked out." When he regained consciousness, he had a hit record on his hands but no recollection of how he had made it.

The Artist: The Tornados
The Song: "Telstar" (1962)
The Story: This landmark recording featured the very first use of a synthesizer and was one of the bestselling instrumentals of all time. The song was recorded in a makeshift studio in producer Joe Meek's apartment: the mixing board was in the living room; the musicians performed in the bathroom, bedroom, and kitchen. Meek came up with the tune, but couldn't read or write music, so he hummed the melody on demo tapes and then played it back to the band. The fact that they were able to discern any tune at all from the tone-deaf Meek's fractured, off-key humming is a testament to their musical talent. Bad luck: The song became a huge #1 hit, but a French film composer sued Meek for plagiarism. Meek lost the suit, which cost him millions of dollars in lost royalties.

The Artist: Serge Gainsbourg
The Song: *"Je T'Aime...Moi Non Plus* (I Love You...Nor Do I)" (1969)

Longest word used by Shakespeare: *honorificabilitudinitatibus.*

The Story: There were several "heavy breathing" songs during the sixties, but none more notorious than this one. Originally written as a love song to sex kitten Brigitte Bardot, Serge rerecorded it in 1969 with his new lover, actress Jane Birkin. It features Birkin panting and moaning, "*Je t'aime, oui je t'aime!*" ("I love you, yes I love you!"), and Serge reciting unromantic lyrics like, "Between your kidneys, I come and go." Moral authorities were outraged; the Pope even excommunicated the record executive who'd released it in Italy. But despite being banned everywhere, the single was a huge international hit. In the United States, the vocals were completely erased and it was issued as an instrumental.

The Artist: The Ramones
The Song: "Blitzkrieg Bop" (1976)
The Story: Sometimes you don't need to be on the record charts to have a hit. This early punk-rock anthem is played during almost every pro football, baseball, and basketball game. Sports fans shout out its chorus of "Hey ho, let's go!" as a rallying cry. But most stadium spectators probably don't realize that the band originally wrote the song as a celebration of gang rumbles, but with lyrics like "Shoot 'em in the back now," it fits right into today's professional sports scene.

The Artist: Patsy Cline
The Song: "I Fall to Pieces" (1961)
The Story: Few singers conveyed emotion the way Cline did, and this anguished ode to the pain of an ended love affair sounded like she'd torn her own heart out during the recording session. Truth was, she hated the tune and didn't want anything to do with it, but her record label was desperate for a hit and tricked her into believing she would be dropped if she didn't record it. It became her first #1 single and stayed on the charts for an amazing 39 weeks. Oddly enough, Cline found out it was a hit after she'd literally fallen to pieces herself. Songwriter Hank Cochran recalls, "Patsy had been in a bad car wreck. It almost killed her. She was in the hospital with her head wrapped with bandages. I told her, 'You got yourself a pop hit, girl.' I think she thought I was just fooling around. When she finally got good enough to look at the numbers, she just laid back and said, 'Damn!' "

There's a replica of Bedrock, the town where the Flintstones lived, in Vail, Arizona.

STRANGE PET LAWSUITS

These days, it seems that people will sue each other over practically anything…including their pets. Here are a few real-life examples of unusual legal battles.

THE PLAINTIFF: Marie Dana
THE DEFENDANT: Samantha, a 15-year-old cocker spaniel
THE LAWSUIT: When Dana's companion, Sidney Altman, died in 1996, he bequeathed his $5 million Beverly Hills mansion and $350,000 in cash to the dog, but left only $50,000 to Dana. The will did offer her $60,000 a year to mind the aging Samantha, but stipulated that upon the dog's death everything was to go to charity. Dana sued the estate for $2.7 million.
THE VERDICT: Unknown. The judge urged the parties to settle out of court.

THE PLAINTIFF: Blackie the Talking Cat
THE DEFENDANT: City Council of Augusta, Georgia
THE LAWSUIT: Carl Miles, Blackie's owner, exhibited the cat on an Augusta street corner and collected "contributions." The city of Augusta said the enterprise required a business license and a fee, which Miles categorically refused to pay. He sued, arguing that such a fee impinged on the cat's right to free speech.
THE VERDICT: The judge actually heard the cat say, "I love you," but ruled that it was not a free speech issue. Because Blackie charged money for his speech, the city was entitled to their fee.

THE PLAINTIFF: Harold Marsh, Esq.
THE DEFENDANT: Mezzaluna Cafe
THE LAWSUIT: Marsh sued the Los Angeles restaurant on behalf of his miniature poodle, after they were asked to leave the outdoor dining section. The suit charged the restaurant with violating the dog's constitutional rights and blamed "idiot tourists and other persons similarly insane" for complaining to the health department about dogs in the restaurant
THE VERDICT: Unknown.

Thick skin: The bark of the giant sequoia can be up to 2 feet thick.

ARE YOU A TORTILLA CHIP?

Snack foods may be junk, but according to Dr. Alan Hirsch's Smell & Taste Treatment and Research Foundation, they can tell a lot about your personality. Want proof? Check out this food-horoscope from Dr. Hirsch's book, What Flavor Is Your Personality?

ARE YOU A Potato Chip? If so... You're an ambitious person, and a high achiever. You enjoy the rewards of success both at work and at home. Not a selfish sort, you enjoy the successes of your spouse and children, too. You also tend to be impatient with less than the best, and you are easily frustrated by life's little blips—traffic jams and waiting in line make you crazy.

ARE YOU A Pretzel? If so... You're a lively sort of person, easily bored with the same old routine. You look for new challenges at work and at home... and can spend hours mulling over abstract concepts while you munch on your pretzels. You are flirtatious and like to dress in a provocative manner, but you quickly tire of a trend and are off to find the latest style. Pretzel lovers are intuitive, make decisions based more on emotion than logic, and they may be overly trusting in romantic relationships. They're fun to be with, but they're vulnerable, too.

ARE YOU A Snack Cracker? If so... You think out problems using a rational logical approach. You tend to be shy, and avoid arguments because you don't like to hurt another person's feelings. Chances are you have many projects going at the same time, and they are competing for your attention. Cracker lovers tend to be loners who prefer private time, so you probably value those relaxing moments with no responsibilities or interruptions. Those who prefer snack crackers may easily find themselves involved in an online romance.

ARE YOU A Cheese Curl? If so... You are conscientious and principled and expect others to be, too. You tend to take the moral high ground. With your finely tuned sense of right and wrong, you treat everyone in the same just and fair manner. You have integrity. You may appear rigid to others, but in reality you just know enough to plan ahead. In your house, the spare batteries and Band-Aids are right where they belong—just like everything on your desk.

ARE YOU Nuts? If so... You tend to be easygoing, empathetic, and understanding. Nut lovers can be counted on to stay calm, even in the midst of upheaval, so even a screaming spouse or a disappointing boss won't ruffle you. They do well in jobs that involve the public. Nut lovers may not be outstanding leaders, but they contribute to a peaceful home and an effective office.

ARE YOU Popcorn? If so... You know how to take charge of a situation, and are usually quick to pick up the slack if the need arises. While these men and women have great self-confidence, they are rather humble—no one would ever call them showoffs. Popcorn lovers may hide their success so well that they appear to be a "poor relation," while they squirrel away their treasures. If you inherit money from a relative you thought was flat broke, he or she was most likely a popcorn muncher.

ARE YOU A Meat Snack? If so... You prefer to be with other people while you indulge. Meat snack lovers are at their best in the company of others because they are so gregarious—and sometimes generous to a fault. If you want a true friend, pick the meat snack lover: they are trustworthy and always loyal. They will go all out for friends and family, even to the point of making sacrifices.

ARE YOU A Tortilla Chip? If so... You're probably a perfectionist; if it's less than perfect, you'll redo it. Not satisfied with a mere A, you want an A+. These individuals are not selfish, so if you want a partner to help you fight an injustice, look to the people with their hands in a bowl of tortilla chips. Invite them over for the weekend, too, because they're likely to be good houseguests. The tortilla chip lover is punctual and conservative. A male tortilla chip lover can slip into a tux or feel just as comfortable in an old T-shirt, but don't look for a tortilla chip–loving woman to dress provocatively—she is rather sexually restrained.

IF YOU...

Life is a series of possibilities.

IF YOU...
are lost near a stream, your chances of finding civilization are much greater if you travel downstream.

IF YOU...
are suddenly buried by a snowstorm and don't know which way is up or down, spit! The spit will always head down. Now you know in which direction to start digging.

IF YOU...
laid all the hot dogs Americans eat between Memorial Day and Labor Day end to end, you'd circle the globe 15 times.

IF YOU...
parachute from a helicopter at random, 7 out of 10 times you'll hit salt water (because 70% of the Earth is covered with salt water).

IF YOU...
eat lots of red beets, your pee might turn pink.

IF YOU...
kiss under mistletoe at Christmas, that's fine. Just don't kiss the mistletoe itself—the berries are poisonous.

IF YOU...
and your friends meet up with a grizzly bear, stay calm and link arms with each other. This makes the bear think he's dealing with one really big creature. Confronted with a larger creature, the bear is likely to retreat.

IF YOU...
can spit a watermelon seed 70 feet, you're in the world-record range.

IF YOU...
have too many mosquitoes in your yard, you need some bats. One bat will eat up to 1,000 bugs per night.

IF YOU...
want to keep leaves out of your rain gutter, secure a slinky in one end, stretch it out, and attach it to the other end. You may need two slinkies if it's a long gutter.

IF YOU...
put a raisin in a glass of champagne, it will sink to the bottom, then float to the top, then sink to the bottom, then float to the top, then sink to the...

The thickest tree on Earth: El Tule, a cypress in Mexico. It has a girth of 138 feet.

YOU'VE GOT MAIL!

Like anyone with an e-mail address, we at the BRI get a lot of unsolicited e-mail that seems to be too good—or bad—to be true. We've looked into the claims made by some of them, and here's what we've found. (Do any of these look familiar? We wouldn't be surprised if you've received a few of them yourself.)

YOU'VE GOT MAIL:

From:	abraxas@cloudten.org
To:	djeff@home.att
Subject:	Fwd: Breasts linked to men's health

This is not a joke: Ogling women's breasts is good for a man's health and can add years to his life, experts have discovered. According to the New England Journal of Medicine, "Just 10 minutes of staring at the charms of a well-endowed female is roughly equivalent to a 30-minute aerobics work-out," declared gerontologist Dr. Karen Weatherby.

THE ORIGIN: The e-mail appeared in March 2000, not long after the *Weekly World News* tabloid ran an article making a similar claim.

THE TRUTH: It is a joke—the *New England Journal of Medicine* never published such a study, and if "Dr. Karen Weatherby" exists at all, she's never had anything published in a medical journal.

YOU'VE GOT MAIL:

From:	Concerned neighbors
To:	My friends
Subject:	Missing 5-year-old

Five-year-old Kelsey Brooke Jones has been missing from her home in southern Minnesota since 4:00 p.m. on October 11, 1999. Please help find her by forwarding this e-mail—and the picture of Kelsey that's attached—to everyone you know.

THE ORIGIN: This e-mail, which originated in southern Minnesota some time after 4:00 p.m. on October 11, 1999, is believed to have been forwarded to millions of people since then.

Count 'em yourself: Every day an adult body produces 300 billion new cells.

THE TRUTH: Kelsey really did "disappear" on October 11— she went a few doors down to a neighbor's apartment to play while her mother was taking a nap, and was still playing there when her mother woke up. Mom called the police before check- ing with the neighbors; officers found Kelsey a few minutes later when they started knocking on doors.

Because Kelsey was never really missing, no missing child report was ever filed. No matter—by then someone had already sent out the first e-mail, and it has been circulating ever since. Apparently, the picture attached to the e-mail isn't even Kelsey... which means that millions of e-mail recipients all over the coun- try may be keeping an eye out for a girl who never disappeared, using a picture that isn't even her.

YOU'VE GOT MAIL:

From:	AllenO@CDC.gov
To:	brmail@mind.net
Subject:	Fwd: Spiked pay phones

Hello, my name is Tina Strongman and I work at a police station, as a phone operator for 911....It seems that a new form of gang initiation is to go find as many pay phones as possible and put a mixture of LSD and strychnine onto the buttons. This mixture is deadly to the human touch, and apparently, this has killed some people....Please be careful if you are using a pay phone anywhere. You may want to wipe it off, or just not use one at all.

THE ORIGIN: The e-mail began circulating in April 1999, fol- lowing months of rumors that HIV-infected drug users were hid- ing contaminated needles in pay phone coin-return slots. The pay phone rumors were so pervasive that the Centers for Disease Control issued an official press release debunking them.

THE TRUTH: The LSD–payphone e-mail is an April Fools' joke that draws its inspiration from a number of classic urban leg- ends, including children's wash-off tattoos that are spiked with LSD; gangs that initiate new members by murdering the occu- pants of vehicles that flash their bright headlights; and AIDS- infected needles hidden in gas pump handles, movie theater seat cushions, and other seemingly innocuous places.

TREKKIES

Star Trek is so integrated into our culture that the word "Trekkie" is now in the dictionary. And there's no more important aspect of Trek culture than Star Trek conventions. We spoke with Trek expert Richard Arnold, of Creation Entertainment, the biggest Trek convention organizers, to get the story of how they started.

STAR WRECK

The vast *Star Trek* empire thrives today, yet back in 1966 the original TV series never did better than 52nd place in the ratings and barely clawed its way through its third season before it was cancelled. After the show's final episode in 1969, the cast and production crew disbanded, never expecting to work together again.

Two years later, Paramount syndicated the series and allowed stations to broadcast it cheaply in order to recoup part of their investment. Stations typically ran it every weekday at dinnertime, and before they knew it devoted watchers were tuning in religiously. Casual viewers also watched, giving the show a much broader audience than it had had in primetime.

Fans wanted more, but Paramount wasn't about to risk another flop by making new episodes. So people had to settle for the next best thing: hearing *Star Trek* creator Gene Roddenberry speak about it. Soon, Roddenberry was swimming in invitations for speaking engagements at colleges and science fiction conventions.

THE WRATH OF CON

Sci-fi conventions had been around since the 1930s, but they focused on books, not movies or television. In fact, the purist organizers of the big sci-fi conventions condemned made-for-TV science fiction as a perversion of the genre. But the droves of sci-fi buffs who packed these conventions had adored Roddenberry's work ever since he previewed the *Star Trek's* pilot episode "The Cage" at the sci-fi convention WorldCon in 1966 to an explosion of cheers.

The more *Star Trek* people wanted, the more resistant organizers became. Finally, their patience ran out. In 1971 at Sci-fi Con, the committee in charge sent a clear message to *Star Trek* fans: "If you want *Star Trek*, put on your own conventions; television is not welcome here."

TO BOLDLY GO WHERE NO SHOW HAS GONE BEFORE

There had never been a convention for only one show before, so the committee thought they were putting a stop to the *Star Trek* madness. But it was a massive blunder: without Roddenberry on the bill, audiences dwindled. Still, Roddenberry was reluctant to put together a convention, so *Star Trek* actors Al Schuster and Joan Winston together with a group of devoted fans decided to do it. The world's first Trek Con was set to take place at New York City's Stadtler Hilton Hotel in January 1972. Roddenberry was to be the keynote speaker and a few actors who had had bit parts were scheduled to make appearances.

Schuster and Winston guessed that maybe 400 fans would show up; a capacity crowd of 800 was a pipe dream. But when convention day arrived, so did 4,000 rabid *Star Trek* fans, who crowded in and around the packed hotel, among them legendary sci-fi author Isaac Asimov (a huge fan). Even NASA sent representatives.

COSTUME DRAMA

Today, a Trekkie can buy almost anything with a *Star Trek* logo on it in the "dealers' room," but in the early days only a few wares were available: T-shirts (two different designs), homemade models, and bumper stickers with phrases like "My other car is a starship" and the infamous "Beam me up, Scotty!"

Some Trekkies showed up to the first convention in full homemade Vulcan or Klingon garb. The person with the best outfit was one of the organizers, Al Schuster, who enlisted the show's head makeup artist to transform him into a Klingon. Once convention organizers realized that fans had no shame about dressing up as their favorite characters, they decided to encourage them by organizing fashion shows and awarding prizes for best costume—human or alien.

Not everyone liked wearing a costume, though. Leonard Nimoy, who played Spock, the show's most popular character, was reluctant to appear at conventions because he didn't want to be typecast. He even wrote a book entitled *I Am Not Spock*. At his first convention in 1973, his presence caused such chaos that he had to be rushed out by an army of security guards. He later came to embrace his popularity, however, and 20 years later wrote another book: *I AM Spock.*

"GET A LIFE!"

The other actors were in great demand as well, and none more than Captain James T. Kirk—William Shatner—but Shatner didn't agree to appear at a convention until 1976. When the time came to go onstage, Shatner was a nervous wreck, says Trek Con organizer Richard Arnold: "I was sort of babysitting him before he went on—for a man who doesn't smoke or drink, he had a cigarette and a drink in each hand." He recovered, then blew the audience away with his over-the-top energy.

But Shatner later turned from fan favorite to hated villain with three little words. When he hosted *Saturday Night Live* in 1986, writers wanted to lampoon Trek conventions in a skit, which ended with an exasperated plea from Shatner: "Get a life!" Shatner was apprehensive about doing the skit, but the people at *SNL* assured him it was all in good fun.

Right before he went on, Shatner remarked: "I hope *Star Trek* fans have a sense of humor, because if not I'm going to be in big trouble." They didn't. According to Arnold, "Some fans are still upset about it to this day because the skit was dead-on. It's true: there are fans who live in their parents' basements and never go out. These people live for the show."

LIVE LONG AND PROSPER

Since the first convention, Trek Cons have grown in frequency and popularity. In fact, it was the popularity of the conventions that convinced Paramount to resurrect *Star Trek* as a movie in 1979. By the mid-70s, Trek conventions were regularly drawing 20,000 people. Chicago's 1975 Trek Con drew a whopping 30,000 Trekkies! Today, every major city has an annual convention; many have several. On an average weekend, there are 10 to 20 Trek conventions taking place in the North America and Europe. Admission prices range from just a few dollars to over $1,000 for front-row seating.

The average office chair with wheels will travel of 8 miles this year.

Astronomical attendance and high ticket prices translate to big bucks for the actors. They used to speak for $500 or less—sometimes even for free. Now big guns like Shatner, Nimoy, and *The Next Generation*'s Patrick Stewart (Captain Picard) and Brent Spiner (Data) pocket as much as $50,000 per appearance. Autographs used to be free; today fans can count on forking over $5 to $30. Shatner and Nimoy charge $50 to $100 for a signature. Many former *Star Trek* actors make a very nice living by appearing at 30-plus conventions per year at $10,000 a pop.

And who is today's biggest draw for Trek conventions? Not Captain Kirk, not Mr. Spock, not even Jean-Luc Picard. It's Seven of Nine—the gorgeous young woman with a painted-on costume played by Jeri Ryan on *Voyager*, ensuring that Trekkies will continue to flock to *Star Trek* conventions for many years to come.

*   *   *

SHIPWRECKS AND ANIMALS—
THE UNTOLD STORIES

A Duck Raises Sheep. In 1964 a freighter carrying 6,000 sheep capsized and sank in Kuwait's harbor. With so many dead animals underwater, Kuwaitis worried that the rotting carcasses would pollute the water. A way had to be found to lift the ship and remove the sheep before the harbor was contaminated. Danish engineer Karl Kroyer remembered a comic book in which Donald Duck and his nephews raised a sunken ship by stuffing it full of ping pong balls. The idea was worth a try, so Kroyer had 27 million polystyrene balls injected into the hull. It worked—thanks in part to Donald Duck.

Moby's Legacy. Two Maori women were the only survivors of a canoe accident off New Zealand. As a dead whale floated by with the harpoon still stuck in it, they used the line from the harpoon to haul themselves aboard the carcass and then floated 80 miles to safety.

Horse Sense. In 1852 the British steamship H.M.S. *Birkenhead* sank three miles off the African coast. Captain Wright was one of the last to abandon ship, and when he finally made it to shore, he was greeted by another of the survivors...his horse.

The Japanese express grief and mourning after the death of a loved one by wearing white, not black.

GENERATION X

In 1990, Douglas Coupland wrote a book called Generation X, *a fictional account of world-weary 20-somethings in the 1990s. It was also a clever—and cynical—glossary of the experiences and people of that generation. Uncle John found it in the...uh...reading room the other day and loved it. He thought you might enjoy it, too.*

McJob: A low-pay, low-prestige, low-dignity, no-future job in the service sector.

Historical Overdosing: Living in a time when too much is happening. Symptoms include addiction to newspapers and TV news.

Occupational Slumming: Taking a job beneath one's skill or education level as a way of retreating from adult responsibilities and avoiding failure.

Knee-Jerk Irony: The tendency to make flippant ironic comments in everyday conversation.

Derision Preemption: A lifestyle tactic; the refusal to go out on any sort of emotional limb so as to avoid mockery from peers. The main goal of *Knee-Jerk Irony.*

Personality Tithe: A price paid for becoming a couple. Formerly amusing people become boring: *"Thanks for inviting us, but Judy and I are going to look at flatware catalogs tonight."*

Cult of Aloneness: The obsessive need for autonomy, usually at the expense of long-term relationships.

Bleeding Ponytail: A Baby Boomer who pines for hippie or pre-sellout days.

Clique Maintenance: The need of one generation to see the next generation as deficient so as to bolster its own collective ego: *"Kids today do nothing. They're so apathetic. We used to go out and protest. All they do is shop and complain."*

Earth Tones: A youthful subgroup interested in vegetarianism, tie-dyed clothes, mild recreational drugs, and good stereo equipment. Earnest, often lacking in humor.

Safety Net-ism: The belief that there will always be a financial and emotional safety net to buffer life's hurts. Usually parents.

Divorce Assumption: A form of *Safety Net-ism,* the belief that if a marriage doesn't work out, there's no problem because partners can simply seek a divorce.

Mid-Twenties Breakdown: A period of mental collapse, often caused by an inability to function outside of school or structured environments coupled with a realization of one's essential aloneness in the world.

Foggiest place in America: Cape Disappointment, Washington.

Now Denial: To tell oneself that the only time worth living in is the past and that the only time that may ever be interesting again is the future.

Lessness: A philosophy whereby one reconciles oneself with diminishing expectations of material wealth: *"I've given up wanting to be a bigshot. I just want to find happiness and open up a little roadside cafe."*

Status Substitution: Using an object with intellectual or fashionable cachet to substitute for an object that is merely pricey: *"Brian, you left your copy of Camus in your brother's BMW."*

Poorochondria: Hypochondria derived from not having medical insurance.

Personal Taboo: A small rule for living, bordering on a superstition, that allows one to cope with everyday life in the absence of cultural or religious dictums.

Voter's Block: The attempt, however futile, to register dissent with the current political system by simply not voting.

Musical Hairsplitting: The act of classifying music and musicians into pathologically picayune categories: *"The Vienna Franks are a good example of urban white acid folk revivalism crossed with ska."*

101-ism: The tendency to pick apart, often in minute detail, all aspects of life using half-understood pop psychology as a tool.

Squires: The most common X generation subgroup; the only one given to breeding. *Squires* exist almost exclusively in couples and are recognizable by their frantic attempts to recreate Eisenhower-era plenitude.

Ultra-Short-Term Nostalgia: Homesickness for the extremely recent past: *"God, things seemed so much better in the world last week."*

Cafe Minimalism: To espouse a philosophy of minimalism without actually putting into practice any of its tenets.

Down-Nesting: The tendency of parents to move to smaller, guest-room-free houses after the children have moved away so as to avoid children aged 20 to 30 who have boomeranged home.

Tele-parablizing: Morals used in everyday life that derive from TV sitcom plots: *"That's just like the episode where Jan lost her glasses!"*

Yuppie Wannabe's: An X generation subgroup that believes the myth of a yuppie lifestyle is both satisfying and viable. Tend to be highly in debt, involved in substance abuse, and show a willingness to talk about Armageddon after three drinks.

Dorian Graying: The unwillingness to gracefully allow one's body to show signs of aging.

Option Paralysis: The tendency, when given unlimited choices, to make none.

It can take up to 12 hours for snails to mate. They mate only once in their lives.

EAT YOUR WORDS

Ever wonder where the names of certain foods or eating utensils come from? At the BRI, it's our job to wonder. Here are some origins for you to chew on:

PLATE. Comes from the Old French *plat*, meaning "flat."

CUP. From the Sanskrit word *kupa*, meaning "water well."

MUSHROOM. An English mispronounciation of *moisseron*, the Old French word for "fungus."

CABBAGE. From the French word for "head," *caboche*.

HORS D'OEUVRE. In French, *hors* means "outside" and *oeuvre* means "work;" literally "apart from the main work."

SALAD. From the Latin *salsus*, meaning "salted."

COLESLAW. Comes from the Dutch terms *kool*, meaning "cabbage," and *sla*, meaning "salad."

SPAGHETTI. From *spago*, the Italian word for "cord" or "string."

CANTALOUPE. From the place it was first grown—Cantalupo, Italy.

GELATIN. Comes from the Latin *gelo*, meaning "to freeze or congeal." So does *jelly*.

DESSERT. *Desservir* is the French word for "to clear (the table)," and that's what you do before dessert is served.

BOWL. Comes from the Anglo-Saxon word *bolla*, meaning "round."

SPOON. From the Anglo-Saxon *spon*, meaning "chip"—a curved chip of wood dipped into a bowl.

*   *   *

Put a pot of chili on the stove to simmer.
Let it simmer. Meanwhile, broil a good steak.
Eat the steak. Let the chili simmer. Ignore it.

—**Recipe for chili from Allan Shivers,
former governor of Texas**

The peanut is one of the most concentrated sources of nourishment.

THE METRIC CLOCK

Uncle John stumbled on a strange-looking timepiece in an antique store. When the dealer told him it was a "metric clock," he just had to find out the story behind it. Here it is.

TIME FOR A CHANGE

Most of the world uses the metric system. But you probably don't know that it was invented by the French and came about as a result of the French Revolution.

After the bloody triumph over the French monarchy in 1792, the French Revolutionary government, known as "the Terror," was intent on cleansing citizens' lives of all influence of the aristocracy and the Church. They were going to create a new society based on reason and rationality.

For many years, French scientists had been trying to replace the traditional arbitrary system of weights and measures with a decimal system. This climate of reform and reason was perfect for implementing their ideas.

REASON PREVAILS

In 1793 the Committee of Public Instruction approved a bold proposal: that the basic unit of distance, the foot, be replaced with the "meter"—a unit equal to one ten-millionth of the length of the arc from the equator to the North Pole. Distance henceforth was measured in multiples of 10: centimeters, millimeters, and kilometers. The quart was replaced with the liter, and the ounce with the gram. And it opened the door for another innovation: metric time.

Under the guidance of mathematician Charles Gilbert Romme, the Committee set about the task of creating a metric clock and calendar that would reflect their belief in science over religion. After a year of tinkering by France's most distinguished poets, scientists, and mathematicians, the French Republican Calendar was officially adopted on October 5, 1793.

The new calendar still had 12 months in a year, but every month had three 10-day weeks, called *decades*. That accounted for only 360 days. The remaining 5 days of the year were celebrated as feast days for the common man: Virtue Day, Genius Day, Labor

Day, Reason Day, Rewards Day, and, in leap years, Revolution Day.

The metric time system was even more confusing than the calendar. Each day was divided into 10 decimal hours, each hour split into 100 minutes, and each minute into 100 seconds. A decimal second was shorter than a traditional second, but a decimal minute was longer than a traditional minute.

THE NAME GAME

The new names for the months and the days were invented by poet Philippe Fabre d'Eglantine. He named the months according to the natural events occurring at that time of year and then rhymed them by season. They were *Vendemiaire* (vintage), *Brumaire* (mist), *Frimaire* (frost), *Nivose* (snow), *Pluviose* (rain), *Ventose* (wind), *Germinal* (sprouting), *Floreal* (blossoming), *Prairial* (meadow), *Moissidor* (harvest), *Thermidor* (heat), and *Fructidor* (fruit). The British press lampooned these as Wheezy, Sneezy, Freezy, Slippy, Drippy, Nippy, Showery, Flowery, Bowery, Wheaty, Heaty, Sweety.

In contrast, d'Eglantine gave the days of the week bland names: *Primidi, Duodi, Tridi, Quartidi, Quintidi, Sextidi, Septidi, Octidi, Nondidi,* and *Decadi.* Translation: "First Day," "Second Day," "Third Day," etc. But every day of the year was named individually, too. D'Eglantine named them for plants, animals, and tools—for example, Olive Day, Goat Day, or Plow Day—but no days were named for saints, popes, or kings.

CONFUSION REIGNS

Despite its nationalistic imagery and scientific convenience, the new calendar was rejected by the common people it was designed to benefit... it was just too confusing.

First strike: The calendar was designed to count from September 22, 1792, the date of the foundation of the French Republic and the abolition of the monarchy. By the time the new calendar was adopted, however, the Republic was already well into the second year, prompting immediate confusion.

Second strike: French workers detested the new calendar because it allotted only 1 rest day in a 10-day week instead of 1 per 7 days. And, to the Terror's chagrin, most people still kept track of Sundays for church.

Third strike: The rest of Europe was still using the Gregorian calendar, which made business increasingly difficult to conduct between French merchants and those in other countries. On top of that, the new metric clocks had faces that included markings for both traditional and metric time, which was confusing even for people who wanted to use decimal hours and minutes.

TICK... TICK... TICK...
As passion for the Revolution faded, aspects of the calendar were slowly abolished. By 1795 the metric clock and the year-end feast days—celebrated only once—were swept away. Napoléon Bonaparte pushed the French senate to reinstate the old calendar as soon as he was crowned emperor. At the beginning of 1806, after only reaching year 13, the French Republican calendar completely disappeared from use.

* * *

WHAT'S IN YOUR DRAIN?
Here are a few items Roto-Rooter claims they've found in clogged pipes:
Home and Garden: Broom handles, doorknobs, garden hoses, bungee cords, and a hummingbird feeder.

Health and Beauty Aids: Glass eyes, gold teeth, dentures, contact lenses, toothbrushes, hearing aides, and toupees.

Clothing and Linens: Women's lingerie, long johns, towels, robes, a complete bedspread, and, of course, a multitude of missing socks.

Electronics: TV remotes, pagers, an alarm clock, a Timex that took a licking and kept on ticking, and a Rolex that took a licking and died.

Sporting Goods and Toys: An eight ball, golf balls (30 in one drain), a shrimp net, a tear gas projectile, and a Teenage Mutant Ninja Turtle doll.

Pets: Birds, bats, beavers, cats, ducks, fish, frogs, possums, skunks, a piranha, a 2½-pound trout, and lots of snakes—including a 6-foot rattlesnake.

Valuables: $400 in coins, $58 in change in a laundromat pipe, cancelled checks, a $4,000 diamond, and $50,000.

Groceries: A Cornish game hen and a six-pack of Budweiser.

CELEBRITY GOSSIP

*Here's our cheesy tabloid section—a
bunch of gossip about famous people.*

LUCIANO PAVAROTTI

When Pavarotti performs for the public, he only does so under very strict conditions. His contract states that during sound check, "there must be no distinct smells anywhere near the artist." In his dressing room, he demands that all sofas be mounted on six-inch risers and that "soft toilet paper" be provided. As for his hotel accommodations, he insists that "the master bedroom must always be kept in total darkness." He refuses to go onstage for a performance before he finds a bent nail somewhere on the stage and pulls it out.

MARLON BRANDO

While filming the 2001 movie *The Score*, Brando refused to be on the set at the same time as director Frank Oz. Brando referred to Oz as "Miss Piggy" (Oz provided the voice of Muppet Miss Piggy many years ago) and teased him with lines like "Don't you wish I was a puppet, so you could control me." Robert De Niro was forced to direct Brando instead, with Oz giving him instructions via headset.

WALT DISNEY

Before Walt Disney's 35th birthday, his brother Roy encouraged employees to throw the boss a surprise party. Two of the animators thought it would be hilarious to make a short movie of Mickey and Minnie Mouse "consummating their relationship." When Disney saw the animation at the party, he feigned laughter and playfully asked who made it. As soon as the two animators came forward, he fired them on the spot and left.

SERENA WILLIAMS

According to London's *Metro* newspaper, tennis star Serena Williams claims to have a six-hour-a-day online shopping addiction. Even while competing in the French Open, she was "stuck" online buying things she didn't need. The source of her compulsion: fame has forced her to avoid shopping in public.

During WWII, the Oscar statue was made of plaster—metal was an essential wartime material.

TIMOTHY DEXTER: AMERICA'S LUCKIEST IDIOT

Have you ever thought about someone: "How could anybody so stupid be so successful?" If not, you will after you read this story is from Zanies: The World's Greatest Eccentrics, *by Jay Robert Nash.*

KING MIDAS

Born in Malden, Massachusetts, on January 22, 1747, Timothy Dexter worked first as a farmer, and then, in Boston, became an apprentice leather tanner. At age 20, with his life's savings in his pocket, all of nine dollars, he moved on to the thriving town of Newburyport, where he met and married a wealthy widow, 31-year-old Elizabeth Frothingham.

Dexter fancied himself a shrewd businessman. Using his wife's money, he copied what other businessmen were doing—he bought stocks. With no understanding of which stocks to buy, he simply bought cheap ones. Somehow, their values rose and Dexter was able to sell at a profit.

Competitors laughed at the semi-illiterate Dexter and amused themselves by giving him lunatic business tips. One merchant told Dexter that the West Indies, where colonization was booming, was sorely in need of warming pans, mittens and Bibles.

Having no idea of the extremely hot weather in the West Indies, Dexter took the tip and proceeded to buy more than 40,000 warming pans, 40,000 pairs of mittens, and 40,000 Bibles and shipped them out. He then waited for fortune to smile on him.

DUMB LUCK

By incredible luck, when Dexter's shipments arrived in the West Indies, there was a religious movement beginning, and his Bibles were purchased at a 100% profit. More luck: A fleet of Russian trading ships visiting ports in the West Indies had their agents immediately buy up the mittens to the last pair. The warming pans sat idly in a warehouse until some inventive planter discovered that they made ideal skimmers with which molasses could be ladled into vats—each and every pan was sold for a profit. These

---

What did Christopher Columbus look like? No one knows—his portrait was never painted.

incredible sales brought Dexter an estimated $150,000, making him enormously wealthy.

CARRYING COAL TO NEWCASTLE

Jealous of Dexter's dumb luck, merchants in his town purposely sought to ruin him by urging him to invest every dime he possessed in shipping coal to Newcastle, England. The unschooled Dexter, not knowing that Newcastle was the center of England's coal-mining industry, hired scores of sailing ships, filled their holds with soft Virginia coal and sent the cargoes to England.

But instead of becoming an international laughingstock, Dexter's amazing good fortune held; a massive strike in Newcastle had left mines empty and there was a shortage of coal in the area. When Dexter's ships arrived, his coal was purchased at enormous profits, making him twice as rich as he had been.

INCREASING ODDITIES

As he grew older, Dexter became more and more eccentric. His wife, Elizabeth, constantly nagged him about his foolish ways. Instead of arguing with her, Dexter pretended that she had died and that her presence in his sprawling mansion was no more than an apparition. When visitors arrived, Dexter would point to her and say: "This is Mrs. Dexter, the ghost that was my wife."

The zenith of Dexter's eccentricities was reached when he decided to publish his memoirs, entitled *A Pickle for the Knowing Ones, or Plain Truths in a Homespun Dress*. The book was, from beginning to end, one long, incoherent sentence, without a single punctuation mark.

Dexter ordered the printing of thousands of copies and had them widely distributed. Few read the book and those who did ridiculed Dexter as a rich buffoon, a self-indulgent idiot who naively destroyed the English language in an expensive fit of egomania. The lack of punctuation in the memoirs was repeatedly pointed out to Dexter as the crowning glory of his moronic gestures.

REVISIONIST

Dexter answered his critics in a revised edition of *A Pickle for the Knowing Ones* some years later. He had the following page reproduced in the second edition:

mister printer the Nowing ones complane of my book the fust edition had no stops I put in A Nuf here and thay may peper and solt it as they plese

,,
,,,;;;;;
;;
....................!!!!!!!!!!!!!!!!!!!!!!!!!!!!....................
....................!!!!!!!!!!!!!!!!!!!!!!!!!!!!....................
....................................!.............................
..................,,,
,,,,,,,,,,,,,,,,,,.....................???????????????????????????......................
....

As a final display of Dexter's golden touch, the book is now considered a valuable collector's item.

*   *   *

MENCKEN'S OBSERVATIONS ON DEMOCRACY

H. L. Mencken (1880–1956) was a writer, editor, and critic for Baltimore newspapers and one of America's wittiest, and most opinionated political commentators.

1. Democracy is the theory that intelligence is dangerous. It assumes that no idea can be safe until those who can't understand it have approved it.

2. Democracy is the theory that two thieves will steal less than one.

3. It is a bit hoggish, but it might be worse. It will be centuries before we are ready for anything better.

4. The principal virtue of democracy is that it makes a good show—one incomparably bizarre, amazing, shocking, and obscene.

5. Democracy is the liberty of the have-nots. Its aim is to destroy the liberty of the haves.

6. Democracy is a sort of laughing gas. It will not cure anything, perhaps, but it unquestionably stops the pain.

7. The Fathers who invented it, if they could return from Hell, would never recognize it. It was conceived as a free government of free men; it has become simply a battle of charlatans for the votes of idiots.

DUMB CROOKS

Here's proof that crime doesn't pay.

YOU'RE SO TRANSPARENT

"A 19-year-old convenience store employee in Shawnee, Kansas, put tape over the security camera, robbed the till, then called police to report a robbery. But since he used transparent tape to cover the camera, it was easy to see that he was the robber and he was quickly arrested."

—*FHM Magazine*

FAT CHANCE

MADRID—"Would-be burglar Pedro Cardona tried to break into a house by squeezing through a doggie door. It was something like putting two pounds of bologna in a one-pound bag as the portly Cardona became wedged in halfway through. Rescuers had to chop the door down with axes to get him out."

—*Bizarre News*

RUN FOR THE BORDER

"A criminal mastermind in a small Iowa town carefully planned a bank robbery and actually got away with the money. But he was arrested the next day at a motel near the state line, only 20 miles away.

"When asked why he had stopped so close to the scene of the crime, he explained that he was on parole and couldn't cross the state line without permission from his parole officer."

—*The World's Dumbest Criminals*, by Daniel Butler

WHAT A DOPE

"A man in Brighton, England, jumped out of a taxi without paying and left behind a bag of marijuana. Amazingly, he called the taxi company to inquire about the bag and was told it had been turned over to the police, so he went to the local police station to claim the bag."

—*Chicago Sun-Times*

MONEY TO BURN

"Six men were charged with attempting Britain's biggest cash robbery. According to court testimony, the gang forced an armored car carrying $18.2 million to be driven to a wooded area, then used high-powered torches to open it. But the torches accidentally set off a 'bonfire' that burned $2.4 million into ashes and caused the men to flee."

—*Dumb Crooks*

BLOCKHEAD

"Seems this guy wanted some beer pretty badly. He decided that he'd just throw a cinder block through a liquor store window, grab some booze, and run. So he lifted the cinder block over his head and heaved it at the window. The cinder block bounced back and hit him on the head, knocking him unconscious. Seems the liquor store window was made of Plexiglas. The whole event was caught on videotape."

—*Darwin Awards*

WANT CHIPS WITH THAT?

"A Subway sandwich shop employee in Edmonton, Alberta, somehow managed to activate the burglar alarm and disarm two men who were attempting to rob him at knife point. Scared by the sandwich-maker's heroics, the felons fled the scene. The Subway employee pursued the would-be thieves, shouting that there was no harm done and that he'd gladly make them free sandwiches if they came back. Amazingly, they did! Police arrived minutes later and arrested the hungry thieves, who were patiently waiting in line for a Cold Cut Trio."

—*Stuff* magazine

*   *   *

ACTUAL JAPANESE CAR NAMES

- Subaru Gravel Express
- Suzuki Every Joy Pop Turbo
- Mazda Proceed Marvie
- Isuzu Mysterious Utility Wizard
- Isuzu 20 Giga Light Dump
- Toyota Master Ace Surf

The good old days: 30 million years ago, there were palm trees in Alaska.

IF YOU BUILD IT, THEY WILL COME

Some people call them roadside attractions. We call them tourist traps. Either way, it's an amazing phenomenon: There's nothing much to see there, nothing much to do there. Yet tourists go by the millions. Think we could get people to come to Uncle John's Bowl of Wonder?

WALL DRUG, Wall, South Dakota
Build It... One summer day in 1936, Dorothy and Ted Hustead had a brilliant idea: they put signs up along highway I-90 advertising their struggling mom-and-pop drugstore. As an afterthought, they included an offer for free ice water. Wall Drug was situated 10 miles from the entrance to the South Dakota badlands, and on sweltering summer days before air conditioning, the suggestion of free ice water made rickety old Wall Drug seem like an oasis. When Ted got back from putting up the first sign, half a dozen cars were already parked in front of his store.

They'll Come: The Husteads knew they were on to something. Ted built an empire of billboards all over the United States, planting signs farther and farther away from his drugstore. There's a sign in Amsterdam's train station (only 5,397 miles to Wall Drug); there's one at the Taj Mahal (10,728 miles to Wall Drug); and there's even one in Antarctica (only 10,645 miles to Wall Drug).

Today, Wall Drug is an enormous 50,000-square-foot tourist mecca with a 520-seat restaurant and countless specialty and souvenir shops; if it's hokey, odds are that Wall Drug sells it. They also have a collection of robots, including a singing gorilla and a mechanical Cowboy Orchestra. Wall Drug spends over $300,000 on billboards, but every cent of it pays off. The store lures in 20,000 visitors a day in the summer and grosses more than $11 million each year. And they still give away free ice water—5,000 glasses a day.

SOUTH OF THE BORDER, Dillon, South Carolina
Build It... Driving south on I-95 near the South Carolina border,

---

Gail Borden (inventor of condensed milk) is buried beneath a headstone shaped like a milk can.

one object stands out from the landscape: a 200-foot-tall tower with a giant sombrero on top. The colossal hat is Sombrero Tower, centerpiece of the huge South of the Border tourist complex.

SOB, as the locals call it, began as a beer stand operated by a man named Alan Schafer. When Schafer noticed that his building supplies were being delivered to "Schafer Project: South of the [North Carolina] Border," a lightbulb lit up over his head and he decided his stand needed a Mexican theme.

They'll Come: Today, SOB sprawls over 135 acres and imports—and sells—$1.5 million worth of Mexican merchandise a year. It has a 300-room motel and five restaurants, including the Sombrero Room and Pedro's Casateria (a fast-food joint shaped like a antebellum mansion with a chicken on the roof). There's also Pedro's Rocket City (a fireworks shop), Golf of Mexico (miniature golf), and Pedro's Pleasure Dome spa. Incredibly, eight million people stop into SOB every year for a little slice of…Mexi-kitsch.

TREES OF MYSTERY, Klamath, California

Build It… When Carl Bruno first toured the towering redwood forests around the DeMartin ranch in 1931, he was awestruck by a handful of oddly deformed trees. Dollar signs in his eyes, Bruno snapped up the property and began luring in travelers to see trees shaped like pretzels and double helixes. He called his attraction Wonderland Park, and for the first 15 years of its existence, it did modest business—but something was missing…

They'll Come: He decided the park needed a 49-foot-tall statue of Paul Bunyan. In 1946 Bruno had the massive mythical logger installed near the highway and changed the park's name to Trees of Mystery. Business began to pick up. He added a companion piece, 35-feet-tall Babe the Blue Ox, in 1949. (When Babe was first introduced, he blew smoke out of his nostrils, which made small children run away screaming. The smoke was discontinued.)

Trees of Mystery prospered and is still open today. It recently added an aerial gondola ride, but the park is primarily a bunch of oddly shaped trees and a tunnel through a giant redwood. The gift shop, which sells cheesy souvenirs and wood carvings, has been hailed as "a model for other tourist attractions." The park was even honored by *American Heritage* magazine as the best roadside attraction for 2001.

Zip s-l-o-w-l-y: According to researchers,

WIDE WORLD OF BATHROOM NEWS

Here are bits and pieces of bathroom trivia we've flushed out of the newspapers of the world over the past couple of years.

GERMANY

Germany's Defense Ministry, which is looking for ways to reduce the country's military costs, has asked soldiers to use less toilet paper. "Lavatory paper is not always used just in the lavatory, it is often also used to wipe things up," a spokesperson explained. "We are asking people to think before they wipe."

UNITED STATES ABROAD

Haliburton, the oil services company that Dick Cheney headed before resigning to run for vice president, admitted during the 2000 presidential campaign that the company "maintains separate restrooms overseas for its American and foreign employees." The company defended its separate-but-equal restroom policy, saying it was done for "cultural reasons," and that Cheney was "unaware" of the practice during his five years as chief executive.

ENGLAND

• The Westminster City Council has decided to erect open-air urinals next to the National Gallery in Trafalgar Square. "Nighttime revelers, waiting at a bus stop outside the gallery, have been relieving themselves against the new wing," the council said in a press release. "The gallery now fears that the stone of the building is being affected by uric acid. Urinals will be placed in problem areas where 'wet spots' have been identified."

• From Scotland Yard: "The Department of Professional Standards is investigating an incivility charge arising from the search of a home under the Misuse of Drugs Act. An allegation has been received from a person in the house that one of the male officers broke wind and did not apologize to the family for his action. The complainant felt it was rude and unprofessional."

every year 100,000 Americans are injured by their own clothing.

CHINA

Archaeologists exploring the tomb of a king of the Western Han dynasty (206 B.C. to 24 A.D.) have unearthed what they believe is the world's oldest flush toilet, one that predates the earliest European water closet by as much as 1,800 years. The toilet, which boasts a stone seat, a drain for running water, and even an armrest, "is the earliest of its kind ever discovered in the world," the archaeologists told China's official Xinhua news agency, "meaning that the Chinese flushed first."

MEXICO

In June 2001, the *Milenio* daily newspaper revealed Mexican president Vicente Fox, who was elected on an anticorruption platform, has furnished the Los Pinos presidential palace with "specially embroidered" bath towels that cost $400 apiece. But they're just a tiny part of the more than $400,000 worth of household items that Fox has purchased during his first six months in office. President Fox admitted to the expenditures and even praised their disclosure by *Milenio*, citing the article as "evidence of progress in bringing transparency to government spending." (The minimum wage in Mexico, where 40 million people live in poverty, is about $132 a month.)

NIGERIA

A Nigerian housewife has reported seeing an apparition of the Virgin Mary in the window of her bathroom in the city of Lagos. "I walked into the bathroom at about five a.m. and was shocked and overwhelmed by fear with the visible appearance of the Virgin Mary," Christiana Ejambi told reporters. Since then the Blessed Virgin has reappeared several times and has given Ejambi messages on a number of subjects, including religious faith and how to control the crowds that have gathered to witness the miracle. Per the instructions of the Virgin Mary, only three people are allowed into the restroom at a time; everyone else has to wait their turn.

*   *   *

"Red meat is *not* bad for you. Now blue-green meat, *that's* bad for you." —Tommy Smothers

On any given day, half the people in the world will eat rice.

SEE YOU IN HELL!

Uncle John was cruising the information superhighway when he crashed into this hilarious article on one of his favorite topics—places with weird names. It's by Kathy Kemp, author of Welcome to Lickskillet: And Other Crazy Places in the Deep South.

ON THE ROAD

Plan to hit the road next summer, but don't know where to go? We don't mean to be rude, but have you considered Hell? Hell, Michigan, that is. (And you thought you had to drive south.) For a different kind of vacation, check out this tour of off-road America, where unusual names are the main attraction:

1. Hell, Michigan. If you've always wanted to see Hell freeze over, visit this place in winter, when the Highland Lake dam often gets icy enough to stop the water flow. In summer, when temperatures are moderate, the town has a "Satan's Holidays" festival and a road race called "Run to Hell." In October is the "Halloween in Hell" Celebration. The town got its name in 1841, when George Reeves, an early settler in this low, swampy place in southeast Michigan, was asked what he thought the town should be named. "I don't care," Reeves said. "You can name it 'Hell' if you want to."

2. Slapout, Alabama. Oscar Peeples, the town grocer in the early 1900s, was forever waiting on customers who asked for things he didn't have. "I'm slap out of it," Peeples would say. This central Alabama community, north of Montgomery, is now little more than a crossroads, with a church, bank, barber shop, and the tumbledown remains of Peeple's old store.

3. Noodle, Texas. In the late 1800s, Texans often used the word *noodle* to mean "nothing," which is exactly what they found when they arrived at this locale near Abilene. Now there are two churches, a store and an old gin. For nearly a century, the population has held steady at about 40 people.

4. Joe, Montana. When quarterback Joe Montana signed on with the Kansas City Chiefs in 1993, a Missouri radio station urged the folk of Ismay, in southeast Montana near the North Dakota border, to change the town's name to "Joe." The sports-minded citizenry,

---

Amen is the same in more languages than any other word. Taxi is second.

all 22 of them, voted in favor of the change, and a new industry was born. In fact, money raised from selling "Joe, Montana" souvenirs enabled the town to build a new fire station.

5. Lizard Lick, North Carolina. Since 1972, the residents of this town, 16 miles east of Raleigh, have held lizard races every fall to herald the farming community's unusual name. It dates back to the days when the area was home to a federally operated liquor still, and lizards were brought in to cut down on the insects. Traveling salesmen noticed the creatures and dubbed the community Lizard Lick.

6. Chicken, Alaska. The village, in the Alaskan wild near the Canadian border, is named for a bird, but not the one you think. In the late 1800s, gold miners found a reliable meal in the abundant *ptarmigan*, a grouse-like critter whose white feathers make it look, from a distance, like a chicken. When the townsfolk decided to incorporate in 1902, none of them knew how to spell *ptarmigan*. So they went with the look-alike Chicken to avoid the jokes a misspelled name would incur. Unfortunately, poultry jokes now abound. The town has a full-time population of about 30 people and mail delivery every Tuesday and Friday. There's a saloon, but no telephones or central plumbing. Incidentally, the *ptarmigan* is now the Alaska state bird.

7. Spot, Tennessee. A dot in the road about an hour west of Nashville, Spot was named by a sawmill operator who was always writing folks about business. One day, pen in hand, the sawmill operator sat at his desk, worrying over a letter from postal authorities wanting to know what to call the town. A spot of ink dropped onto the sawmill operator's white stationery, and the town had its name. By town, we mean a couple of houses and a ramshackle store.

8. Peculiar, Missouri. In spring of 1868, Postmaster E. T. Thomson decided to name his town "Excelsior," but postal officials told him it was already taken. Thomson reapplied with new names, and received the same response time after time. Exasperated, he finally told postal officials to assign the town a unique name, one that was "sort of peculiar." Peculiar, near the Kansas border just south of Kansas City, is home to about 1,800 people.

9. Zap, North Dakota. A Northern Pacific Railroad official, in charge of naming settlements on the line, named Zap after Zapp, Scotland, because both places had coal mines. The city, about 15 miles south of Lake Sakakawea, encompasses one square mile and is home to about 300.

10. Embarrass, Minnesota. If faces are red here, it's only because the town—205 miles north of St. Paul—is typically the coldest spot in the continental United States. The midwinter temperature often drops to –60°F, and snow has been known to fall in June. The name comes from early settlers, who used the French word for obstacle—*embarras*—to describe the hardships they faced in the frigid territory. Today, the population is largely Finnish. They celebrate their thriving community with a Finnish-American Festival every summer.

AND DON'T FORGET...

Think the preceding towns have nutty names? Here are some more.

• Idiotville, Oregon

• Knockemstiff, Ohio

• Monkey's Eyebrow, Kentucky

• Satan's Kingdom, Vermont

• Toad Suck, Arkansas

* * *

ASK THE EXPERTS

Q: *Which weighs more, a pound of feathers or a pound of gold?*

A: "Surprisingly, a pound of feathers weighs more. Feathers are weighed according to the avoir-dupois system, which measures 16 ounces to the pound. Gold is weighed according to the troy system, which measures 12 ounces to the pound.

"Now, which weighs more, a pound of feathers or a pound of lead? Tempted to say lead? Of course, since they are both weighed according to the same system, a pound of lead weighs exactly the same as a pound of feathers." (From *A Book of Curiosities*, by Roberta Kramer)

NFL great Vince Lombardi coined the term "game plan."

IRONIC, ISN'T IT?

There's nothing like a good dose of irony to put the problems of day-to-day life in proper perspective.

CRIMINAL IRONY

• New York State Assemblywoman Nancy Calhoun recently pled guilty to charges that she harassed her ex-boyfriend in 1999. According to the ex-boyfriend, the harassment included "bursting into his home in the middle of the night; tailgating him in a car; and posing as a cosmetics saleswoman in order to get the phone number of the man's new girlfriend." Calhoun was co-sponsor of the state's anti-stalking legislation.

• In 2000 a branch fell off a tree in Nevada City, California, and struck a power line, cutting off power to the town for more than 30 minutes. The outage delayed the courtroom trial of the Pacific Gas & Electric Company, which was charged with "failing to trim vegetation around power lines."

• In October 2000, a gunman armed with a .38-caliber revolver held up a Head Start school in Stapleton, New York, and escaped with $11,000 in cash and jewelry. The man was later arrested... and identified as a local minister, who used the money to pay the rent on his church for the next six months.

MISCELLANEOUS IRONY

• In January 2000, a British professional soccer player named Rio Ferdinand strained a tendon his leg and had to be put on the team's disabled list. Cause of injury: "He left his leg propped for too long on his coffee table while watching the Super Bowl on TV."

• A fire destroyed a $127,000 home in Maui, Hawaii; fire investigators identified the cause as a short in a fire-prevention system. "This is even worse than last year," the homeowner told reporters, "when someone broke in and stole my new security system."

• In October 2000, a British government official rode his bike to a local pub, where he met with citizens to discuss their concerns about crime in the area. During the meeting, his bike was stolen.

Say cheese: Kodak founder George Eastman hated to have his picture taken.

WHY WE HAVE POSTAGE STAMPS

One of the lessons we've learned over and over again at the BRI is that there's a pretty interesting story behind just about everything, no matter how small it is or how ordinary it may seem to be in our lives. We learned it again when we started researching the history of postage stamps.

C OLLECT ON DELIVERY
One afternoon in the mid-1830s, an Englishman named Rowland Hill happened to observe the response of a housemaid when the postman delivered a letter to her. In those days, the recipient of a letter, not the sender, paid the postage due on it—and the recipient could refuse to accept delivery if they wished.

That's just what the housemaid did, but there was something unusual about the way she did it: she studied the outside of the envelope, almost as if she were looking for some kind of hidden message. Then, she handed the letter back to the postman and refused to pay the postage due on the letter.

Hill knew what would happen next: The postman would take the letter back to the post office and throw it onto a pile of hundreds or probably thousands of similar "dead" letters that clogged every English post office in the 1830s. Sooner or later the post office would return that letter to the sender, free of charge.

In other words, every dead letter sent through the English mail in those days was sent through *twice*—first to the recipient (who refused it), and then back to the sender—even though no postage was ever collected from either the sender or the recipient. The enormous cost of delivering, storing, and returning so many dead letters was passed on to paying customers in the form of higher postage rates. Thanks to this and other glaring inefficiencies, in the mid-1830s, sending a letter across England could cost as much as an entire day's wage—historians estimate that those years saw the highest postal rates in the history of the English Post Office.

Translated from Greek, *philatelist* (stamp collector) means "lover of something untaxed."

READING BETWEEN THE LINES

The system was wide open to abuse. It was common for people to hide some kind of coded message on the *outside* of the envelope, which the recipient could read without having to pay the postage on the letter. Hill was sure that this was what the housemaid and the sender of her letter were up to. An educator by profession, he decided to conduct a comprehensive statistical analysis of the British postal system to see if he could improve upon it.

In 1837 Hill completed his study and published his findings in a pamphlet titled *Post Office Reform: Its Importance and Practicability*. In it, he pointed out the obvious problems associated with having the recipient of a letter pay the postage. He also criticized the practice of calculating postage by the mile: In those days a letter that traveled 15 miles or less required 4¢ postage, and a letter that traveled 500 miles or more cost 15¢. But charging by the mile meant that postal employees had to spend time measuring distances between towns and calculating postage due for every letter they delivered, a practice Hill thought was wasteful.

A BETTER SYSTEM

Hill calculated that when all of the inefficiencies were taken into consideration, on average it cost the Post Office about one and one-half cents to deliver a letter. He proposed lowering the postage rate to a uniform price of one cent per letter, regardless of how far it had to travel to get to its destination. And he proposed that the *sender* of the letter pay the postage in advance, so that the Post Office wouldn't waste time or money delivering letters that no one wanted to pay for. Payment in advance also saved postmen from the trouble of calculating postage due, as well as from the hassle of trying to get letter recipients to pay it. They could now devote their time to actually delivering the mail.

Better yet, by wringing dead letters and other inefficiencies out of the system, Hill believed that the Post Office's cost of delivering a letter would drop from one and one-half cents per letter to under a cent, which meant that the penny stamp would cover the entire cost of sending the letter. Reducing postage rates from four to fifteen cents down to a penny would also mean that ordinary people would be able to afford to send a letter for the first time. And with payment required in advance, people couldn't cheat the system.

SEAL OF APPROVAL

But how would the Post Office know for sure whether postage for a particular letter had been paid in advance or not? Hill proposed that the Post Office mark each letter using a special rubber stamp to indicate the postage had been paid. And to save customers the trouble of standing in line every time they needed a post office to stamp a piece of mail, he proposed that the Post Office sell pre-stamped envelopes that people could just drop in a mailbox whenever they were ready to send a letter.

For those who preferred to use their own stationery, Hill proposed that the Post Office sell "a bit of paper just large enough to bear the stamp," complete with gum on the reverse side that, when moistened, would allow the piece of paper to stick to the envelope. Hill didn't realize the significance of his idea at the time—he thought the prestamped envelopes would be a bigger hit than the prestamped "bits of paper," as he called them—but he had just invented the world's first adhesive postage stamp.

England's House of Commons was intrigued enough by Hill's proposals that it formed a committee to study them in 1837. Two years later, the government adopted his proposals, and on January 10, 1840, "universal penny postage" became the law of the land.

IT WORKS!

Just as he'd predicted, Hill's reforms revolutionized mail service in England. The number of letters delivered by the Post Office doubled from 83 million in 1839—the last year of the old system—to nearly 170 million the following year; by 1847 the Post Office was delivering more than 322 million letters a year. And although it had lowered its postal rates in some cases as much as 94%, by 1850 the Post Office was generating just as much revenue as it had in 1839.

The advantages of Hill's system were obvious, and other countries took note. In 1845 the United States reformed its postal rate structure to be in line with England's; Canada and France followed four years later. By 1870, more than 30 countries around the world had adopted Hill's system; for the rest of the world it was just a matter of time.

First stamp design selected by vote of the U.S. public: The 1993 Elvis Presley 29¢ stamp.

DESMOND'S DISCOURSE

*Words of wisdom from one of the world's leading
human rights activists, Bishop Desmond Tutu.*

"History, like beauty, depends largely on the beholder."

"Forgiving means abandoning your right to pay back the perpetrator in his own coin, but it is a loss that liberates the victim....One asks, 'Have you forgiven those who held you prisoner of war?' 'I will never forgive them,' replies the other. His mate says, 'Then it seems they still have you in prison, don't they?'"

"It is very easy to break down something. Throw a stone through that window; that is easy. Try fixing it, and that takes longer."

"When the missionaries came to Africa they had the Bible and we had the land. They said 'Let us pray.' We closed our eyes. When we opened them we had the Bible and they had the land."

"Freedom and liberty lose out by default when good people are not vigilant."

"If you are neutral toward injustice, you have chosen the side of the oppressor. If an elephant has its foot on the tail of a mouse and you say that you are neutral, the mouse will not appreciate your neutrality."

"We are made different not in order to be separated. We're made different to know of our need for each other."

"To be impartial is to have taken sides already...with the status quo."

"I am not interested in picking up crumbs of compassion thrown from the table of someone who considers himself my master. I want the full menu of rights."

"Do your little bit of good where you are; it is those little bits of good put together that overwhelm the world."

"Dream! Dream. And then go for it!"

THE RIDDLER

*What's white and black and read all over? This
page of riddles. Here are some BRI favorites.*

1. What does a diamond become when it is placed in water?

2. What did the big rose say to the little rose?

3. What is it that doesn't ask questions, but must be answered?

4. What does a chicken do when it stands on one foot?

5. What kind of bird has wings, but can't fly?

6. What two words have the most letters in them?

7. What has neither flesh nor bone but has four fingers and a thumb?

8. How many of each animal did Moses bring on the ark?

9. What is it that grows larger the more you take away from it?

10. Poke out its eye and it has nothing left but a nose. What is it?

11. What runs all day and never walks / Often murmurs, never talks / Has a bed and never sleeps / Has a mouth and never eats?

12. Which side of a pitcher is the handle on?

13. What is the difference between here and there?

14. If two is company, and three's a crowd, how much is four and five?

15. What fruit do you find on a dime?

16. How can you divide 10 potatoes equally between three people?

17. What is no larger when it weighs 20 pounds than when it weighs 1 pound?

18. No sooner spoken than broken. What is it?

19. What falls but never breaks? What breaks but never falls?

Answers on page 508.

FAMOUS FOR 15 MINUTES.COM

The stars below are living proof that dot-com fame can be as fleeting as dot-com profits.

THE STAR: Raphael Gray, 18, who lives with his parents in Clynderwen, a tiny village in south Wales.

THE HEADLINE: *Internet Robin Hood Scores the Ultimate Hack*

WHAT HAPPENED: Gray used to perform a "public service" by hacking into websites, downloading customer credit card information, and e-mailing it back to the companies to demonstrate how insecure the sites were. "It was just click, click, click, and I was downloading thousands of credit card numbers," he says. As a direct result of Gray's hacking, Visa and Mastercard had to spend nearly $3 million providing refunds and new credit cards to customers.

But what makes Gray truly unique is that one of the 26,000 credit card numbers he downloaded was for Microsoft founder Bill Gates. Gray used the information to order Gates some Viagra for delivery to Microsoft's world headquarters in Redmond, Washington. When police arrested Gray in March 2001, he became an Internet folk hero overnight. (Ironically, the Bill Gates credit card was a fake—the e-commerce company had created a fake account in Gates's name to test their software. The Viagra was never shipped.)

THE AFTERMATH: In July 2001, Gray pled guilty to 10 counts of hacking and 2 counts of fraud; he was sentenced to three years of probation and ordered to seek counseling for his "low self-esteem."

THE STAR: Baby [Your Name Here], born to Jason Black and Frances Schroeder in New York in 2001.

THE HEADLINE: *Parents Offer Unique Name Game*

WHAT HAPPENED: In July 2001, Black and Schroeder put

After his famous midnight ride, Paul Revere billed

the naming rights to their infant son up for auction on the eBay and Yahoo! auction sites. Their hope was to attract a corporate sponsor for their son: in exchange for naming their son "Nike," "Microsoft," or "A&W Root Beer," they hoped to raise money to buy a new house and save for their children's college education. The couple saw the promotion as a potential media moment for the sponsor: Announcing the name of the child when the auction was over would generate enough "free" publicity for the winning bidder to more than justify the expense.

The couple posted their auction notices on July 18, 2001. Minimum bid: $500,000.

THE AFTERMATH: Nobody bid—so they named him Zane.

THE STAR: Adam Burtle, a 20-year-old student at the University of Washington.

THE HEADLINE: *It's Official: eBay Has No Soul*

WHAT HAPPENED: In February 2001, Burtle put his soul up for auction on the eBay website. "Hardly used," his ad read. "I make no warranties as to the condition of the soul. As of now it is near mint condition, with only minor scratches. Due to difficulties involved with removing my soul [he wasn't dead yet], the winning bidder will either have to settle for a night of yummy Thai food and cool indie flicks, or wait until my natural death."

The bidding started at a nickel; Burtle's ex-girlfriend bid it up to $6.66, the number of "the Beast." In the final hour of bidding, the price rose from $56 to $400, placed by a woman in Des Moines, Iowa...but then eBay officials learned of the auction and removed the listing before bidding closed—not because auctioning a soul over the Internet is improper, but because eBay requires that "you have a piece of merchandise that a seller can deliver to a buyer," says eBay spokesman Kevin Pursglove. (eBay also forbids the selling of drugs, alcohol, guns, and body parts.)

THE AFTERMATH: Burtle, who was suspended from placing any more items for auction on eBay, is philosophical about the canceled sale. "I don't think the winner is going to be able to collect on my soul anyway, to be honest," he says. "I was just happy the bidding rose past $7.50."

THE STAR: DotComGuy, a.k.a. Mitch Maddox, a 26-year-old computer systems manager and self-described "cyberhermit"

THE HEADLINE: *Cyber-Cabin Fever Earns Man New Name, Dog and Fiancée; Not Much More Than That*

WHAT HAPPENED: Maddox legally changed his name to DotComGuy and on January 1, 2000, placed himself in a sort of self-imposed "house arrest" in an empty Dallas townhouse for a year. There, using only a laptop computer and a credit card, he was supposed to furnish the entire "Dotcompound" and meet all of his personal needs: food, clothing, entertainment, pets, etc., without ever leaving the house or his tiny backyard. Twenty web cameras set up all over the house (except the bathroom) would record his every move 24 hours a day and broadcast the action on his website, *www.dotcomguy.com*. If he managed to tough it out the entire year, he would be rewarded with a bonus of $98,289 in cash, raised from the sale of banner advertising on his site.

The year-long publicity stunt had just one flaw: When it was conceived, the idea of buying everything you need online was a novel concept, but by the time DotComGuy moved into his townhouse it was already passé. "The novelty is gone," Internet analyst Patrick Keane told reporters about six months into DotComGuy's confinement. "If I'm an advertiser, there are a lot better places to put my message."

THE AFTERMATH: At one minute after midnight on January 1, 2001, DotComGuy emerged from his townhouse and announced he was changing his name back to Mitch Maddox. Then he hopped on a scooter and rode off into the darkness, having fulfilled his commitment to live in the house for one year. So what did he have to show for his experience? A dog he bought online (DotComDog), a fiancée he met in an online chatroom (Crystalyn Holubeck, a Dallas TV reporter)...but no $98,289. The banner ads barely raised enough money to keep the company afloat, let alone pay a bonus. According to a company spokesman, "DotComGuy 'forgave' his bonus at the end to keep the company's doors open."

The average American is exposed to 1,600 commercials and advertisements a day.

THE HISTORY OF FOOTBALL, PART II

*Uncle John has always wondered why college football is so
popular in the face of the NFL. Answer: tradition.
College is where organized football started.*

LAYING DOWN THE LAW

In 1876 representatives from Harvard, Yale, Columbia, and
Princeton met to form the Intercollegiate Football Association and draft a uniform set of rules that all of the colleges would
play by.

The game would be essentially rugby, with some modifications.
The size of the field was set at at 140 yards by 70 yards (a modern
football field is 100 yards long and 160 feet wide). And as in
rugby, there would be 15 men on each team. The IFA also decided
that one kicked goal counted as much as four touchdowns, and
that whichever team scored the most touchdowns was the winner.
If a game ended in a tie, a kicked goal counted for more than four
touchdowns.

FIGHTING WORDS

The length of the game was set at 90 minutes, which was divided
into two 45-minute halves separated by a 10-minute break (the
clock was only stopped for scoring, injuries, and "arguments," so
the games were usually shorter than football games are today). And
instead of letting team captains resolve game disputes themselves,
the new rules called for one unbiased referee and *two* opposing
umpires, one for each team. That's what led to all the arguments.

"The two umpires discharged their duties like an opposing pair
of football lawyers," gridiron historian Parke Davis wrote in the
1926 Football Guide. "In fact, they were frequently selected more
for their argumentative abilities than for their knowledge of the
game." Arguing with the referee became a common strategy: if an
umpire noticed that his team needed a rest, he could pick a fight
with the referee and drag it out for 5 or even 10 minutes, until his
team was ready to play.

What's the scientific name for any object that's shaped like a football? An "prolate spheroid."

Some more rules:

• Every member of the team played both offense and defense.

• The ball remained in play until it went out of bounds or someone scored a touchdown or goal.

• Forward passes were illegal—the ball carrier could throw the ball to teammates on either side of him or behind him, but not to players ahead of him.

FROM SCRUMMAGE...

In rugby, at the line of play, the ball went into what was known as "scrum" or "scrummage." Neither side had possession of the ball; the ball was tossed in between the rushers on both teams, who heaved and butted against each other as they tried to kick it forward toward the goal.

...TO SCRIMMAGE

Football guru Walter Camp thought the game would be more interesting if, instead of having the forwards on both teams fighting for the ball, "possession" of the ball would be awarded to one team at a time. The team in possession of the ball would have the exclusive right to attempt a touchdown or goal. One forward, called the "snapperback," would be the person designated to put the ball in play, "either by kicking the ball or by snapping it back with the foot," Camp's proposed rule explained. "The man who received the ball from the snapback shall be called the *quarterback.*"

Camp pushed his proposal through in 1880. That same year he succeeded in shrinking the field size to 110 yards by 53 yards and reducing the number of players on a team from 15 to 11. Modern football finally began to diverge from rugby.

A WHOLE NEW BALL GAME

The concept of "possession" changed the nature of football considerably. It vastly increased the role of strategy, elevating the importance of the coach in the process. Because the team in possession *knew* that it was getting the ball, the players could arrange themselves on the field in particular ways to execute planned plays.

But at the same time that possession of the ball increased the sophistication of the offensive strategy, it also weakened it. The defending team knew that every play would begin with the center snapping the ball to the quarterback, so the defensive forwards were now free to move in closer toward the center, ready to move in for the tackle as soon as the ball was snapped.

Football was already a fairly violent sport, but the new rules made it even more so by increasing the concentration of players at the center of the action. "Bodies now bumped together in massed, head-to-head alignments," Stephen Fox writes in *Big Leagues*. "Instead of glancing tackles in the open field, knots of players butted heads, like locomotives colliding, in more dangerous, full-bore contact."

BACK AND FORTH

There was a delicate balance between the strengths of the offense and defense in football, and the rule changes of 1880 upset that balance in ways the rule makers had not foreseen. Within a year they would enact new rules to restore the balance, establishing a pattern that would continue for years to come: 1) New rules to counteract new tactics; and 2) New tactics to counteract new rules.

GOING NOWHERE

The next round of changes was largely the result of outrage over the 1881 Princeton-Yale game. In those days, there was no limit to how long a team could retain possession of the ball and no way the opposing team could force them to give the ball up. A team retained possession until it scored a touchdown, made a field goal attempt, or lost the ball in a fumble. Players quickly realized that if they attempted neither a touchdown nor a field goal, they could retain possession of the ball for the entire half.

In their 1881 game, Princeton and Yale did just that: Princeton, awarded possession of the ball at the start of the first half, scrimmaged back and forth for the entire 45 minutes without attempting to score, and Yale did the same thing in the second half.

The Princeton and Yale players may have felt their do-nothing tactics were fair, but fans were outraged—and so were the newspaper sportswriters who helped whip the controversy into a national story. Within days of the game, football fans all over the country

---

In the United States, more snow falls in February than in any other month.

were writing to newspapers to air their disgust. According to football legend, one such fan, who identified himself only as "an Englishman" wrote a letter to the editor proposing a solution: Instead of letting a team have possession of the ball for an entire half, why not limit possession to four consecutive scrimmages?

USE IT OR LOSE IT

The newspaper printed the letter, and someone sent it to Walter Camp. He was intrigued, but he was opposed to the idea of taking the ball away from a team that was putting it to good use. If the team in possession of the ball wasn't abusing the system, why should they be forced to give it up before they scored?

Camp finally hit upon the idea of giving a team the right to possess the ball beyond three scrimmages, or "downs," but only if they *earned* that right by advancing the ball at least five yards. If they didn't, they'd have to give the ball to the other team. As long as a team continued to gain at least five yards every three downs, they were allowed to retain possession of the ball.

Camp proposed this idea when the Intercollegiate Football Association met in 1882. It passed, as did Camp's proposal that football fields be marked with chalk lines spaced five yards apart, so that it would be easy to tell if a team had gained the yardage in three downs or not. American football moved another giant step away from rugby.

TOUGH GUYS

The introduction of the downs system helped to make the game more interesting, and it changed it in another way that perhaps Camp had not intended: Now that teams had to move forward or lose the ball, agility came to be less valued than sheer mass and brawn, as teams sought to find ways to blast through the opposing team's forward line. Or as Parke Davis puts it, "The passing of the light, agile man of the seventies and the coming of the powerful young giant date from this period."

*Second down. Turn to page 241 for Part III
of The History of Football.*

Buy American? The Liberty Bell was made in England.

NUDES & PRUDES

It's hard to shock anyone with nudity today. But stupidity is always a shock. These characters demonstrate that whether you're dressed or naked, you can still be dumber than sin.

NUDE... In April 2000, a state trooper stopped a car in the Houston suburb of Sugarland and discovered that all four passengers—three women and a three-year-old girl—were naked. God, the women claimed, had told them to burn their clothes and drive to Wal-Mart to get some new clothes. "It's always something," the state trooper says. "No two days are the same in this job."

PRUDE... Police in Brazil arrested a minor league soccer player named William Pereira Farias after he stripped off his uniform and threw it into the crowd to celebrate the scoring of a goal. "He broke the laws of respectful behavior," police officer Alfredo Faria told reporters. "He offended the townspeople and will likely be suspended from the team."

NUDE... Norway's Radio Tango has become the first radio station to offer live nude weather reports. The reports, billed as "more weather, less clothes," air on the station's morning show; listeners can view the naked weather forecasters on the Internet. "This is a world exclusive," says morning host Michael Reines Oredam. "It has never been done before. It brings a certain atmosphere to the studio which we hope our listeners are able to pick up on."

PRUDE... Police in Seremban, a town south of Kuala Lumpur, Malaysia, have raided several cellular phone stores and seized "obscene" plastic cellular phone covers that feature naked images of well-known celebrities. "The phones are modified to light up the private parts of actors or actresses when a user receives or makes a call," says police superintendant Abdul Razak Ghani.

NUDE... Portland businessman Mark Dean hopes to expand his topless nightclub business by running it as a topless doughnut shop during breakfast hours, with his strippers doubling as wait-

---

Fathead: A newborn's brain will triple in weight during the first year of life.

resses. What are the odds that his new venture will succeed? Not as good as you might think—a topless doughnut shop in Fort Lauderdale, Florida, went under after less than a year; a topless car wash operated by the same businessman lasted only a few months.

PRUDE... The executor of the estate of the late basketball legend Wilt Chamberlain reports that he is having trouble selling the Big Dipper's Bel Air estate, even after reducing the price from $10 million to $4.3 million and tearing out the "playroom," which featured a waterbed floor covered with black rabbit fur and a wraparound pink velvet couch. (The retractable mirrored roof over the master bed has been preserved; so has the traffic light in the bedroom that signals either a green light to "Love," or a red light for "Don't Love.") Executor Sy Goldberg admits that Chamberlain's boasting that he slept with more than 20,000 women in his lifetime may be part of the problem, but he says that holding that against the house is "ridiculous."

NUDE... A Dutch telemarketing company has found a novel way around the tight labor market in the Netherlands: they've created a special division of the company that allows employees to work in the nude. "We had about 75 applicants in the first four hours," a spokesman for the company—which did not release its name "for fear of offending existing clients"—told reporters. "With a normal call center, you'd be lucky to get one or two applicants an hour."

PRUDE... Officials at Los Angeles International Airport have covered images of "bounding nude men" with brown paper pending a decision on whether to remove them permanently. The naked men, who are supposed to represent the earliest human attempts at flight, are sandblasted into the granite floor of a newly renovated terminal at the airport. American Airlines paid Los Angeles artist Susan Narduli $850,000 to create the work, which was approved by both the airline and the city's cultural affairs commission. Narduli says the figures' private parts are "completely obscured." No matter: "If the city decides it wants the artwork changed," says an American Airline spokesperson, "we'll change it."

Reykjavik, Iceland, one of the coldest cities on Earth, is heated almost entirely by hot springs.

CHILD'S PLAY

What did children do before there were TVs and computers?
These old children's games are taken from the 1920s book,
Games for the Playground, Home School and
Gymnasium, *by Jessie H. Bancroft.*

HUCKLE, BUCKLE, BEAN STALK
Number of Players: 5 to 30

How It's Played: A thimble, cork, ring, or other small object is used for hiding. All of the players leave the room save one, who places the object in plain sight but where it is unlikely to be seen, as on the top of a picture frame, in a corner on the floor, etc. It may be placed behind any other object, as long as it can be seen without moving any object.

Once the object has been placed, the players are called back to the room, and all begin to look for it. When one spies it, he does not disclose this fact, but quietly takes a seat, and says, "Huckle, buckle, bean stalk!" which indicates that he knows where the object is. The game keeps on until all of the players have located the object, or until the leader calls the hunt closed. The first one to find the object hides it for the next game.

THE MINISTER'S CAT
Number of Players: 5 or more

How It's Played: The first player says, "The minister's cat is an avaricious cat," using an adjective which begins with "a" to describe the cat. The next player makes a remark about the cat, using the same initial letter for the adjective; for instance, that it is an "aggressive" cat. This is continued, each player using a different adjective beginning with the letter "a," until the game has gone entirely around the circle. The first player then makes a similar remark about the cat, using an adjective beginning with "b." This goes around, and so on through the alphabet. Any player who fails, must drop out. The player who lasts longest, wins.

DUMB CRAMBO
Number of Players: 10 to 30

How It's Played: The players are divided into two parties. One party goes outside the room; those remaining choose a verb, which is to be guessed by the other party. The outside party is told a word which rhymes with the chosen verb. They consult among themselves, decide on a verb which they think may be the right one, enter the room, and without speaking, act out the verb they have guessed. The inside party must decide from this pantomime if the correct verb has been guessed. If correct, they clap their hands. If not, they shake their heads. No speaking is allowed on either side. If the outside party is wrong in their guess, they retire and try again, repeating this play until they hit on the right word, when the two sides change places.

ANIMAL BLIND MAN'S BLUFF
Number of Players: 10 to 20
How It's Played: One player is blindfolded and stands in the center of a circle with a stick or cane in his hand. The other players dance around him in a circle until he taps three times on the floor with his cane, when they must stand still. The blind man then points his cane at a player, who must take the opposite end of the cane in his hand. The blind man then commands him to make a noise like some animal, such as a cat, dog, cow, sheep, lion, donkey, duck, parrot. From this the blind man tries to guess the name of the player. If the guess is correct, they change places. If wrong, the game is repeated with the same blind man.

The players should try to disguise their voices as much as possible when imitating the animals, and much sport may be had through the imitation. Players may also disguise their height, to deceive the blind man, by bending their knees to seem shorter or rising on toes to seems taller.

BLIND BANANA FEED
Number of Players: 6 to 20
How It's Played: Blindfold several couples. Give a peeled banana to each person. Have the couples clasp left hands, and at the signal to start they begin trying to feed one another. It may get messy, so it is well to provide bibs for the players by cutting a hole in a sheet of newspaper and dropping it over the head. Whichever team finishes their bananas first is the winner.

FOR YOUR READING PLEASURE...

Recently, we stumbled on Bizarre Books, a collection of weird-but-true book titles compiled by Russell Ash and Brian Lake. Hard to believe, but these titles were chosen and published in all seriousness. How would you like to spend your time reading...

Warfare in the Enemy's Rear, by O. Heilbrunn (1963)

Selected Themes and Icons from Spanish Literature: Of Beards, Shoes, Cucumbers, and Leprosy, by John R. Burt (1982)

What to Say When You Talk to Yourself, by Shad Helmstetter (1982)

What Do Bunnies Do All Day?, by Judy Mastrangelo (1988)

The Romance of Proctology, by Charles Elton Blanchard (1938)

How to Become a Schizophrenic, by John Modrow (1992)

Teach Yourself Alcoholism, by Meier Glatt (1975)

Nasology; or, Hints Towards a Classification of Noses, by Eden Warwick (1848)

Not Worth Reading, by Sir George Compton Archibald Arthur (1914)

Snoring as a Fine Art, and Twelve Other Essays, by Albert Jay Nock (1958)

How I Know That the Dead Are Alive, Fanny Ruthven Paget (1917)

Hepatopancreatoduodenectomy, by F. Hanyu (1996)

Jaws and Teeth of Ancient Hawaiians, by H. G. Chappel (1927)

Who's Who in Barbed Wire, by Anon. (1970)

Your Answer to Invasion—Ju-Jitsu, by James Hipkiss (1941)

Rhythmical Essays on the Beard Question, by W. Carter (1868)

How to Abandon Ship, by Phillip Richards and John J. Banigan (1942)

We would know: *Adoxography* is defined as "good writing about a trivial subject."

WHO FINANCED THE REVOLUTION?

Uncle John was reading an article about the Declaration of Independence and saw a brief mention of "Robert Morris, financier of the American Revolution." Having never heard of Morris, he did some research and discovered some fascinating forgotten history.

UP AGAINST THE WALL

In the late 1770s, a bunch of North American colonists got together, called themselves the Continental Congress, and decided to rid their colonies of British rule. They planned to form an army and a navy to defeat the world's most powerful nation. All they needed was the money to feed, clothe, and arm their men—about $20,000 a day. Oops.

The problems of financing the American Revolution were many. First, half of the colonists—and most of the ones with money—did not support the revolution. Next, the Continental Congress gave itself the right to tax its citizens but no power to collect the tax. And they couldn't borrow money, because no one would lend it to them—they weren't even a real country yet.

Yet behind any successful revolutionary stands a smart financier. In this case, it was Robert Morris.

SELF-MADE MAN

In 1747 Morris, a motherless 13-year-old British boy, arrived in Maryland to join his father. Three years later, Morris was orphaned when his father was killed in a gun accident. Young Morris was packed off to Philadelphia to work with Charles Willing, a shipper and merchant. Morris worked with such dedication and brilliance that at age 20 he was made full partner in the firm.

As a merchant, Morris objected to British policies of taxation more than most colonists. When news of the massacre of the colonial militia at Lexington reached him, it solidified his position against England. In 1776 Morris served in the Continental Congress as a representative from Pennsylvania. He became a signer of the Declaration of Independence and was charged with heading

---

"Battle Hymn of the Republic" was written by Julia Ward Howe. She sold the rights for $5.

Congress's finance committee. Soon, with money borrowed, begged for, and taken from his own wallet, Morris was funding the American Revolution.

FORGOTTEN HISTORY

Coming up with $20,000 a day for more than five years to support the Revolution should have guaranteed Morris the heroic popularity that John Adams, Ben Franklin, and George Washington have today. But it didn't. For example:

- **History tells us...** how George Washington's army crossed the Delaware on Christmas night, 1776, and defeated the British. But what happened next is not so well known. The term of service for most of Washington's soldiers expired a week later, at the end of the year. And, as Morris wrote to John Hancock, "You might as well attempt to stop the winds from blowing... as stop them from going when their time is up." Washington was desperate. He was in a position to gain control of New Jersey, but not if his army disbanded. Worse yet, within a week, the British would regroup, defeat the depleted American army, and recapture Trenton.

  Washington needed $50,000 to buy information on British troop movements and to pay each of his soldiers a $10 bonus to stay for another six weeks. He turned to Morris, who in turn, asked a Quaker merchant to lend him the money. "But what is thy security for this large sum," asked the Quaker. "My word and my honor," replied Morris.

  "Thou shalt have it," the man said. Washington got his needed funds, the soldiers stayed, and New Jersey was soon free of the British.

- **History tells us...** how Washington's army suffered through the winter of 1777 in Valley Forge. But it needn't have been so horrible. Against Morris's advice, Congress had issued worthless paper money and demanded, by law, that it be used. Discouraged manufacturers and sellers chose instead to cease operations, which is why 12,000 soldiers at Valley Forge were without enough shoes, blankets, and food.

- **History tells us...** how Washington's army arrived at the Yorktown, Virginia, peninsula on October 19, 1781, just in time to capture the British army and effectively end the war. But the scenario might have easily played out differently.

Weeks earlier, Washington was without the money to move his army from New Jersey to Virginia. Morris quickly raised $1.4 million for flour, corn, salted meat, rum, tobacco, and hay; boats to carry the men across the many waterways; and a cash inducement for the starving soldiers to march the hundreds of miles to Yorktown. "I advanced not only my credit," Morris wrote, "but every shilling of my own money, and all which I could obtain from my friends, to support the important expedition against Yorktown."

RESIGNATION

His proposed monetary policies repeatedly rejected, a frustrated Morris resigned his position in January 1783. Eventually, in 1789, his friend Alexander Hamilton, the nation's first secretary of the treasury, was successful in securing a feasible plan to repay the huge war debt. (Almost $79 million was owed, mostly to foreign nations.)

By 1795 Morris was again fully engaged in private enterprise. Convinced that immigration would drive the nation's development westward, Morris acquired six million acres of land to resell for a sure financial killing. But the pace of European immigration and settlement slowed, and the taxes and mortgages on the unsold land overwhelmed him. Suddenly, he was broke.

HUMILIATION

In 1798 Morris was arrested and thrown in debtors prison. After more than three years of imprisonment, 68-year-old Morris was released. He died five years later in poverty and obscurity. The patriot upon whom the heroes of popular history depended, the financier who kept the Continental army in the field out of his own wallet and with his private credit, the speculator who once owned more land than any man in America, was quietly buried in a Philadelphia churchyard.

*   *   *

"It is fair to judge people by the rights they will sacrifice most for."
—Clarence Day

AN "UPLIFTING" STORY

*Our long-promised history of the bra may seam padded, but
it is contoured especially for bathroom readers. This is the
real story—but check out the myth of Otto Titzling
on page 434. Thanks for your support.*

MOTHER OF INVENTION

Who invented the bra? Through the 1800s, a number of
people patented items of intimate apparel for women, but
most were just extensions of the corset. In 1893 Marie Tucek was
granted a patent on a crude "breast supporter," which had a pocket
for each breast, straps that went over the shoulders, and a hook-
and-eye fastener in the back.

But the modern bra was really born 20 years later. The fashion
of the early 1910s was to flatten the breasts for a slim, boyish figure;
the fashion also favored plunging necklines. In 1913 a Manhattan
debutante named Mary Phelps Jacobs became frustrated when her
chest-flattening corset kept peaking out above her plunging neck-
line. "The eyelit embroidery of my corset-cover kept peeping
through the roses around my bosom," she wrote in her autobiography, *The Passionate Years*. The sheerness of her Paris evening gown
was ruined by the lumpy, bulky corset.

WHAT'S A DEBUTANTE TO DO?

In frustration, she and her maid designed an undergarment made of
two handkerchiefs and some ribbons that were pulled taut. "The
result was delicious. I could move more freely, a nearly naked feeling, and in the glass I saw that I was flat and proper."

Showing off her invention in the dressing rooms of society
balls, she had her friends begging for brassieres of their own. Jacobs
actually sewed and gave away many bras as gifts. But when
strangers started accosting her, requesting the brassieres and offering money, Jacobs went to see a patent attorney (she had her maid
model the garment discreetly over the top of her uniform).

A patent was granted and Jacobs opened a small manufacturing
facility. She called her invention the "backless brassiere." It was the
first ladies undergarment to dispense with corset-stiffening whale-
bone, using elastic instead. Jacobs sold a number of her brassieres

---

One out of every 270 pregnancies results in identical twins.

under the name "Caresse Crosby," but for all her ability as a designer, she had no marketing instincts. Sales were flat and she soon shelved the business.

A few years later, she bumped into an old boyfriend who happened to mention the fact that he was working for the Warner Brothers Corset Company. Jacobs told him about her invention and at his urging, showed it to his employers. They liked it so much they offered to buy the patent for $1,500. Jacobs took the money—she thought it was a good deal. So did Warner Brothers Corset Company—they went on to make some $15 million from Jacobs' invention.

MAIDENFORM

Ida and William Rosenthal, two Russian immigrants, came to America penniless and set up a dressmaking business in New York with a partner, Enid Bissett. They were constantly dissatisfied with the way dresses fit around the female bosom, so in frustration—and perhaps in rebellion to the popular flat-chested look of the flapper—they invented the first form-fitting bra with separate "cups." And since all women are not built equally, Ida invented cup "sizes."

The Rosenthals gave up the dress shop in 1922 and started the Maidenform Brassiere Company with a capital investment of $4,500. Four years later, they had 40 machines turning out mass-produced bras. Forty years later, they had 19 factories producing 25 million bras annually. Some of their innovations:

• The "uplift bra," patented in 1927.

• The "training bra" (no definitive word on what they were in training for).

• The "Chansonette bra," introduced in 1949. It had a cone-shaped cup stitched in a whirlpool pattern. The bra, which never changed shape, even when it was removed, was quickly dubbed the "Bullet Bra." Over the next 30 years, more than 90 million were sold worldwide.

When William died in 1958, Ida carried on and continued to oversee the company until her death in 1973 at the age of 87. The Maidenform corporation, which started with 10 employees, now has over 9,000.

PLAYTEX

Another major contributor to the development of the bra was Abram Nathaniel Spanel, an inventor with over 2,000 patents (including one for a garment bag designed so that a vacuum cleaner could be hooked up to it to suck out moths). In 1932 Spanel founded the International Latex Corporation in Rochester, New York, to make latex items such as bathing caps, slippers, girdles, and bras, sold under the name Playtex.

Playtex was very aggressive with its advertising. In 1940—an era when underwear ads in print publications were primarily discreet line drawings—Playtex placed a full-page ad in *Life* magazine with photos of models wearing Playtex lingerie alongside a mail-in coupon. Women responded: 200,000 sales were made from the ad. And in 1954 Playtex became the first company to advertise a bra and girdle on TV. Those garments—the Living Bra and Living Girdle—remained part of the line for 40 years.

In 1965 Playtex introduced the Cross Your Heart Bra. Today it remains one of the best-known brands in the United States and is the second bestselling brand of Playtex bra, with the 18-Hour Bra filling out the top spot.

HOWARD HUGHES

The tycoon and film producer also had his hand in creating a bra. In 1941 he was making a movie called *The Outlaw*, starring his 19-year-old "protégé," Jane Russell. Filming was going badly because the bras Russell wore either squashed her breasts or failed to provide enough support to prevent her from bouncing all over the screen.

According to legend, Hughes designed an aerodynamic half-cup bra, so well reinforced that it turned Russell's bosom into a veritable shelf. Censors had a fit. 20th Century-Fox postponed the release date due to the controversy. Millions of dollars stood to be lost, so rather than back down, Hughes went all out. He had his people phone ministers, women's clubs, and other community groups to tell them exactly how scandalous this film was. That prompted wild protests. Crowds of people insisted the film be banned. The publicity machine launched into full gear, and when the film was finally released, it was a guaranteed hit.

On opening night, Hughes hired skywriters to decorate the

Hollywood skies with a pair of large circles with dots in their centers. Jane Russell, an unknown before the film, became a star overnight. Years later she revealed in her autobiography that she had found Hughes's bra so uncomfortable that she had only worn it once...in the privacy of her dressing room. The one she wore in the movie was her own bra. No one—not even Hughes—was the wiser.

THE VERY SECRET BRA
An inflatable bra introduced in 1952, it had expandable air pockets that would help every woman achieve "the perfect contour." The bra could be discreetly inflated with a hidden hand pump. Early urban myth: these inflatable bras sometimes exploded when ladies wore them on poorly pressurized airplanes.

THE JOG BRA
Hinda Miller and Lisa Rosenthal were friends who enjoyed jogging but didn't like the lack of support their normal bras offered. Lingerie stores had nothing better to offer them, so they decided to make their own. In 1977 they stitched together two jock straps and tested it out—it worked. Their original prototype is now displayed in the Smithsonian.

In 1978 the two inventors sold $3,840 worth of their bras to sporting apparel stores. In 1997 Jogbra sales topped $65 million.

THE WONDERBRA
Originally created in 1964 by a Canadian lingerie company named Canadelle, the Wonderbra was designed to lift and support the bustline while also creating a deep plunge and push-together effect, without compressing the breasts. Even naturally flat-chested women could achieve a full-figured look. The bra was popular in Europe but wasn't even sold in the United States because of international licensing agreements.

In 1991 fashion models started wearing Wonderbras they had purchased in London. Sara Lee Corporation (yes, the cheesecake company), who by then had purchased Playtex, bought the license to the Wonderbra and began marketing it aggressively. They spent $10 million advertising the new product, and it paid off. First-year sales peaked at nearly $120 million. By 1994 the Wonderbra was selling at the rate of one every 15 seconds for a retail price of $26.

One newspaper headline described the furor over the Wonderbra as a "Tempest in a D Cup."

UNCLE JOHN'S BOOBY PRIZES

• **Highest-Tech Bra:** A British inventor has come up with a bra that contains a heart rate monitor, a Global Positioning System, and a cell phone. If the wearer is attacked and her heart rate jumps dramatically, the phone will call the police and give her location as determined by the GPS. The electronic components in this "Techno Bra" are removable for laundry day.

• **Most Expensive Bra:** For $15 million you can buy a Victoria's Secret bra inset with over 1,300 gemstones, including rubies and diamonds (with matching panties).

• **Most Cultured Bra:** Triumph International, a Japanese lingerie firm, created a bra to honor Mozart on the 200th anniversary of his death. It plays 20 seconds of his music every time it's fastened and has lights that flash on and off in time to the beat. But perhaps in keeping with Mozart-era hygiene, the bra isn't washable.

• **Smelliest Bra:** In 1998, French company Neyret announced that it was marketing a bra that would release scents when stretched or caressed. Aromas included apple, grapefruit, and watermelon.

• **Biggest Celebrity Bra Collection:** If you're in L.A., visit the Frederick's of Hollywood Bra Museum. It has such items as the bra Tony Curtis wore in *Some Like It Hot*; the bra Milton Berle wore on his TV show; and Phyllis Diller's training bra, marked "This side up."

• **Biggest Bra:** The Franksville Specialty Company of Conover, Wisconsin, manufactures bras for cows in order to prevent them from tripping over their udders. The bras come in four sizes and are available in only one color: barnyard brown. Design extra: They keep the udder warm.

• **Cleverest Dual-purpose Bra:** When public opinion turned against her, former Philippine first lady Imelda Marcos reportedly wore a bullet-proof bra.

*   *   *

"When women's lib started, I was the first to burn my bra and it took three days to put out the fire."

—**Dolly Parton**

Coldest place on Earth: Vostok, Antarctica. Average annual temperature: –72°F.

CIRCUS SUPERSTITIONS

From its earliest days, the circus has been surrounded by traditions and superstitions. Here are some of the most widely known and often-practiced beliefs.

Circus bands play John Philip Sousa's "Stars and Stripes Forever" in emergency situations only. The march is played as a warning signal to circus workers that something is wrong.

Never count the audience.

Accidents always happen in threes.

Always enter the ring with your right foot first.

Never whistle in the dressing room.

Boots, shoes, and slippers should never be seen in a trunk tray or on a dressing table.

Cannon-back (rounded top) tunnels are bad luck.

Never look back during the circus parade.

In pictures, elephants must always have their trunks up.

Never sleep inside the Big Top. (This belief comes from the days when the circus ring was made of dirt and people were afraid it might collapse on them.)

Never eat peanuts in the dressing room.

Never move a wardrobe trunk once it has been put into place; moving it means that the performer who owns the trunk will be leaving the show.

Never sit on the circus ring facing out.

Peacock feathers are bad luck.

Hair from the tail of an elephant is good luck.

*   *   *

AND SOME CIRCUS SLANG...

Nut: The daily cost of operating a show. Legend has it that local authorities would remove a nut from the wagon wheel of the circus office and keep it to ensure that the circus didn't leave town before its local taxes were paid.

Rats can't vomit, which is why they are so susceptible to poison.

THE CURSE OF MACBETH

*Actors won't even call it by its name—they refer to it as
"the Scottish play." Why? Because they say it's cursed.
You may not be superstitious, but after reading this,
you'll never think of this play the same way.*

OUT, OUT DAMN SPOT

In a scene from Shakespeare's *Macbeth*, three witches stand around a bubbling cauldron, brewing up a stew which includes ingredients such as eye of newt and toe of frog, wool of bat, and tongue of dog—"double, double, toil and trouble, fire burn and cauldron bubble"—we all know the scene. But there's a story behind that scene...and a curse on the play.

In 1606 King James I commissioned Shakespeare to write a play in honor of the visit of his brother-in-law, King Christian of Denmark. The play Shakespeare wrote was *Macbeth*.

POOR KING

James was no stranger to tragedy. He was taken from his mother shortly after birth and never knew her. His father was murdered soon after that. His mother was forced from the throne of Scotland, imprisoned for 19 years in England, and beheaded by her cousin, Queen Elizabeth I. James began his rule of Scotland at age 19, married Anne of Denmark, had nine children, and survived a number of assassination attempts. When Queen Elizabeth died, he ascended her throne.

Moving to England from Scotland was like turning on a light in a dark room for James. He was particularly taken with Shakespeare's plays. He gave Shakespeare and his company royal protection in a time when actors were considered scoundrels. Shakespeare now had the security, popularity, respect, and money that he needed. He produced six new plays in the next five years.

HERE COMES TROUBLE

King James was fascinated by witchcraft and obsessed by death and

---

In the 1700s, trappers could get a dollar for a buckskin. Hence the term *buck*.

demons. He wrote a book about demonology and was considered the foremost authority on the subject. With this in mind, Shakespeare sat down to write a play that looked seriously at the king's favorite subject, and he did his homework. The plot was a thinly disguised accounting of the death of James's father; the witchcraft scene was crafted with care and filled with authentic details.

CURSES!

Some say the play's witchcraft spells and incantations were too faithfully reproduced, that they created a curse and that the curse is renewed every time the words are uttered. Others claim that local witches were so incensed at having their secrets revealed that they placed a perpetual curse upon the play. Whatever the case, for 400 years, *Macbeth* has been uncannily surrounded by death and disaster. So malevolent is the spell that it is said that bad luck will befall any actor who merely quotes from the play.

The curse manifested itself immediately. The young actor scheduled to play Lady Macbeth for King James came down with a fever right before the performance. Some accounts say he died. King James, who had a phobia about knives and gore, was horrified by the death scenes, which were realistically portrayed with guts and blood secured from a butcher. He immediately banned preformances of *Macbeth* for five years.

After the ban ended, the play was performed at Shakespeare's Globe Theater. A few days later, the theater burned to the ground and with it all of the company's scenery, props, costumes, and manuscripts.

DISASTER STRIKES

Skeptical? Here is just a sampling of the disasters that have surrounded *Macbeth* in the 20th century:

• In the early 1900s, the Moscow Arts Company was doing a dress rehearsal when actor Constantin Stanislavski forgot his lines in the middle of the murder scene. He whispered for a prompt but the prompter was silent. He *yelled* for a prompt, but the prompter remained silent. Investigating, he found the prompter slumped over the script, dead. The show never opened.

• During a 1937 production at the Old Vic Theatre in England, the theater's founder, Lilian Baylis, suddenly died of a heart attack just before the play opened. Laurence Olivier, who was starring in the lead role, missed death by seconds when a sandbag accidentally fell from the rafters.

• In 1948, during a production at Stratford, Connecticut, Diana Wynyard as Lady Macbeth loudly announced she thought the curse was ridiculous. She also decided it was silly to play her sleepwalking scene with her eyes open, and tried it with her eyes closed. She walked off the edge of the stage during the next performance and fell 15 feet down.

• A version of the play directed by John Gielgud in 1942 was plagued by death. First, Beatrice Fielden-Kaye, in the role of one of the witches, died of a heart attack. Next, Marcus Barron, in the role of Duncan, died of angina pectoris. Another of the witches, Annie Esmond, died on stage one night while she was vigorously dancing around the cauldron. Finally, set designer John Minton committed suicide in his studio, surrounded by his designs for the *Macbeth* sets and costumes. The repainted sets were later sent on tour with matinee idol Owen Nares, who died on the tour.

• A Russian version of the play scheduled to be filmed in Georgia was canceled when nine members of the crew died of food poisoning on location.

• During a 1971 production at the Mercer O'Casey Theatre, no less than seven burglaries and one fire marred the three-month run.

A CURE

To avoid the curse, veteran actors give this advice: Walk out of the dressing room, turn around three times, spit or swear, knock on the door three times, and then humbly ask for readmittance. If that doesn't work, try quoting this line from one of Shakespeare's "lucky" plays, *The Merchant of Venice*: "Fair thoughts and happy hours attend you."

Final note: Abraham Lincoln was quoting passages from *Macbeth* to his friends the evening before he was assassinated.

*   *   *

Random fact: The Cairo Opera House was destroyed by fire in 1970....the Cairo fire station was located in the same building.

A typical American child sees 80,000 TV commercials by the age of 16.

(NOT) COMING TO A THEATER NEAR YOU

You'd be surprised by how many films in Hollywood are started...without ever being finished. Here's a look at a few that will probably never make it onto the big screen.

STAR TREK VI: STARFLEET ACADEMY (1990)

Starring: An entirely new cast of young actors playing James T. Kirk, Mr. Spock, and the other original *Star Trek* characters

Making the Movie: *Starfleet Academy* was intended as an "Episode 1" prequel to the original *Star Trek* TV series: the story of how Kirk, Spock, and McCoy met at Starfleet Academy. The film was the brainchild of Harve Bennett, producer of Paramount's *Star Trek* feature films.

Kiss of Doom: Bennett was also the archrival of Gene Roddenberry, creator of the original TV series. Roddenberry had his own ideas for a *Star Trek* prequel; when he learned of Bennett's plans for *Starfleet Academy*, he set out to destroy the film by spreading rumors that Bennett wanted to model it after the *Police Academy* series.

Actor George Takei (Sulu) did his part by appearing at Star Trek conventions, urging fans to protest if he and his co-stars were replaced with new actors. "This pressure from all sides...doomed the academy idea for the time being," Chris Gore writes in *The 50 Greatest Movies Never Made*. "*Starfleet Academy* as envisioned by Harve Bennett now resides amid the dust of the unproduced story pile over at Paramount."

NATIONAL LAMPOON'S JAWS 3, PEOPLE 0 (1983)

Starring: Jaws

Making the Movie: Disappointed with how poorly *Jaws 2* did at the box office, Universal Studios gave serious thought to handing their killer-shark franchise over to the folks at *National Lampoon* to see if they could do anything with it. Screenwriters John Hughes and Tod Carroll came up with story for *Jaws 3, People 0*, a comedy about the making of a *Jaws* sequel.

Kiss of Doom: In the end, Universal dumped the idea and made *Jaws 3-D* instead. It bombed even worse than *Jaws 2*.

SOMETHING'S GOT TO GIVE (1962)

Starring: Marilyn Monroe and Dean Martin

Making the Movie: By 1962 Monroe's emotional and substance abuse problems had caught up with her. She was in no condition to work on a film, but she had to complete her four-picture deal with 20th Century-Fox. So she signed on to make *Something's Got to Give* under George Cukor, one of the few directors she was still willing to work with.

Sure enough, when filming started in May, Monroe proved impossible to work with: on the days when she bothered to show up at all, she was usually hours late and often unable to do her scenes.

Kiss of Doom: True to the film's title, something did give: Monroe. Her erratic behavior helped to push the film more than $1 million over budget in just a few weeks of filming. 20th Century-Fox was also in deep financial trouble with *Cleopatra*, already well on its way to becoming the most expensive film ever made. They couldn't afford another loser, so they fired Monroe, then rehired her when Dean Martin threatened to walk off the set. By then it was too late: Monroe died of a drug overdose in August 1962, before production could resume.

A DAY AT THE U.N. (1960)

Starring: The Marx Brothers

Making the Movie: Director Billy Wilder (*Sunset Boulevard, The Lost Weekend, Some Like It Hot*) got the idea while filming *The Apartment* near the United Nations building in New York. It occurred to him that the Cold War seriousness of the U.N. would make a great backdrop for a Marx Brothers film, even though the brothers had not worked together since their 1950 film *Love Happy*. He pitched the idea to Groucho Marx; he liked it and told Wilder to work out a deal with his brother (and agent) Gummo Marx.

weather for the filming of *She Wore a Yellow Ribbon* in 1949. It worked.

Kiss of Doom: *A Day at the U.N.* came late in the Marx Brothers' careers...too late: Harpo had a heart attack while the script was being written, and although he got better, insurance companies refused to cover the Marx Brothers for the time that it would take to make the film. Sadly, the insurance companies were right: Chico died in 1961, ending the hope of one last Marx Brothers film.

THE ADVENTURES OF FARTMAN (1996)

Starring: Howard Stern

Making the Movie: *Fartman*, from a simple comedy sketch that Stern invented for his radio and TV shows, was supposed to serve as the film "vehicle" that would give Stern his big-screen debut. Screenwriter Jonathan Lawton (*Pretty Woman*) fleshed out the concept, developing *Fartman* into the story of a New York editor who gains astonishing "colonic powers" when bad guys stuff him full of mysterious goo.

Kiss of Doom: Ironically, *Fartman* was done in by a group of cartoon characters—the Teenage Mutant Ninja Turtles. New Line Pictures, which made the Ninja Turtle movies without obtaining the licensing rights to the characters, had missed out on millions of dollars in merchandising profits and wasn't about to make the same mistake with *Fartman*. The company insisted on controlling the licensing rights, offering Stern only a 5% share in the profits. "The deal fell through over Fartman coffee mugs," Stern said.

*　　*　　*

STAMP OF DISPROVAL

In 1994 the U.S. Postal Service announced that it was issuing a set of ten commemorative stamps to mark the 50th anniversary of the end of World War II. One of the stamps was going to show an atomic mushroom cloud with the caption, "Atomic bombs hasten war's end, August 1945"...but the insensitive message infuriated the Japanese, prompting the Japanese government to launch a formal protest with the Clinton Administration. On December 7, 1994—the 53rd anniversary of the attack on Pearl Harbor—The Postal Service announced that it was dumping the stamp in favor of one showing President Truman announcing the end of the war.

Jaybirds hide their food underground. They can find it even under 1½ feet of snow.

KATE'S GREATS

Thoughts and observations from one of America's best actors, Katharine Hepburn.

"If you obey all the rules, you miss all the fun."

"Love has nothing to do with what you are expecting to get—only with what you are expecting to give—which is everything."

"Life can be wildly tragic at times, but whatever happens to you, you have to keep a slightly comic attitude. In the final analysis, you have got not to forget to laugh."

"If you always do what interests you, at least one person is pleased."

"To keep your character intact, you cannot stoop to filthy acts. It makes it easier to stoop the next time."

"It's life isn't it? You plow ahead and make a hit. And you plow on and someone passes you. Then someone passes them. Time levels."

"I never realized, until lately, that women were supposed to be the inferior sex."

"Never complain. Never explain."

"If you don't paddle your own canoe, you don't move."

"Acting is the most minor of gifts. After all, Shirley Temple could do it when she was four."

"Someone asked someone who was about my age: 'How are you?' The answer was, 'Fine. If you don't ask for details.'"

"If you want to sacrifice the admiration of many men for the criticism of one, go ahead, get married."

"Without discipline, there's no life at all."

"I'm an atheist, and that's it. I believe there's nothing we can know except that we should be kind to each other and do what we can for other people."

"Enemies are so stimulating."

"Life is hard. After all, it kills you."

Galileo called Saturn "the planet with ears."

"MIRRORS WITH A MEMORY"

Here's the story of how photography pioneer Joseph Niepce's partner, a theater owner named Louis Daguerre, turned his name into a household word and began a worldwide obsession with photography. (For the previous part of the story, turn to page 107.)

YOU HAVE TO START SOMEWHERE

The world's first photograph, the one that Joseph Niepce took in 1827, survives to this day. There's a picture of it in just about every book on the history of photography, but it's almost impossible to make out anything that's in it. If there wasn't a caption next to it identifying the objects in the scene (a courtyard, a pigeon loft, and the roofs of some buildings), you would never be able to guess what they are.

Clearly, Niepce's heliographic process was flawed. For one thing, the light-sensitive medium he used, bitumen of Judea, was very slow to react, which meant that long exposure times were required to take pictures. *Very* long exposure times: That first picture required an exposure of more than eight hours, during which time the sun moved most of the way across the sky. So did the shadows, obscuring much of the picture's detail.

And the sloppy way Niepce smeared bitumen of Judea on his metal plates made the resulting image even blotchier and harder to make out than it would have been otherwise.

ENTER DAGUERRE

Niepce couldn't solve these problems himself, so he joined forces with a Parisian theater owner named Louis Daguerre, who was also experimenting with photography. Daguerre's motivation: he thought that photography, if it were perfected, could be used to create better scenery for the theater.

In 1829 the two men signed an agreement to work together for 10 years, but unfortunately Niepce died from a stroke 4 years into the partnership. Daguerre tried to continue the work with Niepce's

son Isidore, but Isidore was convinced that if he contributed anything, Daguerre would take credit for it, so he refused to do any
research on his own.

SERENDIPITY

Daguerre soldiered on by himself, and in 1835 made an amazing—
and accidental—discovery. One sunny morning, the story goes,
Daguerre polished a silvered copper plate and placed it in a box
containing iodine. The iodine combined with the silver in the
plate to form photosensitive silver iodide, which was a significant
improvement over Niepce's bitumen of Judea. Then he loaded the
plate into a camera.

That morning he set everything up and started his exposure,
which he expected to take several hours…but a half hour later
the sun disappeared behind some clouds, ruining everything. So
Daguerre took the plate out of the camera and tossed it into his
chemical cabinet so it would be out of the way.

The following morning, when he took the plate out of the cabinet to polish it for reuse, he saw that it contained a very sharp,
detailed image of the picture he had tried to take the day before.

WORTH A THOUSAND WORDS

How did the picture get there? Thirty minutes of exposure was
nowhere near enough time to create an image. Daguerre guessed
that the short exposure had been enough to create a hidden or
"latent" image on the plate, and that one of the chemicals in the
cabinet must have "developed" it to the point that it was visible to
the naked eye. He tested his theory by taking another 30-minute
exposure and leaving it in the chemical cabinet overnight, as well.

Sure enough, the following morning there was an image on the
plate. By process of elimination, Daguerre discovered that vapors
from mercury, stored in the cabinet, had developed his exposures.

Daguerre made another important discovery: Like Wedgwood
and Schulze, he wanted to arrest the photosensitive reaction to
stop photographic images from being obliterated from further exposure to light. He solved the problem by soaking his developed
daguerreotypes, as he called them, in a saltwater bath to create the
first permanent photographic images. (Well, almost permanent: the
saltwater didn't arrest the photosensitive reaction completely, but it

Sorry, Fido: Animal acts are banned from the Miss America Pageant.

did slow it down enough that daguerreotypes could be viewed in daylight and could even be preserved for many years.)

CREDIT WHERE CREDIT IS DUE

The discovery of "mercurializing," as it came to be called, was Daguerre's and Daguerre's alone—and understandably, he wanted full credit for it. In 1837 he drew up a new contract with Isidore Niepce in which he took credit for the new process, but gave Joseph Niepce credit for the old process. Isidore Niepce objected to the terms, but had little choice in the matter—he had not participated in Daguerre's research, did not know how the new process worked, and could not claim credit for it. So he signed.

They made plans to sell both steps of the photographic process to private investors, but when the French Academy of Sciences caught wind of the idea, it persuaded the French government to purchase the rights and give them away free to the entire world... except their traditional rival, England. Daguerre's process was now free of charge for anyone in the world—except the Brits, who had to pay him a royalty.

NOTHING LIKE IT IN THE WORLD

On January 7, 1839, Daguerre went before the Academy of Sciences to show his daguerreotypes and give a description of his process. The assembled scientists were amazed. Images that detailed did not exist anywhere on Earth and were virtually inconceivable to the 19th-century mind. They were so finely detailed that people called them "mirrors with a memory."

The American inventor Samuel Morse was in Paris when the Academy of Sciences published the news of Daguerre's process; Daguerre invited him to view the pictures. Morse described what he saw in a letter home to his brother:

> The exquisite minuteness of the delineation cannot be conceived. No painting or engraving ever approached it. For example: in a view up the street, a distant sign would be perceived, and the eye could just discern that there were lines of letters upon it, but so minute as not to be read with the naked eye. By the assistance of a powerful lens, which magnified fifty times...every letter was clearly and distinctly legible, and so also were the minutist breaks and lines of the walls of the buildings; and the pavements of the streets.

The effect of the lens upon the picture was in a great degree like that of the telescope in nature....[It is] one of the most beautiful discoveries of the age.

DAGUERREOTYPE-MANIA

On July 7, 1839, six of Daguerre's daguerreotypes were put on public display in Paris; then on August 19, the full details of the photographic process were released to the world. The world's first photography fad started within days, as Parisians descended on the city's lens makers by the thousands to order the equipment that would allow them to make their own daguerreotype images. Eye-witness Marc Antoine Gaudin described the scene:

> Opticians' shops were crowded with amateurs panting for daguerreotype apparatus, and [soon] everywhere cameras were trained on buildings. Everyone wanted to record the view from his window, and he was lucky who at first trial got a silhouette of rooftops against the sky. He went into ecstasies over chimneys, counted over and over roof tiles and chimney bricks, was aston-ished to see the very mortar between the bricks—in a word, the technique was so new that even the poorest plate gave him inde-scribable joy.

A PERMANENT RECORD

Perhaps the most impressive but underappreciated early contribu-tor to photography was Sir John F. W. Herschel, an Englishman. When Herschel learned of Daguerre's discovery, he set out to see if he could duplicate the results without knowing anything about the process, which was still a closely guarded secret.

In several weeks Herschel accomplished what had taken Daguerre several years to do; he even improved on the process by remembering an 1819 experiment in which he had observed that hyposulfate of soda dissolved silver salts. He tried the experiment again, hoping he could use the chemical to "fix" his images perma-nently, something Daguerre had been unable to do. It worked— and hyposulfate of soda, now known as sodium thiosulfate, is used to fix photographic images to this day.

Advance to the next frame of our story, on page 273.

Advance to the next frame of our story, on page 273.

BRI's favorite Barbie accessory: A pink toilet with real flushing action (but no toilet paper).

KITTY LITTER

Sophisticated products for your finicky feline needs.

BOW TIE COLLAR *($15, Classy Cat)*: It's a collar that looks like a bow tie. Perfect for weddings, bar mitzvahs, or parties of any kind. A must for the cat clotheshorse. Comes in red, black, plaid, or leopard-print.

PETALK *($34, Coolpetstuff.com)*: Feel guilty when you leave your cat home alone? PeTalk plays a 10-second recording of your voice every hour while you're gone. Kitty will either be comforted or think she's going crazy.

ME-OW-TRAGEOUS GRAND SOPHISTI-CAT *($589.99, PetsMart.com)*: A cat-sized, solid wood grand piano, (covered in carpeting).

JOANNA SEERE, PET PSYCHIC *($90/hour)*: Ms. Seere helps cats find peace through guided meditations…conducted over the phone. Says Seere: "Meditation is to help animals find themselves, find balance, and find wholeness." Maybe she can help explain why you spent $589.99 on a cat piano.

PET DNA STORAGE *($600 to $1,400, plus annual fees)*: For a fee, PerPETuate will store your cat's genetic information in liquid nitrogen freezers. No one has cloned a cat yet, but once the technology arrives, thanks to PerPETuate, you and Fluffy can be together forever.

MIRACLE BEAM LASER TOY *($9.99, PetsMart.com)*: A standard laser pointer, packaged to look like a cat toy. Buy the optional "mouse hologram" and the red dot becomes shaped like a mouse.

CAT WEDDING GOWN *(PetVogue.com)*: This custom-made Elizabethan-style "gown" embellished with French lace and comes with a crystal tiara. Price: $1,650—probably more than your mother paid for her wedding dress.

KITTY GRASS *($30 plus overnight shipping, Priscilla's)*: No, not that kind of grass. This grass provides "a tender and tasty source of protein, vitamins, nutrients…and chlorophyll."

Cats sleep about 14 hours a day; donkeys only sleep about 4.

FIRSTS

Here's another list of the very first appearance of several things we take for granted. From The Book of Firsts, by Patrick Robertson.

THE FIRST DIET

Date: 1862

Background: The first scientifically planned slimming diet was prescribed by Dr. William Harvey, an ear specialist, for an overweight London undertaker named William Banting. The Banting diet was based on the reduction of carbohydrates and was the precursor of most of today's weight-reducing systems. In Banting's case, it meant that the undertaker was obliged to forgo pastry, potatoes, pies, and all sweetstuffs and restrict himself to lean meat, fish, and fruit.

Within a year Banting had decreased his 203-pound bulk to a svelte 153 pounds. At first dieting tended to be a male preoccupation, but became a fashionable activity among women after 1914, when they ceased to distort their figures with corsets and stays.

THE FIRST ELECTRIC FAN

Date: 1882

Background: The first electric fan to be produced commercially was developed by Dr. Schuyler Skaats Wheeler, chief engineer of the Crocker & Curtis Electric Motor Co., New York. The company's earliest models were two-bladed desk fans.

The first gear-driven oscillating electric fan was produced in the United States by the Eck Dynamo & Motor Co. in 1908. Previous types of "moving" fans were revolving models, which had the disadvantage of blowing in unwanted directions.

THE FIRST HELICOPTER

Date: January 6, 1905

Background: The first helicopter capable of lifting a person off the ground in vertical flight was designed by E. R. Mumbord to a specification titled "The Solution to Aerial Flight," and built by William Denny & Bros., shipbuilders of Dumbarton, Scotland.

Half of all crimes are committed by people under the age of 18.

The machine had six propellers, each 25 feet in diameter, powered by a 25-horsepower engine. Construction was originally of bamboo, but was later replaced by metal, which wouldn't become waterlogged in a storm. By 1912 it had achieved tethered flights of up to 10 feet from the ground.

The first helicopter to achieve free flight was a twin-rotor machine designed by French cycle dealer Paul Cornu and test-flown at Lisieux on November 13, 1907. Powered by a 24 horse-power engine, the machine stayed in the air for 20 seconds at a height of 6 feet.

THE FIRST WOMAN TO MAKE A PARACHUTE JUMP FROM A PLANE

Date: 1913

Background: Mrs. Georgia Thompson of Henderson, North Carolina, joined the Charles Broadwich stunt parachute team as a fifteen-year-old wife and mother in 1908, and made her first jump from a home-built biplane over Griffith Park, Los Angeles. In San Diego, on July 4, 1914, "Tiny" Broadwick, as she was know professionally, made the world's first jump—man or woman—using a manually-operated parachute with a rip-cord.

THE FIRST AIRPLANE WITH A BATHROOM

Date: 1913

Background: The first bathroom in the sky was on the giant Russian passenger transport, *Rusky Vitiaz*, designed by one Igor Sikorski. Whether this was an actual water-closet is doubtful—it is unlikely that Sikorski would have increased the load by carrying unnecessary supplies of water. Nevertheless, he was the first man who concerned himself with the problems of high-altitude sanitation. We salute him.

THE WORLD'S FIRST MOTORIZED HEARSE

Date: 1900

Background: The first motor hearse was an electric vehicle used for a funeral in Buffalo, New York. Fourteen other electric cars made up the funeral procession.

Long story: In England in 1558, beards were taxed according to their length.

WHAT'S IN TOOTHPASTE?

Ever wonder what the different ingredients in your toothpaste do? Here's the basic formula for most toothpastes and how they're supposed to work.

Water. Toothpaste is 30% to 45% water. Which means you're paying about $2 a pound for that water.

Chalk. The same variety that schoolteachers use. What is chalk? It's the crushed remains of ancient ocean creatures. The exoskeletons retained their sharpness during the eons when they were buried, and they are one of the few things tough, yet gentle enough, to clean the hardest substance in the body, tooth enamel.

Titanium dioxide. This stuff goes into white wall paint to make it bright. On your teeth, it paints over any yellowing for at least a few hours, until it dissolves and is swallowed.

Glycerine glycol. To keep the mixture from drying out, glycerin glycol is whipped in. You know it as an ingredient in antifreeze.

Seaweed. A concoction made from the seaweed known scientifically as *Chrondrus crispus* is added. This oozes and stretches in all directions and holds the paste together.

Paraffin. This petroleum derivative keeps the mixture smooth.

Detergent. What good would toothpaste be without the foam and suds? The answer is: It would be perfectly fine...but the public demands foam and suds.

Peppermint oil, menthol, and saccharin. These counteract the horrible taste of detergent.

Formaldehyde. The same variety that's used in anatomy labs. It kills the bacteria that creep into the tube from your brush and the bathroom counter.

Does this recipe for toothpaste turn you off? Take heart. Studies have shown that brushing with plain water can be almost as effective.

29% of men say the unstable economy "is making them watch more cartoons."

THE LEGEND OF KING ARTHUR

What do you think—was King Arthur a real person, or is he purely the stuff of legend? Either way, he makes for a good story.

T ABLE TALK
In England, the most popular tales of chivalry are the Welsh legends of King Arthur and his knights of the Round Table. No one knows for sure if there was a real person who served as the inspiration for Arthur... or if so, which historical figure it was. The earliest known mention of Arthur is a reference to a mighty warrior in "Gododdin," a Welsh poem written about 600 A.D. Another 200 years would pass before Arthur received another mention, this time in *History of the Britons*, which credits him with winning 12 battles against Saxon invaders.

It's likely that tales of Arthur were also spread by word of mouth, because when Geoffrey of Monmouth wrote down the tales of Arthur in his *History of the Kings of Britain* in 1135, he recorded Arthur's birth in the late fourth century, childhood, military conquests, marriage to Guinevere, relationship with his mentor Merlin, and his death in 542 when he was mortally wounded in battle by his treacherous nephew Mordred. Geoffrey is also the first person to identify Arthur as a king, not just a warrior.

COOKING THE BOOKS

So where did Geoffrey of Monmouth get his information? He claimed to have gotten it from a "certain very ancient book written in the British language," but did not identify it by name. Historians now believe there was no such book. They theorize that Geoffrey simply recorded the popular tales of his day, and when needed, made up his own details to fill in any gaps, drawing from legends surrounding leaders like Alexander the Great and Charlemagne. That didn't stop readers from taking *History of the Kings of Britain* seriously—it served as the standard text on British history for more than 600 years.

Geoffrey of Monmouth wasn't the first to invent tales about

Muscle cells live as long as you do. Skin cells live less than 24 hours.

King Arthur, and he certainly wasn't the last. In 1155 another writer, Wace of Jersey, introduced the concept of the Round Table; five years later, the French poet Chrétien de Troyes wrote five Arthurian romances that are credited with introducing the Holy Grail and Sir Lancelot's love affair with Queen Guinevere. A 13th-century French poet, Robert de Boron, contributed the famous story of the orphaned Arthur winning his crown by removing a magic sword from a stone.

TIME WARP

One thing historians agree on is that even if a "King Arthur" really did live in England in the early sixth century, he and his knights did not live in castles, wear suits of armor, or fight in tournaments—because none of those things existed in the sixth century. So why is Arthur so closely associated with them? Because Geoffrey of Monmouth and other contributors to the Arthurian legend had no sense of how different life had been 600 years earlier. They, not Arthur, lived in an age of castles and knights in shining armor, and they filled their stories with the trappings of their own era. In the process they created a world for King Arthur that he, if he did really exist, would never have recognized.

YOU CAN LEAD A KNIGHT TO WATER...

What about the generations of knights that grew up listening to the chivalrous tales of King Arthur and his knights of the Round Table—how well did they live up to the noble example set by their hero? Did they give to the sick and the poor? Did they protect orphans and the elderly? Did they respect women and treat captured knights with the same respect they'd bestow upon guests?

Not quite—medieval knights preached chivalry, but practicing it was another story, as Will Durant writes in *The Story of Civilization*:

> Theoretically the knight was required to be a hero, a gentleman, and a saint. All this, however, was chivalric theory. The hero who one day fought bravely in tournament might on another be a faithless murderer. He might [preach] of protecting the weak, and strike unarmed peasants down with a sword; he treated with scorn the manual worker and with frequent coarseness and occasional brutality the wife whom he had sworn to cherish and protect. He could hear Mass in the morning, rob a church in the afternoon, and drink himself into obscenity at night.

AMAZING LUCK

*Sometimes we're blessed with it, sometimes we're cursed
with it—dumb luck. Here are some examples of people
who have lucked out...for better or worse.*

HEAVY SLEEPER

Keith Quick, 28, a homeless man in Omaha, Nebraska, climbed into a dumpster and went to sleep. Bad move—he happened to do it on garbage pickup day and was still sleeping when the garbage truck emptied the dumpster into its compactor and crushed it. Quick cried out for help but it wasn't until the trash had been compacted two or three more times that the garbage men finally heard him. The trash was compressed so tightly that it took firefighters more than an hour to dig him out. Incredibly, he suffered no serious injuries.

SEEING IS BELIEVING

In 1990, 14-year-old Lisa Reid went permanently blind as the result of a brain tumor. Then one night about 10 years later, she smacked her head on a coffee table as she was bending down to kiss her guide dog goodnight. When she woke up the next morning, 80% of the vision in her left eye had been restored. She celebrated the miracle "by telephoning her mother and reading aloud the health warning on a packet of cigarettes."

NOW THAT'S A HAPPY MEAL

In August 2001, Patrick Collier, 35, walked into a McDonald's restaurant in Holly Hill, Florida, and ordered a meal. As he was sitting down to eat it he was approached by some McDonald's corporate executives. Only weeks earlier he'd been homeless and sleeping in a cardboard box, and he was still down on his luck... and looked it. When the executives approached him, he said, "I thought I had done something wrong."

Not quite—the executives handed him a certificate worth $1 million. A month earlier the FBI had arrested employees of the marketing company that ran the McDonald's "Monopoly" contest for stealing more than $13 million worth of game prizes. McDonald's, concerned that the scandal would harm consumer confidence in its sweepstakes, chose five restaurants at random and instructed each one to award a $1 million prize to someone eating in the restaurant. At random. Apparently, Collier was the first person chosen. "I'm getting a Harley," he said, "and a couple of houses."

BODY ARMOR

In June 2001, Dana Coldwell, 31, of Frankenmuth, Michigan, was mowing her lawn when the mower blade struck a $1\frac{1}{2}$-inch-long nail and sent it hurtling toward her chest. The nail struck her on the right breast, but didn't pierce her heart—an injury that would probably have been fatal. Why? It was deflected by the "liquid-curved" Maidenform bust-enhancing bra she was wearing. "I almost didn't wear the bra, but a higher power told me to put it on," she says. "I don't know if I will be mowing the lawn after this, but if I do, I'll be wearing the bra."

THE PERFECT STORM

In June 2001, tropical storm Allison struck the township of Upper Moreland, Pennsylvania. The storm ruptured a gas main at the Village Green apartment complex, causing an explosion that destroyed much of the building and killed six people. One elderly resident lost everything she owned, but at least she had insurance. When claims adjuster Paul Markloff arrived a few days after, she asked him to search what was left of the apartment to find her purse. The woman was distraught and confused, but she believed the purse might contain as much as $8,000 in cash.

Markloff sifted through the rubble and found the purse. It contained only $35, so he looked around to see if there was any other money in the apartment...and found 181 envelopes filled with $50 and $100 bills stuffed into three drawers of a dressing table. "I was amazed," Markloff says. "The dressing table was the only piece of furniture that hadn't been touched by fire." It took four bank tellers more than three hours to count the money, which came out to more than $420,000.

"Tragedy is when I cut my finger. Comedy is when you fall into an open sewer and die."

—Mel Brooks

SALT WARS

*Today we think of salt as cheap and plentiful. But
before modern mining methods, salt was rare
and valuable—even worth fighting for.*

INDIA VS. BRITAIN

Straining under 300 years of British rule, India badly wanted independence. The movement for self-rule began at the dawn of the 20th century; Mahatma Gandhi led the fight.

Salt was plentiful in India, and because of the tropical climate, where work in the hot sun depletes the body of its reserves, it was an indispensable commodity. But British Colonial law dictated that the sale or production of salt by anyone other than members of the British government was a criminal offense. And British salt was heavily taxed, forcing Indians of all castes to pay high prices for something they could have easily gotten for free at the seashore. Gandhi decided to use this as the focal point of his campaign for freedom.

March to the Sea

In 1930 Gandhi wrote to the British viceroy announcing his intention to break the Salt Laws in a campaign of civil disobedience. On March 12, Gandhi and 78 supporters began a march, walking from the town of Sabarmati to the coastal village of Dandi 240 miles away. Their 23-day journey took them through the center of every town along the way. In each town, speeches were made and people joined the march...until the procession was two miles long.

On April 6, the marchers reached the Arabian Sea, where Gandhi picked up a lump of mud and salt and boiled it to refine it, using the ages-old method of obtaining salt. He consumed the salt and then encouraged his thousands of followers to do the same, all of which was illegal according to British law. By the end of the month, the British had imprisoned over 60,000 people for making salt illegally. Gandhi himself was imprisoned for nine months. The salt march was one of Gandhi's most visible and successful campaigns for independence and was closely followed by the media and the Indian people. The salt tax was eventually repealed, but it was too late for British Colonialists. The image of Gandhi march-

---

The world has been at peace only 8% of the time over the last 3,500 years.

ing to the sea had become a potent political symbol, adding momentum to the independence movement. In 1947 the British gave up and India finally achieved Gandhi's goal—once again becoming an independent nation.

THE REVOLT OF THE SALINEROS

For over 300 years, the Mexican salineros, or "saltmen," had been mining and selling salt from deposits near what is now El Paso, Texas. They didn't understand the concept of private ownership of what they considered public land—anyone who was strong enough to unearth the salt and and sell it was welcome to it.

That all changed in the 1870s when a young Texas district judge named Charles Howard used legal tactics to claim the land surrounding the mines as his own. Now Howard was saying *he* owned the property and no one was allowed to gather salt but him. At first, the salineros ignored him and continued mining as they had always done. Howard made his point clear by shooting one man who opposed him and arresting two others for merely talking about going to get salt.

Outrage spread like wildfire and a plan was made to fight back. When word came to Howard that a train of 16 wagons was being sent to get salt, he realized this meant a showdown and sent for the Texas Rangers. Howard and the Rangers were organizing when their building was surrounded by salineros and a siege began. The battle had dragged on for five days when the salineros sent word: "If Howard gives himself up willingly and gives up all claim to the salt lakes, no harm will come to him." He surrendered, but a mob shouted for his death. Howard and a few of his followers were put in front of a vigilante firing squad and summarily executed. The rest of the Rangers were released, and they fled. They are noted today for being the only Rangers who have ever surrendered.

Federal troops soon arrived, seeking revenge for Howard's murder. Anyone suspected of participating in the siege was shot on sight. Pandemonium broke out, and people began to loot and riot. A larger contingent of Texas Rangers then came on the scene and put an end to the fighting.

At the End of the Day

A full investigation of the affair led to no definite conclusions.

Low profile: The 17-year locust lives 16 years, 9 months underground.

No one was ever arrested or prosecuted. When a new agent was appointed to head up the Texas Rangers, the salineros politely applied for permission to haul salt for a reasonable fee. It was granted.

THE FRENCH REVOLUTION

In 1259, Charles of Anjou, king of Sicily, imposed the first Salt Tax on the people of France. Its original purpose was to finance a war against Naples. Every citizen over the age of eight was required to buy a certain amount of salt at a price determined by the king—but the tax wasn't equitable. People who lived close to salt-production centers paid very little, while those who lived farther away were forced to pay taxes up to 20 times the actual value of the salt, equal to a month's wages for the average family. Some provinces had special treaties that exempted them from the tax altogether, but it was illegal to buy salt in a province you didn't live in. People traveling from one place to another were searched for smuggled salt, and the penalty for possessing it was often death.

Revolt

The Salt Tax, harsh and unfair, plagued the people of France for centuries. But the tax was hardest on butchers, who needed 30 pounds of salt to preserve a single pig. In 1413 butchers formed a union and organized a black market system to avoid the tax. Deadly skirmishes between butchers and tax collectors were common.

Ultimately, the Salt Tax was one of the factors that led to the French Revolution. During the Revolution, 32 Salt Tax collectors were executed by the peasants. The tax was repealed in 1791, but Napoléon reinstated it in 1806 in order to finance his invasion of Italy. It wasn't finally abolished until shortly after World War II ended.

*   *   *

HELL OF A PAGEANT

On April 29, 2001, 17-year-old Carla Renee White beat out 10 other women in a Berkeley County, South Carolina, beauty contest to win the title Miss Hell Hole. Now in its 30th year, the contest is named after a local community's "defining body of water."

It takes 6,000 gal. of paint, 60 people, and 4 months to paint the Eiffel Tower.

THE PROVERBIAL TRUTH

You know that "a bird in the hand is worth two in the bush," but there are countless other proverbs that you may have never heard. Here are some of BRI's favorites from around the world.

"A full stomach likes to preach about fasting."
Russia

"The addition is correct but where is the money?"
Japan

"The archer that shoots badly has a lie ready."
Spain

"The beetle is a beauty in the eyes of its mother."
Egypt

"A beggar who begs from another beggar will never get rich."
Jamaica

"A good bell is heard far, a bad one still farther."
Finland

"Evil knows where evil sleeps."
Nigeria

"If you want a bird and a cage, buy the cage first."
America

"If you want your dinner, don't offend the cook."
China

"Where the body wants to rest, there the legs must carry it."
Poland

"The sweetest grapes hang highest."
Germany

"Patience is an ointment for every sore."
Wales

"What is play to the cat is death to the mouse."
Denmark

"No medicine cures stupidity."
Japan

"Run after two rabbits—you won't catch either one."
Armenia

"He who is free of faults will never die."
Zaire

"Their mosquito won't bite me."
Ivory Coast

"The mud that you throw will fall on your own head."
Iran

"Don't sell the bearskin before the bear is dead."
Holland

"Better to die upright than to live on your knees."
Yiddish

"There is no phrase without a double meaning."
Kenya

Queen Anne of England (1665–1714) had 17 children; they all died before she did.

THANKS FOR YOUR MONEY, HAVE A NICE DAY

Last year our friendly neighborhood bank went global...and unfriendly. They still have tellers, but if you want to do anything beyond cash a check, they point you to "the phone." This satire by Tom McNichol, first published on Salon.com, really rang true for us. Has it happened to you yet?

BRAVE NEW WORLD
Dear Valued Customer: You may have already heard about First National's recent acquisition of Bank of the West and our proposed merger with First Interstate and World Savings to form a new entity, Monolithic Bank, N.A. As a valued customer of the new Monolithic Bank, you may be wondering how this change will affect you.

Let me take this opportunity to assure you that this merger was undertaken solely with you, our valued customer, in mind. As one of the largest financial institutions in the world, Monolithic Bank is now in a position to serve you better than ever. Here's how:

Absolutely Positively Totally Free Checking

Enjoy the convenience of Absolutely Positively Totally Free Checking, a Monolithic Bank exclusive. Just keep a minimum of $10,000 in a savings, money market, *and* time deposit account (or $30,000 in any one of them), and your first three checks each month are absolutely, positively, totally free!

Choose from a wide range of designer check colors, including White, Cream, Albino, Lily-of-the-Valley, Vanilla, and Ivory. And each check is distinctively personalized with your signature at the bottom.

No More Bounced Checks

You can also avoid the inconvenience and embarrassment of bounced checks by signing up for Automatic Overdraft Protection. Qualified customers who keep $5,000 in an easy-to-open Overdraft Protection Account are completely covered against bounced checks—up to $5,000! Automatically. We'll even waive

---

William Henry Harrison's inaugural address was the longest, at 8,443 words.

the annual membership fee if you sign up now.

Best of all, your Absolutely Positively Totally Free Checking account comes with unlimited check-writing privileges. No one will ever come to your door and tell you to stop writing checks. You're free to write as many checks as you want, until the accumulated service charges exceed your balance. That's a Monolithic Bank promise.

Hard-Working Savings

Your money should work as hard as you do. At Monolithic Bank, it works even harder. Simply open a Money-Maker Savings Account and your money goes to work for you 365 days a year—no vacations, no sick days, and no maternity leave. Make additional deposits and watch your account balance go up, up, up. The sky's the limit.

We've also got savings plans designed for special needs, like our Christmas Club account. Just transfer funds from your Money-Maker Savings into a Christmas Club account and your money will still be there when the holidays roll around—guaranteed!

Convenient Locations

Say good-bye to frustrating drives around town looking for a bank branch. Our new Branch Consolidation Plan makes banking easier by significantly reducing the number of bank outlets, making the remaining branches much easier to locate. You'll soon settle on one location as your "home" branch and feel better about it.

And in case you're wondering, most branch closings will be in "bad" neighborhoods, places where you and your loved ones probably wouldn't want to be walking in the first place. We're glad to be doing our part to make banking safe—and fun—once again. Welcome home!

Zero Human Error

You have better things to do than worry about whether the bank has made an error. Our rapidly expanding ATM network is bringing us closer to our goal of Zero Human Error—another Monolithic Bank exclusive. Each teller we replace with an ATM reduces the number of human mistakes, making your banking experience more efficient and pleasurable.

George Washington's second inaugural address was the shortest, at just 135 words.

But don't worry—we haven't forgotten the value of friendly service. Our ATMs always greet you with a neighborly "Welcome" screen, never tire of asking whether you'd like another transaction, and thoughtfully "beep" when you leave your card in the machine. We guarantee a warm "Thank You" and "Have a Nice Day" printed right on every receipt.

Most importantly, our ATM network is designed with your safety in mind. Each machine comes equipped with a state-of-the-art parabolic mirror—simply look straight into the mirror and you'll actually be able to see "behind" you. In the unlikely event of a mishap, our new Crime-Stoppers Hotline makes filling out a robbery report a snap. Just call during regular business hours and follow the easy instructions (touch tone phones only). And don't worry about paying for the call—you'll be billed automatically.

Sound Investment Advice

Whether you're looking for long-term financial gain or short-term windfall profits, Monolithic has a flexible investment plan to suit your needs. Our investment specialists target companies that are aggressively downsizing or shedding unnecessary salary and pension costs, assuring you of a maximized rate of return. At Monolithic, our money managers never forget the time-honored investment maxim: Main Street's pain is Wall Street's gain.

We don't stop at the border, either. Our financial specialists search the globe for investment opportunities that will work harder for you. Ask about our Third World Growth and Income Fund, which seeks emerging companies in China, Indonesia, Cambodia, Albania, and Mexico that have dramatically lowered labor costs. You'll soon become a "slave" to high earnings.

Of course, money doesn't grow on trees. But if it did, there'd be a tree growing beside every Monolithic Bank investment specialist!

No-Hassle Loans

You've told us that banks should make it easy to borrow money, and we've listened. All we need to process your No-Hassle Loan is your application, a credit report, an appraisal, a current pay stub, and your tax returns for the last five years. That's it! No last-minute holdups for "additional" paperwork.

Our No-Hassle Loan Officers will customize a car or home equity loan tailored to your financial requirements, without bothering you with confusing details about "rates," "points," and "collateral." They'll even advise you on public transit options if your car unexpectedly changes hands or help you look for an apartment if you suddenly lose your house.

Our mortgage lenders understand that a house is not merely a house—it's a home. That's why we've developed the Home Sweet Home Mortgage Kit to help you secure the home of your dreams. Be sure to consult the handy Home Buyers Map for your region—applicants within the designated red-lined area may qualify for special treatment.

Commitment to Diversity

At Monolithic, we're committed to diversity. We will not discriminate on the basis of race, gender, age, religion, familial status, sexual orientation, disability, or national origin. Everyone is welcome to deposit his money here.

We're working hard to make our workplace more diverse, too. In many areas, it's not unusual to see women and people of color working at our branch offices, or employed by companies that clean and provide security to those branches. Who knows—someday one of those hard workers may become a branch manager. At Monolithic, anything's possible.

Peace of Mind

Most importantly, your money is safe at Monolithic Bank. It's federally insured by the FDIC for qualified customers. It's also backed by the full faith and credit of the U. S. government—your money is legal tender for all debts public and private.

And thanks to our recent mergers, Monolithic Bank is now officially Too Big To Fail. The feds couldn't shut us down if they tried. Not even if all our investments suddenly went belly up and the board of directors fled to the Cayman Islands. Not that it's going to happen.

You'll sleep better knowing your money's safe at Monolithic. So go ahead—sleep.

We'll handle the rest.

It would take 5,000 strands of spider web to made a ribbon 1 inch wide.

AESOP'S FABLES

Sometimes, the best way to illustrate a point is by telling a story.

THE BUNDLE OF STICKS

An old man once called his sons to him. "I shall soon die," he said, "but before I leave you, I want to show you something of great importance. But first go and gather some thin sticks for me."

His sons did as they were bid.

Then the father gave each of them a stick and said, "Please break this for me." Each of them broke a stick with great ease.

Then the father took all the remaining sticks and placed them together. "Now," he said to one of his sons, "break all these sticks at one time." The son tried and tried but could not do so. Nor could any of the other boys break the bundle of sticks.

"I am sure," said their father, "that you know what I mean to tell you by this. Each one of you, alone, is weak; but if you stay together, you will be strong."

In unity there is strength.

THE BOY WHO CRIED WOLF

There was once a shepherd boy who used to mind his sheep far out of town on a lonely hillside. The days wore heavy on his hands and one day the lad thought of a way to drum up some excitement. He ran down the hill shouting, "A wolf! A wolf!"

At this, the neighboring farmers, thinking that a wolf was devouring the boy's flock, dropped their work and ran to his aid. However, when they got to the hillside, the boy laughed and said, "I was just playing a joke." The men were quite annoyed and went back to their work.

Some few days later, the boy tried the same thing again. Again the farmers dropped their tools and ran to his assistance. When they saw that the boy had fooled them a second time, they were very angry. The next day, however, a wolf did appear.

"Wolf! Wolf!" cried the boy. But this time the farmers did not believe him. They refused to help him, and many of the boy's sheep were eaten.

A liar is not believed even when he tells the truth.

A giraffe can clean its ears with its tongue.

RUMORS OF MY DEATH...

Plenty has been written about how people who nearly die, get a glimpse of the "other side," and then somehow make it back to the land of the living. Here are some examples of another kind of "rebirth": people who were thought to be dead, but were actually quite alive.

DECEASED: Ajay "Happy" Chopra, 34, of New Delhi, India

NEWS OF HIS DEATH: Several weeks after Happy disappeared from his home in 1995, his brother Ashok spotted someone he thought was his brother at a local bazaar. He walked up to the man and—no kidding—asked him, "Are you Happy?" The man nodded "yes." So Ashok took him home and bathed and fed him. He wasn't troubled by the man's apparent inability to speak, because Happy had a history of drug abuse.

That evening "Happy" died. The funeral and cremation took place the following morning.

RESURRECTION: The next evening, the real Happy Chopra returned from a religious pilgrimage, unaware that "his remains" had been cremated just that morning. The Chopra family has no idea who the dead man was, and due to the cremation no one will ever know. "The resemblance was uncanny," Ashok says. "Not only myself, but the whole neighborhood thought Happy had come back." Bonus: Happy Chopra is now seen as a sort of demigod in his neighborhood. "People touch his feet, seek his blessings, and give him offerings of money," Ashok says.

DECEASED: Abdel-Sattar Abdel-Salam Badawi, an Egyptian man suffering from fibrosis of the liver

NEWS OF HIS DEATH: In July 1997, Badawi fell into a deep coma. Thinking he was dead, doctors put his body into a coffin and sent him to the morgue.

RESURRECTION: About twelve hours later Badawi came out of his coma. "I opened my eyes, but I couldn't see anything," he later told a reporter. "I moved my hands and pushed open the coffin lid, to find myself among the dead. I shouted for someone to rescue me. When no one heard me, I started to chant verses from the Koran."

Badawi remained locked in the morgue for more than twelve hours before a nurse unlocked the door. But upon seeing a "corpse" standing up and reciting from the Koran, the nurse dropped dead from a heart attack. "I left the body in the refrigerator," Badawi says, "and got out of that place."

UPDATE: The doctor who declared Badawi dead was reprimanded; Badawi says he will never go to the hospital again.

DECEASED: Jose Estrada, 48, of Baytown, Texas

NEWS OF HIS DEATH: In February 1996, Estrada went for a run on a jogging trail near his house. He didn't know it, but just a few minutes earlier paramedics had taken away the body of a man who had collapsed and died while jogging on the same trail. The dead man wasn't carrying any identification—all he had was a set of General Motors car keys. So a sheriff's deputy went back to the scene to see if the keys fit any of the cars. Somehow, the keys fit in Estrada's GM truck.

The deputy traced the license plate to the Estrada residence, broke the news to Estrada's wife, Herlinda, and took her to the hospital to identify the body. "There was a tube in the man's mouth, and tape over his mouth and eyes, so I couldn't really see his face," Herlinda says. "I thought, 'This must be Jose.' You're in such a state of shock, you're not thinking straight."

RESURRECTION: While all of this was going on, Estrada finished his jog and stopped at the grocery store before heading home. As he was putting away the groceries, his wife's boss called to offer condolences. Informed of his own death, Estrada raced to the hospital to tell his wife it was a mistake, arriving just after she signed the death certificate. "After I stopped hugging him, I started crying," Herlinda says. "And I told him, 'If you ever die on me again, I'll kill you myself.'"

Salt Lake City gets more snow than Fairbanks, Alaska.

FORD'S WORDS

Thoughts and observations from American entrepreneur Henry Ford.

"Thinking is the hardest work there is, which is the probable reason so few engage in it."

"Money is like an arm or a leg—use it or lose it."

"Failure is the opportunity to begin again, more intelligently."

"The man who is too set to change is dead already. The funeral is a mere detail."

"There are two fools in this world. One is the millionaire who thinks that by hoarding money he can accumulate real power, and the other is the penniless reformer who thinks that by taking the money from one class and giving it to another, all the world's ills will be cured."

"If you have an idea, that's good. If you also have an idea as to how to work it out, that's better."

"Before everything else, getting ready is the secret of success."

"If you take all the experience and judgment of men over 50 out of the world, there wouldn't be enough left to run it."

"Whether you think you can or whether you think you can't, you're right!"

"Every piece of work in the shops moves. Save 10 steps a day for each of the 12,000 employees, and you will have saved 50 miles of wasted motion and misspent energy." —*On the theory of the assembly line*

"Even a mistake may turn out to be the one thing necessary to a worthwhile achievement."

"New York is a different country. Maybe it ought to have a separate government. Everybody thinks differently, acts differently. They just don't know what the hell the rest of the United States is."

"Paying attention to little things that most men neglect makes a few men rich."

Bilingual: Woodrow Wilson's typewriter could be altered to print in either English or Greek.

THE DUSTBIN
OF HISTORY

*Think your heroes will go down in history for something they've done?
Don't count on it. These folks were VIPs in their time...but they're
forgotten now. They've been swept into the Dustbin of History.*

FORGOTTEN FIGURE: Vaughn Meader, a comedian and impersonator in the early 1960s

CLAIM TO FAME: In 1961 Meader mimicked President John F. Kennedy while kidding around with friends. His impersonation was so good that they encouraged him to incorporate it into his act. So Meader put a five-minute "press conference" at the end of his routine, taking questions from the audience and responding in Kennedy's Boston accent. The JFK shtick got him a mention in *Life* magazine, which helped him land a contract to record *The First Family*, an entire album of his Kennedy parodies.

The First Family sold more than 10 million copies, making it at the time the most successful record in history. Meader became a superstar overnight. When he appeared in Las Vegas, he pulled in $22,000 a week—not bad for a guy who'd been making $7.50 a night just a few months earlier.

Then on November 22, 1963, a year after *The First Family* made him the biggest name in comedy, Meader climbed into a taxicab in Milwaukee. The driver asked him if he'd heard about Kennedy's trip to Dallas. "No, how's it go?" Meader replied, thinking the driver was setting up a joke. No joke—in an instant Meader went from being one of the most popular acts in show business to being a pariah. No one could bear to watch him perform, even after he stopped doing JFK, the memories were just too painful.

INTO THE DUSTBIN: Meader's career never recovered; by 1965 he was broke. "That was it," Meader told a reporter in 1997. "One year, November to November. Then boom. It was all over."

FORGOTTEN FIGURE: Lucy Stone, mid-19th-century feminist, suffragist, and abolitionist

---

Most wild birds live only 10% of their potential lifespan.

CLAIM TO FAME: When Stone married abolitionist Henry Blackwell in 1855, she became the first woman in U.S. history to keep her own surname. Not a big deal these days, but in 1855 it was shocking. In those days, marriage laws in many states effectively awarded "custody of the wife's person" to the husband, as well as giving him sole control over the wife's property and their children. Stone and Blackwell intended the gesture as a protest against these laws, declaring that "marriage should be an equal partnership, and so recognized by law," not an institution in which "the legal existence of the wife is suspended."

Stone consulted several lawyers before taking the step; they all assured her there was no law specifically requiring her to take her husband's name. But the move was highly controversial, and in 1879 it cost Stone the thing she had fought for years to obtain: her right to vote. That year the state of Massachusetts allowed women to vote in school board elections for the first time, but the registrar refused to register her as anything other than "Mrs. Blackwell." Rather than surrender on principle, Stone chose not to vote.

INTO THE DUSTBIN: Stone died in 1893, 27 years before passage of the 19th Amendment guaranteed women's suffrage.

FORGOTTEN FIGURES: The Dionne quintuplets

CLAIM TO FAME: Born on May 28th, 1934, Yvonne, Annette, Emilie, Cecile, and Marie Dionne became world-famous as the first documented quintuplets. Their miraculous birth and survival, coming in the depths of the Great Depression, captivated the public and provided a welcome distraction from the economic troubles of the day.

What's not as well known is that the "quints" were also five of the most cruelly exploited children of the 20th century. Born to an impoverished French Canadian farm couple who already had six children, the girls were taken from their parents within weeks of birth and made wards of the government under the care of Dr. Alan Dafoe, the doctor who had delivered them. He raised them in "Quintland," a specially constructed "hospital" that was little more than a zoo with five tiny human residents.

Over the next nine years, more than four million tourists—up to 6,000 a day—visited Quintland to view the children from

How did hammocks get their name? They were first made from the fibers of the *hamack* tree.

behind two-way mirrors, pumping $500 million into the Ontario economy and turning Dafoe into one of the most famous doctors in the world. The only people who were discouraged from visiting were parents Oliva and Elzire Dionne; they weren't even allowed to photograph their own children because the rights to their image had been sold off and used to advertise products like Puretest Cod Liver Oil, Lysol, and Palmolive.

INTO THE DUSTBIN: In 1954 one of the quints, Emilie, died during an epileptic seizure. Four surviving quints weren't nearly as interesting as a complete set of five, so their fame began to fade. In 1997 the surviving women wrote an open letter to the parents of the newborn McCaughey septuplets pleading with them not to make the same mistakes.

"Multiple births should not be confused with entertainment, nor should they be an opportunity to sell products," the letter read. "Our lives have been ruined by the exploitation we suffered."

*   *   *

ANIMALS FAMOUS FOR 15 MINUTES

THE STAR: A blind cod living in a fjord in Norway

THE HEADLINE: *For Blind Fish, A Light At End Of Tunnel*

WHAT HAPPENED: In March 2000, Norwegian fisherman Harald Hauso caught a cod in one of the nets he uses to catch crabs and starfish. When Hauso saw that the cod was blind, he let it go out of pity.

A week later the cod was back. He let it go again, but it came back again and again...and again: Hauso estimates that the cod came back and deliberately got himself caught in the net on 35 different occasions. "He's found an easy place to find food," Hauso told reporters. "And he knows I let him go every time." As word of the cod's story spread, he became a local celebrity.

THE AFTERMATH: In January 2001, a marine park in Aalesund, Norway, learned of the cod's plight and gave it a home in their aquarium. Bad news, though: After two months of luxurious aquarium living, the cod suddenly and inexplicably rolled over and died.

"THE BLAST BLASTED BLUBBER BEYOND ALL BELIEVABLE BOUNDS"

We at the BRI are always on the lookout for great urban legends. For years the tale of the Exploding Whale has floated around the Internet. But it's not an urban legend—it's 100% true. Here's the story:

A WHALE OF A PROBLEM

How do you get rid of a 45-foot-long stinking dead whale? That was the bizarre question George Thornton had to answer on the morning of November 12, 1970. A few days earlier, an eight-ton rotting sperm whale carcass had washed ashore on a Florence, Oregon, beach, and the responsibility fell on Thornton—assistant highway engineer for the Oregon State Highway Division—to remove it. His options were limited. He couldn't bury the rapidly decomposing corpse on site because the tides would soon uncover it, creating a health hazard for beachgoers. And because of the whale's overpowering stench, his workers refused to cut it up and transport it elsewhere. He also couldn't burn it. So what could he do? Thornton came up with an unbelievable solution: blow the whale up with dynamite.

WHALE WATCHING

Thornton's expectation was that the whale's body would be nearly disintegrated by the explosion, and he assumed that if any small chunks of whale landed on the beach, scavengers like seagulls and crabs would consume them. Indeed, many seagulls had been hovering around the corpse all week.

Thornton had the dynamite placed on the leeward side of the whale, so that the blast would hopefully propel the whale pieces toward the water. Thorton said, "Well, I'm confident that it'll work. The only thing is we're not sure how much explosives it'll take to disintegrate the thing." He settled on 20 cases—half a ton of dynamite.

As workers piled case upon case of explosives underneath the

A typical 100-ton blue whale eats its own weight in microscopic krill every month.

whale, spectators swarmed around it to have their pictures taken—upwind, of course—in front of the immense carcass, right near a massive gash where someone had hacked away the beast's lower jaw. Even after officials herded the crowds a full quarter of a mile away for safety, about 75 stubborn spectators stuck around, most of them equipped with binoculars and telephoto lenses. After almost two hours of installing explosives, Thornton and his crew were finally ready to blow up a whale. He gave the signal to push in the plunger.

THAR SHE BLOWS!

The amazing events that followed are best described through the eye of a local TV news camera that captured the episode on tape. The whale suddenly erupts into a 100-foot-tall plume of sand and blubber. "Oohs" and "aahs" are heard from the bystanders as whale fragments scatter in the air. Then, a woman's voice breaks out of the crowd's chattering: "Here come pieces of...WHALE!" Splattering noises of whale chunks hitting the ground grew louder, as onlookers scream and scurry out of the way. In the words of Paul Linnman, a Portland TV reporter on the scene, "The humor of the entire situation suddenly gave way to a run for survival as huge chunks of whale blubber fell everywhere."

For several minutes after the blast, it rained blubber particles. Fortunately, no one was hurt by the falling chunks, but everyone—and everything—on the scene was coated with foul-smelling, vaporized whale. The primary victim of the blubber was an Oldsmobile owned by Springfield businessman Walter Umenhofer, parked well over a quarter of a mile away from the explosion. The car's roof was completely caved in by a large slab of blubber. As he watched a highway worker remove the three-by-five foot hunk with a shovel, a stunned Umenhofer remarked, "My insurance company's never going to believe this."

THE AFTERMATH

Down at the blast site, the only thing the dynamite had gotten rid of were the seagulls. They were either scared away by the blast or repulsed by the awful stench, which didn't matter because most of the pieces of blubber lying around were far too large for them to eat. The beach was littered with huge chunks of ripe whale, including the whale's entire tail and a giant slab of mangled whale meat that never left the blast site. And the smell was actually worse than before.

Thornton had hoped his work was done, but it was just beginning—he and his workers spent the rest of the day burying their mistake. His blunder drew the attention of news stations all over the country, but amazingly, he was promoted just six months later.

Twenty-five years later, the tale of the exploding whale is documented all over the Internet. And the Oregon Highway Division still gets calls about it today—many callers hoping to get their hands on the video. The whale is still dead, but the story took on a life of its own.

*　　*　　*

ASK THE EXPERTS

The Heart Was Taken

Q: *Why do people cross their fingers for good luck?*

A: "The practice may have evolved from the sign of the cross, which was believed to ward off evil." (From *The Book of Answers*, by Barbara Berliner)

Yee-Haw!

Q: *In movie Westerns, people fire guns straight up into the air as warning shots or just to make noise during a celebration. But those bullets have to come down somewhere. How dangerous will they be if they hit somebody?*

A: "Physics tells us that when it hits the ground the bullet will have the same velocity it had when it left the muzzle of the pistol, 700 to 800 mph. But that ignores air resistance. Realistically, the bullet's landing speed can be around 100 to 150 mph. That's more than enough speed to do serious or lethal damage to a cranial landing site.

"And by the way, the jerk who fires the bullet isn't very likely to be hit by it. In one experiment, out of 500 machine-gun bullets fired straight upward, only 4 landed within 10 feet (3 meters) of the gun. Wind has a great effect, since bullets can reach altitudes of 4,000 to 8,000 feet (1,200 to 2,400 meters) before falling back down. (From *What Einstein Told His Barber*, by Robert. L. Wolke)

Whales dream.

DUMB JOCKS

*They give an awful lot of interviews, but sports stars
aren't always the most articulate people. Maybe
they should keep their mouths shut...nah.*

"The doctors X-rayed my head and found nothing."
—Dizzy Dean

"Some people think football is a matter of life and death. I can assure you it is much more important than that."
—Bill Shankly

"I want all the kids to do what I do, to look up to me. I want all the kids to copulate me."
—Andre Dawson, Chicago Cubs outfielder

"Nobody in football should be called a genius. A genius is a guy like Norman Einstein."
—Joe Theismann

"I'm not allowed to comment on lousy officiating."
—Jim Finks, New Orleans Saints G.M., when asked-what he thought of the refs

"You guys pair up in groups of three, then line up in a circle."
—Bill Peterson, Florida State football coach

"Better make it six; I can't eat eight."
—Pitcher Dan Osinski, when asked if he wanted his pizza cut into six or eight slices

"We're going to turn this team around three hundred sixty degrees."
—Jason Kidd

"Left hand, right hand, it doesn't matter. I'm amphibious."
—Charles Shackleford, NCSU basketball player

"I'm not an athlete. I'm a professional baseball player."
—John Kruk

"Are you any relation to your brother Marv?"
—Leon Wood, to announcer Steve Albert

"He's a guy who gets up at six o'clock in the morning regardless of what time it is."
—Lou Duva, boxing trainer, on the regimen of heavyweight Andrew Golota

---

More people die playing golf than any other sport. Leading causes: heart attacks and strokes.

UNUSUAL INVENTIONS

Here's living proof that the urge to invent something—anything—
is more powerful than the urge to make sure that the invention
will be something that people will actually want to use.

The Invention: Personal Sound Muffler
What It Does: Have you ever wanted to scream in the middle of a crowded room? With this device, you can... without disturbing others. About the size of a dust mask, the muffler's interior is made of sound-absorbing foam, with a saddle-shaped opening that seals tightly to the user's face. Extra bonus: "A microphone mounted at the bottom of the muffler activates a light, giving the user immediate visual feedback as to the intensity of sound produced."

The Invention: Bulletproof Dress Shirt
What It Does: Just what every well-dressed gangster needs. Wear this with a tie or over a turtleneck, and no one will ever know you're actually wearing a bulletproof garment. Main features: removable bulletproof pads made of "an ultrahigh-molecular-weight extended chain polyethylene fabric for superior bullet-stopping power."

The Invention: Self-Dusting Insecticide Boot Attachment
What It Does: Like a flea collar for people, only you wear it around your boot, not around your neck. It's supposed to prevent ticks and other crawling insects from creeping up your leg.

The Invention: Tool for Imprinting on Hot Dogs
What It Does: No home should be without one. This amazing invention is actually a branding iron for imprinting messages on hot dogs ("Happy Birthday to Frank").

The Invention: Flushable Vehicle Spittoon
What It Does: Designed for use in a car or truck, this device is for anyone who likes to drive and spit at the same time. Mount the cylindrical receptacle anywhere on the dashboard with a conven-

---

Thomas Jefferson invented a coding device called the...

ient Velcro tab. Your "fluids" flow into the funnel-shaped bottom of the spittoon, out a drainage tube, and onto the ground under the car. Then flip a switch and windshield washer fluid is automatically pumped to a spray nozzle that rinses the interior of the spittoon receptacle. You're ready to start spitting again.

The Invention: Life Expectancy Timepiece
What It Does: It looks like a watch and you wear it like a watch, but this timepiece actually displays the approximate time remaining in your life. The wearer determines his or her own life expectancy by referring to a combination of actuarial and health factor tables. How much time do you have left? Just check your watch.

The Invention: Toilet Seat Clock
What It Does: These days people like to know the time every minute of the day, even when they're in the bathroom. But where do you put a clock in the bathroom? This waterproof digital clock is mounted in the front of a U-shaped toilet seat. And the seat cover has a rectangular cutout, so the clock can be seen even when the lid is down. The clock can be reversed, so you can read it either sitting on the seat, or standing facing the toilet.

The Invention: Electrofishing Pole
What It Does: For the modern fisherman, this device is an electrified stainless-steel loop with an insulated fiberglass handle. The user wears a battery-backpack, which is connected to the loop and has another wire in the water, completing the electrical circuit. When a fish swims within the electric field created by the electrodes, ZAP! The fish quickly loses consciousness and can be easily plucked from the water. We recommend using rubber gloves.

The Invention: Electrified Tablecloth
What It Does: Plagued by picnic pests? This tablecloth has a pair of built-in electrical strips, powered by a 9-volt DC battery. An insect trying to cross the strips will get an electrical shock strong enough to discourage further travel across the table, making the world safe for potato salad. Good news: The strips are not strong enough to shock a person who accidentally touches them.

22 THINGS THAT FELL FROM THE SKY

One day, Mrs. Uncle John came home from walking the dog and insisted she had seen small fish all over the ground. Raining fish? Uncle John had to see it for himself. It was true (he still has one in the freezer). Well, after reading this list compiled by David Wallachinsky in the Book of Lists, *raining fish seems tame.*

1. HAY

A great cloud of hay drifted over the town of Devizes, England, on July 3, 1977, and fell to Earth in handful-size lumps. The sky was otherwise clear and cloudless with a slight breeze. The temperature was 26°C (about 79°F).

2. GOLDEN RAIN

When yellow-colored globules fell over suburban Sydney, Australia, in late 1971, the minister for health, Mr. Jago, blamed it on the excreta of bees, consisting mostly of undigested pollen. However, there were no reports of vast hordes of bees in the area and no explanation as to why they would choose to excrete en masse over Sydney.

3. BLACK EGGS

On May 5, 1786, after six months of drought, a strong east wind dropped a great quantity of black eggs on the city of Port-au-Prince, Haiti. Some of the eggs were preserved in water and hatched the next day. The beings inside shed several layers of skin and resembled tadpoles.

4. MEAT

The famous Kentucky meat shower took place in southern Bath County on Friday, March 3, 1876. Mrs. Allen Crouch was in her yard making soap when pieces of fresh meat the size of large snowflakes began to fall from the cloudless sky. Two gentlemen who tasted it said that it was either mutton or venison. Scientists

---

Mosquitoes are attracted to the color blue.

who examined the material found the first samples to be lung tissue from either a human infant or a horse. Other later samples were identified as cartilage and striated muscle fibers. The local explanation was that a flock of buzzards had disgorged as a group while flying overhead.

5. A 3,902-POUND STONE

The largest meteorite fall in recorded history occurred on March 8, 1976, near the Chinese city of Jilin. Many of the 100 stones that were found weighed over 200 pounds; the largest, which landed in the Haupi Commune, weighed over 3,902 pounds. It is, by more than 1,000 pounds, the largest stone meteorite ever recovered.

6. MONEY

On October 8, 1976, a light plane buzzed the Piazza Venezia in Rome and dropped 500-lire, 1,000-lire, and 10,000-lire banknotes on the startled people below. The mad bomber was not found.

7. SOOT

A fine blanket of soot landed on a Cranford park on the edge of London's Heathrow Airport in 1969, greatly annoying the local park keepers. The official report of the Greater London Council said the "soot" was composed of spores of a black microfungus, *Pithomyces chartarum*, found only in New Zealand.

8. HUMAN WASTE

A 25-pound chunk of green ice fell from the sky on April 23, 1978, and landed with a roar and a cloud of smoke near an unused school building in Ripley, Tennessee. The Federal Aviation Administration claimed the green blob was frozen waste from a leaky airplane toilet. These falling blobs are unfortunately quite common, and Denver, Colorado, is the center of such phenomena. At least two Denver families have had ice bombs crash through their roofs. And then there's the story of the unfortunate Kentucky farmer who took a big lick of a flying Popsicle before he discovered what it was.

9. 500 BIRDS

About 500 dead and dying blackbirds and pigeons landed on the streets of San Luis Obispo, California, over a period of several

Thinking a-head: Roman statues were often made with heads

hours in late November 1977. No local spraying had occurred, and no explanation was offered.

10. FIRE

On the evening of May 30, 1869, the horrified citizens of Greiffenberg, Germany, and neighboring villages witnessed a fall of fire, which was followed by a tremendous peal of thunder. People who were outside reported that the fire was different in form and color from common lightning. They said they felt wrapped in fire and deprived of air for some seconds.

11. WHITE FIBROUS BLOBS

Blobs of white material up to 20 feet in length descended over the San Francisco Bay Area in California on October 11, 1977. Pilots in San Jose encountered them as high as 4,000 feet. Migrating spiders were blamed, although no spiders were recovered.

12. LUMINOUS GREEN SNOW

In April 1953, glowing green snow was encountered near Mount Shasta, California. Mr. and Mrs. Milton Moyer reported that their hands itched after touching it and that "a blistered, itching rash" formed on their hands, arms, and faces. The Atomic Energy Commission denied any connection between the snow and recent A-bomb tests in nearby Nevada.

13. MYSTERIOUS DOCUMENTS

The July 25, 1973, edition of the Albany, New York, *Times Union* reported the unusual case of Bob Hill. Hill, the owner of radio station WHRL of North Greenbush, New York, was taking out the station garbage at 4:15 p.m. when he noticed "twirling specks" falling from a distance higher than the station's 300-foot transmitter. He followed two of the white objects until they landed in a hay field. The objects turned out to be two sets of formulas and accompanying graphs, which apparently explained "normalized extinction" and the "incomplete Davis-Greenstein orientation." No explanation has been made public.

14. BEANS

Rancher Salvador Targino of Brazil, reported a rain of beans on his property in Paraíba State in early 1971. Local agricultural authorities speculated that a storm had swept up a pile of beans in West Africa and dropped them in northeastern Brazil. Targino boiled some of the beans, but said they were too tough to eat.

15. SILVER COINS
Several thousand rubles' worth of silver coins fell in the Gorki region of the USSR on June 17, 1940. The official explanation was that a landslide had uncovered a hidden treasure, which was picked up by a tornado, which dropped it on Gorki. No explanation was given for the fact that the coins were not accompanied by any debris.

16. MUSHROOM-SHAPED THINGS
Traffic at the Mexico City airport was halted temporarily on July 30, 1963, when thousands of grayish, mushroom-shaped things floated to the ground out of a cloudless sky. Hundreds of witnesses described these objects variously as "giant cobwebs," "balls of cotton," and "foam." They disintegrated rapidly after landing.

17. TOADS
Falls of frogs and toads, though not everyday occurrences, are actually quite common, having been reported in almost every part of the world. One of the most famous toad falls happened in the summer of 1794 in the village of Lalain, France. A very hot afternoon was broken suddenly by such an intense downpour of rain that 150 French soldiers (then fighting the Austrians) were forced to abandon the trench in which they were hiding to avoid being submerged. In the middle of the storm, which lasted for 30 minutes, tiny toads, mostly in the tadpole stage, began to land on the ground and jump about in all directions. When the rain let up, many soldiers discovered toads in the folds of their three-cornered hats.

18. OAK LEAVES
In late October 1889, a Mr. Wright of the parish of Penpont, Dumfries, Scotland, was startled by the appearance of what at first seemed to be a flock of birds, which began falling to the ground. Running toward them, he discovered the objects to be oak leaves, which eventually covered an area one mile wide and two miles

long. The nearest clump of oak trees was eight miles away, and no other kind of leaf fell.

19. JUDAS TREE SEEDS

Just before sunset in August 1897, an immense number of small, blood-colored clouds filled the sky in Macerata, Italy. About an hour later, storm clouds burst and small seeds rained from the sky, covering the ground to a depth of $1/2$ inch. Many of the seeds had already started to germinate, and all of them were from the Judas tree, which is found predominantly in the Middle East and Asia. There was no accompanying debris—just the seeds.

20. FISH

About 150 perchlike silver fish dropped from the sky during a tropical storm near Killamey Station in Australia's Northern Territory in February 1974. Fish falls are common enough that an "official" explanation has been developed to cover most of them. It is theorized that whirlwinds create a waterspout effect, sucking up water and fish, carrying them for great distances, and then dropping them somewhere else.

21. ICE CHUNKS

In February 1965, a 50-pound mass of ice plunged through the roof of the Phillips Petroleum plant in Woods Cross, Utah. In his book *Strangest of All*, Frank Edwards reports the case of a carpenter working on a roof in Kempten—near Düsseldorf, Germany—who was struck and killed in 1951 by an icicle six feet long and six inches around, which shot down from the sky.

22. SPACE JUNK

In September 1962, a metal object about six inches in diameter and weighing 21 pounds crashed into a street intersection in Manitowoc, Wisconsin, and burrowed several inches into the ground. The object was later identified as part of Sputnik IV, which had been launched by the USSR on May 15, 1960. Since 1959 more than 6,000 parts of spacecraft have fallen out of orbit, and many of them have reached the surface of the Earth. On July 11, 1979, Skylab, the 77-ton U.S. space station, fell out of orbit over the South Indian Ocean and western Australia, The largest piece of debris to reach land was a one-ton fuel tank.

The longest a lunar eclipse can last is 7 minutes, 58 seconds.

THREE NEAR MISSES

Here at the BRI, we never fail to be amazed at the role that chance plays in life. Take these three instances, for example:

JFK'S EAGLES

In 1985 Norman Braman, owner of the Philadelphia Eagles, was visiting the U.S. Senate when Senator Edward Kennedy told him the story of how John F. Kennedy considered buying the Eagles in October 1962. Not yet two years into his first term, JFK was already thinking about what he would do after leaving office. When he learned the Eagles were for sale, he and brother Bobby instructed Ted to go to Philadelphia to meet with the team's management and discuss a possible sale. But Ted never went, and someone else bought the Eagles. "What happened?" Braman asked. "The Cuban Missile Crisis," Ted told him.

POISONING GENERAL WASHINGTON

Phoebe Fraunces, the daughter of a New York tavernkeeper, reportedly saved the life of General George Washington after pretending to sympathize with English spies. When Thomas Hickey, a member of Washington's guard, told her to serve the general a plate of poisoned peas, she did so, and then whispered a warning to Washington. He (or she, depending on the account) immediately flipped the peas out the window, where some chickens ate them and died. Hickey was later executed for treason.

THE HUGHES H-1

In 1934 millionaire aviator Howard Hughes built an experimental plane called the H-1. In January 1937, it set a transcontinental speed record by flying at 332 mph from California to New Jersey, making it the fastest plane on Earth. Hughes proposed to the U.S. Army that they base a fighter plane on the design, but they weren't interested. Japan was. Mitsubishi engineer Jiro Horikoshi designed a fighter plane that incorporated many of the H-1's features: the "Zero" was the premier fighter plane of World War II. The United States and its allies didn't develop a plane that could match it until 1943.

Armed? A 15-year-old burglar was charged with armed robbery after pointing his...

CELEBRITY LAWSUITS

These days, it seems that people will sue each other over practically anything. Here are a few real-life examples of unusual legal battles involving celebrities.

THE PLAINTIFF: Rosie O'Donnell
THE DEFENDANT: KRSK-FM, a Portland, Oregon, radio station
THE LAWSUIT: KRSK gave itself the name "Rosie 105," a reference to Portland's nickname, "the Rose City." But O'Donnell's lawyers sued, claiming that O'Donnell owned the name and that the radio station was trying to cash in on her celebrity. Local newspapers blasted O'Donnell.
THE VERDICT: Not guilty.

THE PLAINTIFF: The Flying Elvi, an amateur skydiving club
THE DEFENDANT: The Flying Elvises, a rival skydiving club
THE LAWSUIT: The Flying Elvi sued the Flying Elvises for trademark infringement: Elvi manager Richard Feeney claimed he was marketing the concept before the Elvises were even formed. But according to the Flying Elvises, both skydiving groups got the idea from the 1992 film *Honeymoon in Vegas*. Furthermore, claimed the Elvises, they have licensing rights from the Elvis Presley estate. The Elvi responded that no such rights exist—Elvis never performed as a skydiver.
THE VERDICT: The Elvi prevailed and are now the only troup of skydivers in wigs, sideburns, and matching jumpsuits.

THE PLAINTIFF: *The New York Times*
THE DEFENDANT: Jake Shubert, Broadway impresario
THE LAWSUIT: In 1915, Shubert decided to ban critics who wrote negative reviews of his productions. The Shubert organization spent a lot on newspaper advertising and felt that it entitled them to preferential treatment. At the very least, they didn't want their advertising dollars to be used to pay critics to pan their plays. It all came to a head when the new *New York Times* critic,

---

pet boa constrictor at a man and ordering him to hand over all his cash.

Alexander Woollcott, was denied admission to a play, even though he'd already paid for a ticket. The *Times* sued.

THE VERDICT: A temporary injunction allowed Woollcott to see and review the play (he liked it). The court later ruled in favor of Shubert, who continued to bar the *Times* critic (it actually helped make Woollcott famous). Ultimately, the New York Legislature passed a bill making it illegal for a theater to refuse admission to any sober ticketholder. The Shuberts contested the law all the way to the Supreme Court (but lost).

THE PLAINTIFF: SPAM Luncheon Meat
THE DEFENDANT: Jim Henson Productions
THE LAWSUIT: Hormel Foods Corporation, makers of SPAM, sued Henson's company over one of the characters in the movie *Muppet Treasure Island*. The character in question is the high priest of a tribe of wild boars that worship Miss Piggy. His name: Spa'am.

Hormel's suit contended that their trademark was damaged because the film "intentionally portrayed the Spa'am character to be evil in porcine form."

THE VERDICT: Not guilty. The court found that although Spa'am was "untidy," he was not evil and that, actually, the character probably enhanced the value of the SPAM trademark.

THE PLAINTIFF: Billie Jean Matay
THE DEFENDANT: Mickey Mouse
THE LAWSUIT: In 1995, Matay brought her grandchildren to Disneyland. The family was returning to their car when they were robbed at gunpoint in the parking lot. The robber got away clean with $165. While Matay reported the crime to D-land security, her grandchildren waited "backstage," where they saw several Disney characters taking off their costumes. Matay, who had actually been a Mouseketeer in 1957, sued, claiming her three grandchildren were traumaized by being exposed to "the reality that the Disney characters were, in fact, make-believe."
THE VERDICT: Case dismissed.

UNKLE JOHN'S
GREATEST BLOOOPERS

One of the BRI's favorite subjects is goofs—especially by celebrities, politicians, and criminals. Napoléon had his Waterloo, Nixon had his Watergate, and guess what…we make mistakes, too. So here's a first—we thought we'd swallow our pride and show you a few of our own bloopers. This article is dedicated to all of you that have taken the time to write in and keep us honest.

A lot of readers pointed this one out to us: On page 88 of *The Best of Uncle John's Bathroom Reader*, in "Famous Last Words," we wrote that Ludwig van Beethoven's final utterance was, "Friends applaud, the comedy is over." But if you skip ahead to page 260, in "Final Thoughts," you'll notice that his last words were "I shall hear in heaven!" Well…he had a lot to say. So which one is correct? We've since discovered that no one really knows. Have proof? Send it along.

• We read that Abraham Lincoln was born in Illinois, so that's what we wrote in *Uncle John's Great Big Bathroom Reader*. But we goofed. A multitude of readers kindly pointed out that Abe was not born in Illinois—he was born in a log cabin near Hodgenville, Kentucky. (OK, but he moved to Illinois when he was very young.)

• If you own the first edition of *Uncle John's Absolutely Absorbing Bathroom Reader*, you might have noticed that there was no running foot on page 398. Actually there was…but it was invisible. We later replaced it with one that people could see.

• BRI member Ed J. pointed out this one: "The one-liner at the bottom of page 77 of *Great Big* is in error. It states that the odds of the average golfer making a hole-in-one are 33,676 to 1. This would make a hole-in-one very commonplace. It should read, 'The odds *against* the average golfer making a hole-in-one are 33,676 to 1.'"

You're right, Ed. But we think people still got the idea.

• In *Uncle John's Giant 10th Anniversary Bathroom Reader*, we state that the fuel economy of an early automobile called the Davis was 65 mph. We meant mpg. Oops.

• And for all of you who wrote in letting us know that the General Sherman tree (*Great Big Bathroom Reader*, page 391) is *not* the oldest living thing on Earth, we know. Well, now we do. The oldest tree is actually a bristlecone pine. Believe it or not, we got the original info from the National Park Service.

• We hoped you enjoyed our article on page 215 in the 1st edition of *Giant 10th Anniversary Bathroom Reader* entitled "Manimals Famous for 15 Minutes." What's a manimal? We don't know either.

• Here's a classic: We once reported that Gandhi was buried in California. Boy, did we hear it on that one. For the record, his ashes were spread in many places all over the world, including California.

• Maybe you're one of the lucky few who have the first printing of *Uncle John's All-Pupose Extra Strength Bathroom Reader*. To find out if you do, check out the copyright page at the beginning and see if yours says *Uncle John's All-Pupose Extra Strength Bathroom Reader* at the top. Just in case you're wondering, we did that on pupose.

• In the *Legendary Lost Bathroom Reader*, on page 73, we didn't mean to say that Mt. Everest, the world's highest mountain, is in India, but that's how it came out. We know it's in Nepal. Really.

• In our *All-Purpose Extra Strength* press release to over 5,000 BRI members, we proudly stated that the book would be available in every state in the U.S. and every providence in Canada. Thank you to everyone who informed us that Canada has provinces, not providences. We knew that.

• This one may be our all-time favorite. In *Great Big*, one running foot says that "Ants don't sleep." Skip ahead a few pages and you'll learn that "Ants yawn when they wake up." Well, do they sleep or not? It turns out that they only rest, but they do stretch before they resume their work.

• And finally, this is for all of you that looked up the word "gullible" and found out that it is indeed in the dictionary: it was a joke, only a joke. Apparently you fell for it.

Tough luck, Lefty: Polo players are not allowed to play left-handed—it's too dangerous.

BRI BRAINTEASERS

We're back with another "regular" installment
of brainteasers. Answers are on page 507.

1. If you went to bed at 8 o'clock at night and wound your alarm clock to go off at 9:00 the next morning, how much sleep would you get?

2. Why can't a man living in North Carolina be buried in South Carolina?

3. If you had only one match and you entered a room in which there was a kerosene lamp, an oil heater, and a wood-burning stove, which would you light first?

4. Two men were playing checkers. Each played five games and each won the same number of games. No draws.
How can this be?

5. You have two coins in your hands equaling 55 cents. One of them is not a nickel.
What are the coins?

6. It is a scientific fact that a person eats over an inch of dirt at every meal.
How is this possible?

7. Jeff bought a word processor small enough to fit in his pocket. It can add, multiply, subtract, divide, and write in all languages. It has a delete device that will correct any error, and no electricity is required to operate it. Amazingly, it costs only 12 cents. How can it be so cheap?

8. A farmer has 17 sheep. All but 9 die. How many sheep are left?

9. A man married 48 women. None of them died, he was never divorced, and he was one of the most admired men in town.
How come?

10. If a doctor gave you 3 pills and told you to take one every half hour, how long would they last you?

11. If a farmer has 5 haystacks in one field and 4 in the other field, how many haystacks would he have if he combined them all in the center field?

THE AMAZING
DR. BAKER

*Of all the incredible women we've ever read about, Dr. Sara
Josephine Baker is one of the most incredible. Her accomplishments
are astounding, especially when you consider the time in which
she lived. Next time you think one person can't make
a difference, remember Dr. Baker.*

RICHES TO RAGS

Sara Josephine Baker was born to a life of privilege in
Poughkeepsie, New York, in 1873. In those days there
were no water treatment plants or indoor plumbing—people
pulled their drinking water right out of the Hudson River. Unfortunately, the Baker family lived downstream from a hospital that
discharged its waste into the same river. The hospital treated people suffering from typhoid fever—and the typhoid germs went
straight into the water. Baker's father and younger brother both
contracted the disease and died when she was 16 years old.

Although the family was left with no income and small savings, Baker announced that she wanted to go to college to become
a doctor, so that she could combat diseases like typhoid. But not
many women became doctors in those days. Nevertheless, the
young woman insisted, and her mother finally agreed.

In 1900, after graduating from the Women's Medical College
of the New York Infirmary and completing her internship, Baker
hung out her shingle in New York City. The next year, she took
the civil service exam and scored very high—high enough to qualify for the job of medical inspector for the Department of Health.

A MISSION

Perhaps because she was a woman, she was given the worst assignment of all: reducing the death rate in Hell's Kitchen—one of the
worst slums in New York. But among rat-infested buildings
crammed with poverty-stricken immigrants, Dr. Baker found her
calling. She went from tenement to tenement, searching for people with infectious diseases.

No kidding—when astronauts returned from the moon, they had to go through customs.

She said, "I climbed stair after stair, knocked on door after door, met drunk after drunk, filthy mother after filthy mother and dying baby after dying baby." Every week, more than 4,500 people in this district died from cholera, dysentery, smallpox, typhoid, and other illnesses, fully a third of them newborn babies. Dr. Baker rolled up her sleeves and went to work.

CHILDREN'S CRUSADE

Focusing on the infant mortality rate, Baker led a team of nurses who went door to door teaching mothers the value of nutrition, cleanliness, and ventilation. She set up milk stations where free pasteurized milk was given away; she standardized inspections of schoolchildren for contagious diseases; she insisted each school needed its own doctor and nurse; she set up a system for licensing midwives; she invented a simple baby formula that mothers could mix up at home; and she devised a widespread club for young girls to teach them how to properly babysit their younger siblings. In short, she set up a comprehensive health-care program for the prevention of disease in children. Her goal: Prevent disease rather than treating it after it occurred.

Baker found that babies wrapped in cumbersome clothing were dying of the oppressive heat or from accidental suffocation. So she designed baby clothing that was light, roomy, comfortable, and opened down the front. This clothing became so popular so quickly that McCall's Pattern Company bought the design, paying Baker a penny royalty for each one sold. The Metropolitan Life Insurance Company ordered 200,000 copies of the pattern and distributed them to policy holders.

She also found that babies routinely received silver nitrate eyedrops to prevent blindness from gonorrhea. But bottles of the solution often became contaminated, or they evaporated so that the concentration of silver nitrate was at a dangerous level, thus causing the blindness it was intended to prevent. Baker invented a foolproof sanitary solution: beeswax capsules, each containing enough solution for one eye. The capsules could not become contaminated and the drops inside could not evaporate. The method was soon being used around the world, and the rate of blindness in babies plummeted.

In ancient Rome, any house hit by lightning was considered consecrated.

CHEATING DEATH

After finding that orphanages had a high rate of infant deaths, Baker became one of the first people to theorize that babies who received no cuddling and cooing simply died of loneliness. After a plan was followed to place orphaned infants with foster mothers, the death rate dropped.

Because of Baker's efforts, the city created the Division of Child Hygiene in 1908 and appointed her the chief. Within 15 years, New York City had the lowest infant mortality rate of any city in the United States or Europe. An astounding statistic: It's estimated that from 1908, when she went to work for the new division, to 1923, when she left, she saved some 82,000 lives.

EXPERT ADVICE

Dr. Baker was without doubt the leading expert of the time on children's health. In 1916 the dean of the New York University Medical School asked her to lecture his students on the subject. She agreed, on one condition—that he allow her to enroll in the school and attend classes. He refused; women weren't allowed at his college. So she told him to find someone else. But there wasn't anyone who knew as much as Baker did. He finally gave in, and because he allowed *her* to attend the college, he had to open the campus to other women as well. In 1917 she became the first woman to receive a doctorate in public health from the school.

World War I strained the U.S. economy, and the poor got poorer. Baker pointed out to a reporter of *The New York Times* that American soldiers were dying at the rate of 4%, while babies in the United States were dying at the rate of 12%, making it safer to be a soldier in the trenches of France than to be born in the USA. Because of the publicity this generated, she was able to start a city-wide school lunch program for older children, which became a model for the world.

WORLD-CLASS

Suddenly, Dr. Baker was in high demand. An international charity asked her to take care of war refugees in France. London offered her the job of health director for their public school system. But she turned the offers down and was appointed Assistant Surgeon General of the United States, the first woman ever to receive a

---

There is a species of butterfly in Brazil that has the color and fragrance of chocolate.

federal government position.

What else did this amazing woman accomplish? Following her retirement in 1923:

• She represented the United States on the Health Committee of the League of Nations, as the first woman to be a professional representative to the League.

• She helped apprehend Typhoid Mary—twice.

• She oversaw creation of the Federal Children's Bureau and Public Health Services, which evolved into the Department of Health and Human Services.

• She helped establish child hygiene departments in every state in the union.

• She served as a member of over 25 medical societies.

• She was a consultant to the New York State Department of Health.

• She served as president of the American Medical Women's Association.

• She wrote over 250 articles and five books, including her autobiography in 1939.

Dr. Baker's enduring legacy: by the time she died in 1945, over half of the babies born each year in New York City were cared for at the health stations she established.

*   *   *

AS GENTLE AS A LAMB?

• "An Egyptian sheep destined for sacrificial slaughter in a religious ceremony forestalled his owner's plans by pushing him to his death from atop a three-story building, police said....Waheeb Hamoudah, 56, was feeding the sheep he tethered on the rooftop, when it butted him."

• "A Bedouin shepherd was shot in the chest and killed... when one of his flock jostled his loaded shotgun as he slept, police said."

—Wire service reports

Athletes? The 1900 Olympic Games included croquet, fishing, billiards, and checkers.

Q & A:
ASK THE EXPERTS

*More random questions, with answers
from the nation's top trivia experts.*

THE BRIGHT STUFF

Q: *How can Day-Glo colors be so brilliant? They look as if they're actually generating their own light.*

A: "They are. There's a chemical in Day-Glo colors that takes invisible ultraviolet radiation out of the daylight and converts it into visible light of the same color as the object. The object is not only reflecting light, it is actively *emitting* light, which makes it look up to four times brighter.

"What's going on is fluorescence, a natural process by which certain kinds of molecules absorb radiation of one energy and emit it as radiation of a lower energy. The molecules in the Day-Glo pigment are absorbing ultraviolet radiation that human eyes can't see, and reemitting it as light that human eyes can see." (From *What Einstein Told His Barber*, by Robert L. Wolke)

WATCHIN' THE WHEELS

Q: *Why do spokes on a wagon wheel appear to move backward on television or movie screens?*

A: "It is an optical illusion. When you watch a movie, you are not watching a continuous flow of action, but rather a series of still shots run at 24 frames per second. The human eye cannot detect the gaps between each frame because they occur so rapidly. You see a smooth-running movie.

"If the spokes were spinning at the same rate as the frames of the movie, the wheels would appear to be stationary. But when the spokes are spinning slower than the speed of the film, they don't make it all the way back to their original position, and as consecutive frames are rolled, the spokes appear to move backward. This illusion is also evident on television, which flashes the picture at 30 times per second." (From *The Book of Totally Useless Information*, by Don Voorhees)

What for? 60% athiests and agnostics say they own at least one Bible.

UNDERWEAR IN THE NEWS

All the undernews that's fit to print.

AROUND THE WORLD
 • **Cambodia:** Police have broken up a notorious gang of criminals that has been terrorizing the Cambodian countryside for more than a year. "They call themselves the Underwear Gang," says Lek Vannak, chief of the country's interior ministry of police. "At night they only wear underwear and carry weapons to rob and assault people in remote villages....People are living in a lot of fear." So far 25 members of the Underwear Gang have been caught; 7 more are still at large.

 • **Colombia:** Maria Fernanda Lopez, winner of the Miss Antioquia Province beauty pageant, was stripped of her title after posing for a magazine advertisement in underpants. Lopez admitted to posing for the ad, but insisted the garment she wore, skintight black shorts similar to the ones cheerleaders wear under their skirts, wasn't a pair of underpants—it was a "multifunctional outerwear garment" that can be worn either as underwear or as outerwear.

 • **England:** The British chain store Tesco has begun sewing labels into its underpants—instructing men on how to examine themselves for testicular cancer. "Men's insight into their own anatomy is very poor," says Ian Banks of the Men's Health Forum in England. "Having labels in their underpants gives them the information they need."

 • **England:** A British company called Brava PLC has introduced a "breast-enlarging bra" that it says can increase size by as much as one cup size. The bra uses vacuum pressure to achieve its results: hard plastic domes ringed with silicon are held in place with a sports bra; a battery-powered suction pump evacuates the air in the domes, creating a low-pressure environment that supposedly stimulates the breasts to grow. The drawbacks: The bras cost $2,000 to $2,500 apiece, and the suction cups have to be worn 10 hours a day for 10 consecutive weeks to achieve any results. "It's like buying a gym

---

Each mile of a four-lane freeway takes up more than 17 acres of land.

membership or an expensive piece of home exercise equipment," says Dr. James Baker, a skeptic. "How many of us have done that and only used it a few times?"

• **Sweden:** An inventor named Per Wallin has invented underwear with "soothing heated inserts" that he says will ease the pain and discomfort of menstruation. The inserts contain chemicals that generate their own heat for up to an hour.

RIGHT HERE AT HOME

• **Orlando, Florida:** Costumed workers at Walt Disney World have won the right to wear their own underwear while on duty and in costume in the company's theme parks.

Why go to court over underwear? Some Disney costumes hug the body so tightly that regular underwear bunches up and can be seen through the costume. To prevent unsightly VPLs (visible panty lines), the company supplies athletic supporters, tights, or cycling shorts that are to be worn in place of undies.

But there's a catch: Employees are not issued their own garments—everyone has to share. Disney is supposed to launder them in hot water and detergent when employees turn them in at the end of a shift *before* they're put back in circulation. That apparently wasn't happening and workers had finally had enough: "Things have been passed around," says stilt walker Gary Steverson. "I don't want to share my tights, and I don't want to share my underwear."

• **Pueblo, Colorado:** Inventor Buck Weimer has come out with underpants containing a powerful charcoal filter that removes the unpleasant smell of intestinal gas. Weimer invented the garment for his wife, who suffers from a gastrointestinal disorder called Crohn's disease. The undies, which the Weimers sell under the brand name Under-Ease, are made from airtight fabric and contain an "exit hole" fitted with a removable filter made of charcoal and Australian sheep's wool. Price: $24.95 a pair. They last for up to six months, but the filters need to be changed every two to three months, "depending on the amount and strength of gas being released."

Does Under-Ease take care of the unpleasant *sounds* associated with intestinal gas? "No," says Weimer, "This is not a muffler."

VIDEO TREASURES

We've shared many of our favorite offbeat films in past Bathroom Readers. This year, we asked our readers to tell us what their favorite movies are. Use this list the next time you're at the video store staring at rows of titles, wondering which film to choose.

BEFORE THE RAIN (1994) *Foreign/Drama*
Review: "Macedonian filmmaker Milcho Manchevski tells a three-part story about the tragic, far-reaching effects of ancient blood feuds and modern-day civil strife in the remnants of Yugoslavia. Riveting and compellingly told." (*Video Movie Guide*)

HAROLD AND MAUDE (1971) *Comedy*
Review: "Oddball black comedy that has become a cult favorite. Harold is a strange young man, rich, spoiled and fascinated with the concept of death. And, that is what draws him to Maude. Maude is old, but she is also eccentric and fun-loving. The two meet at a funeral and fall in love. This is not at all a typical comedy, but the open-minded viewer will be greatly rewarded with insights into human nature." (*Mark Satern's Illustrated Guide to Video's Best*)

LIES MY FATHER TOLD ME (1975) *Drama*
Review: "Simple drama about growing up in the 1920s in a Jewish ghetto. The story revolves around a young boy's relationship with his immigrant grandfather. Quiet and moving." (*VideoHound's Golden Movie Retriever*)

THE LOVED ONE (1965) *Satire*
Review: "Correctly advertised as the picture with something to offend everyone. Britisher Robert Morse attends to his uncle's burial in California, encountering bizarre aspects of the funeral business. Often howlingly funny, and equally gross. Once seen, Mrs. Joyboy can never be forgotten." (*Leonard Maltin's Movie and Video Guide*)

WAKING NED DEVINE (1998) *Comedy*
Review: "Old Ned Devine has the winning ticket for the Irish National Lottery—unfortunately, the shock has killed him. The

---

'Snow joke. Per capita, Alaskans eat twice as much ice cream as the rest of the nation.

residents of Tulaigh Morh conspire to fool a bored lottery official into thinking that Michael O'Sullivan is Devine, so that they can share the wealth. ...Warm and full of blarney, but never becomes too sappy, or contrived." (*VideoHound's Golden Movie Retriever*)

TRULY, MADLY, DEEPLY (1991) *Romantic Fantasy*

Review: "A woman grieving for the death of her husband is visited by his ghost. Unusual story of coming to terms with loss, combining wit, insight, and excellent acting. Intelligent, charming, ironic, and exceptionally well-played." (*Halliwell's Film and Video Guide*)

ROBINSON CRUSOE ON MARS (1964) *Science Fiction*

Review: "Surprising reworking of the classic Defoe story, with Paul Manatee as a stranded astronaut, at first accompanied by only a monkey. "Friday" turns out to be a similarly trapped alien. Beautifully shot in Death Valley; its intimate nature helps it play better on TV than most space films." (*Leonard Maltin's Movie and Video Guide*)

KING OF HEARTS (1966) *Foreign*

Review: "Phillippe de Broca's wartime fantasy provides delightful insights into human behavior. A World War I Scottish infantryman searching for an enemy bunker enters a small town that, after being deserted by its citizens, has been taken over by inmates of an insane asylum. In French with English subtitles." (*Video Movie Guide*)

GATES OF HEAVEN (1978) *Documentary*

Review: "(This film) is surrounded by layer upon layer of comedy, pathos, irony, and human nature. I have seen this film perhaps 30 times, and am still not anywhere near the bottom of it: All I know is, it's about a lot more than pet cemeteries." (*Chicago Sun-Times*)

SHALL WE DANCE? (1996) *Foreign/Drama*

Review: "This film proves that Japanese filmmakers can fashion charming, feel-good movies every bit as effective as their Hollywood counterparts. The film uses ballroom dancing to explore one man's struggle for freedom from the suffocating repression of Japanese society. This is a film for anyone who prefers to leave the theater smiling. Winner of 13 Japanese Academy Awards." (*ReelViews*)

Johnny Carson, Michael Douglas, and Clint Eastwood were all once gas station attendants.

ANIMALS FAMOUS FOR 15 MINUTES

When Andy Warhol said "everyone will be famous for fifteen minutes," he didn't have animals in mind. Yet even they are unable to escape the relentless publicity machine.

THE STAR: A 300 pound hog (name withheld)

THE HEADLINE: *When Pigs Fly, First Class Asks "Why?"*

WHAT HAPPENED: On October 17, 2000, two women and their hog boarded a US Airways flight from Philadelphia to Seattle. They presented a note from a doctor verifying that the animal "was a 'theraputic companion pet,' like a guide dog for the blind," so the airline cleared it to fly.

The hog snoozed through most of the six-hour flight, but got spooked when the plane landed. It charged up and down the aisle, squealing loudly, at one point even trying to smash into the cockpit. Then it hid in the galley until its owners lured it out with food and pushed it off the plane...at which point it fouled the jetway.

THE AFTERMATH: US Airways immediately revised its companion animal policy specifically to exclude hogs. "We can confirm that the pig traveled," a spokesperson told reporters, "and we can confirm that it will never happen again. Let me stress that. It will never happen again."

THE STARS: Drag racing hamsters of London

THE HEADLINE: *When The Chips Are Down, Bet On Hamsters*

WHAT HAPPENED: In February 2001, the highly contagious foot-and-mouth disease struck English livestock, resulting in a ban on horse races.

What was an obsessed gambler to do? The Internet betting site Blue Square, Ltd. created something new for desperate bettors—hamster drag racing. "You put an exercise wheel in the middle of a 10-inch-long dragster," a company spokesperson told reporters. "As they run in the wheel, it moves the whole thing forward."

Each race featured six hamsters in tiny plastic hot rods running along a six-foot wooden track; video cameras broadcasted the action live over the company's website. More than 2,000 people around the world logged on to watch and bet on each race.

THE AFTERMATH: The epidemic slowed, the horse races resumed, and the hamsters were put out to tiny little pastures.

THE STARS: As many as 500 Barbary apes smuggled into France from North Africa

THE HEADLINE: *Dearth Of Dogs Leads To Mobs Of Monkeys*

WHAT HAPPENED: In the late 1990s, French authorities began cracking down on youth gangs that used vicious dogs—Rottweilers, Dobermans and Pit Bulls—to intimidate rival gangs. The crackdown was working…until gangs began switching to monkeys. "The apes are becoming the new weapon of choice. They're ultra-fashionable," says Didier Lecourbe, a police officer in Aubervilliers, a suburb of Paris.

THE AFTERMATH: The apes turn out to be even tougher than the attack dogs. "Removed from their natural habitat," natural historian Marie-Claude Bomsel told the *London Guardian*, "they can become highly aggressive. They bite, and their favored method of attack is to hurl themselves at people's heads."

THE STAR: A dinosaur the size of a German Shepherd

THE HEADLINE: *Dinosaur Found In Rock Named In Honor Of One Of Rock's Dinosaurs*

WHAT HAPPENED: In early 2001, paleontologists digging on Madagascar discovered a new species of dinosaur that lived 65 to 75 million years ago. "It had bizarre teeth," paleontologist Scott Sampson told reporters. "They're long and conical with hooked tips. They protrude straight forward, so it might be easier to catch fish or used to spear insects."

While digging for dinosaurs, Sampson and his colleagues listened to the music of Dire Straits, so they named the species *masiakasaurus knopfleri* in honor of Dire Straits singer/guitarist Mark Knopfler. "If it weren't for his music, we might not have found the animal in the first place," Sampson explained.

THE AFTERMATH: "I'm really delighted," Knopfler told reporters when he learned of the honor. "The fact that it is a dinosaur is certainly apt, but I'm happy to report that I'm not in the least bit vicious."

WORD ORIGINS

Ever wonder where words come from?
Here are some more interesting stories.

BOULEVARD

Meaning: A broad avenue, often with one or more strips of plantings (grass, trees, flower beds) on both sides and/or down the center

Origin: "The name originally came from the Middle Low German *Bolwerk*, the top of the wide rampart—often 20 or more feet wide—that served as the defensive wall of medieval towns. As more sophisticated weaponry rendered such structures obsolete, they sometimes were razed to ground level and used as a wide street on the town's perimeter. Vienna has such a broad boulevard, called the Ring, circling the old town on the site of its original city walls." (From *Fighting Words*, by Christine Ammer)

QUEEN

Meaning: The wife or widow of a king

Origin: "*Queen* goes back ultimately to prehistoric Indo-European *gwen-*, 'woman' (from which English gets *gynecology*), Persian *zan*, 'woman,' Swedish *kvinna*, 'woman,' and the now obsolete English *quean*, 'woman.' In its very earliest use in Old English, *queen* (or *cwen*, as it then was) was used for a 'wife,' but not just any wife: it denoted the wife of a man of particular distinction, and usually a king. It was not long before it became institutionalized as 'king's wife,' and hence 'woman ruling in her own right.'" (From *Dictionary of Word Origins*, by John Ayto)

PARASITE

Meaning: An organism that lives in or on another organism at the other's expense

Origin: "In ancient Greek it meant a professional dinner guest. It came from the Greek *para* ('beside') and *sitos* ('grain, food'). Put together, *parasitos* first meant 'fellow guest' and acquired, even then, its present-day meaning." (From *Dictionary of Word and Phrase Origins*, Vol. III, by William and Mary Morris)

Buzz Aldrin's mother's maiden name: Moon.

TADPOLE

Meaning: The larva of an amphibian

Origin: "*Tad* was an early spelling for 'toad,' and *pol* meant 'head' in 17th-century speech. Therefore, *tadpole* means 'toad head,' an appropriate name for the early stage of a frog when it is little more than a big head with a small tail." (From *The Facts on File Encyclopedia of Word and Phrase Origins*, by Robert Hendrickson)

NAMBY-PAMBY

Meaning: Weak, wishy-washy

Origin: "Derived from the name of Ambrose Philips, a little-known poet whose verse incurred the ridicule of two other 18th-century poets, Alexander Pope and Henry Carey. In poking fun at Philips, Carey used the nickname *Namby Pamby*: Amby came from Ambrose; Pamby repeated the sound and form, but added the initial of Philips's surname. After being popularized by Pope in *The Dunciad*, *namby-pamby* went on to be used for people or things that are insipid, sentimental, or weak." (From *Word Mysteries & Histories*, by the Editors of The American Heritage Dictionaries)

BLESS

Meaning: To consecrate or invoke divine favor

Origin: "A gracious word with a grisly history. Its forefather was Old English *bledsian*, a word that meant 'to consecrate with blood,' this, of course, from the blood sacrifices of the day. In later English, this word turned into *blessen*, and the term finally came to mean 'consecrated.' So today when we give you the greeting, 'God bless you,' we are actually saying, 'God bathe you in blood.'" (From *Word Origins*, by Wilfred Funk)

KALEIDOSCOPE

Meaning: A tubular optical toy; a constantly changing set of colors

Origin: "In 1817 Dr. David Breuster invented a toy which he called a *kaleidoscope*. He selected three Greek words that when' combined had a literal meaning of 'observer of beautiful forms.' The words were *kalos* ('beautiful'), *eidos* ('form'), and *skopos* ('watcher'). The term has come into prominent use in its figurative sense; namely, a changing scene—that which subtly shifts color, shape, or mood." (From *The Story Behind the Word*, by Morton S. Freeman)

Margaret Hamilton, who played the Wicked Witch of the West, was once a kindergarten teacher.

OOPS!

*More tales of outrageous blunders to let us know that
other people are screwing up even worse than we are.*

A MOVING EXPERIENCE

MISHAWAKA, Ind.—"An Indiana couple should seriously consider hiring professional movers next time. Marsha
and Niles Huntsinger threw their futon mattress out the window
and it fell between two buildings. Niles lowered Marsha down on a
rope to try to get the futon, but she became wedged in the 16-inch
gap between the walls. Huntsinger had to be rescued by a fire crew
after she spent half an hour jammed 20 feet off the ground. The
rescuers also managed to save the futon."

—Bizarre News

ANGRY, ANGRY HIPPO

"During a 60 *Minutes* interview, Mike Wallace meant to ask
former Russian president Boris Yeltsin, 'Is Yeltsin thin-skinned
about the press?' But the question was mistranslated as: 'Is Yeltsin a
thick-skinned hippopotamus?' Yeltsin responded by saying that
Wallace should 'express himself in a more civilized fashion.'"

—San Francisco Chronicle

STANDING ROOM ONLY

"A visitor at a Minneapolis art gallery sat in and broke a chair,
which he did not realize was part of an exhibit dating to the Ming
Dynasty. Value of the chair: $100,000."

—"The Edge," The Oregonian

SNIP-SNIP

"A minor league baseball team in Charleston, South Carolina,
recently came up with a novel promotion for Father's Day. The
River Dogs offered fans the chance to win a free vasectomy. They
immediately withdrew the offer, however, when fans protested.
Among those who complained was the Roman Catholic Diocese of
Charleston, led by season ticket holder Bishop David Thompson.

'People didn't like the idea,' General Manager Mark Schuster

Don't believe the Scots. The kilt originated in France.

said, noting the team never meant to offend anyone. 'We are sensitive to our fans' wants.'"

—*Wacky News*

SOFA, SO GOOD

"After a long night of drinking, Casey Adams ate some leftover lasagna, took off his clothes and made himself at home on the sofa. The problem? It was the wrong sofa—the wrong house, too.

"At about 6:00 the next morning, Frances Brown, the Edgewater homeowner, discovered Mr. Adams, 26, lounging on the sofa in his gray boxer shorts, fast asleep. A shocked Mrs. Brown quickly called the police.

"Police found no signs of forced entry on the home; residents said a door may have been left unlocked. They charged him with fourth-degree burglary and had his Jeep towed from the driveway.

"Mr. Adams didn't know how or when he arrived there, but he gave police a statement saying he was extremely intoxicated and nothing like this had ever happened to him before.

"'He kept saying he was sorry,' Mrs. Brown said."

—*The Capital*

NOUVEAU SCROOGE

"A Louisville, Kentucky, man who won $65 million in the state lottery recently filed suit against a woman seeking reimbursement after he met her in a bar and, 'while in an intoxicated state,' accidentally gave her $500,000."

—*Bloomington-Normal Daily Pantograph*

BETTER LATE THAN NEVER

EDINBURGH—"Postmen in the Scottish city of Aberdeen did their very best to deliver a letter from Australia—112 years late.

"'The card was posted on the fourth of January in 1889 and it arrived in Aberdeen a few days ago. We have absolutely no idea where it's been,' said Aberdeen postmaster Pete Smith.

"'Whoever has this postcard should get in touch with us because we might start a new category,' a spokesman for the *Guinness Book of Records* said. 'We've got a record for a parcel but that's only about two or three years.'"

—*CNN Fringe*

Largest city without a major league sports team: El Paso, Texas (pop. 612,000).

CREME *de la* CRUD

From the BRI files, a few samples of the worst of the worst.

WORST FOOD PRODUCT INVENTED BY MILTON HERSHEY
Beet Sherbet

Like many Americans, Milton Hershey went on a vitamin kick in the early 1940s, and he started experimenting with vegetable juices. "It's much easier to drink raw vegetables than to eat raw vegetables," he explained. Surely vegetable juice sherbets were even better.

Hershey tested onion, carrot, and celery sherbets before concluding that beet sherbet tasted the best and adding it to the menu at the Hershey Hotel. Those brave few who ordered the stuff couldn't stomach it—it tasted *terrible*, which had completely escaped the man who gave us the Hershey bar. How'd that happen? Former CEO Samuel Hinkle blamed the cigars that Hershey, then in his mid-80s, had smoked for more than 60 years. "After smoking six, eight, ten cigars a day, Mr. Hershey had absolutely burned out his taste buds," Hinkle recalled. "He couldn't taste or smell a thing."

WORST PULP FICTION NOVEL
Killer in Drag, *by Ed Wood, Jr.*

Yes, *that* Ed Wood, Jr. When he wasn't making movies like *Plan 9 From Outer Space, Glen or Glenda,* and *Bride of the Monster,* Wood was hard at work cranking out books that were every bit as bad as his films. *Killer in Drag* is the story of a transvestite assassin who "goes straight (criminally speaking) and tries to get a shady sugar daddy to pay for his sex-change operation."

WORST HOLE OF GOLF
Mrs. J. F. Meehan, Shawnee Ladies Invitational

When she got the 16th hole (126 yards, par 3), Meehan teed up, swung...and hit her ball into the water. The ball was floating on the surface of the water, but rather than use another ball, Meehan got her husband to find a boat and row her out to the ball. She leaned over the front of the boat and took her swing...and another…and another. It took her more than 40 strokes just to hit the ball onto land; then she had to play through a thickly wooded area to get back to the green. Final score for the hole: 161 strokes.

WORST CHOICE OF PROPS IN A LONDON PLAY
Real champagne, in a scene of the first (and last) performance of "Ecarte" at the Old Globe Theatre

Playwright Lord Newry was a stickler for authenticity, so when his play called for a picnic, he used a real picnic basket filled with roast chicken, pies, truffles…and several bottles of champagne, which the actors drank to the last drop. Leading lady Nita Nicotina was soon too drunk to remember her lines; her leading man kept track of his by shouting them out at the top of his lungs. That tired him out, so he laid down in the middle of the stage and fell fast asleep as the other actors worked around him, tripping over props and leaning against scenery that was not designed to support their weight.

By now the audience had lost its composure; when Nicotina walked out onstage at the beginning of the next scene wearing one red and one green boot, the audience lost itself in howling waves of laughter. That made her mad—"What are you laughing at, you beastly fools?" she screamed. "When you have done making idiots of yourselves, I will go on with this—*hiccup*—beastly play." She never got the chance—the audience laughed and booed the entire cast off the stage. (Except for the leading man, who was still asleep.)

WORST FROZEN BREAKFAST FOOD PRODUCT
IncrEdibles Breakaway Foods

Remember those "push-up" ice cream and frozen yogurt pops? IncrEdibles, introduced in 1999, were scrambled egg push-up breakfast pops designed for eaters on the go. They came in three flavors: cheese, sausage and cheese, and bacon and cheese. The concept may seem disgusting, but what really killed IncrEdibles was the fact that when you heated them up in the microwave, the eggs became so soft, it was almost impossible to eat them without the whole superheated mess spilling onto your lap. Ouch!

THE HISTORY OF FOOTBALL, PART III

In this part of our football saga, we contemplate the mysteries of safeties, offensive interference, and tackling below the waist.

MAKING HIS POINT(S)
In the early days of football, games often ended in a tie, and the referee decided the winner. Yale coach Walter Camp thought that instituting a *point* system, something more sophisticated than just counting touchdowns and field goals, would solve the problem by making tied games less likely. He pushed his proposal through the Rules Committee in 1883.

Beginning that year, a touchdown counted for two points, a goal kicked following a touchdown was worth four points, and a field goal was worth five points. Then there was the "safety." Whenever the ball came within 25 yards of the offensive team's own goal line, it was common practice for them to touch the ball down behind their own goal line "for safety," because this meant that the ball would be brought back out to the 25-yard line for a free kick. Henceforth, if a team was forced to resort to a safety, one point was awarded to the other team.

The new point system lasted only a year—by 1884 it was obvious that touchdowns were harder to score than field goals, so their value was raised to four points. The goal after touchdown was lowered to two points, the safety was raised to two points, and the field goal remained unchanged at five points.

GETTING IN THE WAY

Technically, "interference," or protecting the ball carrier from incoming tacklers, was illegal, just as it was in rugby. But because the introduction of the system of downs was thought to have weakened the offense, enforcement of the rules against interference began to decline.

As early as 1879, Princeton protected the ball carrier by running two players alongside him, one on either side. These shielders didn't actually block the incoming tacklers—that was still against

---

...Robert Louis Stevenson wrote *Travels with a Donkey.*

the rules—but they were an intimidating presence. Rather than complain, other teams adopted the tactic themselves.

They also began testing the limits of what else they could get away with—and quickly discovered they could get away with a lot. "A few years later," Stephen Fox writes in *Big Leagues*, "the shielders had moved out ahead of the runner, using their arms and hands to shed tacklers. The old offside rule was no longer enforced. Barely a decade old, football had lost this final vestige of rugby."

LOW BLOW

The gradual acceptance of offensive interference served to strengthen the offense, so in 1888 Walter Camp pushed through two new rules that helped strengthen the defense in response: The first banned blocking "with extended arms," a tacit acknowledgment that other forms of blocking had become legal; the second legalized tackling below the waist, as far down as the knees. The new rules shifted the balance so firmly over to the defense that the offense had to completely rethink its game.

The low tackle proved to be much harder to defend against than tackles above the waist, so forwards had little choice but to move in closer around the center, until they were literally standing shoulder to shoulder, as they do today. The backfield (halfbacks and fullbacks) moved further up to provide additional protection. Now, instead of being spread out all over the field, players were clumped together in the middle. It was also about this time that centers started using their *hands* instead of their feet to snap the ball back to the quarterback.

THE V-TRICK

With so many players crowded together, it was probably just a matter of time before someone hit upon the offensive tactic of everybody locking arms and slamming into the defense in one single, devastating mass.

One of the earliest examples of such a "mass play," as it came to be known, was the V-trick, which Princeton invented on the spur of the moment in 1884, during the second half of a game against the University of Pennsylvania. (Lehigh University claims to have invented a similar version at about the same time.)

Princeton wasn't having any luck advancing the ball with its

In a 1936 ping pong tournament, the players volleyed for over 2 hours on the opening serve.

usual strategy of having a halfback carry the ball down the field behind seven other players. Then it occurred to quarterback Richard Hodge that the seven interferers might be more effective if they locked arms together and formed a V, with the point of the V pointing downfield and the ball carrier running safely inside the formation. It worked: Princeton scored a touchdown, and went on to win the game, 31–0.

SECOND TRY

It wasn't until 1888 that Princeton used the V-trick again. This time they sprang it on Yale at the start of the second half. But it was not nearly as effective has it had been four years before, because one of the Yale guards instantly figured out a way to counter it. Author Parke Davis described the scene in his 1911 book *Football: The American Intercollegiate Game:*

> The Princeton players formed themselves into a mass of the shape of the letter V....The ball went into play and away went the wedge of men, legs churning in unison like the wheels of a locomotive.
>
> But on the Yale team was a young giant by the name of Walter "Pudge" Heffelfinger. He rushed at the mighty human engine, leaped high in the air, completely clearing its forward ramparts, and came down on top of the men inside the wedge, whom he flattened to the ground, among them the ball-carrier.

HUMAN CANNONBALL

Yale won the game, 10–0, and went on to win every game of its 1888 season, racking up 694 points to 0 for its opponents. Nevertheless, the V-trick was so effective that other teams quickly adopted it and began inventing other mass plays. Likewise, they adopted the defensive tactics of Pudge Heffelfinger, perfecting the art of cannonballing knees-first into chest of the lead man in the wedge. The best players were able to vault the wedge entirely to slam full force into the ball carrier.

Tactics like these led to an increase in the number of serious injuries and even deaths in the game, which led to a general increase in brutality and foul play. "We were past masters at tackling around the neck," Georgia Tech's John Heisman recalled of the period. "There was a rule against it, but that rule was broken often....Fact is, you didn't stand much of a chance making the

How many leaf-cutter ants does it take to lift a 10-pound picnic basket? 60,133.

line in those days unless you were a good wrestler and fair boxer."

THE FLYING WEDGE

In 1890 a Boston lawyer and chess expert named Lorin F. Deland happened to see a Harvard football game. He'd never played football, but had became a fan of the sport, in large part because the strategy seemed to have a lot of parallels with battlefield tactics. His interest in the sport prompted him to read books on Napoléon Bonaparte.

One of the little emperor's favorite tricks was massing the full strength of his troops at the enemy's weakest points; Deland thought this would also work well in football. He pitched his idea for what became known as the "flying wedge" to Harvard in 1892. The flying wedge applied the principles of speed and momentum to the Princeton V-trick; Deland proposed using it during kickoffs, which would allow the wedge to get a 20-yard running head start before slamming full-speed into the opposing team.

Harvard agreed to try it against Yale in the fall and spent much of the summer secretly practicing the move. On game day they introduced it at the start of the second half, when Harvard had the kickoff. The beefiest players gathered on the right side of the field 20 yards away from the ball; the smaller players gathered 15 yards further back on the left side. When the signal was given, both groups converged in front of the ball at full speed and locked arms to form the wedge as the kicker, Bernie Trafford, tapped the ball with his foot (still legal in those days), then picked it up and passed it to teammate Charlie Brewer running alongside him.

FOOT FAULT

Running from inside the safety of the flying wedge as it plowed into Yale's defensive line, Brewer managed to advance as much as 30 yards and might even have gone all the way for a touchdown, had he not tripped over a teammate on Yale's 25-yard line. Harvard never did score a touchdown—Yale won, 6–0, but the effectiveness of the flying wedge was obvious to everyone. By 1893 almost every college football team in the country had adopted "mass momentum" plays. The golden age of football violence had arrived.

Halftime: After the BRI Marching band performs, turn
to page 331 for Part IV of our History of Football.

Dallas was named after George Mifflin Dallas. Who was he? U.S. vice president 1845–1849.

BUSHISMS

Some "deep" thoughts from George W. Bush.
Frankly, we don't understand them, either.

"Families is where our nation finds hope, where wings take dream."

"I know how hard it is for you to put food on your family."

"What I am against is quotas. I am against hard quotas, quotas they basically delineate based upon whatever. However they delineate, quotas, I think vulcanize society."

"I know the human being and fish can coexist peacefully."

"I will have a foreign-handed foreign policy."

"I would have to ask the questioner. I haven't had a chance to ask the questioners the question they've been questioning."

"I am mindful of the difference between the executive branch and the legislative branch. I assured all four of these leaders that I know the difference, and that difference is they pass the laws and I execute them."

"They want the federal government controlling Social Security like it's some kind of federal program."

"One of the common denominators I have found is that expectations rise above that which is expected."

"The California crunch really is the result of not enough power-generating plants and then not enough power to power the power of generating plants."

"The senator has got to understand—he can't have it both ways. He can't take the high horse and then claim the low road."

"I am mindful not only of preserving executive powers for myself, but for predecessors as well."

"How do you know if you don't measure if you have a system that simply suckles kids through?"

"They misunderestimated me."

President Busch: In a survey, U.S. children 8–12 could name more brands of beer than presidents.

THE OTHER TEXANS

George W. Bush's verbal blunders are well-known.
But is he the only Texas politician who has a flair
for the English language? Nope. Read on for
more fun from the Lone Star state.

"It just makes good sense to put all your eggs in one basket."
— **Rep. Joe Salem, on an amendment requiring all revenues to go into the state treasury**

"I want to thank each and every one of you for having extinguished yourselves this session."
— **Speaker Gib Lewis**

"Lemme give ya' a hypothetic."
— **Rep. Renal Rosson**

"Well, there never was a Bible in the room."
— **Gov. Bill Clements, on repeatedly lying about the SMU football scandal**

"I am filled with humidity."
— **Speaker Gib Lewis**

"It's the sediment of the House that we adjourn."
— **Speaker Wayne Clayton**

"This is unparalyzed in the state's history."
— **Speaker Gib Lewis**

"Oh good. Now he'll be bi-ignorant."
— **Ag. Commissioner Jim Hightower, when told that Gov. Bill Clements was studying Spanish**

"Let's do this in one foul sweep."
— **Speaker Wayne Clayton**

"There's a lot of uncertainty that's not clear in my mind."
— **Speaker Gib Lewis**

"No thanks, once was enough."
— **Gov. Bill Clements, when asked if he had been born again**

"If it's dangerous to talk to yourself, it's probably even dicier to listen."
— **Ag. Commissioner Jim Hightower**

Alaska alone has as much coastline as the rest of the United States.

VOLCANIC ACTION

Look out the window: everything may look calm and serene—but what's going on below the surface? The answer is...a lot. Here's some basic Earth sciences.

K ABLOOM!
Why do volcanoes explode? Simply stated, because the center of the Earth is hot, while the crust is (relatively speaking) cold. This causes different pressures, which need to be equalized.

The Earth is covered by a crust of solid rock, 20 miles thick over the average continent, twice that thick under mountain ranges, and only 5 miles thick under the oceans. It's about 4,000 miles to the center of the Earth, and the deeper you go, the hotter it gets—90°F for every mile. The high temperature is generated by a concentration of radioactive materials, which give off heat as they deteriorate.

Gold miners in South Africa work at 11,736 feet below the Earth's surface—just a little more than two miles deep—where the rocks are hot enough to burn a naked hand. The average temperature of a typical rock on the surface is 55°F, but deep in the gold mines it is 125°. Forty miles under the surface, the heat is so great that rocks melt, forming magma. At the core, temperatures may reach 13,000°F. (Compare that to the melting point of pure iron, a mere 2,795°.)

AT THE BIRTH OF THE EARTH

In the planet's infancy, the outer part may have been a solid shell. But as it cooled, the shell cracked like an egg into nine main pieces and about a dozen smaller ones, called tectonic plates. They fit together like a jigsaw puzzle and float on top of a layer of molten magma. The plates move at the average rate of one inch per year, which is about as fast as fingernails grow. (The hour hand of a clock move 10,000 times faster.)

Each of the tectonic plates rubs against three or more other plates. The points where the plates meet are where magma is most likely to find an escape route. Eighty percent of the world's volca-

---

If you work nights, you're nearly twice as likely to have an accident than if you work days.

noes and 90% of its earthquakes occur along the edges of these plates. That's also where we find the Earth's tallest mountains and deepest trenches.

WORLD IN MOTION

Magma is not stagnant; it moves. The same way that differences in hot and cold air cause wind, and differences in hot and cold water cause currents, differences in hot rocks in the center of the Earth and cold rocks at the surface of the Earth cause magma to move.

In addition, when rocks melt, their various materials naturally sort by weight, with heavy elements, such as iron and nickel sinking, and lighter elements rising. This also produces motion in magma. Furthermore, the gases produced when rocks melt rise to the surface, pushing magma upward. The magma forces its way through any fissure it can find. When a weak spot in the surface of the Earth is found, a pipeline forms and everything spews out. But when a pipeline becomes clogged—for example, by a plug of hardened lava from a previous explosion—nothing can escape. In that case, the pressure of the gases and magma continues to increase until it's strong enough to blow out the plug. Obviously, the tighter the plug and the greater the pressure, the more devastating the explosion.

HOT STUFF

When magma comes to the surface, it's called lava. The average temperature of lava is about 1,800°F, although it can be much hotter. When lava is churned violently, mixed to a froth with air and gases, and then thrown into the atmosphere, it comes down as pumice. When magma cools beneath the surface, it forms dense rocks such as granite and basalt. Fully 80% of the Earth is volcanic in origin.

There are about 600 active volcanoes in the world and an average of 20 explosions per year around the planet. North America has about 20 volcanoes, all on the west coast. Japan has over 70. (Australia has none at all, because it sits in the middle of a tectonic plate.) Over the last 10,000 years, about 1,500 different volcanoes have exploded. Over the last 1,000 years, approximately 300,000 people have died due to volcanic eruptions.

Burning truth: Nearly 1,000 people per year die as a direct result of volcanic activity.

BRINGER OF LIFE

The amount of destruction that volcanoes have caused, however, is infinitesimal compared to the bounty they've given us. Basically, without volcanos there'd be no life on Earth.

When our planet was very young, it was very hot. As the outer crust cooled, volcanoes spewed out enough gas over the first billion years to create a swirling, dynamic atmosphere. The cycle kept going...and going...and going. Weather systems formed and eons of rain eventually created the oceans.

What happened next is not known for certain—here are two theories:

• Lightning may have caused certain simple chemicals, like ammonia, to form into more complicated chemicals which, in turn, may have hooked together in chains, forming molecules such as RNA and DNA, the building blocks of life.

• Fats in the primitive seas may have formed large globules enclosing "life-directing" chemicals, and these structures eventually may have formed primitive living cells.

In either case, most scientists agree that volcanoes were the spoon that stirred the primordial soup long enough to allow the chemistry of life to succeed. And they're still stirring it today. For evidence, look at any volcanic region on Earth and you'll find some of the greenest and most fertile land anywhere.

WHAT'S OUT THERE

Knowing what volcanoes have done for Earth, astronomers have looked for them on other planets. Mars has the largest known volcano in the solar system, Olympus Mons, three times higher than Mount Everest and as wide as Arizona. Samples taken from the Martian surface show trace amounts of water and biogenic elements that suggest life once existed there.

Farther away, scientists are eyeing Jupiter's moon Europa, which also shows evidence of volcanism and water. Who knows—before the 21st century is complete, we may find some new friends in the neighborhood.

Back on Earth, nothing can be done to stop volcanoes from exploding. Scientists can usually predict explosions using seismology, gas monitoring, and satellite technology. Meanwhile,

---

Grocer's dozen: 90% of the world's food crops come from only 12 species of plants.

mankind constantly works to reduce the impact of volcanoes on the population. Sometimes, it works. Sometimes, it doesn't.

BOILING RAIN

The Kelut volcano on the Indonesian island of Java tended to collect water in its crater, creating a huge lake. So, whenever the volcano erupted, an avalanche of boiling water and mud would sweep down the mountain, destroying everything in its path. In 1919 104 villages were buried and more than 5,000 people killed. Engineers decided to drain the lake. They began digging a series of tunnels through the side of the volcano, each one 30 feet lower then the last. By 1926, the lake was reduced from 85 million cubic yards of water to 4 million. When the volcano erupted again in 1951, the much smaller lake simply evaporated.

Unfortunately, the explosion also ruined the drainage system and deepened the crater. Once again, massive amounts of water collected. In 1963 an explosion killed thousands. A new drainage system was begun. Since then, the lake has been maintained at a safe level. When Kelut erupted in 1990, only 32 people were killed.

SAVING HELGAFELL

In 1973 the Helgafell volcano off the coast of Iceland began erupting. The 5,300 residents of Heimaey Island were evacuated, but 300 people remained to try to save the town. A wall of lava 120 feet high and 1,000 feet wide threatened to seal off the town's only harbor, which would effectively destroying the local economy. In desperation, the remaining citizens used their fire engines to pump water on the advancing flow. Small tongues of lava solidified under the steady barrage of water, and a small dam built up, slowing the flow. Then they used a sand dredger to pump sea water onto the flow. More high-pressure pumps were sent from the United States, and workers discovered that by piping water to points behind the flow's front, a series of small dams could be created to form internal barriers. Nineteen miles of pipe and 43 pumps were used to move water for nearly four months straight. Finally the volcano settled down. The harbor—and the town—had been saved.

For more about volcanoes, check out the stories of Mount St. Helens on page 302, Mount Peleé on page 72, and The Lost City of Pompeii on page 376.

A cubic foot of gold weighs more than half a ton.

TOILET TECH

Better living through bathroom technology.

WHY PIT-STOP...WHEN YOU CAN PIT-GO?
Inventor: Aston Waugh of East Orange, New Jersey
Product: An automobile urinal that flushes. The urinal consists of three parts: a hanging water tank, a miniature padded toilet bowl that the driver sits on while driving, and a waste storage tank that stows neatly beneath the driver's seat.
How It Works: After use, the driver flushes the device by opening a valve; water from the hanging tank flows through a tube into the toilet bowl, and from there into the storage tank underneath the seat. "For privacy," the inventor advises, "the user may wrap a large towel around him or herself from the waist to the knees before undoing the clothing to facilitate urination." (Not recommended for use while operating a cell phone.)

PET-O-POTTI
Inventor: Floraine Cohen of New York City
Product: A toilet conversion kit that allows dogs and cats to use the facilities just like any other member of the family.
How It Works: A ramp leads up to a trapdoor that's installed over the toilet bowl. An electronic sensor detects when the animal has come and gone, so to speak; then, after the animal has left, it opens the trapdoor, allowing the waste to fall into the bowl. "Encircling the trap door is a perforated tube into which water is fed, for purposes of flushing the waste material into the toilet."

PORT-O-PET-O-POTTI
Inventor: Angela Raphael of New York City
Product: A strap-on animal waste collector for dogs owned by people too squeamish to use a pooper-scooper.
How It Works: It looks kind of like a pet harness, only backward with two add-ons. One waste receptacle attaches beneath the dog's tail, and one attaches beneath the dog to capture urine. Extra bonus: Both receptacles are disposable.

Ross' loss: Ross Perot lost $450 million on the stock market in a single day—April 22, 1970.

GIVES YOU STRONG MOUTH AND REFRESHING WIND

In Japan, English words are "cool"—it doesn't even matter whether they make sense, which is why they're so funny. Here are some actual English phrases found on Japanese products.

On Fresh Brand Straws: Let's try homeparty fashionably and have a joyful chat with nice fellow. Fujinami's straw will produce you young party happily and exceedingly.

Warning on a toy box: A dangerous toy. This toy is being made for the extreme priority the good looks. The little part which suffocates when the sharp part which gets hurt is swallowed is contained generously.

On Koeda brand chocolate-covered pretzels: The sentimental taste is cozy for the heroines in the town.

On a fondue set: When all family members are seated around the table, dishes are all the more tasteful. If dishes are nice, the square ceiling becomes round.

Advertisement for a restaurant: No one really goes to Aqua Bar for the drinks, but we make sure our drinks won't kill you.

On a paper coffee cup: The Art of Hot. Side by side, I'll be yours forever. Because please don't weep.

Sign for Café Miami: We established a fine coffee. What everybody can say TASTY! It's fresh, so-mild. With some special coffee's bitter and sourtaste. "LET'S HAVE SUCH A COFFEE! NOW!" is our selling copy. Please love Café Miami.

On a coat label: Have a good time! Refreshed and foppish sense and comfortable and fresh styles will catch you who belong to city-groups. All the way.

Good thing they're hauling gas: Giant oil tankers get about 31 feet per gallon.

On a package of prawn-flavored crackers: Once you have opened the packing it will be entirely impossible for you to suppress the desire to overcome such exciting challenge of your tongue. However, don't be disappointed with your repeated failure, you may continue with your habit.

In a Honda repair manual: No touching earth wire, fatal eventuarity may incur.

On a toothbrush box: Gives you strong mouth and refreshing wind!

On a package of bath salts: Humanity are fighting against tired. Charley support you.

On a washing machine: Push button. Foam coming plenty. Big Noise. Finish.

On the front of a datebook: Have a smell of panda droppings. This one is very fragrant.

On children's play microphone: Mom ma! Pap Pap! I and Lady Employees to play with it together!

On a photo developing envelope: Takes the thirst out of everyday time. A pure whiff of oxygen, painting over a monochrome world in primary colors. We all know that. It's why everyone loves fruit.

*   *   *

THE WRITING'S ON THE WALL

In Pompeii, the walls of every building were used as billboards on which anyone was allowed to write whatever they wanted. When the buried city was excavated, archaeologists found notices of upcoming plays at the theater, the schedule of games at the stadium, the price of goods in the market, and the comments of passersby. One message declared, "Everybody writes on walls but me."

The elections in Pompeii were coming up when the city was destroyed, so thousands of political ads were found, including this one: "Vote for Vatia, who is recommended by sneak thieves, the whole company of late drinkers, and everyone who is fast asleep."

Pigeons have three sets of eyelids.

THEY ALWAYS GET THEIR MAN

For people who grew up on John Wayne movies, where the cavalry always fought the Indians, this may be hard to believe, but Canada's cavalry, the Royal Canadian Mounted Police, was actually started to protect the Native Americans. Here's the story.

THE WESTERN FRONTIER

Canada only became an independent nation in 1867. After the American Civil War, the British colonies that now form Canada viewed the U.S. as a potential threat: America was a powerful nation, equipped with the tools of war and possibly willing to use them to annex Canada. Already, several fur-trading forts had been established in Western Canada and some were even flying flags that resembled the American flag. These traders posed a real threat to Canadian sovereignty, because the prairie border was not firmly established or enforced at that time. For their own protection, the colonies banded together as a single Dominion of the British Crown.

The newly formed Canadian government knew it needed a national police force to maintain friendly relations with Native American tribes and to maintain the borders at the Western territories. But there were other pressing matters, so the organization of such a police force was repeatedly postponed.

CYPRESS HILLS MASSACRE

In May 1873, a group of hunters from Fort Benton, Montana, crossed the Canadian border in search of animal pelts. One night while they slept, a band of thieves invaded their camp and stole their horses. When the hunters awoke, they were furious. They followed the tracks to the Cypress Hills in Saskatchewan and confronted a local tribe, the Assiniboine. The tribe didn't have the horses, but the hunters wanted revenge and cared little who paid for it. They raped the Assiniboine women and massacred most of the tribe.

When news of the Cypress Hills Massacre reached the east, government officials were appalled. Organizing a police force to patrol the western territories immediately became the Dominion's top priority.

UPHOLD THE RIGHT

The government sought an educated group of men with "good moral character." By September, the recruits, called the North West Mounted Police, or "Mounties" for short, totaled 300 men. Mounted on horseback and wearing scarlet coats that mimicked the uniforms of British soldiers, the new force was stationed throughout western Canada. Their primary job: To stop Americans from slaughtering game and selling whiskey to native tribes.

By protecting the First Peoples (as the native tribes are now known) from U.S. poachers and expansionists, the Mounties quickly became friends with the Canadian Indians. In fact, by the early 1890s, there was almost no need for a mounted police force. Then gold was discovered in the Yukon.

By 1899 thousands of Canadian and U.S. citizens had invaded the Yukon in search of gold. The Mounties dispatched 250 officers to the Yukon to keep the peace and again protect Canadian sovereignty. American prospectors returning home told stories of the courageous officers on horseback who managed the potentially explosive situation with an iron fist. The romantic image appealed to newspapers, which, in turn, inspired Hollywood. Then came "Sergeant Preston of the Yukon" on radio, in comic books, and on television. The Mounties had become a Canadian icon.

MAY THE FORCE BE WITH YOU

• The Royal Canadian Mounted Police aren't mounted anymore, and they haven't been since 1966, when routine equestrian training was abandoned.

• Mounties are still issued the traditional scarlet jacket, blue jodhpur pants with gold stripes, and brown Mountie hat. But they only wear them on ceremonial occasions; most of the time they just wear standard police uniforms.

• "We always get our man" is not the RCMP motto and never has been. The phrase was invented in 1877 by an American reporter. Their real motto: "Maintain the Right."

• For that matter, Mounties don't even call themselves "Mounties." They prefer to think of themselves as "the Force."

8 streams, 9 colleges, 10 lakes, 33 counties, and 121 towns across the world.

DOG DOO! GOOD GOD!

Palindromes are phrases or sentences that are spelled the same way backward and forward. Who comes up with these things? Don't they have jobs...or families...or any other way to spend their time? Well, whether they're weird or not, we're hooked. Here are some of Uncle John's favorites.

Ana, nab a banana.

Campus motto: Bottoms up, Mac!

Dog doo! Good God!

No, Mel Gibson is a casino's big lemon.

Pasadena, Ned—ASAP!

Straw? No, too stupid a fad. I put soot on warts.

Too far, Edna, we wander afoot

He lived as a devil, eh?

Pull up, Eva, we're here! Wave! Pull up!

I saw desserts; I'd no lemons, alas no melon. Distressed was I.

Marge lets Norah see Sharon's telegram.

Ned, go gag Ogden.

No evil Shahs live on.

No lemons, no melon.

Now, sir, a war is won!

A dog! A panic in a pagoda!

Star? Come, Donna Melba, I'm an amiable man— no Democrats!

Step on hose-pipes? Oh no, pets.

Too bad, I hid a boot.

Was it a rat I saw?

We'll let Dad tell Lew.

Kay, a red nude, peeped under a yak.

Yawn. Madonna fan? No damn way.

Red rum, sir, is murder.

Don't nod.

Some men interpret nine memos.

Dammit, I'm mad!

Ed, I saw Harpo Marx ram Oprah W. aside.

Evil I did dwell, lewd did I live.

Gert, I saw Ron avoid a radio-van—or was it Reg?

Lew, Otto has a hot towel!

Lonely Tylenol.

O, stone, be not so.

Re-paper.

So, G. Rivera's tots are Virgos.

Too hot to hoot.

Was it Eliot's toilet I saw?

In 1939 Gerald Ford appeared in *Look* magazine, modeling ski clothing.

FAMILY FEUD

Here's an example of what happens when families are more interested in money and power than they are in each other.

CULKIN VS. CULKIN

The Contestants: Child actor Macaulay Culkin, his father and onetime manager, Kit Culkin, and his mother, Patricia Brentrup.

The Feud: Culkin and Brentrup and their seven children were living in a one-room tenement when Macaulay was cast in the 1990 film *Home Alone*. Nine-year-old Macaulay suddenly found himself the biggest Hollywood child star since Shirley Temple.

"Big Mac" made only $100,000 on *Home Alone*, but made $27 million on *Home Alone 2* and went on to command huge salaries in the other roles his father chose for him. But nearly all the films that followed (*The Pagemaster*, *Getting Even with Dad*, and *Richie Rich*) were flops, and Kit Culken, "universally reviled as the stage father from hell," had burned his bridges with just about every director in Hollywood. Not that it really mattered: by 1995 the 14-year-old Macauley was so burned out—having made 14 films in less than 10 years—that he told his parents he was through with movies. "I'd been wanting to stop since I was about eleven," he says.

As if his career problems weren't enough, Macaulay's parents split up and began a long and ugly battle for custody of the children, which included control of Macaulay's estimated $50 million in assets. Brentrup accused Kit Culkin of punching her when she was pregnant and threatening to toss her off a balcony; he accused her of being an adulterous drunk who neglected her children. Brentrup eventually won custody of the kids, and in 1997 a judge awarded oversight of Macaulay's assets to his accountant.

And the Winner Is: Macaulay, sort of: He still has plenty of cash in the bank, and after a four-year break from acting, landed the lead in a play in London's West End. As of October 2000, he and his father had not seen or spoken to each other for nearly four years. "Hopefully someday he'll realize some of the things he's done," Culkin says. "But I understand my parents put me in the financial position where I am today, and I'm grateful for that."

Male monkeys go bald just like men.

MYTH-CONCEPTIONS

*"Common knowledge" is frequently wrong. Here are
some examples of things that many people believe...
but that according to our sources, just aren't true.*

Myth: "Give me a home where the buffalo roam, and the
deer and the antelope play..."
Fact: There are no antelope in North America. The animal the song probably refers to is the pronghorn, which resembles an antelope. Real antelope only live in Asia and Africa.

Myth: The forbidden fruit eaten by Eve was an apple.
Fact: The Bible makes reference to the "fruit of the tree" (Genesis 3:3), but names no particular fruit. Horticulturists say that apple trees have never grown in the area where the Garden of Eden supposedly existed. She probably ate a pomegranate.

Myth: Blood is red.
Fact: This is only true part of the time. Blood is red in arteries because it is loaded with oxygen. After the oxygen is used up, blood travels through veins back to the heart and is usually a purplish-blue. When the blood in a vein hits the air because of a cut, it instantly oxidizes and turns red again.

Myth: Hunger is triggered by an empty stomach.
Fact: Hunger is set off when nutrients are absent in the bloodstream. In response to this, the brain begins rhythmic contractions of the stomach and intestines, which causes stomach grumbling and the feeling of hunger.

Myth: A limb "falls asleep" because its blood supply gets cut off.
Fact: This feeling of numbness—called *neurapraxia*—happens when a major nerve is pinched against a hard object or bone. This causes the harmless temporary sensation of numbness, but the blood continues to flow normally.

Myth: Pandas are bears.
Fact: The panda is an extremely large cousin of the raccoon.

Homebodies: 75% of migrating robins will return to within 5 miles of where they lived before.

MAKING HIS MARK

*Sometimes being in the right place at the right time makes
all the difference. Here's a great story submitted by
our official BRI coincidencologist, Janet Spencer.
(See if you can guess the surprise ending.)*

A YOUNG WRITER'S BIG BREAK

In 1866, the clipper ship *Hornet* was sailing from California to New York with a cargo of kerosene and candles. A thousand miles from land and 108 days into the voyage, a careless sailor accidentally set the cargo on fire. The 33 men abandoned the ship in three life boats, each with a 10-day supply of rations. They drifted apart, and two of the lifeboats were never seen again. The third one, piloted by the captain floated 4,000 miles in 43 days until it landed safely in Hawaii.

A correspondent for a California newspaper was in Hawaii at the time, and went to the hospital to interview the men. He worked on the story all night and sent the article out on a California-bound ship the next day. His account was the first detailed report to reach the mainland—and it was a scoop. He was paid an astounding $300 bonus for it. On his return trip to California, he found that two of his fellow shipmates were survivors of the *Hornet*. He interviewed them and compiled an even more detailed article. The prestigious magazine *Harper's Monthly* purchased it.

OR WAS IT?

The writer expected to achieve instant fame and worldwide name recognition with the article's publication. Unfortunately, *Harper's* goofed—they misprinted his name. The correspondent was Samuel Clemens using his pen name, Mark Twain. But *Harper's* listed the author as "Mac Swain." Twain's dreams of fame were dashed. "I was not celebrated," Twain later lamented, "I was a Literary Person, but that was all—a buried one; buried alive."

Not quite. Within months of the Harper's debacle, Clemens' short story "The Celebrated Jumping Frog of Calaveras County" became a national hit. This time, the publisher got his name right—and Mark Twain became a star.

U.S. city with the highest percentage of cell phone users: Anchorage, Alaska, with 56%.

NAME A FAMOUS JOHN

Where do game shows go when they die? It's called the Game Show Network, and it's where you can catch reruns of the Family Feud. (No cable? Don't fret—there's a new version of the Feud in syndication.)

LET'S START THE FAMILY FEUD!

In 1976, game show guru Mark Goodson (*The Price Is Right, Concentration, Password, I've Got a Secret*) had an inspiration. One segment of another of his hits, *Match Game*, featured an Audience Match round, in which a panelist—usually Richard Dawson—and a contestant tried to match responses to an audience survey. The segment was so popular that Goodson decided to spin it off as a regular show, starring Dawson as host.

Richard Dawson was a British comedian who got his first big break in 1965 playing "Newkirk" on the classic TV sitcom *Hogan's Heroes*. When the show was cancelled in 1971, he landed a gig on *Rowan & Martin's Laugh-In*, and when that show died he went on to *Match Game 73*. Then came the *Feud*.

MATCH THIS

Family Feud premiered on ABC on July 12, 1976 and quickly surpassed *Match Game* as the top-rated daytime game show, even winning an Emmy Award. And Dawson's easygoing manner, sharp wit, and style were central to the show's success. He kissed every female contestant, joked with the families and with the camera, and did it with such style that audiences couldn't help but like him. The show became so popular that Goodson created a primetime version, featuring popular celebrities feuding for charity. And that show was so popular that he expanded it from one night a week in 1977 to two nights a week in 1979 to five nights a week in 1980. At its peak, the *Feud* with Dawson appeared 15 times per week.

But fame went to Dawson's head. Behind the scenes he was not so easygoing. He fought constantly with the *Family Feud* and *Match Game* staffs. On *Match Game*, he stopped making jokes and even refused to smile on camera. Frustrated producers were happy to let him out of his contract when he left in 1978.

Bank robber John Dillinger used Ford cars exclusively for his getaway vehicles.

But Dawson stayed with the *Feud*, and the *Feud* stayed on top, maintaining its #1 status for years. Then, in 1983, it was eclipsed by a new show, *Wheel of Fortune*, and that was the beginning of the end. The nighttime *Family Feud* was cancelled in 1984; the daytime *Feud* was cancelled a year later. Dawson's career pretty much ended, too. His reputation for being difficult preceded him, and work was hard to find. But his rep did help him land one part: that of the evil game show host Damon Killian in the 1987 Arnold Schwarzenegger's film *The Running Man*.

NEW LEASE ON LIFE

In 1988 Mark Goodson talked CBS into reviving the *Feud*. It was the same old show, with a new host—Ray Combs, a furniture salesman turned stand-up comic. Then Goodson freshened it up by renaming it *Family Feud Challenge*, lengthening it to one hour, and adding some new features. Combs was no Dawson, but the show continued to do reasonably well until 1992, when Goodson died and ratings started to slip.

Goodson had once remarked that while he was alive, Dawson would never work with his company again, but his son, Jonathan, was desperately looking for a way to save the *Feud*. In 1994 he fired Ray Combs and asked Dawson, now 62, to return as host. It didn't help—bringing back the veteran wasn't enough to save the show, and it was cancelled a year later.

I WANT MY *FAMILY FEUD!*

Family Feud was off the air for four years. In 1997 the British conglomerate Pearson Television acquired the U.S. syndication company All American Communications, which owned the Goodson library of game show formats. Now the Brits owned the show, and they decided to bring it back once again. They needed a warm and friendly host who could work well with families. After looking at lots of options, they chose another stand-up comic, Louie Anderson. According to Tony Cohen, Pearson president, "Louie appeals to that kind of Middle American audience which we think is the *Family Feud* heartland."

In September 1999, Anderson took the helm. The revamped set, new theme music, and dollar amounts aside, the *Feud* today is played pretty much the same as it always has been. The show with

Anderson gets consistently high ratings.

One Final Note: What happened to Ray Combs? In 1993 his 18-year marriage collapsed. Two years later, he was involved in a serious car crash, which left him partially paralyzed. He had earned $800,000 per year for his six-year stint as host of *Family Feud*, but the money was gone. In 1995 he finally landed another game show—a *Double Dare* wannabe called *Ray Combs' Family Challenge*—but it lasted only six months. In 1996, out of work, alone, and destitute, the 40-year-old Combs committed suicide.

FEUD FACTS

• The original *Feud* theme song was actually a *Price Is Right* new-car song, redone with banjos.

• In 1981 a 27-year-old *Feud* contestant, Gretchen Johnson, received more than a kiss from Dawson: the couple had a child and married 10 years later.

• Given serious consideration for *Family Feud* host: Dolly Parton.

• Louie Anderson was the victim of extortion after he allegedly propositioned a man named Richard Gordon at a California casino in 1993. Anderson reportedly agreed to pay the man $100,000 in hush money, fearing for his career. But Gordon upped the ante to $250,000, so Anderson went to the police. Gordon was convicted of extortion and sentenced to 21 months in a federal penitentiary.

*   *   *

SIGHT FOR SOAR EYES

Mr. See and Mr. Soar were old friends. See owned a saw and Soar owned a seesaw. Now, See's saw sawed Soar's seesaw before Soar saw See, which made Soar sore. Had Soar seen See's saw before See saw Soar's seesaw, then See's saw would not have sawed Soar's seesaw. But See saw Soar and Soar's seesaw before Soar saw See's saw, so See's saw sawed Soar's seesaw. It was a shame to let See see Soar so sore just because See's saw sawed Soar's seesaw.

SURVEY SAYS...

Remember the Fast Money round on Family Feud? *Answers come easily when you're sitting on your sofa...but imagine the pressure you'd feel on national television. You might even say something stupid.*

Q: Name a fruit that is yellow.
A: Orange.

Q: Name something that floats in the bath.
A: Water.

Q: Name a famous cowboy.
A: Buck Rogers.

Q: A number you have to memorize.
A: Seven.

Q: Name a part of the body beginning with "N."
A: Knee.

Q: Something you do before going to bed.
A: Sleep.

Q: Name a bird with a long neck.
A: Naomi Campbell.

Q: Name something with a hole in it.
A: Window.

Q: Name a sign of the zodiac.
A: April.

Q: Name something you might accidentally leave on all night.
A: Your shoes.

Q: Name a holiday when the stores are always busy.
A: Monday.

Q: Name something some people do clothed that others do without clothes.
A: Ride a motorcycle

Q: Name something you do in the bathroom.
A: Decorate.

Q: Name the first thing you take off after work.
A: Underwear.

Q: Something that flies that doesn't have an engine.
A: A bicycle with wings.

Q: Name an occupation where you need a torch.
A: A burglar.

Q: Name an animal you might see in the zoo.
A: A dog.

Q: A job around the house that has to be done every fall.
A: Spring cleaning.

Q: Something you might be allergic to.
A: Skiing.

Q: Name a famous bridge.
A: The bridge over troubled waters.

Q: Name something a cat does.
A: Goes to the toilet.

Q: Name a song with moon in the title.
A: Blue suede moon.

Q: Name an item of clothing worn by the three Musketeers.
A: A horse.

Q: Name a famous group of singers.
A: The Simpsons.

Two countries are actually smaller than New York's Central Park: Monaco and Vatican City.

THE SAGE OF ATHENS

*Thoughts and observations from the ancient
Greek philosopher, Socrates.*

"The only good is knowledge and the only evil ignorance."

"Let him that would move the world first move himself."

"What you cannot enforce, do not command."

"Remember that there is nothing stable in human affairs; therefore avoid undue elation in prosperity, or undue depression in adversity."

"He who is not contented with what he has, would not be contented with what he would like to have."

"The unexamined life is not worth living."

"I know I am intelligent, because I know that I know nothing."

"Wisdom begins in wonder."

"Beauty is a short-lived tyranny."

"To do is to be."

"The way to gain a good reputation is to endeavor to be what you desire to appear."

"Fame is the perfume of heroic deeds."

"From the deepest desires often come the deadliest hate."

"If all our misfortunes were laid in one common heap, whence everyone must take an equal portion, most people would be content to take their own and depart."

"Nothing is preferred before justice."

"Better do a little well, than a great deal badly."

"As to marriage or celibacy, let a man take the course he will. He will be sure to repent."

"Life contains but two tragedies. One is not to get your heart's desire; the other is to get it."

GENUINE FAKE: LINCOLN'S LOG CABIN

*This is the story of Lincoln's birthplace—built 30 years after his death!
It comes from one of our favorite books,* Lies Across America:
What Our Historic Sites Get Wrong, *by James W. Loewen.*

ONE CABIN IS AS GOOD AS ANOTHER
Thomas Lincoln bought Sinking Spring Farm near Hodgenville, Kentucky, in December 1808. His son Abraham was born in a small cabin on the farm on February 12, 1809. A little more than two years later the family moved to another farm 10 miles away. By the time Lincoln was assassinated, according to three different people who visited the farm looking for it, the cabin had disappeared. Either it had fallen into ruin or nearby farmers had recycled its logs into their buildings.

In 1895 New York entrepreneur Alfred Dennett bought Sinking Spring Farm and instructed his agent, James Bigham, to build a log cabin on it, according to National Park Service historian Dwight Pitcaithley. Bigham bought a two-story cabin from a neighboring farm and used the best of its logs to build a cabin on the Lincoln farm. Dennett then widely circulated photographs of this new cabin, which he tried to pass off as the actual cabin in which Lincoln was born.

"Lincoln was born in a log cabin, weren't he?" said Bigham, defending himself to a skeptical newspaperman. "Well, one cabin is as good as another!"

SOME ASSEMBLY REQUIRED
Despite Bigham's efforts, few made the trek to rural Hodgenville to see the "historic" structure. Undaunted, Dennett and Bigham decided to take the cabin to the people, so they took it apart and reassembled it at the Tennessee Centennial Exposition in Nashville in 1897. To make the exhibit even better they bought another old log cabin and proclaimed it the birthplace of Jefferson Davis!

Next the cabins traveled to the 1901 Pan-American Exposition in Buffalo, where they found themselves between "Bonner, the Edu-

---

Shut up! Giraffes have no vocal chords. How do they communicate? With their tails.

cated Horse" and Esau, a trained chimpanzee billed as the "Missing Link." As an added feature, 150 African-Americans billed as "Old Uncles and Aunties, formerly slaves," were on display "living in the genuine cabins in which Abraham Lincoln and Jefferson Davis were born."

Then the cottages went to Coney Island, where the "Lincoln cabin" was to become an attraction. "But alas," as Pitcaithley puts it, "during the journey to Coney Island, the logs of the cabins became intermingled." So it became much larger and was briefly known as the "Lincoln and Davis Cabin!"

BRING ON THE LAWYERS

Meanwhile Robert Collier, publisher of *Collier's Weekly*, acquired the farm in Hodgenville, set up a Lincoln Farm Association, bought the logs for $1,000, and shipped them to Kentucky. The train stopped in major cities along the way to let people touch the logs. The Association then selected architect John Russell Pope to design a memorial building in which to enshrine the reassembled cabin and engaged lawyers to produce affidavits from three residents that claimed the cabin was authentic. (No one now believes these affidavits, collected a century after the original cabin's construction.)

The logs arrived in Louisville in June 1906, and the cabin was built in a local park. Because its logs were originally from two cabins it was twice as large as might be expected, in the tradition of the "Lincoln and Davis Cabin." Nevertheless, it was so popular that an armed guard had to be posted to stop visitors from taking pieces off it as souvenirs. After just a week it was dismantled for safekeeping.

PRESIDENTIAL SEAL

Three years later the association used some of the logs to reerect the cabin, now back to solo cabin size, at Hodgenville for the centennial of Lincoln's birth in 1909. President Theodore Roosevelt came to lay the cornerstone for the Greek temple that Pope had designed to house it.

"The crude log cabin in which Lincoln was born in Hodgenville, Kentucky, is a symbol of his bonds with the common people, and it has come to mean to them as Americans what the humble stable in Bethlehem means to them as Christians," Roosevelt proclaimed. "But just as the world's faithful have sanctified the birthplace of

Abraham Lincoln was the first president to wear a beard in office.

Christ by housing it within an impressive Church of the Nativity, so the American people have ennobled the birthplace of Lincoln by housing it within a marble Temple of Fame."

When the temple was finished in 1911 however, it was too small to let visitors move easily around the outside of the cabin. Rather than enlarge the temple, Pope shrank the cabin! He took a couple of feet off its length and three or four feet from its width. Now just 12 by 17 feet, it fits fine. It also fits well with the nation's ideological needs. Americans want to believe in the "log cabin myth," and the tinier the cabin, the bigger the myth. Now the site offers the ultimate expression on the landscape of the "rags to riches" story that Lincoln's life exemplifies: the cabin is even smaller than the one in which he was born, and the Greek marble-and-granite temple makes a grander effect even than the White House to which he rose. Also, the 56 imposing steps—one for each year of his life—symbolize Lincoln's upward mobility.

THE STAMP OF POVERTY

Harold Holzer, writing in *The New York Times*, confirmed the power of the two structures in combination: "The shrine's almost oppressive formality cannot mask the rawness and shockingly tiny size of the airless, one-room cabin it contains. Picturing a family living in such a place tests the imagination, and touches the heart." But Lincoln's own son Robert Todd Lincoln discouraged preserving the cabin, complaining that it falsely bore the "stamp of poverty" when in fact the Lincolns owned two farms, livestock, and a lot in nearby Elizabethtown.

For a time the Park Service was fairly forthright about the building it presents at Hodgenville. Now it pretends the cabin is real, even admonishing visitors not to use flash cameras—as if their light could damage logs that have seen so many journeys. The National Park Service labels the little building "Traditional Lincoln Birthplace Cabin," which gives "traditional" a new definition: "hoax over time."

THE POWER OF THE ICON

Long ago, a lad at the University of Wisconsin answered a class assignment for Prof. Helen White with the blooper, "Abraham Lincoln was born in a log cabin which he built with his own hands." The reality is even sillier: Abraham Lincoln had been dead 30 years when his birthplace cabin was built!

The geodesic dome is the only structure that becomes stronger as it increases in size.

Even more bizarre, Americans have built more birthplace cabins for him ever since—in Fort Wayne, Indiana; in heiress Mary Forbes's backyard in Milton, Massachusetts—indeed, upon request the National Park Service will send you a handout so you can build one in your backyard!

Beginning in 1920, children built miniature replicas all across the country. In that year John Lloyd Wright, son of Frank, invented Lincoln Logs, named after these logs in Kentucky. Lincoln Logs originally came with instructions on how to build Uncle Tom's cabin as well as Lincoln's log cabin! The power of the icon is uncanny: Americans seem to need this structure, so we copy and cherish it even though it is fake.

*   *   *

ON SECOND THOUGHT...

"I share your view that the urgent problem of species extinction and the conservation of biological diversity should be addressed. The first step in saving any plant or animal from extinction is to become aware of and respect the fragile ecosystems that make up our environment."
—Vice president Al Gore, in 1996, in a letter to a Dallas couple who complained about the elimination of the "Texas Eagle." Gore didn't realize the "Texas Eagle" was an Amtrak train connecting Dallas to Chicago and the West Coast

"You know, I once played Grover Cleveland in the movies."
—Ronald Reagan, 1981, commenting on House Speaker Tip O'Neill's desk, which had belonged to President Cleveland. Reagan had actually played Grover Cleveland Alexander, the baseball player

"An island of stability."
—President Jimmy Carter, 1979, describing the Shah of Iran, a few months before the Shah was overthrown

"The fire of an election no longer burns in me."
—Arkansas Governor Bill Clinton, 1990, explaining why he would not run again

The common housefly can carry more than 25 different diseases.

UNCLE JOHN'S BOTTOM 10 RECORDS

If cream rises to the top, what sinks to the bottom? These do: records so bad, they're good. Here's this year's official BRI count-down—and we do mean down. They don't sink any lower...

10. EILERT PILARM: Greatest Hits. Anyone who's expecting this Swedish Elvis impersonator to resemble the King will be very disappointed. Wearing white leather and rhinestones, he comes across like somebody's Uncle Olaf after a drunken weekend in Vegas. His singing sounds as if he hit puberty around age 60. Our favorite: "Yailhouse Rock."

9. MAE WEST: Way Out West. Is that an electric guitar in your pocket, or are you just glad to see me? On this 1969 album, the then-70-year-old former sex symbol tries to prove she's still relevant by talking her way through rock classics like "Day Tripper" and "Twist and Shout."

8. PADDY ROBERTS: Songs for Gay Dogs. Roberts sings about the sex life of fish in "Virgin Sturgeon" and serves up a steaming pile of potty humor with "Don't Use the WC," a song about dirty bathrooms. It's not just in bad taste—it's bad. By the way, this LP has nothing to do with Spot's alternative lifestyle. So what does the title mean? Well, most of the songs are drinking songs—maybe he was under the influence when he picked it.

7. SAMMY PETRILLO: My Son, the Phone Caller. Petrillo was an awful Jerry Lewis impersonator who starred in a few el cheapo flicks, including the memorable *Bela Lugosi Meets a Brooklyn Gorilla.* This album features him doing moronic phone pranks like calling hospitals and saying that he's got a pregnant pet gorilla in labor, then asking how to deliver the baby.

6. THE NATIONAL GALLERY: Performing Musical Interpretations of the Paintings of Paul Klee. Four beatniks from Cleveland introduce us to the German Expressionist painter by

---

Number of "real" haunted houses in the U.S., according to the Ghost Research Society: 789.

performing "rock-art" song versions of his paintings. Complete with acid-drenched lyrics like "Boy with toys, alone in the attic / Choking his hobby horse, thinking of his mother."

5. HELEN GURLEY BROWN: *Lessons in Love.* The editor of *Cosmopolitan* magazine gives advice to swinging singles on the finer points of adultery. It may have been edgy back in 1963, but today it sounds like Martha Stewart reading *Affairs for Dummies.* Side 1 (for men) covers topics like "How to get a girl to the brink and…keep her there when you're not going to marry her."

4. LITTLE MARCY: *Little Marcy Visits Smokey the Bear.* A creepy singing ventriloquist's dummy visits Smokey and his animal pals in the woods. Part of an evangelical Christian children's act, Little Marcy had an eerie grin and a high-pitched singing voice that were probably responsible for frightening thousands of kids into becoming atheists.

3. MR. METHANE: *Mr. Methane.com.* The masked Mr. Methane is a "fartiste" in the style of Frenchman Le Petomaine. He breaks new wind by pooting his way through classics like "The Blue Danube," Beethoven's Ninth Symphony, and "Greensleeves," proving conclusively that he doesn't have to be silent to be deadly.

2. LUCIA PAMELA: *Into Outer Space with Lucia Pamela.* A former Miss St. Louis, Pamela claims she and her band flew to the moon in her own rocket ship to record this concept album about her trip to "Moontown." Sounding like an off-key Ethel Merman, she clucks like a chicken when she forgets the words.

1. MUHAMMAD ALI: *The Adventures of Ali and His Gang vs. Mr. Tooth Decay.* Recorded in 1976. Ali assembled an all-star bicentennial cast, including Frank Sinatra, Richie Havens, and Howard Cosell, for this "Fight of the Century" against Mr. Tooth Decay and his evil sidekick, Sugar Cuba. Old Blue Eyes sounds like he's working on his fifth martini as a shopkeeper who offers Ali's gang of hyperactive kids free ice cream. The Champ sends Frankie packing back to Vegas to "tell Sammy, and all them cats like old Dino" about the horrors of periodontal disease.

LUCKY FINDS

*Ever found something really valuable? It's one of the best
feelings in the world. Here's another installment of
a regular Bathroom Reader feature.*

A SHAKY PROSPECT

The Find: A dirty, moldy, wobbly old card table

Where It Was Found: At a lawn sale, for $25

The Story: In the late 1960s, a woman named Claire (no last
name—she prefers to remain anonymous) moved to a new house
and needed a small table for one of the rooms. She found one at a
yard sale but it was dirty and it wobbled; a friend advised against
buying it, telling her that "it would never hold a lamp." She
bought it anyway—after bargaining the price down from $30 to
$25, because that was all the money she had in her purse. When
she cleaned the table up, she noticed a label on the underside of it
that read "John Seymour & Son Cabinet Makers Creek Square
Boston." Claire did some research on it, but didn't learn a lot.

Nearly 30 years passed. Then in September 1997, Claire took
her table to a taping of the PBS series *Antiques Roadshow*. There
she learned that Seymour furniture is among the rarest and most
sought-after in the United States; until Claire's table showed up,
only five other pieces in original condition with the Seymour label
were known to exist. Claire thought the table might be worth
$20,000; the *Antiques Roadshow* appraiser put it at $300,000. Not
even close—the table sold at auction at Sotheby's for $490,000.
A pretty good price for a table that can't hold a lamp.

I YAM WHAT I YAM

The Find: A diamond

Where It Was Found: In Sierra Leone...under a yam

The Story: In 1997 three hungry boys were scrounging for food
near the village of Hinnah Malen in the African country of Sierra
Leone. The boys, orphaned since 1995 when their parents had
been killed in a rebel attack, had gone two days without food.
They spent three unsuccessful hours searching for yams that morning and were on their way home when their luck changed. They

found a yam under a palm tree and dug it up. Right under the yam they found a flawless 100-carat diamond. Estimated value: $500,000. "It was easy to see," according to the oldest boy, 14-year-old Morie Jah. "It was shining and sparkling."

NOT BAA-AA-AD

The Find: A lost Hindu shrine

Where It Was Found: In a cave in the Himalayas, in India

The Story: In September 2001, a shepherd named Ghulam Qadir lost some of his sheep and set out to look for them. He crawled into a small cave, thinking they might be there...but instead of his sheep, he found a 12-inch idol of the Hindu god Shiva. The cave turned out to be a 1,500-year-old shrine, one that had been forgotten and undisturbed for centuries. Government officials were so excited by the discovery that they have promised to pay Qadir 10% of the cash offerings left at the shrine from 2002 to 2007, followed by a large final payment when the five years are up. (He never did find his sheep.)

UNLUCKY FIND

The Find: A swastika and a pile of pornographic magazines

Where They Were Found: In a brand-new Jaguar automobile—the magazines were stuffed into an interior cavity; the swastika was painted underneath a seat panel.

The Story: The discovery was made accidentally when the car was being taken apart for bomb-proofing, because this car happened to be purchased by Queen Elizabeth. The magazines and the swastika were put there during assembly by an autoworker who had no idea of the car's final destination. "It is one of those old traditions where people used to write things behind the seat panel of cars and they were never discovered unless there was an accident," another factory worker told the British newspaper *The Guardian*, "only this time it wasn't funny."

Update: The worker responsible for the "factory extras" lost his job over the incident...but that probably won't stop the practice of hiding things in new cars. "The chaps go to an awful lot of trouble to do the car," says the Jaguar employee. "They're there all day. What else have they got to do?"

HERE'S LOOKING AT YOU

It's easy to forget that just 160 years ago, most people lived and died without leaving a single visual record of themselves for posterity. Here's how photography began to change that.

NO-MAN'S-LAND
In 1837 Louis Daguerre discovered how to create a lasting detailed photographic image. Within months of the groundbreaking publication of his photographic process in 1839, people started taking cameras to Greece, to the Middle East, to Africa, to Central and South America, and to every other corner of the world to photograph the wonders they saw there.

But if you look at these early photographs, you'll notice that no matter what the scene, there's always one thing missing from the picture: *people*. These first photographs appear barren and empty, completely devoid of human or even animal life. It's as if each had been taken in a ghost town.

STILL SHOTS
It turns out that there were plenty of people in these scenes when the pictures were taken; they just can't be seen because they were *moving*. The early photosensitive chemicals took so long to form an image—30 minutes on a sunny day, an hour or more when it was cloudy—that pedestrians and street traffic passed in and out of the picture without registering.

The American inventor Samuel Morse noted this when he was invited to look at some of Daguerre's first photographs in 1839. One daguerreotype was a view of a busy Paris street, taken in the middle of the day when there must have been hundreds of people out. Only one person—quite possibly the first ever to be captured on film—was visible in the picture, and this only because he had been standing relatively still. Morse wrote to his brother:

> Moving objects leave no impression. The boulevard, though constantly crossed by a flood of pedestrians and carriages, appeared completely deserted, apart from a person who was having his boots polished. His feet, must of course, have remained immobile for a certain time, one of them being placed on the boot-black's box, the other on the ground.

A hippo's stomach is 10 ft. long and can hold 400 lb. of food.

FACE TIME

The irony was that people living in the late 1830s and early 1840s wanted pictures of themselves and their loved ones more than any other photographic subject. Mortality rates were much higher then, and the pain of a death in the family was made worse by the fact that families frequently had no images of the deceased to remember them by. Only the wealthy were able to commission portraits of themselves. Now photography, with its promise of "automatic" portraits, seemed to offer the possibility of making portraiture available to everyone.

Understanding this need, photographers started looking for ways to take photographic portraits. They located their studios in rooftop glass houses to maximize available sunlight; they crammed those studios with mirrors to bring in even more light. They even filtered the sunlight through blue glass or bottles of blue liquid to take advantage of the fact that early photographic plates were especially sensitive to blue light. (Remember, the lightbulb wasn't invented until 1879.)

SAY "CHEEEEEESE"

Even with all of these measures, exposure times remained quite long—20 minutes or more—leaving the aspiring portraitist little choice but to resort to desperate measures. Since there was no easy way to stare at a fixed point in space for such a long time, many photographers instructed their subjects to pose with their eyes closed...and that was just the beginning: "Paint the face of the patient dead white," one daguerreotypist advised in 1839. "Powder his hair, and fix the back of his head between two planks attached to the back of an armchair and wound up with screws."

Posing for a portrait in such a studio was almost unbearable, something akin to having your picture taken inside a hot car with the windows rolled up and your head in a vise. The heat trapped by all that glass sent the temperature soaring, and the light from the mirrors was blinding. Looking "natural" under these conditions—sweating profusely, eyes squinting or closed, hair powdered, face painted white, head held immobile by boards while sitting perfectly still for 20 minutes or more—was just about impossible. Even when the pictures did come out, they were usually disappointing.

The U.S. has almost 4 million miles of roads and streets.

NEW AND IMPROVED

Fortunately, the first major improvements in daguerreotype photography came quickly. In 1840 Hungarian mathematician Jozsef Max Petzval invented a lens that let 22 times more light into the camera, reducing exposure times from 40 minutes to $2\frac{1}{2}$ minutes. That same year, English scientist John Frederick Goddard discovered that exposing daguerreotype plates to bromine vapors increased their photosensitivity, further shortening exposures to under a minute.

So what does Daguerre's process have to do with the modern photograph? Almost nothing. Daguerre became world famous, but his process was flawed—it only resulted in a single unique image. Daguerreotypes couldn't be reproduced, and ultimately the process fell into disuse.

The true father of modern photography was English physicist William Henry Fox Talbot. In a sense, what Talbot did was invent the negative—a reverse image on photosensitive paper that could be used to make any number of positive prints, or "calotypes" as they came to be called. Talbot invented his process in 1835, but never published his findings or patented his original process. So when Daguerre came along two years later, he got all the credit for inventing photography. It turns out that Daguerre wasn't just smart, he was also very lucky.

OPEN FOR BUSINESS

In 1840, a photographer named Alexander Wolcot opened America's first portrait studio in New York City; the following year a coal merchant named Richard Beard opened one in London. The "nobility and beauty of England" were soon flocking to his studio to have their pictures taken; by 1842 he was making as much as £35,000 a year (in today's currency, £1,820,400, or $2,653,415) .

Other studios soon sprang up in the major cities of Europe and the United States. By the late 1840s, nearly every city in the U.S. had a "daguerrean artist," and smaller towns were served by itinerant photographers traveling by wagon. Photography was starting to realize its promise.

Click to page 348 for the next part of the story.

Julius Caesar wore a laurel wreath crown to hide the fact that he was balding.

TESTOPHOBIC?

Do you have testophobia, the fear of taking tests? If you don't, then test your skills at the meanings of these other fears. They're 100% real.

1. coulrophobia
2. phalacrophobia
3. automatonophobia
4. liticaphobia
5. myxophobia
6. geniophobia
7. cacophobia
8. atychiphobia
9. selenophobia
10. coprastasophobia
11. phobophobia
12. Francophobia
13. didaskaleinophobia
14. caligynephobia
15. arachibutyrophobia
16. decidophobia
17. automysophobia

A. failure
B. slime
C. making decisions
D. France
E. the moon
F. ventriloquist dummies
G. beautiful women
H. lawsuits
I. clowns
J. phobias
K. being dirty
L. becoming bald
M. school
N. ugliness
O. constipation
P. chins
Q. peanut butter sticking to the roof of your mouth

Answers:

1-I; 2-L; 3-F; 4-H; 5-B; 6-P; 7-N; 8-A; 9-E; 10-O; 11-J; 12-D; 13-M; 14-G; 15-Q; 16-C; 17-K.

The enamel on a human tooth is only 1/1,000th of an inch thick.

THE ORIGIN OF SOAP OPERAS

Soaps—you either love 'em or hate 'em. Either way,
you might be interested to learn where they come from.

SOAP DUD

In the early 1930s, Richard Deupree, the president of Procter & Gamble, had to make one of the most important and most difficult decisions in the history of the company: Should they continue to advertise their products, even though the country was suffering through the Great Depression?

Times were tough. Financially strapped customers were defecting to cheaper brands, forcing P&G to introduce less profitable "price brands." But for all the good that did, P&G's sales still dropped 28% in 1933, and the price of their stock fell more than 70%.

What was the point of advertising when customers (not to mention the company) were going through such hard times? Maybe it made more sense to conserve cash and wait for things to improve. A lot of the company's shareholders argued that Procter & Gamble should do just that, but Deupree had other ideas.

GOTTA HAVE IT

Deupree noticed that despite the Depression, some companies were actually prospering. The Fuller Brush Company, famous for selling its line of household brushes door-to-door, was thriving; so were many other companies that sold basic household necessities. And as crazy as it sounded, people were still buying radios even though they were a luxury. What on Earth were people doing buying luxury items in the middle of a depression?

Deupree concluded that no matter how much people had to cut back on their household expenses, some items—like soap—were so essential that families would not go without them. And if they really *wanted* something—like a radio—they were willing to scrimp and save their pennies for as long as it took to get one.

If people were going to spend money on things they needed or

Elephant tusks continue to grow as long as the animal lives.

wanted, Deupree figured that Procter & Gamble had no choice but to advertise…or lose business to competitors that did.

ON THE AIR

And since the number of households with radios was increasing, Deupree believed P&G should continue experimenting with the new medium.

Radio broadcasting was barely a decade old—KDKA, the country's first commercial radio station, had only been broadcasting since November 1920. During the day, audiences were smaller because husbands were at work and children were at school. Those few daytime shows that did exist, such as *Live Stock Reports*, *Our Daily Food*, and *Mouth Hygiene*, didn't attract very large audiences. Most broadcasters focused on providing evening programming, when everyone could listen.

Procter & Gamble was one of the first companies to realize that housewives working at home during the day represented a huge and potentially lucrative listening audience for the products it sold.

Remember, this was the era when most household chores had to be done by hand—few homes had washing machines or automatic dishwashers, and nearly all cooking was done from scratch. After a housewife finished preparing breakfast for her family and doing the dishes, she might spend hours washing clothes by hand with bar soap and a washboard; when she finished, she spent what was left of the afternoon cleaning the house or doing other chores. Then she prepared dinner; after that she did the dishes. Each day was filled with hours and hours of backbreaking, tedious work, and there was little to ease the boredom. Until radio.

LEARNING CURVE

Deupree and other executives understood that if they created programming that women could listen to while they were doing their chores—many of which required the use of soap—they could advertise and sell a lot of Proctor & Gamble products in the process. But what kind of shows would work the best? It would take nearly a decade of experimentation for P&G to figure that out.

As far back as 1923, the company had created a recipe show called *Crisco Cooking Talks*, in which every single recipe, naturally, called for Crisco shortening. The show was successful, and P&G

What's special about Mount Irazú in Costa Rica?

followed up with shows teaching people how to use Camay soap, and Chipso laundry soap, as well as a second show (one apparently wasn't enough) on how to use Crisco.

Today these shows would probably be considered "infomercials"—their purpose was not to entertain the listener, but rather to teach them new ways to use the product being advertised. It worked, but Deupree and other executives knew the shows didn't come close to realizing radio advertising's full potential.

In 1930 Procter & Gamble created a show that featured a singer named George the Lava Soap Man. George didn't teach listeners about Lava soap; all he did was sing. It didn't matter—sales of Lava went up anyway, and the experience taught P&G execs that entertaining listeners made more sense than instructing them.

TUNE IN TOMORROW

But George the Lava Soap Man was missing something—a hook. If a listener missed George's show one day, what difference did it make? They could always tune in the next day without feeling like they'd missed anything, because one day's singing was as good as any other.

There had to be a way to create a format that would compel listeners to tune in every single day, maximizing the number of P&G ads they heard and keeping them from straying to shows sponsored by the competition.

One technique that had proven effective in Proctor & Gamble's newspaper advertising was the comic strip serial. Ivory soap's ad campaigns featured "The Jollyco Family." Each week the strip featured a member of the Jollyco family or a neighbor using Ivory soap. There was even a snooty villainess named Mrs. Percival Billington Folderol who used colored, scented soaps instead of good old-fashioned Ivory. The story line continued from one week to the next, so people had to read the strip every week to keep up with what was going on.

The campaign was effective: Readers responded to the ads as if they were just another comic strip. They also bought soap—lots of it. After "The Jollyco Family" strip premiered in a New York newspaper, sales of Ivory soap jumped 25% in only six months.

If a continuing newspaper serial could sell soap, what about a

---

It's the only point in the Americas where one can see both the Atlantic and Pacific oceans.

radio serial? By 1932 Proctor & Gamble was ready to find out.

AND NOW A FEW WORDS FROM OUR SPONSOR

In 1932 they introduced a 15-minute radio serial called *The Puddle Family* on WLW in Cincinnati to advertise Oxydol laundry detergent. But that flopped. The following year they tried again with a show called *Ma Perkins*, the continuing saga of a widowed lumber mill owner who mothers her employees and helps them solve their problems. Once again Oxydol was the sponsor.

In every 15-minute show, Ma Perkins or the other characters managed to plug Oxydol 20 to 25 times, or nearly twice a minute. "We knew the repetition would be very irritating and we'd get complaints," one P&G executive said, "but the business was bad enough that we decided to try it."

Sure enough, P&G received 5,000 letters of complaint that first week alone. Within a few weeks, however, reports of another kind began arriving at company headquarters: all over the country, P&G salespeople were reporting that sales of Oxydol were picking up. Way up—in Ma Perkins's first year on the air, sales of Oxydol more than doubled, and they kept on climbing.

MOTHER OF HER COUNTRY

In a very short time, *Ma Perkins* grew into a national phenomenon. To many listeners, she was more than just a radio character: she was a member of the family, a close confidant, a best friend. An astonishing number of people actually believed she was real, Alecia Swasy writes in *Soap Opera*:

> Ma Perkins became America's beloved "mother of the air." Fans wrote asking her advice on their personal lives. Some sent her pot holders. One older woman suggested in a letter that the two could be companions in their "fading days." She asked Ma for directions to "Rushville Center," so she could begin packing her bags.

Proctor & Gamble had finally found a radio formula that really hooked the listening audience. The "washboard weeper," or "soap opera," as it would soon become known, had arrived.

ON A ROLL

Ma Perkins sold so much Oxydol that Procter & Gamble decided

A dragonfly can use its feet for perching but not for walking.

to create shows for their other products. Camay soap sponsored one called *Forever Young*; Chipso soap flakes was advertised on *Home Sweet Home*; and P&G White Naphtha laundry detergent sponsored *The Guiding Light*.

By producing its own shows and advertising on them as well, Procter & Gamble cut out so many middlemen that it saved as much as 75% of its advertising costs. So they kept creating more shows, and so did competitors like Colgate and American Home Products. By the early 1940s, there were 33 different soap operas on the radio, creating a solid block that started each morning at 10:00 a.m. and ran straight through till 6:00 p.m. Listening to the soaps during chores became a pop-culture institution—more than 40 million people were tuning in every day.

HAPPY ENDING

Richard Deupree's advertising gamble had paid off. Thanks to soap operas, Procter & Gamble not only survived the Great Depression, it thrived: Between 1933 and 1939, sales of Ivory soap nearly doubled, and sales of Crisco nearly tripled. These and other brands like Camay and White Naphtha became household words. And on the strength of their sales, Proctor & Gamble was well on its way to becoming the largest soap manufacturer in the country.

Will Proctor & Gamble stay on top? Will Ma Perkins ever be on television? Will Uncle John ever leave the bathroom? Tune into page 439 for part II of our saga.

*   *   *

SOAPY SALES

In 1951 the Swedish Film Industry was on strike and Ingmar Bergman—already an established director—needed work. So he signed on to direct nine commercials for a new Swedish deodorant soap called *Bris* (Breeze). The words were the ad company's: "Bris kills bacteria!" How to get that message across was entirely up to Bergman. So how did the director of such somber classics as *Smiles of a Summer Night* and *Wild Strawberries* do it? He used his cinematic talents to create little movies in which actors dressed as microbes were defeated by Bris Man, Sweden's first antibaterial superhero.

The world's largest zipper: The one that zips the turf together in the Houston Astrodome.

FIRSTS

*Here are some more stories of when and how things
we take for granted came to be created, from
The Book of Firsts, by Patrick Robertson.*

THE FIRST TOOTHPASTE TUBE

Date: 1892

Background: The first collapsible metal toothpaste tube
was devised by Dr. Washington Sheffield, a dentist of New London, Connecticut, and manufactured by his Sheffield Tube Corp.

THE FIRST LAWN MOWER

Date: 1830

Background: The first mower was invented by Edwin Budding of
Stroud, Gloucestershire, England. He signed a contract for the
manufacture of machinery for the purpose of cropping or shearing
the vegetable surface of lawns. Previously Budding had been
employed at a textile factory, and is said to have been inspired with
the idea of the lawn mower from using a machine designed to shear
the nap off cloth.

The first recorded customer for the new contraption was Mr.
Curtis, head gardener of Regent's Park Zoo, who bought a large
model in 1831. A smaller mower was available for the use of country gentlemen, who, said Budding, "will find in my machine an
amusing, useful, and healthful exercise." Just how "amusing" anyone found the heavy and inefficiently geared machine is open to
doubt, but it was clearly an improvement on cutting the lawn with
scythes. The growth of the new industry was slow, until the advent
of lawn tennis in the 1870s, which brought an influx of mowers
into backyards all over games-loving Victorian England.

THE FIRST NEWSPAPER PHOTOGRAPH

Date: March 4, 1880

Background: The first newspaper photograph was actually a
halftone illustration by Stephen H. Horgan, from Henry J. Newton's photograph of New York's Shantytown, which appeared in
the *New York Daily Graphic*.

In the Old West, more cowboys died crossing swollen rivers than during gunfights.

STRANGE LAWSUITS

These days, it seems that people will sue each other over practically anything. Here are a few more real-life examples of unusual legal battles.

THE PLAINTIFF: Janette Weiss

THE DEFENDANT: Kmart Corporation.

THE LAWSUIT: Weiss was shopping for a blender. But the blenders were stacked on a high shelf, just out of her reach. Ignoring the laws of gravity, Weiss jumped up and grabbed the bottom box. Predictably, when she yanked it out, the three blenders on top came crashing down on her head. Claiming to be suffering from "bilateral carpal-tunnel syndrome," Weiss sued Kmart for "negligently stacking the boxes so high on the upper shelf."

THE VERDICT: Not guilty. After Weiss admitted on the stand that she knew the boxes would fall, it took the jury half an hour to find in favor of Kmart.

THE PLAINTIFF: Dr. Ira Gore

THE DEFENDANT: BMW America

THE LAWSUIT: In 1990, Gore purchased a $40,000 BMW. After he got it home, he discovered that the dealer had touched up a scratch in the paint on a door and never bothered to tell him he was buying damaged goods. Outraged, Gore sued.

THE VERDICT: The jury awarded Gore $4,000 compensation, even though the actual repair cost only $600. And then they slapped BMW with an unbelievable $2 million in punitive damages.

THE PLAINTIFF: Jeffrey Stambovsky

THE DEFENDANT: Helen V. Ackley

THE LAWSUIT: Stambovsky purchased Ackley's house in Nyack, New York, for $650,000. When he later discovered that the house was "haunted," he sued Ackley for failing to disclose the presence of poltergeists.

THE VERDICT: Guilty. Unfortunately for her, Ackley had bragged to friends for years that the place was spooked. She was even interviewed by *Reader's Digest* for an article on haunted houses. The judge found that Ackley should have told Stambovsky everything about the house, noting that the existence of ghosts meant that she had actually broken the law by not leaving the house vacant.

THE PLAINTIFF: Chad Gabriel DeKoven
THE DEFENDANT: Michigan Prison System
THE LAWSUIT: DeKoven, a convicted armed robber who goes by the name "Messiah-God," sued the prison system, demanding damages that included thousands of trees, tons of precious metals, peace in the Middle East, and "return of all U.S. military personnel to the United States within 90 days."
THE VERDICT: Case dismissed. While noting that all claims must be taken seriously, the judge ultimately dismissed the suit as frivolous. DeKoven, the judge said, "has no Constitutional right to be treated as the 'Messiah-God' or any other holy, extra-worldly or supernatural being."

THE PLAINTIFF: Louis Berrios
THE DEFENDANT: Our Lady of Mercy Hospital
THE LAWSUIT: Berrios, a 32-year-old quadriplegic, entered the hospital complaining of stomach pains. Doctors took X-rays to determine the cause of his pain and then called the police when the film revealed what they thought were bags of heroin in Berrios's stomach. The police interrogated Berrios and kept him handcuffed to a gurney for 24 hours, only to discover that the "bags of heroin" were actually bladder stones. Berrios, "shamed, embarrassed and extremely humiliated," sued the hospital for $14 million.
THE VERDICT: Unknown.

THE PLAINTIFF: Judith Richardson Haimes
THE DEFENDANT: Temple University Hospital
THE LAWSUIT: Haimes claimed to have had psychic abilities… until a CAT scan at the Philadelphia hospital "destroyed her powers." The hospital's negligence left her unable to ply her trade as a clairvoyant, she said.
THE VERDICT: Amazingly, the jury awarded Haimes $986,465. The judge disagreed and threw out the verdict.

HOW SOAP WORKS

There's so much going on in the bathroom. Take that bar of soap next to the sink, for example. For a dollar you can buy three bars. But in every bar is a thousand years of science and history. Think about it—it's amazing.

OPPOSITES DON'T ALWAYS ATTRACT

Oil and water don't mix; they repel each other like opposite ends of a magnet. When you wash your skin with water alone, the oil or "sebum" in your skin repels the water and keeps it from cleaning the skin effectively. That's where soap comes in.

Primitively speaking, soap is oil plus alkali. For centuries, that meant fat plus lye. American colonists and pioneers saved fat scraps from cooking. They also saved the ashes from their fireplaces, which they placed in a barrel with a spigot at the bottom. Water poured over the ashes and left to soak would form lye, which was then drained off from the bottom. The cooking fat would be rendered in a vat over a fire, then the lye would be added. After much stirring and cooking, a chemical reaction would take place and soap was the result. Too much lye, and the soap would be harsh on the skin. Too much fat, and the soap would be greasy. The newly formed soap would then be poured into boxes to harden and cure for several months.

But how does a combination of fat and ash take away dirt? Let's get out the microscope.

CHEMISTRY MADE SIMPLE

Water is a molecule composed of hydrogen and oxygen. The hydrogen end of the molecule has a positive charge, and the oxygen end has a negative charge. Oil has neither a positive nor a negative charge—it carries a uniform electrical distribution. That's why water and oil repel each other. Soap is actually a compound called sodium stearate and has the properties of both oil and water: partly polar, partly nonpolar. That's how it brings oil and water together.

A molecule of soap is shaped like a snake, with the head being

---

Israel is one-fourth the size of Maine.

the water-loving sodium compound, and the tail being the water-hating stearates. Add soap to water, and the tail end tries to get away from the water. Now add something oily to the water. The stearate tail of the soap molecules will rush to cling to the oil molecules. The oil molecule bonds with the tail and floats away, led by the water-loving sodium head.

THE HISTORY OF SOAP

So how did humans discover soap? The legend is that some time around 1000 B.C., Romans performed many animal sacrifices to the gods on Mount Sapo. The fat from the animals mixed with the ashes of the sacrificial fires. Over time, this mixture of fat and alkali flowed down to the Tiber River and accumulated in the clay soils. Women washing clothing there found that the clay seemed to help get things cleaner. Whether or not this story is true, experts say Mount Sapo is the origin of our word "soap."

The manufacture of soap actually predates this legend by a number of centuries. A recipe for soapmaking was discovered on Sumerian clay tablets dating back to 2500 B.C. And during excavations of ancient Babylon, archaeologists uncovered clay cylinders containing a soaplike substance that were around 5,000 years old. The Phoenicians were making soap around 600 B.C., and Roman historian Pliny the Elder recorded a soap recipe of goat tallow and wood ashes in the first century. A soap factory complete with finished bars was found in the ruins of Pompeii.

OUT OF REACH

In Spain and Italy, soapmaking did not become an established business until about the 7th century. France followed in the 13th century and England a century after that. Southern Europeans made soap using olive oil. Northern Europeans used the fat from animals, including fish oils.

In most places, soap was a luxury item because it was so difficult to manufacture correctly. And it was often so heavily taxed that it was beyond the budgets of most people. Furthermore, bathing was out of fashion for many centuries, being considered sinful, even unhealthy. But when Louis Pasteur proved that cleanliness cuts down on disease in the mid-1800s, bathing and the use of soap for personal hygiene began to become an accepted practice.

COUNTRY HITS

You've probably hummed some of these songs to yourself at one time or another. Here are the stories behind them.

Mammas, Don't Let Your Babies Grow Up to Be Cowboys (1978). After nearly 20 years of writing songs without producing a hit, 35-year-old songwriter Ed Bruce was ready to give up. He set out to write a song called "Mammas, Don't Let Your Babies Grow Up to Be Guitar Players," as a warning to others... but his wife suggested that a song about cowboys might sell more records. (She was right.)

Folsom Prison Blues (1956). Johnny Cash didn't get the idea for this song while doing time. He got it while watching a documentary titled *Inside the Walls of Folsom Prison.* It struck him that most people live in a prison of one kind or another, and that they would relate to a song about prison as much as they would to a song about drinking, trains, or broken hearts.

If You've Got the Money, I've Got the Time (1950). In 1950 a friend of Lefty Frizzell drove all the way from Oklahoma to West Texas to hear him sing in a nightclub. He'd come so far that when Frizzell was finished singing, the friend asked him to play a little longer. "Well," Frizzell joked, "if you've got the money, I got the time!" Frizzell knew right then he had the makings of a hit song.

Tumbling Tumbleweeds (1934). In the mid-1930s, a Los Angeles songwriter named Bob Nolan wrote "Tumbling Leaves," a song inspired by the blowing autumn leaves he'd seen in Arizona. His group, Sons of the Pioneers, performed the song on the radio, and it became a hit—of sorts: listeners requested "Tumbling *Tumbleweeds,*" not "Tumbling Leaves." Nolan got so tired of correcting people that he rewrote the song. (It was Gene Autry's first big hit.)

Your Cheatin' Heart (1953). Hank Williams came up with the idea while he and his fiancée Billie Jean Eshlimar were driving to Louisiana to visit her family. After rambling on about how his ex-wife Audrey had mistreated him, Williams concluded with, "Her cheatin' heart will pay!" He thought for a moment and then said, "That would make a good song!"

Cost of the Louisiana Purchase: $15 million; cost of the New Orleans Superdome: $75 million.

CALVIN AND HOBBES

*Words of wisdom from one of the BRI's favorite
comic strip duos, Calvin and Hobbes.*

"School's out! Free at last!
And just six precious hours to
forget everything I learned
today."

"My parents are the two stu-
pidest people on Earth. Just my
luck they'd get married and
have me."

Calvin: "It must be awful to be
a girl. I'm sure it's frustrating
knowing that men are bigger,
stronger and better at abstract
thought than women. Really, if
you're a girl, what would make
you go on living?"

Susie: "The thought of a jerk
like you begging one of us for a
date when you're 17."

"I wonder if my life will flash
before my eyes. That's the problem with being six years old...
my life won't take very long to
watch. Maybe I can get a few
slow-motion replays of the time
I smacked Susie upside the
head with a slushball."

"The secret to enjoying your
job is to have a hobby that is
even worse."

"True friends are hard to come
by... I need more money."

"Leave it to a girl to take
the fun out of sex discrimina-
tion."

"The way I see it, God put me
on Earth to achieve a certain
number of things. By now I'm
so far behind, I'll never die."

"I'm at peace with the world.
I'm completely serene. I've
discovered my purpose in life.
I know why I was put here
and why everything exists....
I am here so everybody can do
what I want. Once everybody
accepts it, they'll be serene
too."

"You can present the material,
but you can't make me care."

"It's an outrage how grown-
ups have polluted the Earth!
I refuse to inherit a spoiled
planet. I'm leaving!"

"I hate to think that all my
current experiences will someday become stories with no
point."

Handyman: In 1907, Theodore Roosevelt set a record by shaking hands with 8,513 people.

MYSTERIOUS RAPPINGS

*Have you ever participated in a séance or tried to contact the
"spirits" using a Ouija board? You probably don't realize it,
but the modern conception of communicating with the
dead only dates back to the late 1840s. Here's the
story of the hoax that started spirit-mania.*

BUMP IN THE NIGHT

In 1848 a devout Methodist farmer named John Fox and
his family began to hear strange noises in their Hydesville,
New York, farmhouse. The noises continued for weeks on end,
until finally on one particularly noisy evening, Mrs. Fox ordered
the two children, 13-year-old Margaret and 12-year-old Kate, to
stay perfectly quiet in bed while Mr. Fox searched the house from
top to bottom. His search shed no light on the mystery, but afterward, Margaret sat up in bed and snapped her fingers, exclaiming,
"Here Mr. Split-foot, do as I do!"

"The reply was immediate," Earl Fornell writes in *The Unhappy
Medium: Spiritualism and the Life of Margaret Fox*. "The invisible
rapper responded by imitating the number of the girl's staccato
responses."

Mrs. Fox began to make sense of what she was hearing.
"Count ten," she told the spirit. It responded with 10 raps. So she
asked several questions; each time the spirit answered correctly.
Next, Mrs. Fox asked the spirit if it would rap if a neighbor was
present; the spirit said yes. So Mr. Fox ran and got a neighbor, the
first of more than 500 neighbors and townspeople who visited the
home over the next few weeks to watch Margaret and Kate inter-
act with the spirit. As long as either Margaret or Kate was present, the spirit was willing to communicate.

MURDER MYSTERY

Using an alphabetic code that Margaret and Kate devised, "Mr.
Split-foot" explained that in his Earthly life he'd been a peddler,
murdered by the person who lived in the farmhouse. The spirit

identified the killer as "C. R." Some citizens tracked down a man named Charles Rosana, who'd lived in the house years earlier, but with no body and no evidence other than the testimony of a ghost, he was never charged.

At that point, Mrs. Fox decided to send Margaret and Kate to live with their older sister, Leah Fish, in Rochester. As soon as the girls left Hydesville, the strange noises and spirit visitations stopped.

KID STUFF

When they arrived in Rochester, Margaret and Kate let their older sister, Leah, in on a secret: the whole thing—the rappings, the spirits, "Mr. Split-foot," the "murder," and everything else—was a hoax. "We wanted to terrify our dear mother," Margaret told the *New York Herald* in 1888.

The girls started out by tying a string to an apple and bouncing it repeatedly on the floor, but soon discovered that they could make loud popping noises by cracking the joints in their big toes. They also figured out how to project the sounds around the room, in much the same way that ventriloquists throw their voices, which helped to make the rapping sounds convincing.

THE SOUND OF MONEY

By now the prank had gone on too long; Mrs. Fox was so upset by the idea of her two young girls talking to dead people that Margaret started feeling guilty and decided to put an end to it. She and Kate staged one last "farewell" rap session, then had the "spirits" announce that their Earthly work was done and that they would no longer try to make any contact with the living.

The only problem was that their sister Leah made her living running a music studio, and when Margaret and Kate had come to live with her, their notoriety scared away all of her pupils. So Leah convinced them to help her by forming a spiritualist society and staging a series of public demonstrations of spirit rapping in Corinthian Hall, the town's largest auditorium. Price of admission: $1 per person.

The audiences of these shows were fooled by the mysterious rappings, and within weeks a number of "spirit circles" formed in Rochester and began hiring the Fox sisters to perform séances in

The language of Taki, spoken in parts of Guinea, consists of only 340 words.

private homes. When people began to tire of listening to Mr. Split-foot, the sisters discovered they could communicate with the spirits of such luminaries as Benjamin Franklin, Thomas Paine, and William Shakespeare.

It was from this modest beginning—two young girls figuring out how to make mysterious noises by popping their big toes, and and an intimidating third sister figuring out how to exploit it— that "Split-foot" spiritualism went on to become what may have been the fastest-growing spiritual movement in the history of the United States.

IN THE RIGHT PLACE, AT THE RIGHT TIME

The Fox sisters didn't know it, but they were perfectly poised to fill the spiritual void created by advances in 19th-century science and the Industrial Revolution. According to Earl Fornell:

> The appearance of these emissaries from another world was particularly welcome, for the rise of science in the early decades of the 19th century had, to some extent, brought into question the validity of older religious dogmas. Such reform movements as Utopian socialism, temperance, abolitionism, and feminism arose from a demand for a better life on earth, since science seemed to promise no afterlife....Still another endeavor was a frenzied search for positive and immediate proof of the immortality that science seemed then to set aside.

TRUE BELIEVERS

The possibility of talking to the departed took the public imagination by storm. Here are a few examples of how deeply "spiritualism" pervaded the culture:

• A judge in upstate New York developed a reputation for consulting the spirits before handing down rulings.

• Some enthusiasts became so convinced that life was better "on the other side" that they commited suicide rather than waste a lifetime waiting for paradise.

• In 1853 some New Yorkers formed a group called the Free Spirit Love Society, which forbade extramarital affairs in all instances...except those in which the adulterer "entered into a new relation under the guidance of spiritual affinities or attractions." At its peak the society boasted more than 600 members.

Most likely items involved in accidents at home: bicycles, stairs, and doors (in that order).

• In 1856 a Bordentown, New Jersey, man died just days before he was supposed to marry his fiancé. Rather than cancel the wedding, the man's family and his bride-to-be turned it into a wedding-funeral, hiring a medium to marry the bride to her fiancé's corpse before it was laid to rest.

SHE KEEPS GOING...AND GOING...AND GOING...

The public's desire to believe was so great that the Fox sisters were able to keep their hoax going for more than 40 years. The spiritualism craze faded somewhat in the late 1850s but came roaring back following the outbreak of the Civil War, as thousands of bereaved families tried desperately to get in contact with loved ones killed in battle.

Even First Lady Mary Todd Lincoln brought spiritualists to the White House so that she could speak to her dead sons Tad and Willie. In 1872, seven years after President Abraham Lincoln was assassinated, Mrs. Lincoln visited Fox several times and each time came away convinced that, through Margaret, she'd made contact with "the real presence of the spirit of her husband."

UNHAPPY MEDIUMS

One of the curses of founding this fraudulent movement was that Margaret and Kate had to spend most of their time in the presence of true believers. Both women grew to hate their lives; both became alcoholics. And though Leah Fish had grown rich off years of public performances, Margaret and Kate had not.

By the late 1870s, Margaret was still giving public performances, but she was suffering from depression and working only a few hours each week—just long enough to make the money she needed to "drown my remorse in wine," as she put it. Somehow, she managed to keep going for another 10 years.

Then in September 1888, a reporter for the *New York Herald* asked Fox to comment on the case of another spiritualist, who'd recently been exposed as a fraud. Margaret told the reporter that spiritualism was bogus and promised to one day give "an interesting exposure of the fraud."

On July 4, 1776, King George III of England noted in his diary:

BAD RAP

Rather than wait, the *Herald* sent a reporter the next day. As promised, Fox delivered—and over the next few hours laid out her bizarre life story in lurid detail. There was no truth to spiritualism, she told the reporter, and she said she more than anyone else should know it.

"I have explored the unknown as far as a human can," she told the reporter. "I have gone to the dead so that I might get from them some little token....I have tried to obtain some sign. Not a thing! No, the dead shall not return."

And in case anyone didn't believe her—in fact, many spiritualists blamed booze for the "false confession"—Fox gave a public confession and demonstration of her methods at New York's Academy of Music. The *New York Herald* described the scene:

> Everybody in the hall knew they were looking at the woman principally responsible for spiritualism. She stood upon a pine table, with nothing on her feet but stockings. As she remained motionless, loud distinct rappings were heard, now behind the scenes, now in the gallery. She had a devil's gift in a rapping ventriloquism, from which spiritualism had sprung to life, and here was the same toe rapping it out of existence.

DIDN'T SEE THIS COMING

The cash Margaret Fox made selling her story didn't last long. Neither did the money she made on tours exposing the fraud of spiritualism. When the public's interest in her exposé dried up, she became so desperate for money that she recanted her confession and went back out on the séance circuit. She toured the country for the next five years, until finally in 1893, like her sister Kate, she died drunk, broke, and alone.

The funeral arrangements were handled by a friend of Margaret's, Titus Merritt, "the mortician," Fornell writes, "at whose establishment she had often spent long nights, sitting among the corpses watching for some signs of spirit life."

The signs never came.

*   *   *

"The guy who invented the first wheel was an idiot, the guy who invented the other three, *he* was a genius."   —**Sid Caesar**

VERY SUPERSTITIOUS

Just to be safe, Uncle John only works on his superstition pages only while wearing his lucky underwear. Here are some more classic folk superstitions.

• To tell who will be elected U.S. president, take two roosters, the evening before election, and name each for the respective candidates of the leading parties; place them together under a tub. Leave them overnight. the following morning uncover them and notice which crows first; the one crowing will indicate the election of the candidate for which he was named. It's as good a way as any...

• When you get dressed in the morning be sure to put on your right sock and right shoe before you put on your left sock and left shoe, and you will have a good day.

• If a red-headed woman comes to your house on Monday, there will be confusion all week.

• Never sleep with the moon in your face. It will draw your mouth over and make it crooked.

• Cutting a baby's nails before he is a year old makes a thief of him. Bite them off.

• When sitting in on a card game, get up and twist your chair three times on its forelegs—in the direction of the sun.

• If your left palm itches, money will come to you. But don't under any circumstances scratch the itch. That will break the enchantment.

• If you dream of fresh pork and fish it is a sign of impending death.

• If by mistake you put on a sweater or some other clothing backward or inside out, it brings good luck. But you must wear it that way all day or your good luck will turn bad. The only exception to this rule is your underwear. You can turn it right side out just after lunch.

• If birds weave some of your hair into their nests, you will go crazy.

• Never take a broom along when you move. Throw out your old broom and buy a new one for your new home.

THE POLITICALLY CORRECT QUIZ

Here are eight real-life examples of "politically correct" behavior. How sensitive are you? Try to guess which answer is the "correct" one. Answers are on page 512.

1. In 2001 Carol Ann Demaret launched a boycott of a film that offended her. Which film and why?

a) *A.I.: Artificial Intelligence.* "Abusing children, even robot children, is wrong."

b) *Planet of the Apes.* "Ape actors should play the ape parts."

c) *Bubble Boy.* "It mocks people without immunities."

2. The Brazilian city of Cascavel has banned municipal workers from engaging in what practice?

a) Praying. "Religion has no place in the workplace. Do it on your own time."

b) Spreading gossip. "Public employees have moral rights."

c) Drinking French roast coffee during breaks. "French roast encourages the perception that Brazilian roast is inferior."

3. A high priest of the British White Witches is protesting the Warner Bros. film *Harry Potter and the Sorcerer's Stone* for what reason?

a) It shows witches in school. "Witches are born, not taught."

b) It shows witches riding brooms with the brush end in the back—real witches ride brooms brush-end forward.

c) It shows several black witches.

4. An organization in Florida launched a petition campaign to amend the state constitution to protect which of the following?

a) Pregnant pigs, to protect them from "chronic stress."

b) Brahma bulls, to protect them from "anti-Hindu terrorism."

c) Human souls, to protect them from "abuse by atheists."

X-rays of the *Mona Lisa* show that there are three different versions underneath.

5. College professor Jon Willand, who has taught American history for more than 30 years, was reprimanded for doing what?

a) Displaying an old recruiting poster that depicts General George Custer and seeks soldiers to fight "militant Sioux."

b) Stating that the civil rights movement was "all about ego."

c) Arranging the seating chart so that all the "hot babes" sat in front.

6. Protestors outside the U.S. Embassy in Bombay, India, criticized the Bush administration's White House website (*www.whitehouse.gov*) for which of the following reasons:

a) Describing a rash as an "Indian burn" in a press release describing George Bush's first presidential medical exam.

b) Showing a picture of the entire Bush family—parents, daughters, two dogs…and a cat named India.

c) Stating that Bush "feels the same way about Indian food that his father feels about broccoli."

7. A Canadian activist organization seeks to change Canada's national anthem in what way?

a) Replace "Canadians" with "North Americans." (Endorses ethnic diversity…and better for tourism.)

b) Remove the reference to the "milk of our sacred land." (Offends vegans and the lactose intolerant.)

c) Remove the phrase "all thy sons." (Sexist.)

POLITICALLY INCORRECT BONUS ROUND

8. According to scientific research conducted by the Australian Wine Research Institute, which of the following is "the best way to preserve the quality of white wine?"

a) Use screwcaps instead of corks; they work better, plus they're easier to open and cheaper, too.

b) Drink it straight out of the bottle, wrapped in a small paper bag. The bag protects the wine against the sun.

c) Mixing a little beer into the unfermented wine, before the bottle is corked and aged at the winery. Foster's Lager works best.

Comic relief: What do you call a baby potato? A small fry.

DUBIOUS ACHIEVERS

People do some pretty strange things. Here are a few of the oddest records we've ever seen.

LONGEST DISTANCE TRAVELED BY MARSHMALLOW FROM A NOSE INTO ANOTHER PERSON'S MOUTH

Record Holder: Scott Jeckel

The Story: Blessed from birth with the amazing ability to launch items from his nose with great precision, Jeckel once fired a marshmallow a distance of 16 feet, 3½ inches into the waiting mouth of partner Ray Persin—who ate it.

MOST ACCOMPLISHED SEWER FISHERMAN

Record Holder: Larry Harper

The Story: Oshkosh, Wisconsin, native Larry Harper has been fishing his town's sewers in his spare time for seven years and has caught 74 fish, 13 rats, 5 old shoes, and 1 tennis racket to date. Harper has even reeled in a small alligator, using a tuna sandwich as bait.

LARGEST MASS WEDDING HELD IN PRISON

Record Holders: Inmates of Carandiru Prison, Sao Paulo, Brazil

The Story: On June 14, 2000, a record 120 prisoners and their lucky fiancées tied the knot simultaneously in a massive ceremony in romantic Carandiru Prison. Why did they do it? Carandiru was built for 3,000 inmates, but houses 7,500. Weekly riots and jailbreaks led authorities to organize the wedding, with the hope that prisoners with family ties would be less violent.

LONGEST DISTANCE TRAVELED BY FOOT WHILE CARRYING A BRICK

Record Holder: Manjit Singh

The Story: A regulation-size brick—weighing exactly nine pounds—has never traveled farther "in an ungloved hand in an uncradled downward pincer grip" than when Manjit Singh lugged one 82.2 miles on foot from November 6 to 7, 1998.

GREATEST NUMBER OF CITATIONS FOR INDECENT EXPOSURE

Record Holder: Helga Svenstrup

The Story: Notorious in her hometown of Copenhagen, Denmark, 67-year-old Svenstrup has been arrested 45 times for indecent exposure. At one of her hearings, she even flashed the presiding judge. Her greatest stunt: At a sold-out soccer match, she ran onto the field dressed as a cheerleader and performed cartwheels without underwear before 50,000 cheering spectators.

FASTEST PEOPLE WEARING A HORSE COSTUME

Record Holders: Geoff Seale and Stuart Coleman

The Story: At a school playground in 1999, dozens of pairs of Elmbridge, England, citizens raced neck and neck in two-man horse costumes for the title of World's Fastest Horse Impersonators. The fleet-footed victors were Geoff Seale and Stuart Coleman, who "galloped" 328 feet in a record-breaking 16.7 seconds.

MOST WORMS CHARMED FROM THE GROUND

Record Holder: Tom Shufflebotham

The Story: At the first World Worm Charming Championship in Cheshire, England, in 1980, entrants tried to entice as many worms out of the ground as possible on a 32.3-square-foot lot. Using his amazing powers of worm appeal, Shufflebotham charmed 511 worms from the ground in just 30 minutes. How does he do it? He coaxes them to the surface by "vibrating garden forks."

LONGEST TIME SPENT SITTING ON A BLOCK OF ICE

Record Holder: Gus Simmons

The Story: During the Depression, people would do almost anything for fun—if it was cheap. On October 17, 1933, at Chicago's White City Casino, contestants tested the warmth of their nether regions in an "ice sitting" championship. Contest winner Simmons sat on a two-foot cube of ice for 27 hours, 10 minutes before finally being disqualified for having a 102-degree fever.

AMAZING ANAGRAMS

In previous BRs, we've included a page of anagrams...words or phrases that are rearranged to form new words and phrases. We particularly like the ones that end up with more or less the same meaning.

THE ACTIVE VOLCANOS
*becomes...*CONES
EVICT HOT LAVA

ADOLF HITLER
*becomes...*HATED
FOR ILL

AN ALCOHOLIC
BEVERAGE *becomes...*
GAL, CAN I HAVE
COOL BEER?

THE ASSASSINATION OF
PRESIDENT ABRAHAM
LINCOLN *becomes...*
A PAST
SENSATION
CHILLS ME, OR
A FIEND SHOT
IN A BARN

CLOTHESPINS *becomes...*
SO LET'S PINCH

THE COMING
PRESIDENTIAL
CAMPAIGN
*becomes...*DAMN!
ELECTING TIME
IS APPROACHING

MUTTERING *becomes...*
EMIT GRUNT

NOVA SCOTIA AND
PRINCE EDWARD
ISLAND *becomes...*
TWO
CANADIAN
PROVINCES:
LANDS I DREAD

POSTPONED *becomes...*
STOPPED? NO.

RECEIVED PAYMENT
*becomes...*EVERY CENT
PAID ME

A ROLLING STONE
GATHERS NO MOSS
*becomes...*STROLLER
ON GO, AMASSES
NOTHING

SLOT MACHINES
*becomes...*CASH LOST
IN 'EM

A STRIPTEASER
*becomes...*ATTIRE
SPARSE

THE PUBLIC ART
GALLERIES *becomes...*
LARGE PICTURE
HALLS, I BET

Jet set: A typical banana travels 4,000 miles before being eaten.

MODERN QUACKERY

*Though the days of such gruesome 19th century medical practices as
bloodletting and blistering are over, quack medicine is still going strong.
Do oxygen bars battle the effects of air pollution? Do magnetic
bracelets cure arthritis pain? We can't say for sure, but here
are a few modern "treatments" that leave us wondering.*

EAR CANDLING

Description: The user sticks a hollow, cone-shaped candle
into their ear canal and lights it. As the candle burns, it
supposedly creates a vacuum that sucks out earwax, debris and
other "toxins." Claimed benefits include improved senses of smell
and taste, clearer eyesight, purified blood, and even a "strengthened brain."

Truth: Sure enough, when you stick the candle in your ear, light
it, and let it burn down, some crud forms inside the cone. What's
it made of? Candle wax. If there was any crud in your ear to begin
with, it's still in there.

FRESH CELL THERAPY

Description: "Fresh cell therapy, also called live cell therapy or
cellular therapy, involves injections of fresh embryonic animal cells
taken from the organ or tissue that corresponds to the unhealthy
organ or tissue in the patient." Some reported recipients: Marlene
Dietrich, Winston Churchill, Nelson Mandela, and Fidel Castro.

Truth: If you're having trouble with your rump, injecting cells
from a rump roast isn't going to do you any good and may do
harm. According to the American Cancer Society, the therapy
"has no benefit, and has caused serious side affects such as infection, immunologic reactions to the injected proteins, and death."

PSYCHIC SURGERY

Description: This procedure takes the power of positive thinking
to extremes: the "surgery" is performed by a healer, using psychic
powers alone.

Truth: It's pure slight of hand. The most skilled "psychic surgeons"
go as far as to use a false fingertip filled with artificial blood so

---

Get moving: To lose 1 lb. of fat, you need to walk at least 35 miles (briskly).

that when they draw the finger across your skin it leaves a red, "bloody" line that has the appearance of a surgical incision. Then they supposedly reach into your body and present you with what they claim are "diseased organs" or other body parts. What are they really? Usually chicken guts or cotton wads soaked in the fake blood. According to the American Cancer Society, "all demonstrations to date of psychic surgery have been done by various forms of trickery."

COLON HYDROTHERAPY

Description: Also called colonic irrigation, this one plays on the theory that if a treatment hurts, it must be doing some good: A rubber tube is passed into the rectum for a distance of up to 30 *inches* (ouch!). Then as much as 20 gallons of warm water, coffee, herbal tea, or some other solution is gradually pumped in and out through the tube to remove "toxins."

Truth: "No such 'toxins' have ever been identified; colonic irrigation is not only therapeutically worthless, but can cause infection, injury, and even death from fatal electrolyte imbalance."

TREPANATION

Description: Trepanation, also known as "drilling holes in your head," is believed to be the oldest surgical practice in history. Archeologists have found skulls with holes drilled in them dating as far back as 5,000 B.C. Modern advocates of the procedure claim that drilling holes "relieves pressure permanently," and in the process increases blood flow to the brain and expands consciousness. One Englishwoman named Amanda Fielding performed the "surgery" on herself in 1970; she not only lived to tell the tale but ran for Parliament in 1978...and received 40 votes. "Although I trepanned myself in 1970, having unsuccessfully for several years looked for a doctor to do it for me, I have always been very against self-trepanation," Fielding says now. "It is a messy business, and best done by the medical profession."

Truth: This form of treatment is not just dangerous, it's also totally unnecessary. "This is nonsense," says Dr. Ayub Ommaya, professor of neurosurgery at George Washington University.

Doctors in the 1700s prescribed ladybugs, taken internally, to cure measles.

MOUNT ST. HELENS

May 18th, 1980 was a day that people living in southern Washington state will never forget—the day that Mount St. Helens literally blew its top. Here's the story.

FIRST COME, FIRST SERVED

In 1774, Spanish captain Juan Josef Perez Hernandez sailed the harbors along the coast of what is now Washington State and British Columbia. Apparently he didn't see much of interest and never bothered to stop. Four years later, English captain James Cook dropped anchor in one of those harbors, now known as Nootka Sound. Cook landed to stock up on fresh water and to trade with the natives. He took a few sea otter pelts back to the Old World, and soon otter pelts were being sold in Europe for $4,000 each, worth more than their weight in gold. Thus began the Otter Rush.

The Spanish claimed that since they had been the first to sail through the sound, the Nootka area belonged to them. The English said that since they had been first to set foot on the land, they owned the territory. The English built a fort; the Spaniards seized an English ship in retaliation. War seemed certain until England sent Ambassador Alleyne Fitzherbert, Baron St. Helens, to Spain to negotiate a treaty. In 1790, the Nootka Convention was crafted to give both countries access to the area. Several years later, Captain George Vancouver was exploring the Northwest, he saw a majestic mountain in the distance and named it after St. Helens. The natives name was *Loo-wit-lat-kla*, meaning "keeper of the fire." It was an appropriate name for a volcano.

On May 18, 1980, it exploded.

IMPENDING DOOM

Scientists knew an explosion was imminent in April of 1980, when a bulge 320 feet high appeared on the side of the mountain, indicating that magma was pressing outward. The bulge was moving up at the sustained rate of 5 feet per day. Finally, the movement triggered an avalanche, which shook off the top of the bulge, exposing the white-hot interior to the air.

Under normal conditions, water can't be heated beyond the boiling point because then it turns to steam. But when it's kept under pressure (as in a pressure cooker) it can be heated beyond the boiling point and still remain liquid. When the pressure is removed, the super-hot water flashes into steam. Because steam takes up a lot more room than water, an explosion occurs. It's like carbon dioxide in soda: shake the bottle or can, and the gas wants to escape. Pop the top, and the release of pressure results in a mini-volcano of soda. That's what happened to Mount St. Helens.

AMAZING STATISTICS

The blast was heard all the way to Canada. The main eruption continued for 10 minutes, followed by 9 hours of explosive ashfall. The energy released was equal to 27,000 Hiroshima-sized bombs dropped at the rate of one per second, for 9 hours. The volcano hurled 1.3 billion cubic yards of ash and rock into the air, enough to cover a piece of land a mile wide, a mile long, and as high as three Empire State Buildings.

The volcanic ash mixed with the water of surrounding rivers and lakes to form mud the consistency of wet concrete; it flowed downstream, wrecking everything in its path. An area stretching 8 miles out from the volcano and fanning to a width of 15 miles was flattened. But the damage extended much farther than that. Eleven hundred miles of Washington roads were impassable, stranding 10,000 people. Police cars were stalled, train service halted, shipping channels clogged, and power lines knocked out.

GONE IN AN INSTANT

Two hundred square miles of wildlife habitat were destroyed. A million and half animals and birds lay dead, as well as half a million fish. A hundred miles of streams were wiped out entirely, and another 3,000 miles of streams were contaminated by ash. Twenty-six lakes were removed from the map. One hundred twenty-three riverside homes were washed away, and 75 cabins were wrecked. More than 1,000 people were left homeless. In all, $2.7 billion in damage was caused in a single day.

Fifty-seven people died; the only survivor in the blast area was a dog who had been on a camping trip with his family. One man who died instantly when the blast hit was found in the front seat

---

After spending 84 days in *Skylab*, astronauts found that they were two inches taller.

of his car with his camera still held up in front of his face. Two young lovers in a tent were blown into a mass of fallen trees hundreds of feet away. They were found with their arms still around each other. Two other people were killed in their car as they tried to outrace the ash cloud. Most of those who died in the explosion were killed by inhaling hot, toxic volcanic gases and ash. And most had violated orders to stay away from the area.

ASH FALLOUT

Nearly half the state of Washington received visible ashfall. As much as 800,000 tons of it fell on the city of Yakima alone, 85 miles east of the volcano. In fact, so much ash was flushed into the Yakima sewer system that the treatment plant was shut down for fear of permanent damage. All over the region, water reservoirs were drained by communities trying to clean city streets and water rationing had to be imposed.

In Pasco, Washington, paper envelopes full of ash (mailed from residents to friends and relatives around the country) kept breaking open during processing, ruining the machinery. Someone in Seattle suggested dropping the "W" from the state's name and calling it Ashington. The ash cloud from the blast took 17 days to go completely around the globe. One disc jockey joked, "If you were planning on visiting Washington this year, don't bother. Washington is coming to visit you!"

BACK TO NATURE

Today, bluebirds are plentiful as they nest in the abundant cavities found in the mountain's snags. Pocket gophers dig holes in the ash, tilling it. Elk, which returned to the area only a few weeks after the blast, leave droppings, which fertilize the ash. Fireweed, with roots that reach the fertile soil beneath the ash, turns entire hillsides pink with flowers. Mosses, grasses, shrubs, and trees all took root again soon after the blast. The trees now stand over 20 feet tall in some areas. Nature recovers, and the moutain is heading back to normal. Except for one thing: the majestic vista that inspired Vancouver is not quite as majestic now. Mount St. Helens is 1,200 feet lower than it was before the eruption.

Your brain operates on the same amount of power that would light up a 10-watt light bulb.

MOTHER OF THE BOMB

You've heard of physicist J. Robert Oppenheimer, the "father of the A-Bomb." But have you heard of Lise Meitner? Her discovery of nuclear fission opened the door to the creation of the atom bomb, much to her regret. Here's her story.

O**UT OF SCHOOL**

Lise Meitner was born in 1878 in Vienna, Austria. She was very bright, but in those days it didn't matter—education was for boys only. People thought that if the delicate female brain was subjected to too much education, the result would be mental illness and infertility. (Schooling for girls ended at age 13.) Fortunately for Meitner in the 1890s, the Viennese government began to permit women to attend high school and college, making it possible for her to pursue her passion—physics.

After graduating from the University of Vienna in 1906, Meitner went to Berlin to attend lectures by Max Planck, later winner of the Nobel Prize for his work in quantum mechanics. The existence of the atom had only recently been discovered and the study of radiation was new and exciting—and Berlin was where these sciences were being advanced most vigorously. She decided to stay.

A WOMAN'S PLACE

At the University of Berlin, Meitner had to ask permission to attend classes. Planck was reluctant to allow a woman in, but begrudgingly gave his permission, saying, "It cannot be emphasized strongly enough that Nature itself has designated for woman her vocation as mother and housewife, and that under no circumstances can natural laws be ignored without grave damage." Planck later recognized that Meitner had great talent, and she became his assistant. Eventually she was offered a position doing research…though she was not allowed to work in the same lab as the men and was instead given a makeshift workshop in the basement. Her parents supported her financially, but she wrote scientific articles to earn additional income, signing her name "L. Meitner." (Journals would not publish work written by a woman.)

At the university, Meitner began working with another scientist, Otto Hahn. Together they made numerous discoveries about the

---

If you had a million $1 bills, you'd need a box as big as a small coffin to carry them in.

nature of the atom and radiation. They remained scientific partners for the rest of their lives.

SECOND-CLASS CITIZEN

When the modern Kaiser-Wilhelm Institute opened a new wing devoted to radiation research, Hahn was offered a job and Meitner accompanied him...officially listed as his "unpaid guest." (Hahn got paid for his work; she did not.) At the institute, Meitner discovered the element *protactinium*. Though she did the majority of the work, Hahn's name appeared as the senior author on their scientific papers. Consequently, the Association of German Chemists presented him with their highest award, the Emil Fischer Medal. Meitner received only a copy of his medal.

It was only after World War I that Meitner's value began to be recognized: She became the first woman professor ever in Germany and was finally paid a living wage (though still less than Hahn). In 1926 she was appointed full professor of physics at the University of Berlin. There, she continued to study beta and gamma rays, isotopes, atomic theory, radioactivity, and quantum physics.

A NEW COUNTRY

By 1937 Meitner and Hahn had identified at least nine different radioactive elements. A scientist named Fritz Strassmann joined them, and together the three of them began working to find out what happens when the nucleus of an atom splits. But at this time, the Nazis were rising to power. Meitner was forced to fill out papers admitting that her grandparents were Jewish. It didn't matter that she was raised a Protestant—she was fired from her job.

Jews made up less than 1% of the German population, yet they accounted for 20% of the scientists. Researchers all over Germany began to follow Albert Einstein's lead, and fled the country. Meitner announced that she was taking a "holiday," but instead escaped to safety in Sweden. At the age of 59, after living and working in Germany for 31 years, she was forced to leave her money, possessions, research papers, friends, and career. Starting over from scratch, she went to work at the Nobel Institute of Physics in Stockholm, where she spent the next 22 years. It was there that she made the discovery that literally rocked the world.

SPLIT DECISION

Scientists knew that radiation is released when the nucleus of an atom decays. Every nucleus has protons, which have a positive charge, and electrons, which have a negative charge. When a nucleus loses protons, radiation is emitted and the atom transforms into a new kind of atom. This new atom, or "daughter atom," splits and spirals away with enough force that the original atom recoils, like a rifle recoils after firing a bullet. (Radium releases a million times more energy during radioactive decay than when it is burned like coal.) Then scientists discovered that every atom also has a neutron, which has no electrical charge at all. Enrico Fermi discovered that when he bombarded heavy elements such as uranium with neutrons, he ended up with new elements that were even heavier than the ones he started with.

Protons and neutrons in a nucleus cling very tightly together, but they cling more tightly in some elements than in others. Iron is the most stable element and therefore the hardest to split. Uranium is the least stable and the easiest to split. When Meitner and Hahn had tried bombarding uranium with slow-speed neutrons, they ended up with barium—which is lighter than uranium, not heavier. They were confused: neither of them realized they had just split the atom.

EARTH-SHATTERING

In Sweden, Meitner discovered that when a nucleus splits, the mass of the two new atoms added together is less than that of the original atom, because some of the mass is released as energy. That energy is what causes the two pieces of the split atom to repel from each other. She calculated, using Einstein's formula of $E = MC^2$, exactly how much energy would be given off every time a single atom split and predicted that this could happen in a chain reaction, releasing an enormous amount of energy in a very short period of time. If millions of atoms could be split at once, the power would be unimaginable: splitting the nucleus of a uranium atom, for example, releases 20 million times more energy than exploding an equal amount of TNT.

When she shared this news with Hahn, he did experiments to prove her theory. Then he published a paper (leaving her name off, for fear he would get in trouble if the Nazis found he was still in contact with her). Meitner also published a report in a British journal in 1939. Suddenly the world was in a race to see who would be first to harness atomic energy in the form of a bomb.

Einstein wrote a letter to President Roosevelt warning him about what would happen if Germany got the bomb first. Roosevelt set American scientists to work on the project—called the Manhattan Project—and invited Meitner to help. She turned the job down, repulsed by the idea that her discovery might be used to kill people. She told them she hoped they failed.

BAD CREDIT

The Nazis, in the meantime, had been removing all traces of the Jews, and Meitner's name was erased from all the research she had done. Perhaps because of this, Otto Hahn managed to convince himself—and the world—that the discovery of nuclear fission (Meitner coined the term) had been his. Hahn received the Nobel Prize in 1944. (Meitner never did.) For years, Hahn was listed at the inventor, with Lise Meitner occasionally mentioned as his assistant.

When the atom bomb was dropped on Japan, Meitner was upset, not only by the devastation but also by the sudden publicity: reporters on her doorstep; cameras in her face; phone messages and telegrams waiting for her reply. She had little to say. The bomb had killed 100,000 people, and suddenly she was being portrayed in the media as the person who had come up with the blueprint for it.

RECOGNITION

Lise Meitner finally did receive her share of attention for her discoveries. She was named "Woman of the Year" by the Women's National Press Club; received the Max Planck Medal from the German Chemical Society; received honorary doctorates; published 135 scientific papers; won the Enrico Fermi Award; and was elected to the Swedish Academy of Science—only the third woman in history to achieve that honor. She was even offered a movie deal by MGM. (She turned it down, horrified that the script called for her to flee from Germany with an atom bomb hidden in her purse!) Meitner continued her research into her mid-70s and helped Sweden design its first nuclear reactor, which was the way she wanted her discovery to be used. Despite continual exposure to massive amounts of radiation, she lived to be nearly 90 years old, dying in 1968, just three months after Otto Hahn. In 1992 physicists named the newly discovered 109th element in her honor: meitnerium.

FABULOUS FLOPS

Next time you see the hype for some amazing, "can't-miss" phenomenon, hold on to a healthy sense of skepticism by remembering these duds.

THE NATIONAL BOWLING LEAGUE

If people were willing to pay to watch professional football, baseball, and basketball teams, they'd pay to watch teams like the New York Gladiators and the Detroit Thunderbirds compete against each other, right? That was the thinking behind the 10-team National Bowling League, founded in 1961. The owner of the Dallas Broncos poured millions of dollars into his franchise, building a special 2,500-seat "Bronco Bowl" with six lanes surrounded by 18 rows of seats arranged in a semicircle; space was also set aside for a seven-piece jazz band to provide entertainment between games. But he couldn't even fill the arena on opening night, and things went downhill after that. The league folded in less than a year.

GERBER SINGLES

This was Gerber Baby Food's attempt to sell food to adults. Launched in the 1970s, the line of gourmet entrees like sweet-and-sour pork and beef burgundy had two major problems: the food came in baby food–style jars, and the name "Singles" was a turnoff to customers who were lonely to begin with.

HERSHEY'S CHOCOLATE SOAP

Milton Hershey didn't like to let anything go to waste. There were times in the chocolate business when he found himself with millions of pounds of cocoa butter that he didn't know what to do with, and he spent years trying to find a product that would put it to use. In the early 1930s, he finally settled on cocoa butter soap.

Three months later, the factory that he built behind the Cocoa Inn in Hershey, Pennsylvania, began producing 120 bars of chocolate-scented soap a minute. Finding 120 customers a minute to buy the stuff proved to be much more daunting: people were used to *eating* their chocolate, not bathing in it, and were put off by the

---

Why swat, when you can wait? A housefly born today will be dead within 2 months.

strong chocolate smell of the soap. (Some even tried to eat the bars, thinking it was candy.)

More than a million bars of the stuff piled up in the basement of the Hershey Sports Arena waiting to be sold; nevertheless, Hershey kept the assembly line running at full speed. "Don't worry about my money," he told his executives, "You just sell all you can." Seven years and several million dollars later, he finally pulled the plug. Ironically, cocoa butter—unscented—is a popular ingredient in soap today.

SOLAR-POWERED PARKING METERS

City officials in Nottingham, England, spent more than £1 million (about $1.5 million) installing solar-powered parking meters on city streets after reading reports that the meters saved a fortune in maintenance costs in Mediterranean countries. The only problem: Mediterranean countries get a lot of sun...and England doesn't, not even in summer. As of August 2001, more than 25% of the parking meters were out of commission, allowing hundreds of motorists to park for free.

HITS SNACK FOOD

One of the few products whose demise can be blamed solely on the packaging. When lined up end-to-end on store shelves, the packages read: "HITSHITSHITSHITSHITSHITSHITS."

NO FURTHER EXPLANATION REQUIRED

See if you can figure out why these products bombed:

• Buffalo Chip chocolate cookies

• Mouth-So-Fresh Tongue Cleaner

• Incredibagels—microwave bagels "stuffed with egg, cheese, and bacon"

• Gillette's For Oily Hair Shampoo

• Hagar the Horrible Cola

• Burns & Rickers freeze-dried vegetable chips

• Jell-O for Salads (available in celery, tomato, mixed-vegetable)

• Tunies (hot dogs made from tuna fish)

Germans eat more potatoes per capita than any other people, averaging 370 lbs. per year.

THE FINAL EDITION

Still waiting for your 15 minutes of fame? Don't worry—
as these folks would attest (if they could), you don't
have to be alive to get your name in the paper.

NO DEPOSIT, NO RETURN

In January 1995, a small-claims court commissioner in Mill Valley, California, ruled that the landlord of a man who died in his apartment could keep the $825 security deposit. Tenant James Pflugradt passed away from a heart attack in 1994; his son Rick cleaned out the apartment five days later and then asked for the security deposit back...but landlord Fred Padula refused to hand it over, arguing that the deposit was needed to cover rent during the time it would take to find a new tenant.

Court Commissioner Randolph Heubach sided with landlord Padula. "I am not unsympathetic, but it is really a straightforward financial situation," he said after making his decision. His reason: The deceased "failed to give the 30-day notice required before vacating his apartment." Rick Pflugradt didn't see it that way. "This sends my faith in the human race to an all-time low," he said.

FAIRWAY TO HEAVEN

In 2001 the city of Columbia, South Carolina, began building a driving range on what they thought was an open field; but it wasn't long after construction got underway that they discovered the plot was actually the unmarked graveyard of a 19th-century insane asylum. At last count there were at least 1,985 graves of mental patients at the site, some dating as far back as 1848. Rather than abandon its plans, city officials simply redesigned the driving range "to ensure that no golf balls land on graves."

HE URNED IT

In August 2001, a two-bedroom apartment in London was put up for sale after the previous owner, described in newspapers as an "unnamed pensioner," passed away. Asking price: $728,000, not a bad amount for apartments in the area. Added "bonus": The apart-

---

Number please: Dustin Hoffman used to type entries for the yellow pages.

ment comes complete with the dead man's ashes, in a stone urn on the mantlepiece. In his will, the man stipulated that he wanted the apartment to serve as his final resting place. "I have to tell people before they go to view the flat," realtor James Bailey told *The Sun* newspaper. "Luckily most just laugh."

STARTING OVER

When 70-year-old James Ross asked girlfriend Maryo Griffin to marry him in 1993, there was just one thing keeping her from saying yes: more than 12 years after the death of his first wife, Judy, Ross still had her ashes, which he kept in his home. Ross and Griffin decided to solve the problem by getting married in Las Vegas and then scattering Judy's ashes in the Grand Canyon.

Everything was going according to plan...until a thief broke into Ross's car in the Las Vegas World Casino parking lot and stole the box containing Judy's ashes. At last report the wedding was postponed, perhaps indefinitely, until the ashes are returned. "They got Judy," said Griffin. "I don't see how we can be married until we get Judy taken care of."

BODY OF EVIDENCE

When Rodney Williams, 21, appeared in Washington State's Cowlitz County District Court in April 1994 to explain why he'd missed an earlier court date on an assault charge, he brought an unusual witness to substantiate his claims—the cremated remains of his mother, which he carried in a plastic box. Williams explained that he had missed the earlier court appearance because he was caring for his mother during her final illness.

Judge Robert Altenhof, who accepted Williams's excuse, said he'd never seen anything like it in 12 years on the bench. "They bring engine parts, rugs that are urine stained, but this is the first time they've brought in human remains," he said. "You think you've heard it all, but somebody always comes up with something new."

*   *   *

BEARS REPEATING

"We don't know one millionth of one percent of anything."
—Thomas Alva Edison

BATHROOM FACTS AND FIGURES

Amazingly, someone—besides us—cares what goes on in the throne room. Yes, government agencies, public interest groups, and private industry all collect statistics on bathrooms and the people who use them. Here is some of what they've found:

PASSING TIME

• According to a study by the National Association for Continence (NAFC), the average American spends about an hour in the bathroom per day, including time spent bathing. That comes to about two weeks total per year.

• How do people pass the time in the bathroom? About half of survey respondents said they thought about "serious issues." A third said they were daydreaming, making phone calls, or singing in the shower.

• Nearly two-thirds of Americans surveyed say they engage in "toilet mapping" when they're out in public—scouting out the locations of restrooms in advance of actually needing them, just in case nature makes an unexpected call. People over 50 are more likely to engage in this practice than people under 50.

• The majority of people think of their bathrooms at home as a relaxing place to get away from the stress of life.

HOME AND AWAY

• Do you avoid using public restrooms? According to Quilted Northern's 2001 "Bathroom Confidential" Survey, 30% of Americans avoid public restrooms, citing "fear of germs" as the primary reason.

• Of those who do venture in, up to 60% say they don't sit—they hover over the public toilet without ever touching it.

• Then, when the deed is done, 40% say they flush the toilet by kicking the handle with their feet, rather than touching it with their bare hands. Another 20% reach for paper to "protect" themselves before touching the handle.

How did the golden silk spider get its name? It's the only spider that spins a gold colored web.

• What about when you're at home—are you bashful? Hard to believe, but 70% of Americans say they always close the bathroom door even if they live alone or are the only ones at home.

• Once they're behind closed doors, people are a little more at ease—50% of Americans talk on the phone in the bathroom and more than 90% read on the pot or in the tub. Meditating, balancing checkbooks, and even eating are also popular bathroom activities.

NEWS FROM ENGLAND

• British tax dollars at work: England's Department of Trade and Industry conducted a survey of emergency room admissions for the year 1999. Among their findings: "trouser accidents" (when anatomy and zippers collide) resulted in more visits to the country's emergency rooms—5,945—than any other bathroom-related accident. That's up from 5,137 in 1998.

• Other winners: Accidents involving sponges resulted in 787 trips to the hospital; accidents involving toilet roll holders, 329.

MODERN PLUMBING

• According to the U.S. Census Bureau, Alaska ranks first among the 50 states in the percentage of homes *without* indoor plumbing. The bureau estimates that in 2000, 3.83%, or 8,269, of Alaska's occupied homes lacked "complete plumbing" (hot and cold running water, a flush toilet, and a tub or shower). That's a significant improvement from just 10 years earlier, when an amazing 12.5%—more than 1 in 10 Alaskan homes—were without.

• The remoteness of many small Alaskan towns is a big part of the problem; so is the state's arctic climate. "At the risk of stating the obvious, water is a solid in our communities for up to nine months a year, and that makes it hard to transport," says Dan Easton, an official with the state. In many parts of the state, water pipes have to be installed above ground, with their own heating systems and plenty of insulation to keep the water from freezing and bursting the pipes.

• New Mexico has more homes without complete plumbing than Alaska—14,228—but they make up only 2.2% of the total number of households in the state.

HANG UP AND DRIVE!

Every year, BRI member Debbie Thornton sends in a list of real-life bumper stickers. Have you seen the one that says...

As long as there are tests, there will be prayer in public schools

Forget About World Peace....Visualize Using Your Turn Signal!

Consciousness: That annoying time between naps

I Are Illeterate And I Vote

SO MANY CATS, SO FEW RECIPES

THERE'S NO SUCH THING AS A DUMB BLONDE (*seen placed upside down on the bumper*)

Jesus is coming... everyone look busy.

A bartender is just a pharmacist with a limited inventory.

Out of my mind...back in five minutes.

VEGETARIAN: Indian Word for "Lousy Hunter"

Warning: I have an attitude and I know how to use it.

PLEASE DON'T MAKE ME KILL YOU.

Meandering to a different drummer.

I drive way too fast to worry about cholesterol.

DON'T PISS ME OFF! I'M RUNNING OUT OF PLACES TO HIDE THE BODIES.

You are depriving some poor village of its idiot.

Everyone has a photographic memory, some just don't have film.

Why am I the only person on Earth who knows how to drive?

Don't like my driving? Then quit watching me.

I may be slow, but I'm ahead of you.

Yak, yak, yak! The average person speaks 450 words in a typical 3-minute phone call.

LOONEY LAWS

Believe it or not, these laws are real.

In Tuscumbia, Alabama, it is against the law for more than eight rabbits to reside on the same block.

In Birmingham, Alabama, it is illegal to drive a car while blindfolded.

In Arizona it is illegal to hunt or shoot a camel.

In Atlanta it is illegal to make faces at school children while they are studying.

In Hawaii no one may whistle in a drinking establishment.

A law in Zion, Illinois, prohibits teaching household pets to smoke cigars.

According to Kentucky law, women may not appear on the highway in bathing suits unless they carry clubs.

In Marblehead, Massachusetts, each fire company responding to an alarm must be provided a three-gallon jug of rum.

It is illegal to fish for whales in any stream, river, or lake in Ohio.

Undertakers are prohibited from giving away books of matches in Shreveport, LA.

It is unlawful to tie a crocodile to a fire hydrant in Detroit.

In Minnesota it is illegal to dry both men's and women's underwear on the same clothesline.

In Natchez, Mississippi, it is unlawful for elephants to drink beer.

It is illegal for barbers in Waterloo, Nebraska, to eat onions between 7 a.m. and 7 p.m.

In Yukon, Oklahoma, it is illegal for a patient to pull a dentist's tooth.

In Portland, Oregon, it is illegal to shake a feather duster in someone's face.

A South Carolina statute states that butchers may not serve on a jury when a man is being tried for murder.

In Knoxville, Tennessee, it is illegal to lasso a fish.

Tendons—which anchor muscle tissue to bones—have half the tensile strength of steel.

LAWYERS ON LAWYERS

Believe it or not, some lawyers are actually quite clever. Here are some quotes from the world's most famous lawyers.

"I bring out the worst in my enemies and that's how I get them to defeat themselves."
—Roy Cohn

"The court of last resort is no longer the Supreme Court. It's *Nightline*."
—Alan Dershowitz

"We lawyers shake papers at each other the way primitive tribes shake spears."
—John Jay Osborn, Jr.

"[The] ideal client is the very wealthy man in very great trouble."
—John Sterling

"An incompetent lawyer can delay a trial for months or years. A competent lawyer can delay one even longer."
—Evelle Younger

"I've never met a litigator who didn't think he was winning...right up until the moment the guillotine dropped."
—William F. Baxter

"I'm not an ambulance chaser. I'm usually there before the ambulance."
—Melvin Belli

"This is New York, and there's no law against being annoying."
—William Kunstler

"I get paid for seeing that my clients have every break the law allows. I have knowingly defended a number of guilty men. But the guilty never escape unscathed. My fees are sufficient punishment for anyone."
—F. Lee Bailey

"I don't want to know what the law is, I want to know who the judge is."
—Roy Cohn

"The 'adversary system' is based on the notion that if one side overstates his idea of the truth and the other side overstates his idea of the truth, then the truth will come out....Why can't we all just tell the truth?"
—David Zapp

Blue eyes simply have less pigment in them than brown eyes.

THE REAL
STAR-SPANGLED BANNER

"The Star-Spangled Banner" became the official United States National Anthem in 1931. Did you know there was—and is— an actual banner? Here's the story of the flag and battle that inspired Francis Scott Key to write the song.

THE WAR OF 1812

When England and France went to war in 1803, each country tried to prevent the other from trading with neutral countries, such as the United States. As the conflict dragged on year after year, England's powerful navy interfered with American shipping to such a degree that the new nation's entire economy was threatened. On June 18, 1812, seeing no other recourse, the United States Congress declared war on England.

As the war began, the port city of Baltimore, Maryland, third largest city in the United States, was a likely target for attack. And if such an attack ever did come, Fort McHenry, which guarded the entrance to Baltimore harbor, would be one of the first targets, a fact that prompted the fort's defiant commander, Major Armistead, to ask for an American flag so big that "the British would have no trouble seeing it from a distance."

PUTTING IT TOGETHER

Two military officers paid a visit to the Baltimore home of Mary Young Pickersgill, a widow and "a maker of colors," and hired her to sew the flag. Mrs. Pickersgill and her 13-year-old daughter, Caroline, spent the next several weeks measuring, cutting, and sewing the fifteen stars and fifteen stripes that comprised the American flag at that time. They used more than 400 yards of English wool bunting, cutting stars that were two feet across from point to point, and eight red and seven white stripes, each of which were also two feet across.

The flag would measure 30 feet by 42 feet, much larger than the bedroom the Pickersgills were sewing it in. So they brought the pieces to the nearby Claggett's Brewery, where they laid them out on the malthouse floor and sewed them into the flag. The completed flag was delivered to Fort McHenry on August 19, 1813. Pickersgill charged the military exactly $405.90 for her services. But it would be a year before the flag would see any action.

BY THE ROCKETS' RED GLARE
In August of 1814, British warships entered Chesapeake Bay, landed in Benedict, Maryland, and attacked Washington, D.C. It wasn't much of a battle—American soldiers broke and ran and the British set fire to the Capitol, the White House, and other public buildings.

From Washington, the British moved north to mount an attack on Baltimore. But Armistead was ready with a strong defense and the British had to rely on their most formidable weapon, the bomb vessel, to try to take the fort.

At 6:30 a.m., September 13, they started bombarding Fort McHenry. The battle lasted 25 hours, with aerial bombs and rockets exploding through the night, showering sparks and schrapnel on the fort. (A young American lawyer and amateur poet named Francis Scott Key watched in wonder from the deck of one of the British ships.) But in the end the British couldn't dent the American defense and had to withdraw. According to Robert Barrett, midshipman on the British frigate *Hebrus*, "As the last vessel spread her canvas to the wind, the Americans hoisted a splendid and superb ensign on their battery."

American Private Isaac Munroe saw it, too. He later wrote, "At dawn on the 14th, our morning gun was fired, the flag hoisted, Yankee Doodle played, and we all appeared in full view of a mortified enemy, who calculated upon our surrender in 20 minutes after the commencement of the action." The "splendid ensign" was the Star-Spangled Banner, the largest battle flag ever flown.

FAMILY FLAG
Sometime prior to his death in 1819, Armistead acquired the flag. How he got it is unknown—he probably just took it. But he was a hero, so no one protested. It passed to his widow and remained in his family for almost ninety years until 1907, when Armistead's grandson, Eben Appleton, donated it to the Smithsonian Institution.

BITS AND PIECES

If you've ever seen Mrs. Pickersgill's flag at the Smithsonian, you may have noticed that a significant portion of the flag is missing. Some of this was due to the damage it received during the bombardment of Fort McHenry, but not all of it. After the battle, a soldier's widow asked for a snippet of the flag to bury with her husband, and Armistead himself cut off a piece for her. He granted numerous similar requests, as did Mrs. Armistead and her daughter, Georiana Armistead Appleton, after his death. Mrs. Appleton wrote in 1873, "Pieces of the flag have occasionally been given to those deemed to have a right to such a memento. Had we given all that we had been importuned for, little would be left to show."

Still, Georiana Appleton continued giving away fragments of the flag—including one of the stars—and by the time it was brought to the Smithsonian, eight feet of material were missing from the end.

PUTTING IT TOGETHER

In 1924 the Smithsonian hired a team of eleven "needlewomen" to sew a linen backing on the flag so that it could be displayed hanging. It took 1.7 million stitches.

For the next 70 years it hung in the Smithsonian. Then in 1998 they took it down, moved it to a lab, and began an $18 million, 3-year restoration of the flag. Using forceps, scissors, and tweezers, six restorers—lying on their stomachs on a platform suspended a foot above the flag—proceeded to surgically remove the linen backing. Then they started analyzing the fabric, along with some of the snippets, which the museum had actually been able to purchase at an auction. Their conclusion, two years into the project: the material was in worse shape than they had originally thought. The flag will have to be displayed in a gas-filled case and at a slight incline so as not to stress the fabric. But the Star-Spangled Banner will never be hung again.

*　　*　　*

Final Irony: Francis Scott Key, author of the United States' national anthem and the words, "O'er the land of the free," was a slave owner.

URBAN LEGENDS

Here's our latest batch of urban legends—have you heard any of these? Remember the BRI rule of thumb: If a wild story sounds a little too "perfect," it's probably an urban legend...or is it?

THE LEGEND: Chocolate milk is made from tainted milk. Dairies too cheap to throw away unusable milk add chocolate to hide the bad taste.

HOW IT SPREAD: This story started out as a schoolyard rumor, spread by kids. But it took on new life in the 1990s, when the introduction of prepared coffee drinks in bottles and cans inspired people to extend the children's tale to adult beverages.

THE TRUTH: The milk in chocolate milk and coffee drinks is as carefully tested and regulated by the U.S. Food and Drug Administration as any other form of milk.

THE LEGEND: When the Missouri Ku Klux Klan won a lengthy court battle to participate in the Adopt-a-Highway program—which would have required the state to use taxpayer dollars to "advertise" the KKK on those little roadside Adopt-a-Highway signs—the state legislature responded by naming the Klan's designated stretch of road after civil rights activist Rosa Parks.

HOW IT SPREAD: By word of mouth and over the Internet.

THE TRUTH: What makes this urban legend different from most others? It's true. In March 2000 the Missouri KKK really did win a legal battle to adopt a mile-long stretch of I-55 south of St. Louis, and the state legislature really did name it the Rosa Parks Highway in response.

PROBLEM SOLVED: No one ever showed up to clean the road either before or after the name change, so the state dropped the KKK from the program in April 2000.

THE LEGEND: A few years before the Gulf War, Barbara Walters did a news story on gender roles in Kuwait in which she reported that Kuwaiti wives traditionally walk several paces behind their husbands. She returned to Kuwait after the war and

---

There are 27 chemicals that can be added to bread without being listed on the label.

noticed that women were now walking several paces *ahead* of their husbands. When Walters asked a Kuwaiti woman how so much social progress had been accomplished in so little time, the woman replied, "Land mines."

HOW IT SPREAD: By word of mouth and e-mail, starting shortly after the end of the Gulf War.

THE TRUTH: This is the latest version of a classic urban legend that has been around as long as landmines themselves. The subjects of the story—Kuwaitis, Korean and Vietnamese peasants, and in the case of World War II, nomads in North Africa—change to fit the circumstances of each new war.

THE LEGEND: You can help oil-soaked Australian penguins by knitting tiny sweaters for them to wear and mailing them to an address in Tasmania, off the southern coast of Australia.

HOW IT SPREAD: By word of mouth, e-mail, and cable news broadcasts, following an oil spill near Tasmania on New Year's Day 2000.

THE TRUTH: Another example of an urban "legend" that's actually true. This one is a request for public assistance that snowballed out of control. In 2001 the Tasmanian Conservation Trust and State Library asked knitters to put their leftover yarn to good use by knitting it into penguin sweaters. It even posted a pattern on the Internet so that knitters would know how to make one in just the right shape and size. (The sweaters keep oil-soaked penguins warm and prevent them from ingesting oil until they regain enough strength to be scrubbed clean.)

The story received international news coverage, prompting concerned knitters all over the world to begin sending penguin sweaters to Tasmania. The Conservation Trust had hoped to create a stockpile of 100 in preparation for the next oil spill, but more than 800 arrived in the first few weeks alone; from there the number just kept growing. "They're all one size," says a volunteer. "But at least the penguins have a choice of color."

*   *   *

"Life is tough, but it's tougher when you're stupid."
—John Wayne

AUTOMOBILE FIRSTS

Here are the stories behind several car-related firsts.
From The Book of Firsts, by Patrick Robertson.

THE FIRST WOMAN DRIVER
Date: 1891

Background: The first woman to drive a car was Madame Levassor, wife of one of the partners in the Paris motor manufacturing concern Panhard et Levassor, but better known by her former name of Madame Sarazin. After the death of her first husband, Madame Sarazin had acquired the French and Belgian rights of manufacture for the Daimler gas-powered engine. The following year, she married Emile Levassor, and the patent rights passed to her new husband's firm. They began manufacturing cars under their own name in 1891, the year Madame Levassor learned to drive. The earliest evidence of her becoming a chauffeuse is a photograph showing her at the tiller of a Panhard car, dated 1892.

THE FIRST TWO-CAR GARAGE
Date: 1899

Background: In 1899, Dr. W. W. Barrett of Southport, England, erected the first garage specifically for cars. It was joined to his house and was equipped with engine-pits and facilities for repairing his two cars, an 1898 Daimler and an 1898 Knitley Victoria. Dr. Barrett was also the first man in England to own a totally enclosed car, and the inventor of the first practical jack for lifting cars.

That same year, a Dr. Zabriskie of Brooklyn, New York, built a brick garage measuring 18 by 22 feet for a cost of $1,500. He had purchased his Winton Road-Wagon in 1898, but it is not known whether his garage was completed before or after Dr. Barrett's.

THE FIRST CAR THEFT
Date: June 1896

Background: The first recorded car theft occurred in Paris, when the Baron de Zuylen's Peugeot was stolen by his mechanic from a repair garage, where it was undergoing repairs. Thief and vehicle were apprehended.

The horseshoe crab has sky-blue blood.

THE FIRST POLICE CAR
Date: 1899

Background: The first occasion in which a car was used in police work occurred when Sgt. McLeod of the Northamptonshire (England) County Police borrowed a Benz vehicle to pursue a man who was selling forged tickets for the Barnum and Bailey Circus. Top speed: 12 mph. The first car *regularly* employed in police work was a Stanley Steamer acquired by the Boston Police Department in 1903. It replaced four horses.

THE FIRST TAXICAB
Date: 1896

Background: The first taxicabs for hire were two Benz-Kraftdroschkes purchased for 8,000 marks each by Droschkenbesitzer Dutz of Stuttgart. In 1897 Friedrich Greiner started a rival service, giving Stuttgart the distinction of having two cab companies running gas-driven taxis before any other city—with the exception of Paris—had even one. But in a literal sense, Greiner's were the first true "taxis," because they were the first motor cabs fitted with taximeters.

THE FIRST CAR RADIO
Date: May 1922

Background: The first known car radio was fitted to the passenger door of a Ford Model T by 18-year-old George Frost, president of the Lane High School Radio Club, Chicago.

THE FIRST AUTOMOBILE FATALITY
Date: August 17, 1896

Background: The first automobile fatality occurred at the Crystal Palace in London, when Mrs. Bridget Driscoll was run over and her skull fractured by a wheel of the car. The driver was Arthur Edsell, an employee of the Anglo-French Motor Co. Edsell's vision was obstructed by two other cars and Mrs. Driscoll, in a state of panic, stood still in the path of the approaching vehicle. At the inquest it was stated that Edsell was driving at 4 mph at the time of the accident. The verdict was Accidental Death.

Sun-light: The weight of the sun's light on the Earth's surface: 2 lbs. per square mile.

THE CHOCOLATE HALL OF FAME

In previous Bathroom Readers we've told you the stories of Milton Hershey, Henri Nestlé, Frank Mars, and other notables in the chocolate world. Here are a few more.(Hint: Baker's chocolate wasn't named with bakers in mind, and German chocolate doesn't come from Germany.)

HARRY BURNET REESE

In the early 1920s Reese worked in one of the dairies owned by Milton Hershey. Inspired by Hershey's success, he decided "if Hershey can sell a trainload of chocolate every day, I can at least make a living making candy." Reese struck out on his own and by the mid-1920s had an entire line of candies, including dinner mints, dipped chocolates, caramels, and coconut candies. In 1928 he added peanut butter cups; they were so popular that when World War II rationing put a dent in his business in 1942, he dumped the rest of his product line and focused exclusively on them. Today Reese's Peanut Butter Cups are part of Hershey Foods.

L. S. HEATH

In 1914 an Illinois schoolteacher named L. S. Heath mortgaged his house for $3,000 to buy his sons a soda shop. A year later he quit his teaching job to join them and expanded the business into homemade ice cream and candy. One afternoon in the mid-1920s a salesman told them about a candy called Trail-Toffee that he'd seen in another store. The Heath brothers took the basic recipe—almonds, butter, and sugar—and spent the next several months experimenting. In 1928 they finally came up with a chocolate-covered English toffee bar—the Heath Bar.

DR. JAMES BAKER

In 1765 Dr. Baker and an Irish immigrant chocolate-maker named John Hannon formed a chocolate company in Dorchester, Massachusetts. In 1772 they started advertising their chocolate under the brand name Hannon's Best Chocolate... but when Hannon

---

Heavy, man: In 1907 egret plumes were worth twice their weight in gold.

was lost at sea in 1799, Dr. Baker assumed full control of the company and renamed the product Baker's Chocolate.

SAM GERMAN

The guy that German chocolate is named after worked for the guy that Baker's chocolate is named after. No kidding. Sam German was an employee of the Baker Chocolate Company in the 1850s, when he created a mild dark chocolate bar for baking. The bar was named Baker's German's Sweet Chocolate in his honor.

About a century later in 1957, a Dallas, Texas, newspaper published a recipe for German Chocolate Cake, sparking a local baking craze. When General Foods, then-owner of the Baker's Chocolate company, noticed a spike in German's Chocolate sales, they investigated... and when they learned that German Chocolate Cake was responsible, sent copies of the recipe and photos of the cake to food editors all over the country. Sales of German's Chocolate jumped 73% in the first year alone, and German Chocolate Cake became an American dessert classic.

JOHN AND RICHARD CADBURY

In 1822 John Cadbury opened a tea and coffee shop in Birmingham, England. He expanded into chocolate manufacturing, and in 1853 became purveyor of chocolate to Queen Victoria. In 1861 his son Richard Cadbury hit upon the idea of increasing sales of Valentine's Day chocolate sales by packaging Cadbury chocolates in the world's first heart-shaped candy box.

DAVID LYTLE CLARK

In 1883 Clark, an Irish immigrant, hired a cook and started a candy business in Pittsburgh. While the cook prepared the candy, Clark sold it out of the back of a wagon to local merchants. In 1886 he tasted chewing gum for the first time; a short while later he added it to his product line. Countless other products followed; in time Clark became known as the Pittsburgh Candy King. But his biggest claim to fame came in 1917, when he invented a nickel candy bar similar to a Butterfinger—honeycombed ground, roasted peanuts coated with milk chocolate—that America's World War I fighting men could carry with them into battle. Clark liked his new product so much he named it after himself: the Clark Bar.

World's most recognizable smell? Coffee.

IRONIC, ISN'T IT?

*Some more irony to put the problems of
day-to-day life in proper perspective.*

VOCATIONAL IRONY
* In August 2000, a 44-year-old woman named Angel Destiny fled for her life dressed only in pajamas after half of her house in Cardiff, Wales, collapsed into rubble. Destiny, who makes her living as a psychic, told reporters, "I just didn't see it coming."

* A circus contortionist who goes by the name Berkine got his right foot stuck on his left shoulder...and did not immediately receive the medical attention he needed to get unstuck. Reason: Circus workers who heard him screaming for help "thought he was joking."

* In May 2000 a save-the-whales activist was forced to call off his sailing voyage across the Pacific Ocean, which he had hoped would call attention to his cause. Reason: "His 60-foot boat was damaged by two passing whales."

* In an unrelated incident, in July 2001, the 50-foot yacht *Peningo* was struck by a whale while sailing about 350 miles off the coast of Newfoundland. What was crew member John Fullerton doing when the incident occurred? Reading a copy of *Moby Dick*.

* According to *Industrial Machinery News*, an (unnamed) company with a five-year perfect safety record tried to demonstrate the importance of wearing safety goggles on-the-job by showing workers a graphic film containing footage of gory industrial accidents. Twenty-five people injured themselves while fleeing the screening room, 13 others passed out during the film, and another required seven stitches "after he cut his head falling off a chair while watching the film."

GOVERNMENTAL IRONY
* In June 2000, an 87-year-old man dropped dead while standing in line at a government office in Bogotá, Colombia. Reason for visiting the office: To "apply for a government certificate to prove he was still alive."

Toilet Rock, a natural rock formation shaped like a flush toilet, is in City of Rocks, NM.

- In 1919 *The New York Times* commissioned a poll asking people who they thought were the 10 most important living Americans. Herbert Hoover won first place. Franklin Roosevelt, then assistant secretary of the Navy, saw the poll and wrote a colleague, "Herbert Hoover is certainly a winner, and I wish we could make him President of the United States."

- In January 2000 a Florida seventh-grade teacher had his 70 students write their elected representatives a letter. Purpose of the exercise: To demonstrate that "their opinions matter." As of the end of the school year, none of the students had received a reply.

HOLLYWOOD IRONY

- *Hellcats of the Navy*, a 1957 film starring Ronald Reagan and Nancy Davis (the future Mrs. Reagan), was co-written by screenwriter Bernard Gordon. Gordon used the name Raymond T. Marcus because he'd been blacklisted during the McCarthy era, during which Reagan had served as a government informant.

- A production company won a $1.8 million judgment against a former employee accused of stealing the concept for a television game show. Name of the stolen show: *Anything for Money.*"

MISCELLANEOUS IRONY

- A 15-year-old Zimbabwe boy named Victim Kamubvumbi lived up to his name when he became stranded on an island in the middle of the Ruya River during a flood. Victim's last name, when translated into English: "slight drizzle that does not end."

- In 1982 Bill Curtis, an electronic technician at the Vancouver airport, became convinced that a nuclear war was imminent. So convinced, in fact, that he moved his family to the place his research told him would be the safest on Earth: The Falkland Islands, an English colony off the east coast of South America. The following April, 4,000 Argentinian troops attacked the islands and claimed them for Argentina, in the process starting a shooting war with England that lasted more than three months.

*　　*　　*

"I've always hated that damn James Bond. I'd like to kill him."
—Sean **Connery**

RUMORS
OF MY DEATH...

Here are more examples of "rebirth": people who were thought to be dead, but were actually quite alive.

DECEASED: Jayaprakash Narayan, Indian "patriot and elder statesman"

NEWS OF HIS DEATH: On March 22, 1979, Prime Minister Morarji Desai announced to the nation that Narayan had died. Desai delivered an emotional eulogy; Parliament was adjourned. Flags were lowered to half-mast nationwide, schools and shops closed, and funeral music was broadcast over All-India Radio in honor of the fallen giant.

RESURRECTION: Later that day, Jayaprakash Narayan heard the news of his own death while convalescing in the hospital, where he was still very much alive. Prime Minister Desai apologized for the mistake and brought the official mourning to an end, blaming the false report on the director of the Indian Intelligence Bureau, "one of whose staff had seen a body being carried out of the hospital."

DECEASED: Sam Kalungi, a private in the Ugandan army

NEWS OF HIS DEATH: In the late 1990s, Private Kalungi was one of more than 10,000 Ugandan soldiers sent to the Congo to aid rebels trying to overthrow Congolese president Laurent Kabila. Several months later the Ugandan Army contacted Kalungi's family, telling them that Kalungi had died in battle. Family members went to the morgue of the Mbuya military hospital, positively identified the body, and had it delivered to their home village of Mbukiro for burial.

RESURRECTION: When his two-year tour was up, Kalungi returned home to Mbukiro, where shocked and relieved relatives took him to see the grave that bore his name. So who's buried there? Private James Kalungi (no relation), delivered to the wrong family and misidentified by Sam Kalungi's own parents. "The body

---

The flowers of Africa's baobab tree open only in the moonlight. They are pollinated by bats.

had spent one and a half months in the military hospital. It had an ice coating on the face which made us believe it was our son," Sam's mother explained.

DECEASED: An unidentified man from Almaty, Kazakhstan

NEWS OF HIS DEATH: According to the Reuters news agency, the man was trying to steal electrical power cables in eastern Kazakhstan, when he touched a live wire and was electrocuted. Thinking he was dead, his family wrapped him in a cloth shroud and buried him in a shallow grave.

RESURRECTION: The grave must have been really shallow, because two days later the man "regained consciousness and rose naked from the ground," whereupon he hitched a ride back to his village…and got there just in time to attend his own funeral feast. That was no easy task—according to local news reports, the naked, electrocuted man "had trouble flagging down a vehicle to take him home."

DECEASED: Cesar Aguilera, 58, of Nicaragua

NEWS OF HIS DEATH: In May 2001, Aquilera went to tend some property he owned in the countryside. More than a week passed and he did not return. His relatives, fearing the worst, went around to local morgues looking for his body…and thought they had found it when they discovered a man about Aguilera's height and weight who'd been run over by a car.

RESURRECTION: Aguilera returned home from his trip just as his family was preparing to bury the deceased. You would expect they would have been happy to see him, but they didn't exactly show it. "One kid screamed at me, 'Are you from this life or the other?'" Aguilera said.

*   *   *

A REAL SHOW STOPPER

In a version of the opera *Carmen* performed in Verona in 1970, 38 horses were used live on stage. All went well until the conductor gave a violent upswing of his baton, startling a horse and causing a stampede. Sole fatality: One of the horses jumped into the orchestra pit and landed on top of the kettledrum.

Lincoln survived two assassination attempts before being killed by John Wilkes Booth.

THE HISTORY OF FOOTBALL, PART IV

*Here's the part of our story on the history of football that "red-meat"
sports fans have been waiting for: how one of America's most violent
sports became even more violent. So violent in fact, that for
a time it looked like some colleges would ban it forever.*

FOOTBALL IN THE NEWS
The "Hospital Box Score" printed by the *Boston Globe* following the Harvard-Yale game of 1894 (Yale won, 12–4):

> **YALE:** JERREMS, KNEE INJURY; MURPHY, UNCONSCIOUS FROM A KICK IN THE HEAD; BUTTERWORTH, CARRIED FROM THE FIELD.
>
> **HARVARD:** CHARLEY BREWER, BADLY BRUISED FOOT; WORTHINGTON, BROKEN COLLARBONE; HALLOWELL, BROKEN NOSE.

By the mid-1890s, due in large part to the introduction of mass plays like the V-trick and the flying wedge, serious injuries had become such a routine part of football that newspapers began publishing injury reports as part of their sports coverage. How violent was it? In the early 1890s, a player was actually allowed to slug another player three times with a closed fist before the referee could throw him out of the game.

THE NAKED TRUTH

The situation was made even worse by the fact that players wore almost no protective padding—not even football helmets, which were not mandatory until 1939. The football players of the late 1880s and early 1890s wore little more than canvas or cotton knickers, a football jersey, high-top shoes with leather spikes, and hard leather shin guards worn underneath wool socks. They topped off the look with a knitted cap with a tassle or pom-pom on top. If a player was worried about getting his ears torn from the grabbing style of tackling popular at the time, he could wear earmuffs. "Anyone who wore home-made pads was regarded as a sissy," early football great John Heisman remembered.

Football has more rules than any other American sport.

One acceptable piece of protective wear: If a player worried about breaking his nose, he could wear a black, banana-shaped rubber nose mask. "Sometimes all 11 players wore them," Robert Leckie writes in *The Story of Football*. "They were indeed a ferocious sight with the ends of their handle-bar mustaches dangling from either side of that long, black, banana-like mask, and their long hair flying in the breeze."

GAME OVER

Thanks to the introduction of mass-momentum plays, the 1893 season was surprisingly brutal, even to hardened football fans. That year's Purdue-Chicago game was so violent that the Tippecanoe County District Attorney, who was watching from the stands, ran out onto the field in the middle of the game and threatened to indict every single player on charges of assault and battery. The departments of the Army and Navy were so disturbed by the violent direction that football was taking that they abolished the annual game between their military academies.

Public sentiment was also beginning to turn sharply against mass-momentum plays—not just because people were being hurt and killed, but also because they made the games boring to watch (unless you were there to watch people break bones). So many players crowded around the ball during the mass plays that it was difficult for spectators to see what was going on.

MAKING SOME CHANGES

In 1894 the University Athletic Club of New York invited the "Big Four" football powers—Yale, Princeton, Harvard, and Pennsylvania—to meet in New York to form new rules that would curb the violence in football.

Banning mass-momentum plays outright was out of the question—they were too popular with too many football teams—but the Big Four did agree to a few restrictions. They limited the number of players who could gather behind the line of scrimmage in preparation for a play, and they passed a rule requiring that a ball had to travel at least 10 yards at kickoffs to be considered in play, unless it was touched by a member of the receiving team.

They also made it illegal to touch a member of the opposing team unless the opponent had the ball, and reduced the length of

---

Seventy-five percent of all murder victims knew their killer.

the game from 90 minutes to 70, in the hopes that shorter games would mean less violence.

The new restrictions effectively banned the flying wedge and similar plays during kickoffs, but in the end they were not very effective, because teams kept inventing new mass plays that got around the rules. Injuries continued to mount.

THE BIG TEN IS BORN

The following year, Princeton and Yale proposed banning mass-momentum plays altogether, by requiring a minimum of seven players on the line of scrimmage and by allowing only one back to be in forward motion before the snap. Harvard and Penn refused to go along, and rather than sign on to the new rules they broke off from the Big Four and drafted their own set of rules, allowing mass-momentum plays.

When the Big Four split in 1895, the presidents of Chicago, Illinois, Michigan, Minnesota, Northwestern, Purdue, and Wisconsin universities stepped in to fill the breach by meeting and forming what grew into the "Big Ten" Western Conference. (Iowa and Indiana joined in 1899, and the 10th school, Ohio State, signed on in 1912.)

The rise of a competing football conference motivated the students of the Big Four to resolve their differences. In the summer of 1896, Harvard and Pennsylvania returned to the fold, and the Big Four moved a step closer to banning mass-momentum plays with a rule that forbade players from taking more than a single step before the ball was in play, unless they came to a complete stop before taking another step. But it wasn't enough, as Robert Leckie writes in *The Story of Football*:

> As the twentieth century began, football was still a game of mass-momentum....The flying wedge was not completely gone. Hurdling and the flying tackle were common. Slugging was still a familiar tactic up front, and the most acceptable method of getting the ball carrier through the line was to push, pull, or haul him through. Thus the only participant surviving the contest undamaged was apt to be the ball.

Fortunately, reading is not a contact sport, so while we go off to the infirmary to get a few bandages, you may turn to page 389 for Part V of The History of Football.

Q & A:
ASK THE EXPERTS

Everyone's got a question or two they'd like answered—basic stuff, like "Why is the sky blue?" Here are a few of those questions, with answers from some of the nation's top trivia experts.

SEA-SONING

Q: *Why are the oceans salty?*

A: One theory: "When rain falls on rocks it dissolves some of the minerals in them, particularly salt. The rainwater washes into streams and rivers, carrying away the salt with it. There is not enough salt in most rivers to make them taste salty, but after millions of years the salt carried to the oceans has made them quite salty. During all these years, ocean water has been evaporating, leaving the salt behind, increasing the saltiness of the oceans. There are beds of salt throughout the world, sometimes hundreds of feet thick, probably formed by the evaporation of ancient seas." (From *The Question and Answer Book of Nature*, by John R. Saunders)

ESSENTIAL BATHROOM KNOWLEDGE

Q: *Why is there a crescent moon on outhouse doors?*

A: "The main reasons for carving anything into an outhouse door are light and ventilation.

"In olden times, outhouse builders used cutouts of the moon and sun to let people know which outhouse to use. The moon represented women, the sun represented men. The symbols also helped foreign travelers. It didn't matter what language they spoke because the symbols were universal.

"But if one of the outhouses at an inn was damaged and could no longer be used, it was automatically assumed to be the men's outhouse. The reasoning was that men could always go behind a tree, so the crescent moon was put on the remaining usable structure for use by women. For economy, many inns only constructed an outhouse for women. This custom soon became so widespread that eventually the moon became the symbol used for all outhouses." (From *What Makes Flamingos Pink?*, by Bill McLain)

Hot commodity: Pound for pound, radium is worth more than gold.

FROZEN STIFF

Q: *Why do ice cubes crack?*

A: "They're trying to shrink! When water freezes, it gets bigger and lighter. As soon as you put an ice cube in a drink, the outside of the cube wants to turn back into water. So the cube tries to shrink—quickly. The shrinking squeezes hard on the inside of the ice cube and, all of the sudden...the inside part goes crack." (From *Why Does Popcorn Pop?*, by Catherine Ripley)

STALE MATE

Q: *Why don't birds sing in the winter?*

A: "One reason is that many species are gone, having migrated south for the winter. But some birds, such as starlings, mourning doves, and sparrows, are around all winter. Yet even they are silent.

"For birds, singing is associated with mating. As birds mate and begin to build their nests, one of their first tasks is to stake out a territory where other birds are not welcome. By keeping competitors away from a particular area, a nesting bird ensures that there will be enough food for both parents and the growing chicks. Singing is a very efffective way of announcing to other birds, 'This territory is occupied.'

"Since most birds set up territories and mate in the spring, this is the time you are most likely to hear birdsong." (From *101 Questions and Answers About Backyard Wildlife*, by Ann Squire)

CAUGHT A LIGHT SNEEZE

Q: *How come whenever I go out into bright light I sneeze?*

A: "You say you don't have this problem? Well, between one-sixth and one-quarter of the population do. They have what's known as photic sneeze reflex ('sneeze caused by light').

"What causes it? Nobody knows. What we do know is that the nerves for the eye and the nose run pretty close together. Some think what we've got here is a case of nerve signals getting crossed. If it bugs you...well, there's always brain surgery. But personally, I'd learn to live with it." (From *Know It All!*, by Ed Zotti)

If you feed a rhesus monkey a "typical American diet" it will die within 2 years.

WOMAN TO WOMAN

Some thoughtful observations on womanhood from some of the world's most interesting women.

"From birth to age 18 a girl needs good parents. From 18 to 35 she needs good looks. From 35 to 55 she needs a good personality. From 55 on, she needs cash."
—Sophie Tucker

"Whatever women do they must do twice as well as men to be thought half as good. Luckily, this is not difficult."
—Charlotte Whitton

"The hardest task in a girl's life is to prove to a man that his intentions are serious."
—Helen Rowland

"My idea of a superwoman is someone who scrubs her own floors."
—Bette Middler

"We haven't come a long way, we've come a short way. If we hadn't come a short way, no one would be calling us 'baby.'"
—Elizabeth Janeway

"I refuse to think of them as chin hairs. I think of them as stray eyebrows."
—Janette Barbery

"I will feel equality has arrived when we can elect to office women who are as incompetent as some of the men who are already there."
—Maureen Reagan

"Woman's virtue is man's greatest invention."
—Cornelia Otis Skinner

"Who ever thought up the word 'mammogram'? Every time I hear it, I think I'm supposed to put my breast in an envelope and send it to someone."
—Jan King

"I'm furious about the women's liberationists. They keep getting up on soapboxes and proclaiming women are brighter than men. That's true, but it should be kept quiet or it ruins the whole racket."
—Anita Loos

"The especial genius of women I believe is to be electrical in movement, intuitive in function, spiritual in tendency."
—Margaret Fuller

BEHIND BAR CODES

*We see them on every item we buy, but we don't know
what they mean or what they're used for. Here's
the story of the Universal Product Code.*

STEP UP TO THE BAR

The story of the bar code begins in 1948, when the president of the Food Fair chain of grocery stores went to see the dean of Philadelphia's Drexel Institute of Technology. Food Fair wanted Drexel to do research into the feasibility of some kind of device that could collect product information automatically at checkout counters. The dean said no—but a graduate student named Bernard Silver overheard the conversation. Silver was intrigued and mentioned it to his friend Joseph Woodland, a teacher at Drexel. The two men decided to work together on creating a device.

After some moderately successful experiments using ultraviolet light, Woodland quit his teaching job and moved to his grandfather's apartment in Florida to devote more time to the project. One day while lounging on Miami Beach, Woodland was thinking about the problem and absentmindedly pulled his fingers through the sand, leaving lines. That gave him the brainstorm to work with Morse code and to extend the lines, so that dots would become skinny lines and dashes would become fat lines—the prototype of the first bar code.

OPTICAL ALLUSION

To read the code, Woodland used technology from another project he was working on—improving Muzak using the technology from movie sound tracks. Sound for movies was printed in a light-and-dark pattern along the edges of film, read by a light, transformed to electric waveforms, then converted to sound. Woodland and Silver adapted the technology to read their morse code lines and filed a patent application on October 20, 1949.

In 1951 Woodland got a job with IBM, where he hoped to push his invention forward. In his spare time, he and Silver built the first actual bar code scanner in the middle of Woodland's living room. The finished product was the size of a desk, and used a

---

A snapping turtle can only swallow when its head is under water.

500-watt lightbulb and a "photomultiplier tube" designed for movie sound systems, hooked up to an oscilloscope. When the bar code on a piece of paper was moved across the beam of light, it caused the oscilloscope signal to move. It was crude, it was huge, and it was so hot that it set the paper on fire...but it worked. Woodland and Silver had created an electronic device that could read a printed code. Their patent was granted in 1952.

In 1962 IBM offered to buy the patent, but Woodland and Silver thought the offer was too low. A few weeks later, Philco made a better offer and they sold it. Philco later sold it to RCA.

UNMARKED CARS

At the same time, the railroad industry was developing its own bar-code system. Tracking freight cars created an impossible tangle of paperwork; bar coding each car looked like a cheaper, easier way to do it. Unfortunately, it wasn't (and eventually they scrapped the idea)—but by the time that became obvious, technology had progressed significantly and it could be used to address some of the bugs in Silver and Woodland's system.

By the late 1960s, lasers and microchips made it possible to greatly reduce the size of the code reader. The bars of the code were also revised to record the numbers 0 through 9 instead of Morse code dots and dashes.

In 1969 the General Trading Company of New Jersey started using bar codes to direct shipments to their loading docks. Then the General Motors plant in Michigan began to use them to monitor production of axle units. Meanwhile, RCA was working on a bull's-eye-shaped code for grocery stores. IBM saw a huge potential market and wanted to get into it, too. Then someone at IBM remembered that the bar code's inventor, Joseph Woodland, was still working for IBM. Woodland was transferred to the project and became instrumental in developing what we know today as the UPC—the Universal Product Code.

STANDARD RESPONSE

In 1973 the Uniform Grocery Product Code set nationwide standards for bar coding. National Cash Register began building efficient scanners and introduced their first model at the 1974 convention of the Super Market Institute. Six weeks later, on June

A cashier entering digits by hand will average one error for every 350 characters,

26, 1974 at the Marsh Supermarket in Troy, Ohio, a package of Wrigley's chewing gum was the first item ever scanned. Why a pack of gum? It just happened to be the first item out of the shopping cart of a now-nameless shopper. Today it is on display at the Smithsonian Institute.

HOW IT WORKS

The UPC is composed of 12 digits. A single digit on the left identifies which type of product the item is: meat, produce, drug, etc. The next five digits identify the manufacturer, followed by five digits that identify the actual product. Every item scanned has its own unique ID number. A single digit on the right acts as a "check digit." It adds up some of the previous numbers to come up with a magic "everything's OK" number. For example, if someone has altered the code with a marker, the numbers won't add up and the product will be rejected.

The identifying numerals are also printed along the bottom of the bar code for the sake of the cashiers, in case the scanner is down or the bar code has been partially obscured and the numbers need to be entered by hand.

The UPC only contains the manufacturer and the product, but this information is fed to a computer (the cash register), which knows the price of the item. It also acts as an inventory system, telling management how much of any given item is still on hand, how fast it's being sold, when it will need to be reordered, how many coupons have been redeemed, and community purchasing patterns.

CHECK THIS OUT

Bar codes are not just for pricing products. They are used:
• For tracking inventory on aircraft carriers
• For coding blood in blood banks
• For following applications in the Patent Office
• For identifying people in places like hospitals, libraries, and cafeterias
• For sorting baggage at airports
• For monitoring radio-collared animals

but a bar code scanner will make an error only once every 3,500,000 characters.

- For keeping track of logs in lumberyards
- For tracking the mating habits of bees (researchers put tiny bar codes on their backs)
- For tracking packages (Federal Express is probably the world's biggest single user of bar code technology)
- For identifying ships in the Navy
- By runners in the New York City Marathon—they don bar codes on their vests and the computer records the order in which they cross the finish line
- To prevent scalping and theft of badges at the Masters Golf Tournament in Georgia
- By NASA to make sure the backs of heat-resistant tiles are installed on the correct spots of the space shuttles
- By the Occupational Safety and Health Administration to track the characteristics of hazardous materials (such as whether they're explosive and how to control them), in case there's an accident

MONETARILY SPEAKING

Over a million companies worldwide use the UPC to identify their products. Equipment used to print, scan, and program bar codes amounts to a $16 billion-a-year business. It's estimated that the codes are scanned five billion times a day across the planet.

Bernard Silver, who died in 1963 at the age of 38, never got to see his invention reach such phenomenal proportions. But Joseph Woodland was awarded the National Medal of Technology by President Bush in 1992. Neither man made very much money from their invention.

*   *   *

HOW DO THEY KNOW WHAT IT IS?

Scientists in Spain have discovered what they believe to be dinosaur vomit. According to a paleontologist from the Natural History Museum of Los Angeles County, it is the world's oldest specimen. Age of the prehistoric puke: about 120 million years.

—**Wireless Flash News Service**

THE BIGGEST CULT MOVIE OF ALL TIME

Imagine the boy next door trading in his Levi's for fishnet stockings, his all-American sister sporting a sexy French maid's outfit. It's a scene that's played out at movie theaters around the world every Saturday at midnight—all because starving actor/playwright Richard O'Brien needed to pay the rent.

DON'T DREAM IT, BE IT

In the early 1970s, Richard O'Brien had just been fired as a chorus boy in a musical on London's version of Broadway, the West End. With no money and a wife and child to support, and lots of time on his hands, O'Brien penned a bizarre musical about cross-dressing, sex-starved aliens. He called it *The Rocky Horror Show*. And somehow, this weird show actually got produced. It opened at London's Royal Court Theatre in 1973 and was an amazing success; it was even named the best musical of the year.

Shortly after its debut, producer Lou Adler bought the play and moved it across the Atlantic to Los Angeles' Roxy Theater, where it met with critical and audience acclaim. It also caught the eye of filmmakers at 20th Century Fox, who were sure they they could transform it into a hit movie. The film version starred newcomers Tim Curry, Susan Sarandon, Barry Bostwick, and the singer Meat Loaf. It took eight weeks to shoot and cost $1 million to make. But before the movie was released, the play opened in New York...and flopped.

COLD FEET

Because the play had bombed, 20th Century Fox spent very little on publicity for the film, and it played in very few theaters. The movie initially had about as much success as the Broadway show—critics hated it and audiences stayed away in droves. It appeared that *The Rocky Horror Picture Show* was dead in the water.

But because of the play's early success at the Roxy, the movie

---

A butterfly's taste organs, located on its feet, are 2,400 times as sensitive as the human tongue.

did well in Los Angeles, so Adler was convinced that the film just hadn't found its audience. In 1976 he persuaded New York's Waverly Theater, in the heart of bohemian Greenwich Village, to begin midnight showings. The tactic was tried in a few other select cities across the country as well. The hope was that it would catch on with cult audiences, just as offbeat films like *El Topo* and George Romero's horror classic *Night of the Living Dead* had done.

JUST A JUMP TO THE LEFT

Within months, a phenomenon began to take hold. Audiences decided to tear down the invisible wall that separated them from the on-screen action. They weren't content just watching the movie from their seats—they began to dress as their favorite characters and perform along with the film, creating a show within a show. Seeing the movie became an interactive adventure; the *Rocky* experience was now part movie, part sing-along, part fashion show, and all party. Being in the audience at *The Rocky Horror Picture Show* now involved shouting lines at the screen, covering up with newspapers during scenes with rain, squirting water pistols to simulate rain in the theater, throwing rice during the wedding sequences, and dancing in the aisles doing the "Time Warp," the film's contagious anthem.

The *Rocky* phenomenon spread across the United States, giving birth to a midnight movie industry that spanned from major metropolitan areas right through to the straightlaced suburbs of America's heartland.

Almost 30 years after its initial debut in the attic of London's Royal Court Theatre, *Rocky* still plays every weekend at midnight in dozens of theaters across the United States and around the world. And in November 2000 *The Rocky Horror Show* returned to Broadway...this time to critical praise and commercial success. It was nominated for several Tony Awards, including Best Revival.

Launching Pad

Can you picture actor Russell Crowe in high heels and a black bustier? In the 1980s, the Academy Award–winning star of *Gladiator* toured Australia and New Zealand singing and dancing through more than 400 performances of *The Rocky Horror Show* as the cross-dressing Dr. Frank N. Furter.

Hedging bets: There are more churches per capita in Las Vegas than in any other U.S. city.

YUPPIE PUPPIES

Sophisticated products for the discriminating dog, sent in by BRI fan, Joe Atkins.

DOG DOORBELL ($29.95, *Hammacher Schlemmer*): When doggie wants to go out, he can trigger this device by stepping on a paw-shaped radio transmitter, which activates a remote chime—letting master know that nature is calling.

EXCLUSIVE MEMORY FOAM DOG BED ($139.95, *Hammacher Schlemmer*): Using space-age technology, the Memory Foam Bed reacts with your dog's body heat, molding itself to the animal's contours, promoting healthy circulation, and eliminating stress on pressure points.

IONIC BATH PET BRUSH ($49.95, *The Sharper Image*): If you love your puppy but not his smell, this brush showers your pet with safe amounts of ozone particles, neutralizing odors and conditioning his fur.

DELIGHTED DOGGY PET TUNES ($9.99, *PetsMart*): A CD for dogs? Yes, and it's not just for your pooch: "Try sitting and listening to it together—you'll both benefit from relaxing and hearing these timeless selections."

OH MY DOG! EAU DE TOILETTE SPRAY ($38, *Saks Fifth Avenue*): The world's first top-quality fragrance crafted especially for canines! "Top notes of rosewood and orange leaves suggest happy barking while the heart notes evoke a boisterous tussle in the grass." Also available: Oh My Cat!

BOW-LINGUAL DOG TRANSLATOR (*About $100—Japan only*): This amazing device translates barks, growls, and whines into common emotions, using a 200-word vocabulary. With a tiny microphone that attaches to the dog's collar, this pager-sized device generates sentences like "I feel lonely" and "Mega happy day!"

MUTTLUKS BOOTIES ($40, *In the Company of Dogs*): If you worry about your dog pal getting hypothermia in cold winter weather, Muttluks Booties can help. Their water- and salt-resistant leather soles will shield his paws from the cold as he plays in the snow, and reflective straps make sure he can be seen at night. Available in Yellow All-Weather and Black Fleece.

When given unlimited access to mice, cats will kill about 15 before stopping.

HIGH VOLTAIRE

Some enlightening thoughts from, Voltaire, France's premier philosopher and satirist from the Age of Enlightenment.

"Judge a man by his questions rather than by his answers."

"One day everything will be well, that is our hope. Everything's fine today, that is our illusion."

"I have never made but one prayer to God, a very short one: 'O Lord, make my enemies ridiculous.' And God granted it."

"Prejudice is the reason of fools."

"If you have two religions in your land, the two will cut each other's throats; but if you have thirty religions, they will dwell in peace."

"The biggest reward for a thing well done is to have done it."

"Common sense is not so common."

"History is little else than a picture of human crimes and misfortunes."

"The art of medicine consists of amusing the patient while nature cures the disease."

"The progress of the rivers to the ocean is not so rapid as that of man to error."

"Our wretched species is so made that those who walk on the well-trodden path always throw stones at those who are showing a new road."

"When it's a question of money, everybody is of the same religion."

"One owes respect to the living, to the dead one owes only truth."

"If God did not exist, it would be necessary to invent him."

"One great use of words is to hide our thoughts."

"A witty saying proves nothing."

"It's dangerous to be right when the government is wrong."

Stand tall: First person to stand during the national anthem: Daniel Webster.

IRONIC DEATHS

You can't help laughing at some of life's—and death's—
ironies... as long as they happen to someone else.
These stories speak for themselves.

BOB TALLEY, *centenarian*
Final Irony: Talley passed away in London during his
100th birthday party, moments after receiving a telegram of
congratulations from the Queen and telling friends, "Yes, I made it
to 100."

RALPH BREGOS, *heart patient*
Final Irony: Bregos, 40, spent more than two years wondering if a
suitable donor heart would ever become available. Finally in 1997,
doctors told him that one had been found. Bregos became so excited at the news that he suffered a massive heart attack and died.

STANLEY GOLDMAN, *candidate for mayor of Hollywood*
Final Irony: At one campaign stop, Goldman chided his opponent for being "too old for the job." Moments later, he dropped
dead from a heart attack.

ROBERT SHOVESTALL, *gun enthusiast in Glendale, California*
Final Irony: Shovestall, 37, died from an accidental gunshot
wound. According to news reports, he placed a .45-caliber pistol he
thought was unloaded under his chin and pulled the trigger. The
incident took place "after his wife's complaints about his 70 guns
prompted him to demonstrate they were safe."

ANONYMOUS MAN, *from West Plains, Missouri*
Final Irony: According to news reports, the suicidal man set himself on fire, only to change his mind moments later and jump into
a pond to extinguish the flames. Cause of death: drowning.

ELIZABETH FLEISCHMAN ASCHEIM, *pioneering X-ray tech-*
nician at the turn of the 20th century
Final Irony: Ascheim often X-rayed herself to show patients that
the treatment was safe. Cause of death: "severe skin cancer."

Happy Hour: Most ice cream is eaten in the evening, between 9:00 and 11:00 p.m.

CLASSIC HOAXES

Here are a few more of our favorite classic hoaxes.

THE WAR IS OVER!

Background: On November 8, 1918, the United Press Association became the first news organization to report that Germany had signed an armistice agreement, bringing World War I to an end. From there the news spread quickly, as papers all over the country ran the story beneath banner headlines. "The public response was what might have been expected," Curtis D. MacDougal writes in *Hoaxes*. "Factory whistles blew, church bells rang, parades were organized, public leaders addressed jubilant crowds, and bonfires were lighted. It was a wild, nationwide demonstration."

Exposed: Unfortunately, it was also a deliberate hoax, which started when "someone, now commonly believed to have been a German secret agent," telephoned the French and American intelligence offices to report that Germany had signed the armistice. From there the story was passed to United Press president Roy Howard in Europe, who cabled the story back to his offices in the United States.

Within the hour, Howard discovered the story was false, but it was too late—cable traffic was backlogged and a second message with instructions to disregard wasn't delivered until 24 hours later. By then, MacDougall writes, the story had became "the most colossal journalistic blunder" of World War I. The real armistice was signed a few days later, on November 11, 1918.

MESSAGES FROM GOD

Background: In 1725 Dr. Johannes Beringer, dean of the medical school at the University of Würzburg, astonished the scientific world by announcing the discovery of hundreds of tiny fossils as well as a number of clay tablets, "including one signed by Jehovah." In 1726, Dr. Beringer published a book theorizing that the tablets and the fossils had been carved from solid stone by God.

Exposed: Beringer's book took the academic world by storm...

Cornucopia: A typical supermarket displays more than 25,000 items.

until rumors began to surface that the tablets were fakes, the work of two of Beringer's enemies on the faculty of the University of Würzburg: J. Ignatz Roderick, a geography professor, and Georg von Eckhart, the university's librarian. When Roderick and von Eckhart confessed to staging the hoax, Beringer accused them of spreading false rumors to undermine the importance of his discovery. Then he examined the tablets a little more closely and found his own name inscribed on some of them.

Rather than admit he'd been had, Beringer tried to cover up the scandal by buying all outstanding copies of his book. He might have succeeded, had word of what he was doing not leaked out. Suddenly, the book became a collector's item. Beringer's professional reputation was destroyed and the man once considered "one of the preeminent scholars of the day" went to his grave a laughingstock.

Final Note: Ironically, the hoax actually contributed to the advancement of science: Beringer's theory of the divine origin of fossils (which unlike the tablets, *were* authentic) was so thoroughly discredited, Carl Sifakis writes in *Hoaxes and Scams*, that "scholars began more and more to embrace Leonardo da Vinci's suggestion that fossils were the remains of a former age."

HARVARD'S ANTI-SMUT WEEK

Background: In 1926 a Harvard University student newspaper announced an "Anti-Smut" campaign, calling it "an organized attempt to aid the police in their diligent prosecution of filth in Harvard University." They sponsored a campus rally and hung posters reading HELP THE OFFICERS TO KEEP YOU CLEAN and DON'T BE DIRTY! all over campus.

Exposed: The newspaper sponsoring Anti-Smut Week was actually the *Harvard Lampoon,* and the campaign was their prankish response to the Boston Police Department's seizure of the *Lampoon* parody of the *Literary Digest,* after the *Boston Telegraph* attacked it as "obscene."

The *Telegraph* fell for the stunt, crediting their own "vigorous denunciations of the moral uncleanness in the atmosphere of Harvard, as shown by the publication of obscenity that nauseated the public," as the inspiration for Anti-Smut Week.

In the densest jungle, only 1% of sunlight ever reaches the forest floor.

PHOTOMANIA

If you had lived in the 1840s, you probably wouldn't have owned even a single photograph. Here's the story of how—and why—photos became affordable. (Turn to page 273 for the previous part of this history.)

GETTING IT BACKWARD

For all of the improvements that had been made to them, daguerreotypes and calotypes still had a lot of problems. Daguerreotype images not only could not be duplicated, they were also reverse images: any writing that appeared in the picture, be it on a street sign, in a shop window, or on the stern of a ship, appeared backward, something that was terribly distracting to the viewer.

Calotype images didn't have those problems—they were printed from negatives, so 1) the images were not reversed, and 2) you could make as many prints as you wanted. But calotype negatives were made of opaque paper. The resulting image was blurrier than a daguerreotype, and the grainy surface of the photographic paper used to make prints only made things worse.

People wanted the best of both worlds: pictures as sharp and clear as a daguerreotype that could be easily duplicated like a calotype. The obvious solution was to replace the calotype's paper negatives with negatives made of smooth-surfaced glass. Figuring out how to do this was a challenge, however, because the nonporous surface of the glass was so slippery that photographic chemicals wouldn't stick to it. Scientists tried everything to get them to stick (including smearing glass with snail slime), but nothing seemed to work.

EGGING THEM ON

Then in 1847, Claude-Félix-Abel Niepce de Saint-Victor, nephew of photographic pioneer Joseph Niepce, finally found something that did the trick: egg whites, also known as albumen. It got the chemicals to stick, and the images that resulted were as crystal clear as daguerreotypes and as easy to duplicate as calotypes. But the exposure times for albumen plates were so long that the plates couldn't be used for portraits.

There are 3 x 10 to the 33rd power (3,000 quintillion) individual living things on this planet....

In 1851 English sculptor and photography buff Frederick Scott Archer used a substance called collodion to glue together some broken glass photographic plates. Made from guncotton (an explosive) dissolved in ether and alcohol, collodion formed a tough, waterproof skin when it dried; doctors used it to seal burns and wounds while new skin grew in underneath.

As Archer pieced together the broken glass, it occurred to him that collodion might be as good as egg whites for getting photosensitive chemicals to stick. He used it to apply a photosensitive emulsion to some photographic plates... and it worked. Not only that, but the plates had exposure times that were 20 times shorter than daguerreotypes (two minutes) or calotypes (one and a half minutes). With good lighting, an exposure of just a few seconds would result in a good picture.

THE WET LOOK

The only drawback to the collodion process was that the photographic plates only worked while the collodion was still wet, because once it dried into its tough waterproof skin it was impervious to the developing chemicals. Photographers had to prepare their plates before they took photographs, and develop them immediately afterward. There was no time to waste.

That meant that a photographer had to bring all necessary equipment—chemicals, darkroom, and everything else—along for every picture. This, of course, was a huge hassle, but the "wet-plate process," as it came to be known, produced such beautiful photographs that it quickly passed the daguerreotype and the albumen calotype to become the most popular form of photography. It remained so for more than 30 years.

Now there was only one thing left that kept people from having their pictures taken: the price.

ACCENTUATE THE NEGATIVE

As he worked on his wet collodion process, Archer noticed that when he held one of his negatives against a black piece of paper, it didn't look like a negative—it looked like an ordinary photograph, very similar to a daguerreotype.

Archer made note of his observation, but didn't do much with it. But other photographers did—they grabbed the idea as a way to

(Of these, 75% are bacteria, and 0.000000,000,000,000,000,00013% are human beings.)

make portraits cheaper. Why go to the trouble and expense of making a positive print, when a negative backed with black paper or some other dark material—soon to become known as an "ambrotype"—worked just as well?

In 1854 Boston photographer James Cutting patented an improved method of making ambrotypes and began selling them. Other photographers followed suit, and in the price war that followed, pressure from ambrotype photographers drove the price of a single daguerreotype from $5 down to 50 cents. Ambrotypes sold for as little as a dime, and though they were lower in quality they were much easier and quicker to produce: a person could pose for an ambrotype and receive the finished portrait in less than 10 minutes. Higher-quality daguerreotypes quickly began to lose ground to the speed and affordability of the ambrotype.

THE TINTYPE

If viewing a glass negative against a black background gave it the appearance of a photograph, why not just make the negative out of something black to begin with, like a thin sheet of tinned iron painted with black varnish? You'd get the same effect for less money because you would be leaving out the glass, which was expensive.

That's what Hamilton Smith was thinking when he invented what became known as the "tintype process" in 1856. Tintypes were cheap—they sold for a fraction of the cost of an ambrotype—and because they were made of iron they could take a lot of abuse. You could carry them in your pocket, send them through the mail, and collect them in photo albums. The images were still reversed, but with simple portraits no one seemed to mind.

As it turned out, you could even carry tintypes into war: In four years' time, Union and Confederate soldiers would bring tintypes of their loved ones with them into battle; between skirmishes they would line up outside the photographer's tent to pose for pictures of themselves to send back home.

MULTIPLE PERSONALITIES

As popular as they were, tintypes never came close to matching the craze of another type of photograph, the *carte-de-visite*. Invented by French photographer Andre Disdéri in 1854, the *carte-de-vis-*

ite was, like the ambrotype and the tintype, an extension of the collodion process. Disdéri's idea was to use a special camera with four lenses to divide a single large photograph into many smaller photographs. Some *carte-de-visite* cameras only let the subject pose for one photograph, which was then duplicated eight or more times; others allowed several poses. Either way the effect was the same: for the price of a single photograph, the customer got as many as 24.

Disdéri intended that the tiny pictures, which were printed on paper and backed by stiff cardboard, would serve as photo versions of traditional calling cards to be given as a memento of a visit with friends.

THE ROYAL TOUCH

Then in 1860, Queen Victoria, her husband Prince Albert, and their children posed for some *cartes-de-visite*. These images were the first photographs of the royal family ever commissioned for the public. They were sold individually, in sets, and in a book called the *Royal Album*. And they were hugely popular.

Photo studios took note. They started printing photographs of other famous people—Sarah Bernhardt, Abraham Lincoln, and Gen. Ulysses S. Grant among them—to see if they would sell. They did, prompting what came to be known as "cardomania." *Cartes-de-visite* covered a huge variety of subjects, including animals, politicians, military leaders, famous works of art, scenes of faraway places...even Barnum's circus freaks. Collectors bought them all. During the Civil War, people bought pictures of Maj. Robert Anderson, the hero of the battle of Fort Sumter, at a rate of 1,000 prints a day.

HOUSE OF CARDS

Cardomania was so powerful that it may be the reason the White House still stands in Washington D.C. The Founding Fathers never intended the White House to be a permanent presidential residence; it was just supposed to serve until something bigger and better would be built.

Few Americans had ever seen the White House, until Lincoln's assassination in 1865, when photos of the fallen president—as well as of the house where he had lived—circulated in great numbers.

Bird brain: Researchers have been able to teach ravens to count as high as six.

These popular images established the White House as a symbol of the presidency...and of the United States. After that, no one would have suggested tearing it down.

PICTURES, PICTURES, EVERYWHERE

After decades of development and innovation, photographs had become part of pop culture. They sold for only pennies apiece. People wore them as jewelry in brooches, lockets and pocket watches. They projected them onto the walls of their homes using gas-lit "photographic lanterns," and drank from china cups decorated with photographic images fired into the porcelain. They bought picture postcards of the places they visited and mailed them home to friends.

Huge albums overflowing with photographs were as common a fixture in late-19th-century households as televisions are today. So were stereographs, double pictures about the size of postcards that, when viewed through a special viewer (like a View-Master), formed a single 3-D image. Portraits were still popular, too, especially now that photographers could retouch negatives to remove wrinkles, moles and other blemishes.

Journalists incorporated photographs into news coverage, publishers pasted them into books, cartographers used them to improve maps, and Scotland Yard fought crime by photographing criminals for the first time. Photographs were everywhere.

LEAVE IT TO THE PROFESSIONALS

These pictures all had one thing in common: They were taken by professionals, or by serious amateurs. If you wanted to be a photographer in the 1860s, you had to be a chemist, too. And you had to have a fair amount of money. This began to change in 1871, when a British physician named Richard Leach Maddox decided he'd had enough of the wet-plate process and started looking for something better.

Part VI of the photography story is on page 400.

*　　*　　*

"You don't take a photograph, you make it."
—*Ansel Adams*

Larger than life: Frank Lloyd Wright wore elevator shoes.

WHY ASK WHY?

Sometimes the answer is irrelevant—it's the question that counts.
These cosmic queries have been sent in by BRI readers.

Do hungry crows have ravenous appetites?

If a lawyer can be disbarred and clergymen defrocked, can electricians be delighted, musicians denoted, cowboys deranged, models deposed, and tree surgeons disembarked?

When cheese gets its picture taken, what does it say?

Why is *brassiere* singular and *panties* plural?

Why are builders afraid to have a 13th floor, but book publishers aren't afraid to have a chapter 11?

If a word is misspelled in a dictionary, how would we ever know?

Why is it that writers write but grocers don't groce and hammers don't ham?

Why do "slow down" and "slow up" mean the same thing?

Why doesn't onomatopoeia sound like what it is?

Why do *fat chance* and *slim chance* mean the same thing?

If humans evolved from monkeys and apes, why do we still have monkeys and apes?

How can the weather be hot as hell one day and cold as hell another?

Why doesn't glue stick to the inside of the bottle?

Why don't you ever see the headline "Psychic Wins Lottery"?

Why is it called *lipstick* if you can still move your lips?

When you lose your temper, shouldn't that mean that you get happy?

If someone is deceased, did they just come back from the dead?

How do you get off a non-stop flight?

If blind people wear dark glasses, why don't deaf people wear earmuffs?

Stand-up act: Lewis Carroll wrote *Alice's Adventures in Wonderland* standing up.

NOT EXACTLY PRINCE CHARMING

Ever heard of Prince Philip? He's the Duke of Edinburgh and husband of Queen Elizabeth II of England. About the only time he makes headlines is when he, as one newspaper puts it, "uses his royal status to insult and belittle people." His public gaffes are so frequent that they've earned him the title "The Duke of Hazard."

To a driving instructor in Scotland: "How do you keep the natives off the booze long enough to get them through the test?"

To a Nigerian diplomat in traditional Nigerian garb: "You look as if you're ready for bed."

On seeing a fuse box filled with wires, during a visit to an electronics company: "This looks like it was put in by an Indian."

To a chubby 13-year-old boy at a space exploration exhibit, pointing to a space capsule: "You'll have to lose weight if you want to go in that."

To a smoke-detector activist who lost two of her children in a house fire: "My smoke alarm is a damn nuisance. Every time I run my bath, the steam sets it off and I've got firefighters at my door."

To members of the British Deaf Association, while pointing to a loudspeaker playing Caribbean music: "No wonder you are deaf."

To a tourist, during a state visit to Hungary: "You can't have been here long, you've no potbelly."

Speaking to British students studying in China: "If you stay here much longer, you'll all be slitty-eyed."

On the "key problem" facing Brazil: "Brazilians live there."

On his daughter Princess Anne: "If it doesn't fart or eat hay, she isn't interested."

On seeing a picture once owned by England's King Charles I in the Louvre in Paris: "So I said to the Queen, 'Shall we take it back?'"

Henry Kissinger's real name: Heinz Kissinger.

WHY IS *CITIZEN KANE* THE MOST IMPORTANT MOVIE OF ALL TIME?

In 2000, Kane was voted the best film of all time by the American Film Institute. Good choice. Here's why.

BACKGROUND
When *Citizen Kane* premiered on May 1, 1941, the *New York Times* film critic called it "far and away the most surprising and cinematically exciting motion picture in many a moon. As a matter of fact, it comes close to being the most sensational film ever made in Hollywood."

But in early 1941 it seemed like the film would never even make it to the theaters, let alone win public acclaim. Newspaper baron William Randolph Hearst, the inspiration for the film's main character, Charles Foster Kane, waged a no-holds-barred campaign to destroy the film. He offered RKO president George Schaefer $800,000 to burn the negative and all the prints in a bonfire; Schaefer refused. When that failed, Hearst tried to prevent it from being widely released.

For the most part, he succeeded: because of Hearst's influence the major theater chains refused to book it, forcing *Kane* to premiere in smaller, independent theaters. The film was a commercial flop, and Orson Welles—the genius who made it—never recovered from the disaster. RKO never again gave him the artistic freedom he'd had in making *Citizen Kane*, and most of his later film projects were commercial flops.

RESURRECTION

To the few who saw *Citizen Kane* in its initial run, it was a masterpiece. To the rest of America, it was quickly forgotten. As Harlan Lebo writes in *Citizen Kane: The Fiftieth Anniversary Album,*

> Through 1950, *Citizen Kane* played here and there, principally in the scattered revival theaters in larger cities that showed "oldies." But that was all. *Citizen Kane* disappeared in the United States almost entirely, and it didn't emerge again for more than five years.

Why is honey so easy to digest? Because it has already been digested by the bee.

In the United States, *Citizen Kane* finally reappeared in 1956—on *television*. And there it developed a following. "Its time had finally come with the general audience," Lebo writes. "Several polls of film fans placed *Citizen Kane* at the top of the picks of screen favorites."

Citizen Kane's TV showings also made it a hit with a new generation of film critics. Over the next several years, the film's stature continued to grow. In 1962 the British magazine *Sight and Sound* released a critics' poll of the best films of all time. *Citizen Kane* was #1.

WHAT'S THE BIG DEAL?

In a world where no one can agree on anything, most serious critics seem to agree that *Citizen Kane* is the best film ever made. Why?

For one thing, "talkies" had only been around for 14 years when *Kane* made its debut, and in that time filmmaking had become predictable. Virtually all movies used the same stale camera angles, the same lighting, and the same types of sets. *Citizen Kane* broke all the rules. It introduced avant-garde storytelling and cinematography methods to Hollywood. And the film was crafted with Welles' incredible attention to detail, from the music to the lighting.

INNOVATIVE FILMMAKING

• Before *Citizen Kane*, most films were organized chronologically: they began at the beginning and ended at the end. *Kane* famously begins at the end, when a dying Charles Foster Kane whispers "Rosebud." From there the film moves back to Kane's childhood, and tells the story of his life...from the perspectives of five different people. Welles explains: "They tell five different stories, each biased, so that the truth about Kane, like the truth about any man, can only be calculated, by the sum of everything that has been said about him."

• Welles also compressed much of Kane's life story into a fictional newsreel segment that was incredibly realistic for its time. Editor Robert Wise blended 127 different clips of film into the newsreel: Some were clips of actual news footage, others were staged shots of Welles and other actors. Wise "aged" the new footage by dragging the negatives across a concrete floor, giving them authentic-looking scrapes.

• In another famous sequence, Welles illustrates the breakdown of Kane's first marriage with a montage of scenes of Kane and his wife at the breakfast table. The first shot shows the newlyweds madly in love with each other; over the next several scenes, they age gradually, denoting the passage of time, and become increasingly distant. In the last scene, they sit at opposite ends of a long table in stony silence. The sequence is less than three minutes long, but it took six weeks to put together.

• Welles and cinematographer Gregg Toland spent weeks setting up *Citizen Kane*'s scenes and planning camera angles. "This is unconventional in Hollywood," Toland wrote in *Popular Photography* in 1941, "where most cinematographers learn of their next assignments only a few days before the scheduled shooting starts."

• Toland used "deep-focus" camera techniques, including special film, lenses, and lighting developed especially for *Citizen Kane*, that made everything on screen appear in focus at the same time, an unheard-of practice in Hollywood. "The normal human eye sees everything before it clearly and sharply," Toland wrote. "But Hollywood cameras focus on a center of interest and allow the other components of a scene to 'fuzz out'.... The attainment of approximate human-eye focus was one of our fundamental aims...in some cases we were able to hold sharp focus over a depth of 200 feet."

Musical Score

It was no accident that the musical score fit the film like a glove: unlike other films, *Citizen Kane* and its music were created side by side. "I worked on the film, reel by reel, as it was being shot and cut," composer Bernard Herrmann wrote in 1941. "Most musical scores are written after the film is entirely finished, and the composer must adapt his music to the scenes on the screen. In many scenes in *Citizen Kane*, an entirely different method was used, many of the sequences being tailored to match the music."

Makeup

Since the story takes place over 50 years, the actors age greatly throughout the film; Kane, for example, ages from 25 to 78. Makeup artist Maurice Seiderman invented many techniques to age the characters in the film. Rather than just cover Welles with latex wrinkles and gray hair, he made a complete body cast and used it to create custom-fitting body pads and facial appliances that show Kane aging gradually over 27 different stages of his life.

The level of detail is astonishing: Welles wore special milky, bloodshot contact lenses to make his eyes look old, and 72 different facial appliances, including hairlines, cheeks, jowls, bags under his eyes, and 16 different chins. Some pieces even had artificial pores that matched those in Welles's own skin.

Ceilings

If you look for ceilings in most movie scenes, you won't find them. The powerful lamps needed to light a scene are usually hung above the set, where a ceiling would normally go. But scenes in *Citizen Kane* used a cloth canopy that simulated an actual ceiling. "The sets have ceilings," Toland wrote, "because we wanted reality, and we felt it would be easier to believe a room was a room if its ceiling could be seen in the picture. Furthermore, lighting effects in unceilinged rooms generally are not realistic because the illumination comes from unnatural angles." Since ceiling lights were not possible, most shots were lit using floor lights.

Acting

• Most of the actors in *Citizen Kane*, Welles included, had never been in a movie before. They had only appeared on stage and on radio as members of Welles's Mercury Theater company. They were not a part of the Hollywood culture and did not feel bound by the conventions of 1940s filmmaking.

• *Citizen Kane* had almost no close-up shots of the actors, which were extremely common at the time. But the Mercury actors were used to performing with the audience at a distance. Welles was afraid their exaggerated gestures and boisterous theatrical acting style—which were calculated to be seen and heard in the most distant seats of a large theater—would look artificial at close range. So he left the close-ups out.

FINAL WORD

"Fifty years later, Citizen Kane is as fresh, as provoking, as entertaining, as funny, as sad and as brilliant as it ever was. Many agree it is the greatest film of all time. Those who differ cannot seem to agree on their candidate."
                                              —**Film critic Roger Ebert**

Story most often made into a movie: *Cinderella* (59 times).

IT'S A WEIRD, WEIRD WORLD

More proof that truth really is stranger than fiction.

I'M NOT DEAD YET

TOPEKA, Kansas—"A 53-year-old Kansas woman reportedly shot herself in the head and then called 911 for help. Firefighters found her unconscious and assumed she was dead, without checking for a pulse. An ambulance was cancelled, and firefighters and deputies waited outside the home to protect it as a crime scene. Meanwhile, the woman regained consciousness and called 911 again. Firefighters outside the home were told of the call and rushed inside to provide medical care."

—*Bizarre News*

ADDING INSULT TO INJURY

"A 51-year-old London man, out of work 14 weeks with broken ribs after being hit by a bus, was billed $850 for damage to the bus."

—*Funny Times*

COME TOGETHER...

"In one of the strangest alliances ever, members of the Pagans Motorcycle Club allegedly conspired with some young Amish men to sell cocaine to Amish youth groups. According to their plan, the drugs were to be sold during hoedowns."

—*Wacky News*

N IS FOR NUTJOB

"Prominent Vermont hunter Thomas Venezia, 41, was finally brought to justice after several shooting sprees, marauding through Canadian woods. An undercover agent quoted Venezia after one illegal shooting: 'I have the K chromosome. I love to kill. I have to kill.' Once, Venezia spontaneously leaped from a truck and started firing at ducks, then later at pigeons because, he said, he had gone an hour without killing anything. At a hearing in Saskatoon, Saskatchewan, Venezia, sobbing, admitted the incidents and was

---

A third of the Earth's land surface can be classified as desert.

permanently barred from Canada. However, he remains licensed to hunt in Vermont."

—*News of the Weird*

KINDERGARTEN COPS

"Children at a kindergarten in Nelson, New Zealand, are now required to carry a pretend weapon permit if they want to carry a pretend weapon to play pretend cops and robbers."

—"Quick Takes," *Chicago Sun-Times*

AWW, YEAH BABY

"According to Sasquatch researcher David Shealy, who also owns an RV park in Ochopee, Florida, love is in the air for a Florida Bigfoot known as the 'skunk ape.' Shealy claims as many as nine of the creatures roam the Everglades, and reports their love calls sound 'something like Barry White doing a dove call.'"

— "The Edge," *The Oregonian*

HOLE IN THE HEAD

"Poet William Adrian Milton, 59, told reporters that his recent CAT scan revealed to his complete surprise that he had a bullet in his head. Searching his memory, Milton recalled a 1976 incident in which he wandered too close to a street fight, heard a noise, and was knocked down. He said he staggered home bloody and went to bed, but failed to seek medical treatment because the bleeding soon stopped and the remaining lump was consistent with being hit by a brick. Milton said he'll leave the bullet there."

—*New York Post*

SWING YOUR TRACTOR...

"Eight farmers in the town of Nemaha, Iowa, have taught themselves to perform various square-dancing routines (do-si-dos, promenades, etc.) on their tractors. However, since all the farmers are men and square-dancing is a couples activity, four of the dancers operate their tractors while dressed in calico skirts."

—**Universal Press Syndicate**

THE NAME GAME

Did you hate your name when you were growing up? Maybe that's because you didn't know what it means. See if you can match the following names with their meanings.

NAME	MEANING
1) George	**a.** God is gracious
2) Amy	**b.** Farmer
3) Michael	**c.** Beloved
4) Barbara	**d.** Worthy to be loved
5) Daniel	**e.** Bright fame
6) Edward	**f.** Bee
7) Amanda	**g.** Foreign
8) Henry	**h.** Lily
9) Joel	**i.** God is God
10) Susan	**j.** Beautiful
11) Linda	**k.** God is my judge
12) Melissa	**l.** Grace
13) Ann	**m.** Ruler of the home
14) Robert	**n.** Rich guard
15) Stephen	**o.** Who is like God
16) John	**p.** Crown

Answers:

1) b; 2) c; 3) o; 4) g; 5) k; 6) n; 7) d; 8) m; 9) i;
10) h; 11) j; 12) f; 13) l; 14) e; 15) p; 16) a

For more info about the answers, see page 511.

Ladybugs are named after the Virgin Mary; they used to be called "beetles of Our Lady."

DISGUSTING FACTS

We know—with a title like this one, you can't help yourself...
you have to read them. They really are disgusting, but, well,
now you have something to share as dinner conversation.

• The average human foot has about 20,000 sweat glands and can produce as much as half a cup of sweat each day.

• Cockroaches can flatten themselves almost to the thinness of a piece of paper in order to slide into tiny cracks, can be frozen for weeks and then thawed with no ill effect, and can also withstand 126 g's of pressure with no problem (people get squished at 18 g's).

• Most of the dust in your house is made up of dead human skin cells—every day, millions of them float off your body and settle on furniture and floors.

• The average municipal water treatment plant processes enough human waste every day to fill 72 Olympic-sized swimming pools.

• According to a recent survey, over 10% of Americans have picked someone else's nose.

• Tears are made up of almost the exact same ingredients as urine.

• Most people generally fart between 10 and 20 times a day, expelling enough gas to inflate a small balloon.

• Your mouth slows production of bacteria-fighting saliva when you sleep, which allows the 10 billion bacteria in your mouth to reproduce all night; "morning breath" is actually bacterial B.O.

• Leeches have mouths with three sets of jaws and between 60 to 100 teeth.

• A tapeworm can grow to a length of 30 feet inside human intestines.

• The crusty goop you find in your eyes when you wake up is the exact same mucus you find in your nose—boogers.

• Spiders don't eat their prey; they paralyze the victim with venom, vomit a wad of acidic liquid onto them, and then drink the dissolved body.

• The average person will produce 25,000 quarts of saliva in a lifetime—enough to fill up two swimming pools.

Three out of every 4 creatures living on Earth are insects.

HIDDEN ADVERTISING

The 30-second TV spot ain't what it used to be. So sneaky TV executives are doing whatever they can to make sure we get the advertising message. This piece by Terry Lefton first appeared in the Industry Standard *on March 26, 2001.*

THE TRIBE HAS SPOKEN

It was a bad night for Ogakor. In the fifth episode of the CBS TV phenomenon *Survivor: The Australian Outback,* the remaining members of the hapless "tribe" competed to win a crate full of luxuries like toilet paper, blankets, spices, shampoo, and toothpaste, but lost out to rival tribe Kucha. "I am getting very frustrated," said Ogakor member Colby Donaldson. "If we don't turn up the heat and turn this runaway train around, there may be a meltdown for the Colbster."

So, while the metaphor-happy Colbster was off under a eucalyptus tree bumming, Kucha was celebrating. Its members descended on the box of goodies. Painted on the crate was a huge red bull's-eye, the unmistakable logo of one of the show's main sponsors, Target.

Welcome to the future of television advertising, where old-fashioned commercial breaks are giving way to experiments in "product integration"—advertisers paying to place their goods into the plots of TV shows. Target's campaign on *Survivor* is just one example. AT&T shows up on *Who Wants to Be a Millionaire,* Campbell's Soup made a high-profile appearance on daytime chat-fest *The View* (co-hosts Meredith Vieira, Star Jones, Joy Behar, and Lisa Ling sang the product's theme song). Corona beer appears on *Blind Date.* And later this month, *The Drew Carey Show* will devote a two-minute interlude to the video game SimCity. (The gang will be transported to a virtual metropolis. Cue laugh track.)

ME DE-MAND

Advertisers and TV networks are pushing their marketing messages right into the heart of the programming for one simple reason: Technology is making traditional commercials obsolete. With hundreds of cable and satellite channels, viewers have more reason than ever to surf during commercial breaks. Recording technologies

---

Lobsters and jellyfish never stop growing.

like TiVo and ReplayTV enable couch potatoes to zap commercial breaks altogether. And before long, viewers will be able to order their favorite programs on demand. It will be the death blow to traditional commercial breaks. "If the audience isn't watching your messages, marketers will put them in places where they will," says Brett Shevack, president of Wolf Group New York, an ad agency whose clients include Space.com and Häagen-Dazs.

LIKE THE GOOD OLD DAYS

If all this seems vaguely familiar, it should. In the early days of television, advertisers sponsored whole programs, and their products got plugs throughout each show. *The Camel Cavalcade of News* doesn't seem so far-off anymore. "TV partnerships are changing," says Mark Owens, senior VP at entertainment marketing agency Davie-Brown. "We're going back to more of a 1950s model as marketers look to find places for messages viewers can't zap."

Survivor is the poster child for this trend. Every advertiser that buys airtime in the top-rated show's commercial breaks also gets prime placement in the program. *Survivor* contestants munch Doritos, guzzle Mountain Dew, wear Reebok sneakers, and win prizes from Budweiser, Dr. Scholl's, Pontiac, and Visa.

The strategy works especially well for targeting the ultimate jaded consumers: teenagers. "Some contestants were really admiring our apparel and footwear on camera," says John Wardley, Reebok's VP of global advertising. "That's the kind of exposure you just can't buy."

Well, actually, you can. Like the other *Survivor* sponsors, Reebok negotiated its product placement in the show along with its commitment to buy a certain number of commercials. And the phenomenon is spreading, Wardley says. He gets proposals offering to feature Reeboks in programs at least once a week. "There are a lot of producers trying to figure out how they can build this kind of marketing into existing shows," he adds.

BREAKING NEW GROUND

The technique goes way beyond "product placement." On television, product placement might involve a show staffer slipping a product into a scene as an informal thank-you for buying an ad. These arrangements are generally finalized after scripts are written and advertising deals are struck. "Product integration," on the other hand, is built into television programs early on. In some cases, like *Survivor*, it's part of the creation of the show itself. In others, like *The View* or *Drew Carey*, it shapes individual episodes or segments. And the products aren't just props like a bottle of Snapple or a box of Special K on *Seinfeld*; they are built into the action of the shows.

LEAGUE LEADER

Product integration took root and thrived on another kind of reality programming—sports. There, sponsor "enhancements"—from electronically superimposed logos on the playing field to sponsored highlights—are routine. For the last two seasons, ESPN has used video insertion technology to create the illusion of a billboard behind home plate during Major League Baseball telecasts. They've also inserted a sponsor's logo inside the goalposts during field-goal attempts in college football broadcasts. "We all have to get more inventive about creating ways to get the advertising message across without insulting the viewer," says Ed Erhardt, president of customer marketing for ESPN/ABC Sports.

And therein lies an obvious danger. If networks and advertisers shoehorn too many commercial messages into programming, viewers are likely to tune out. Here again, sports may lead the way. In its most recent TV contract signed with four networks, the National Football League barred sponsored highlights and other enhancements—the Bud Light play of the game, the Nike starting lineup—from its telecasts.

MILK IT

Over at CBS, network executives are limiting product integration to *Survivor*. It's a way to milk its hit show without cluttering the rest of the lineup—for now. Marketers are also leery of making too much of a good thing. "It's a new phenomenon for entertainment programming," says Owens, the entertainment marketer. "And we are all trying to be careful and not make it as crowded as sports has become."

Still, he admits, "When digital cable gives us the capacity, it's entirely possible we'd recommend a dedicated cable network for a client with a really strong brand." Bring on the Dr. Scholl's Channel.

CIRCUS SLANG

Uncle John was at the circus earlier this summer, when it occurred to him that circus performers probably have their own language. Well, it turns out they do. Here's a list of his favorite terms.

Clown Alley: The dressing area for the clowns.

Blow Off: Immediately following the end of a performance, when the crowd mills out of the tent and onto the midway.

Butcher: A concessionaire who sells food—hot dogs, sodas, ice cream, etc.—to the audience.

Dry Butcher: A butcher who sells toys and souvenirs.

Groundhog: A slow butcher.

Greyhound: A fast butcher.

Razorbacks: The workers who set up the big tents.

Roustabout: A laborer for the circus.

Deemer: A dime; 10 cents.

Mud Show: A small circus or carnival.

Cloud Swing: Aerial act performed on a loop of rope suspended from the top of the tent.

Kinker: Any circus performer.

Grease Joint: A food stand.

Grubers: Peanuts.

Spool Truck: Truck that carries the tent canvas.

Joey: Any clown, after Joseph Grimaldi's character, Joey.

Fine Ways: Twenty-five cents.

The Disaster March: "Stars and Stripes Forever" (see "Circus Superstitions," page 172).

Fancy Pants: The master of ceremonies (often incorrectly referred to as the *ringmaster*).

First of May: A rookie on the circus.

John Robinson: A shortened performance.

Pie Car: Place where circus people eat. Also *cookhouse*.

Risley: An acrobatic act in which one person juggles another on their feet.

Cherry Pie: Extra work for extra pay.

Home Sweet Home: Last show of the season.

Straw House: A sold-out performance.

Windjammer: Circus musician.

Twenty-Four-Hour Man: The scout who plans the route to the next town and determines where the circus will be set up.

How many hair follicles on an average adult? **5 million.**

THREE'S COMPANY

Critics called Three's Company "mindless" and "smarmy." But it was one of the longest running and highest rated shows in TV history. We're not sure why, either, but here's the story.

COME AND KNOCK ON OUR DOOR

You might not know it, but two popular American TV shows were actually rip-offs of British sitcoms: *All in the Family* is an Americanized version of *Till Death Do Us Part*, and *Sanford and Son* is a copy of *Steptoe & Son*.

Donald Taffner, U.S. representative for Thames Television, wanted to export other shows for American audiences so he hooked up with American TV executive Ted Bergmann. In 1975 Bergmann took a Thames hit, *Man About the House*, to the networks. ABC's programming chief, Fred Silverman, ordered a pilot.

He advised Bergmann to get an experienced television writer, and he found one in Larry Gelbart, developer of the TV show *M*A*S*H*. Gelbart declined at first, but an unprecedented offer of $50,000 convinced him. Gelbart devised characters in their late 20s who were intelligent and witty: David Bell, an aspiring filmmaker; Jenny, a witty brunette who worked at the DMV; and Samantha—Sam for short—a cute blonde model aspiring to be an actress. And of course there was a landlord, George Roper, and his sex-starved wife, Mildred.

FALSE START

But Gelbart's pilot didn't make the 1976 fall season lineup—Silverman wanted the show recast. He'd already picked John Ritter for the male lead. A relatively unknown Norman Fell was cast as the nosy landlord, with veteran actress Audra Lindley as Mildred. But the original female leads were fired and another pilot was ordered.

Before moving to ABC, Silverman was president of CBS Entertainment. So Silverman got NRW Company, producers of *All in the Family* and *The Jeffersons*, to develop *Three's Company*. He instructed them to make it "the same kind of breakthrough in sexiness that *All in the Family* was in bigotry."

NRW renamed the roommates and gave them ordinary jobs that

people could relate to: David Bell became cooking student Jack Tripper; civil servant Jenny became florist Janet Wood, played by Joyce DeWitt; and aspiring actress Sam became naive jiggle queen Christmas Snow—Chrissy for short—played by an unknown Suzanne Somers.

A SMASH HIT

The show premiered on March 15, 1977—and ABC's ratings immediately went through the roof: *Three's Company* ranked #11 among all the network shows for the 1976–77 season. Combined with *Happy Days* and *Laverne & Shirley*, the show made ABC's Tuesday-night lineup the most-watched night on TV from 1977 to 1980.

The success of *Three's Company* astounded ABC execs. It broke ratings records, even beating CBS's *M*A*S*H*, a feat no other show could accomplish—but critics hated it. The *New York Times* suggested that a blank television screen was better than tuning in to the show.

THE KISSES ARE HERS, HERS, HERS!

In February 1978, the same week that *Three's Company* hit #1 in ratings, *Newsweek* magazine did a feature on the trio that would forever mar the ensemble's relationship. The article reported that the National Religious Broadcasters was lobbying against the show's "immoral programming." But it wasn't the negative publicity that bothered Ritter and DeWitt, it was the cover—featuring Suzanne Somers most prominently, with the two others behind her.

The veteran actors feared that Somers was compromising the cooperative effort to secure her own stardom. She was being aggressively marketed by her star-maker agent, Jay Bernstein—who had helped launch Farrah Fawcett's career—and began hawking hammers for Ace Hardware, posing for *Playboy* (twice), and performing in Las Vegas and Atlantic City. But when she fired Bernstein in 1980 so hubby Alan Hamel could take over, it was the beginning of the end. "After that, it all went to hell in a handbasket," said Ted Bergmann. "Hamel was about as ill-equipped to do the job as anybody could be."

The husband-and-wife team pushed for more money: they wanted $150,000 per episode, the same amount Alan Alda was getting for *M*A*S*H*, and demanded part ownership of the show. Somers believed she was the secret of the show's success, but the producers said it was the pratfalling Ritter...and he was only getting $50,000 an episode.

CHRISTMAS PAST

So Somers went on strike—she didn't show up for work, claiming "back injuries," which infuriated her co-stars. Then she threatened to sue the producers and her on-screen roommates for conspiracy. Negotiations crumbled, and by the time Somers did return to work, the producers had had it—they wanted to get rid of her.

But ABC execs feared ratings would drop if the jiggle queen was dropped completely, so her role was cut to one minute a week. Chrissy suddenly went away to care for her sick mother. Somers was secluded to a small set, where Chrissy talked to Janet on the telephone from her mother's. Slowly and quietly, Chrissy Snow was phased out of the show.

Somers left the show in 1981, but it proved a costly mistake: She walked away from $4.5 million in residuals, and DeWitt and Ritter wouldn't even speak to her.

WE'VE BEEN WAITING FOR YOU

Somers's replacement, ex-L.A. Rams cheerleader Jenilee Harrison, played Chrissy's country cousin, Cindy Snow, and the writers tried to develop her character without using the trademark suggestive jokes. Bad move: ratings dropped. Harrison was dropped, too.

A new blonde was brought in to facilitate the dirty talk. As Terri Alden, Priscilla Barnes gave *Three's Company* the shot in the arm it needed to regain its #1 status. But the success was short-lived: the producers didn't want to repeat the experience they had had with Somers, so they didn't let the writers develop Barnes's character. Another bad move. The show couldn't sustain its ratings, and ABC cancelled it.

The one-hour series finale aired on May 15, 1984 as a hurried attempt to provide closure to the millions of viewers who had watched the show and the characters develop over the years. Janet married her boyfriend Phillip, Jack fell in love with their neighbor Vicky, and Terri moved to Hawaii to care for sick children.

WHERE ARE THEY NOW?

John Ritter went on to star in more than 20 TV projects, including the spin-off bomb, *Three's a Crowd*. He's also appeared in motion pictures, most notably Billy Bob Thornton's *Sling Blade*. Joyce DeWitt dropped out of sight after *Three's Company*, going on a 13-year spiritual odyssey around the world.

Audra Lindley and Norman Fell were lured off *Three's Company* to star in their own show, *The Ropers*. They left at the height of *Three's Company*'s popularity; *The Ropers* flopped after a single season. Throughout the 1980's, Fell worked steadily in supporting roles on the big and small screens. Lindley returned to the stage and made guest television appearances on *Friends* and *Cybill*. She died of complications from leukemia in 1997. Fell died of natural causes the following year.

When Fell and Lindley left *Three's Company*, they were replaced by Don Knotts. Knotts played the leisure suit–wearing bachelor, Mr. Furley, and the audience loved him. The producers actually had to edit Knotts's lines because his laughs were so long. After *Three's Company*, Knotts made several films, including *Return to Mayberry*.

And Suzanne Somers? The networks wouldn't touch her for almost a decade after her battle with ABC. She rehabilitated herself as a bankable commodity when she became the spokesperson for the ThighMaster exerciser in 1990. The attention landed her the lead in the sitcom *Step By Step* in 1991 and a job as co-host of *Candid Camera* in 1998. But since then she's been marketing a line of exercise equipment...the FaceMaster and the ButtMaster.

*　　*　　*

Place-Name Origin: "California was named by the Spanish, not from their language but from their literature. In 1510 Garcia Rodriquez de Montalvo wrote a book entitled *Sergas de Esplandian* (*Feats of Esplandian*), in which he created the imaginary realm of *California*: an island ruled by Black Amazons 'at the right hand of the Indies...very close to that of the Terrestrial Paradise.' When the first Spaniards arrived in the southern portion of California in the 1530s, they believed it to be an island and so called it California." (From *Inventing English: The Imaginative Origins of Everyday Expressions*, by Dale Corey)

One out of every 14 women in America is a natural blond (and one out of every 16 men).

THE PRICE WAS RIGHT

You've heard people talk about how much things cost back in the "good old days"—heck, you might even remember them yourself (Uncle John does). Talk about nostalgia...check out these prices.

IN 1900:

Seven-shot revolver: $1.25

Bicycle: $20

Grand piano: $175

Men's leather belt: 19¢

Alligator bag: $5

IN 1910:

All-expenses-paid trip to Bermuda for nine days: $37.50

Bottle of Coke: 5¢

Imported spaghetti: 12¢/box

Cigarettes: 10¢/pack

Wage for postal workers: 42¢/hr.

IN 1920:

Life insurance premium: $16.40/yr.

Chocolates: 89¢/lb.

Eggs: 64¢/doz.

Box of 50 cigars: $2.98

Public school teacher's salary: $970/yr.

IN 1930:

Christmas tree light set (eight bulbs): 88¢

Electric toaster: $1

Motor oil: 49¢/gal.

Washing machine: $58

IN 1940:

Coffeemaker: $2

Movie ticket: 25¢ (day); 40¢ (night)

Golf balls: $1.88/doz.

Bayer aspirin: 59¢

Minimum wage: 30¢/hr.

IN 1950:

Jackie Robinson's salary ('51): $39,750/yr.

Roll of film: 38¢

Toilet paper (20 rolls): $2.39

Corvette ('53): $3,498

Combination 19" television/FM radio/phonograph: $495

IN 1960:

Refrigerator: $200

Polaroid Camera: $100

Mercedes Benz 220S: $3,300

Breakfast (two hot cakes and two strips of bacon): 33¢

Clearasil: 98¢/tube

IN 1970:

Answering machine: $50

Sirloin steak: 97¢/lb.

Tennis racket: $25

Movie projector: $80

Orange juice: 35¢/qt.

IN 1980:

Cordless telephone: $300

Six-pack of Budweiser: $1.99

Video camera: $360

Cadillac El Dorado: $19,700

Herbert Hoover never accepted his presidential salary.

AMERICAN CANNIBAL

Our previous Bathroom Reader included an "Oops!" about a government cafeteria named after Alferd Packer. After our friend Jeff Cheek read it, he sent us this amazing story.

A DUBIOUS DISTINCTION

Alferd G. Packer holds a unique spot in American jurisprudence. He is the only U.S. citizen ever charged, tried, and convicted for the crime of murder and cannibalism.

Born in rural Colorado in 1847, Packer drifted into the Utah Territory, supporting himself as a small-time con artist, claiming to be an experienced "mountain man." In the fall of 1873, he persuaded 20 greenhorns in Salt Lake City to grubstake an expedition to the headwaters of the Gunnison River in Colorado Territory. He swore that the stream was full of gold and promised to lead them to it if they would finance the operation.

GOLD FEVER

With Packer leading, they plunged into the San Juan Mountains and promptly got lost. The party was near starvation when they stumbled into the winter quarters of the friendly Ute tribe. The Indians nursed them back to health, but the leader, Chief Ouray, advised them to turn back. Winter snows had blocked all trails. Ten of the party listened and returned to Utah. The other 10, still believing Packer's tales of gold-filled creeks, stayed with him.

Ouray gave them supplies and advised them to follow the river upstream for safety, but Packer ingored this counsel and plunged back into the mountains. The party split up again. Five turned back and made their way to the Los Pinos Indian Agency. Fired up with gold fever, the others continued on with their con man guide. Days later, exhausted, half frozen, and out of food, they found refuge in a deserted cabin. Most of them were now ready to give up and go back to Salt Lake City.

The exception was Alferd Packer. He was broke, and returning to Salt Lake City would cost him his grubstake. When the others fell asleep, Packer shot four of them in the head. The fifth woke and tried to defend himself, but Packer cracked his skull with the barrel of his rifle. Then, he robbed them.... He also used them for food.

When his strength returned, he packed enough "human jerky" to get back to the Los Pinos Agency. Several miles from the agency, he emptied his pack to conceal his crime. He was welcomed by General Adams, commander of the agency, but shocked everyone by asking for whiskey instead of food. When he flashed a huge bankroll, they started asking questions.

WELL, YOU SEE, OFFICER...

Packer's explanations were vague and contradictory. First, he claimed he was attacked by natives, then he claimed that some of his party had gone mad and attacked him. On April 4, 1874, two of Chief Ouray's braves found the human remains Packer had discarded. General Adams locked him up and dispatched a lawman named Lauter to the cabin to investigate. But while Lauter was away, Packer managed to escape.

He made his way back to Utah and lived quietly for 10 years as "John Schwartze," until a member of the original party recognized him. Packer was arrested on March 12, 1884 and returned to Lake City, Colorado, for trial.

Packer claimed innocence but as the evidence against him mounted, he finally confessed. Apparently, he reveled in the attention his trial gave him and even lectured on the merits of human flesh. The best "human jerky," he said, was the meat on the chest ribs. The judge was not impressed.

"Alferd G. Packer, you no good sonofabitch, there wasn't but seven Democrats in Hinsdale County, and you done et five of 'um," he thundered. "You're gonna hang by the neck until dead!"

SAVED BY A TECHNICALITY

His lawyer appealed the decision, citing a legal loophole. The crime was committed in 1873, in the *territory* of Colorado. The trial began in 1884, in the new *state* of Colorado. The state constitution, adopted in 1876, did not address such a heinous crime, so the charge was reduced to manslaughter and Packer was sentenced to 40 years in prison. He was a model prisoner and was paroled after 16 years. Freed in 1901, he found work as a wrangler on a ranch near Denver.

On April 21, 1907, Alferd G. Packer, horse wrangler and cannibal, died quietly in his sleep.

The only fish that swims upright: the seahorse.

OOPS!

*It's comforting to know that other people are screwing
up even worse than we are. So go ahead and
feel superior for a few minutes.*

LIGHT MY FIRE

JERUSALEM—"It was, to say the least, a very unfortunate
mistake. German chancellor Gerhard Schroeder accidentally extinguished Israel's eternal memorial flame for the six million
Jews killed in the Nazi Holocaust.

"At a somber ceremony in Jerusalem's Yad Vashem Holocaust
Memorial, Schroeder turned a handle that was supposed to make
the flame rise. It went out instead. Israeli prime minister Ehud
Barak stepped forward to try to help, but was unsuccessful. Finally,
a technician used a gas lighter to bring the flame to life again, but
by then the damage had been done."

—Reuters

REAL-LIFE LESSON

"A Grand Rapids, Minnesota, SWAT team, scheduled a drill at a
local high school with actors and actresses playing the part of ter-
rorists. But they mistakenly stormed another school next door.
One of the teachers terrorized in the 'raid' said she was sure she
was about to be killed as she was led from the building at gunpoint
by the officers, who never identified themselves."

—Bonehead of the Day

SANTA CROOK

PHILADELPHIA—"Construction workers recently did a 'chimney sweep' of a vacant building and found the remains of a serial
burglar who had tried to rob the place several years ago. According to Detective Romonita King, workers were knocking down
the chimney Saturday when they smelled a foul odor. On closer
inspection, they noticed a pair of sneakers, jeans, a Phillies cap,
and what appeared to be human remains. The medical examiner's
office tentatively listed the cause of death as accidental compres-
sion asphyxia. It was reported that the remains could be at least

five years old and it was not known how long the business—ironically, a theft-prevention business—was closed."

—*Bizarre News*

THREE STRIKES, YOU'RE OUT

"Lorenzo Trippi, a lifeguard in Ravenna, Italy, lost his job when three people drowned after he hit them with life preservers. Police said his aim was too accurate."

—*Strange World #2*

HOE NO!

"Leonard Fountain, 68, got so fed up with having his gardening tools stolen from his shed that he rigged a homemade shotgun booby trap by the door. A year later, he was in a hurry to get some pruning done and opened the door, forgetting about the modification. He received severe flesh wounds to his right knee and thigh from the ensuing blast, and was charged with illegal possession of firearms."

—*Stuff* magazine

THE YOUNG AND THE WRESTLESS

TACOMA, Wash.—"A seven-year-old boy practicing wrestling moves he had seen on TV bounced off his bed and tumbled out a second-story window. The boy sustained minor cuts and bruises after smashing through the bedroom window and tumbling two stories onto a cushion of grass. 'He was jumping from the dresser and doing a back-flip to the bed and went straight out the window,' said his mother.

"The boy was treated for minor internal injuries and hospitalized in satisfactory condition Friday. 'It hurts to wrestle,' he said. 'I'm not doing any more wrestling moves.'"

—*CNN Fringe*

*   *   *

"I watched the Indy 500 and I was thinking—if they left earlier they wouldn't have to go so fast."

—Steven Wright

had died, making Tyler president? He was on his knees playing marbles.

THE LOST CITIES

Everyone fantasizes about accidentally uncovering a treasure.
Pompeii and Herculaneum were such treasures. They existed for
a thousand years until, in one brief moment, they disappeared.
Here's the story of how they were lost…and found.

VESUVIUS BLOWS

Two thousand years ago, the prosperous cities of Pompeii and Herculaneum thrived near Rome, 10 miles from the foot of the volcano Mount Vesuvius. Vesuvius hadn't exploded for over 1,000 years; no one even knew it was a volcano. Then on August 24 in the year 79 A.D., it erupted, completely burying both cities under mountains of ash—Pompeii and Herculaneum were lost.

Mount Vesuvius continued to erupt sporadically over the centuries that followed, each time adding to the volcanic debris that covered the former town sites; each layer leaving the two cities more hidden than before. Four hundred years later, the Roman Empire collapsed, and legends about the two lost cities went with it. For 15 centuries, they lay forgotten and undisturbed, their stories untold. Then clues about their existence began to turn up. For example, around 1594, a Roman architect named Domenico Fontana was digging a canal to supply water to a rich man's home when workmen uncovered pieces of ruined buildings and a few ancient coins. But nothing much came of the discovery.

RUMORS OF TREASURE

In 1707 part of Italy came under Austrian rule, and Prince d'Elboeuf came to command the cavalry. He heard rumors of treasures being brought up from underground, so he promptly purchased a large parcel of land in the immediate vicinity. Oven the next 30 years, he had shafts and tunnels dug and uncovered vases, statues, and even a number of polished marble slabs—once the floor of the theater in Herculaneum—all of which he used to decorate his villa.

Word of the prince's finds spread, and other treasure hunters came looking. When the first skeleton—complete with bronze and silver coins—was unearthed in 1748, treasure fever hit hard. For

---

A museum dedicated to nuts in Old Lyme, Connecticut, also has the world's largest nutcracker.

the next several years, artifacts were continually looted from the area. But it wasn't until 1763, when workers unearthed an inscription reading *"res publica Pompeianorum"*—meaning "the commonwealth of Pompeians"—that the ancient city was identified.

SAVED AT LAST

The looting of Pompeii and Herculaneum continued for 100 years until a new ruler, King Victor Emmanuel II, became interested in preserving the sites. In 1860 he put archaeologist Giuseppe Fiorelli in charge of excavations. From that time until the present, the treasures of Pompeii have been treated with the care and respect they deserve, and, in turn, they have taught much about daily life in ancient times.

Ironically, the explosion of Vesuvius occurred the day after the annual celebration of Volcanalia, festival of the Roman god of volcanic fire. When Vesuvius began quaking, spouting ash, and spewing rivers of lava on August 23, 79 A.D., most of Pompeii's 20,000 inhabitants fled the area. For the next 12 hours, ash and pumice rained down on the town, accumulating at the rate of six inches per hour. About 2,000 people remained in the city. Perhaps they refused to abandon their treasures. Or possibly they were slaves ordered to stay behind. Early in the morning of August 24, Vesuvius really blew its top. By then, it was too late.

GHOSTS

Crouching, crawling, and clinging to loved ones, the people were buried by ash, which perfectly preserved their positions at the moment of death. When rain came, the layer of ash turned to concrete, entombing the bodies in an undisturbed environment. The bodies themselves then slowly decayed. When archaeologist Fiorelli found the hollow cavities where the bodies had once been, he realized that by pumping wet plaster into what were essentially molds and letting it harden, he could make perfect casts of the dead.

A beggar with a new pair of shoes died at the city gate. Perhaps he had recently swiped the shoes from a corpse. The owners of a house were hiding their valuables in their well when they fell in and died. A dog was still chained up to a fence. A woman held an infant in her arms while two young girls clung to the hem of her dress. A man was trying to pull a goat by its halter outside the city

The seed cones of the cycad tree can weigh up to 90 lb.

wall. Thirty-four people were hiding in a wine vault with food that they never got a chance to eat.

A man, seeking refuge in a tree, died holding a branch. A young girl clutched a statue of a goddess. A man, laying next to a woman seven months pregnant, reached out to cover her face with his robe in the moment before death. A group of priests were about to sit down to a meal of eggs and fish. One of the priests had a hatchet and chopped his way from room to room as lava rushed after him. He was trapped in the last room, which had walls too thick to chop through. The remains of a woman were found next to a wine vat. Inside the vat were over 100 silver dishes and 1,000 pieces of gold. One of the silver cups bore this inscription: *Enjoy life while you have it, for tomorrow is uncertain.*

CIVILIZATION INTACT

Here was an entire thriving city, caught exactly at the peak of its prosperity and perfectly preserved: eggs unbroken; bread baking in an oven; coins left on a countertop. Pots on cookstoves still contained meat bones. Shops displayed onions, beans, olives, nuts, and figs. A heap of discarded fish scales was uncovered near a fish shop. A meal of bread, salad, cakes, and fruit was set on a table. Ropes and nets used by unknown fishermen were preserved, as was the straw padding recently removed from a shipment of glasswares.

Papyrus scrolls, charred but still readable, revealed dissertations on music and other subjects. There were taverns, snack shops, gambling halls, a stadium that could hold 20,000 spectators, theaters, public baths, streets with sewer systems and raised sidewalks, homes with plumbing, and thousands of works of art. Everyday objects such as perfume bottles and glass jars, sewing needles and brooms, muffin pans and cooking pots were found in the homes. Also uncovered: glass vases, tile mosaics, painted murals, marble statues, golden jewelry, bronze lanterns, jeweled amulets, religious icons, and exquisite furniture.

POMPEII TODAY

The excavation of Pompeii continues today—it's estimated that only about a third of the town has been uncovered. Yet Vesuvius continues to rumble, most recently erupting in 1944.

Will it bury Pompeii again?

IT'S A DOG'S LIFE

A page of canine quotes for dog lovers.

"Ever consider what they must think of us? I mean, here we come back from a grocery store with the most amazing haul—chicken, pork, half a cow. They must think we're the greatest hunters on Earth!"
—**Anne Tyler**

"Women and cats will do as they please, and men and dogs should relax and get used to the idea."
—**Robert A. Heinlein**

"They fight for honor at the first challenge, make love with no moral restraint, and they do not for all their marvelous instincts appear to know about death. Being such wonderfully uncomplicated beings, they need us to do their worrying."
—**George Bird Evans**

"I've seen a look in dogs' eyes, a quickly vanishing look of amazed contempt, and I am convinced that basically dogs think humans are nuts."
—**John Steinbeck**

"To a man the greatest blessing is individual liberty; to a dog it is the last word in despair."
—**William Lyon Phelps**

"I don't eat anything a dog won't eat. Like sushi. Ever see a dog eat sushi? He just sniffs it and says, 'I don't think so.' And this is an animal that licks between its legs and sniffs fire hydrants."
—**William Coronel**

"If dogs could talk it would take a lot of the fun out of owning one."
—**Andy Rooney**

"Dear Lord, help me to be the kind of person my dog thinks I am."
—**Anonymous**

"Don't make the mistake of treating your dogs like humans, or they'll treat you like dogs."
—**Martha Scott**

"Whoever said you can't buy happiness forgot about puppies."
—**Gene Hill**

On January 20, 1973, it was −16°F in Deadwood, SD, but 52°F in Lead... only 1½ mi. away.

MAKING SMALL TALK

Here are the origins of some common abbreviations.

£ or lb.

Meaning: Pound

Origin: The abbreviation originates with the Latin phrase *libra pondo*, which means "a unit of measurement by weight." The Romans shortened the phrase to *pondo*, which ultimately became *pound* in English, but the abbreviation of the first word—*lb.*, for *libra*—endured. The symbol for British currency is a stylized L, or £, which comes from the same source. The value of the British pound was originally equal to one pound of silver.

V.I.P.

Meaning: Very important person

Origin: This frequently used contraction was created during World War II by a British officer in charge of organizing flights for important military leaders. In order to conceal the names from enemy spies, each of these were referred to as a "V.I.P." in the flight plan.

Mrs.

Meaning: A married woman

Origin: Originally, *Mrs.* was a shortened version of *mistress*, a word that used to mean "wife" but has since acquired a very different meaning. Strictly speaking, because the word it once abbreviated has changed its meaning, *Mrs.* is no longer an abbreviation—unlike *Mr.*, its male counterpart, which can be spelled out as *Mister*.

K

Meaning: A strikeout in baseball

Origin: In the 1860s when a batter struck out, it was proper to say that he "struck." It was during this era that a newspaperman named Henry Chadwick created symbols for use with his new invention—the box score. He gave each play a letter: S for sacrifice, E for error, and so on. Since S was already taken, he used the last letter of "struck" instead of the first to abbreviate it: K.

Rx

Meaning: A drug prescription

Origin: Actually, there is no *x* in *Rx*. In Medieval Latin, the first word in medicinal prescriptions directing one to take a specific quantity of a concoction was *recipe*, meaning "take" or "receive." This was later symbolized as an R with a slash across its leg. The spelling *Rx* is an attempt to represent this symbol in English letters.

B.O.

Meaning: Body odor

Origin: In 1933 the Lifebuoy Health Soap Company ran a series of radio advertisements containing their new slogan: "Lifebuoy stops B--- O---." A heavy two-note foghorn warning was synchronized with the "B.O.," giving the phrase a negative spin it has retained ever since.

D-Day

Meaning: June 6, 1944, the day Allied forces invaded France during WWII

Origin: The *D* in D-day does not stand for "designated" or "defeat," as many believe, but simply for "day." *D-day* actually means "day day." The redundancy comes from the common practice in army correspondence of referring to a top secret time as *H-hour* or *D-day*.

XXX

Meaning: Marking on bottles in cartoons to indicate that they contain alcohol

Origin: During the 19th century, breweries in Britain marked their bottles X, XX, or XXX as a sign of alcohol content. The number of Xs corresponded to the potency of the drink.

*   *   *

"What a life. When I was a kid, I asked my dad if I could go ice skating. He told me to wait until it gets warmer."

—**Rodney Dangerfield**

Cyclospporine, which prevents organ transplant rejections, comes from a fungus grown in dirt.

THE BOOB TUBE

*It seems that anything goes on television these days. But this
wasn't always the case. We recently found this timeline
in an old issue of* The Wall Street Journal.

LETTING DOWN THE GUARD
With legislators railing about excessive sex and violence on
network television, questions about what should be seen on
shows and what should be cut continue to preoccupy producers and
the public. But this much is certain: each season's new series will
contain scenes that were unthinkable and dialogue that was unmentionable in the early days of television.

To reach the 18 to 49-year-olds coveted by advertisers, networks
in recent years "have had to open up to dealing with relatively controversial issues," says Lynn Spigel, a professor at the University of
Southern California School of Cinema-Television. Each network
has a standards-and-practices department overseeing programming
content and presentation, but "there's no such thing as broadcast
standards" today, says Steven Bochco, co-creator of *NYPD Blue* and
Hill Street Blues. He adds: "It's really what you can get away with.
Then it becomes a new standard."

SHOCKING!

It is illuminating to see how much primetime standards have loosened since the 1950s, when the word "damn" shocked viewers, and
the 1960s, when network executives refused to air an episode of *Dr
Kildare* because it involved rape.

1939: NBC begins the first regular network broadcasts.

1950: Arthur Godfrey becomes one of the first people to swear on
national TV when he utters the words "damn" and "hell" during a
live CBS program.

1950: The first bare breasts appear—unintentionally—when talk-
show host Faye Emerson accidentally falls out of her plunging neck-
line. (The 1977 miniseries *Roots* is the first to intentionally show
bare breasts.)

1951: TV's first pregnant character in primetime is a woman on

One Man's Family, a long-running radio program that made its way to TV in 1949.

1952: Ozzie and Harriet Nelson are the first TV couple shown sleeping in the same bed. "There was no controversy—they were so darn wholesome," says Alex McNeil, author of *Total Television.*

1952: Lucille Ball's pregnancy is featured in seven episodes of *I Love Lucy*—without the word "pregnant" uttered once.

1961: Actress Yvette Mimieux wears a scanty bikini and bares her navel in a *Dr. Kildare* episode. No other navels are shown for the next decade: *I Dream of Jeannie* is launched in 1965 and runs for five years without showing Barbara Eden's, which is hidden under waist-high harem pants. Cher ends the taboo on the *Sonny and Cher Comedy Hour* in the 1970s.

1962: In an episode of *The Defenders,* a doctor speaks out in favor of abortion, which at the time is illegal in all 50 states. Some stations refuse to air the episode, and the show's regular sponsor pulls out. More than 10 years later, *Maude* experiences a similar backlash when its two-part abortion episode airs.

1968: *Star Trek* features the first interracial kiss. In an episode titled "Plato's Stepchildren," a man who has the power to control the actions of others forces Captain Kirk and Lieutenant Uhura to kiss.

1970: ABC's *The Odd Couple* features the first lead characters who are divorced. Ironically, *The Mary Tyler Moore Show,* which premiered on CBS five days earlier, was originally to have been about a divorced woman. But CBS told the show's creators that a divorcee was too controversial to be the main character of a weekly comedy, so Mary Richards was rewritten as a woman who had recently ended a long engagement.

1971: During its first season, *All in the Family* brings one of the first homosexual characters to primetime. In the episode, "Judging Books by Covers," Archie Bunker scorns his son-in-law's effeminate friend, unaware that one of his own tough beer-drinking buddies is gay.

1973: In another episode of *All in the Family,* titled "Gloria, the Victim," Gloria is almost raped and suffers through the aftermath of reporting the crime.

UNCLE JOHN'S PAGE OF LISTS

Uncle John has a list of ten reasons why the Bathroom Reader *should have lists in it. (The list is confidential.)*

7 "Official" Attributes of the Pillsbury Doughboy:
1. His skin must look like dough: "off-white, smooth, but not glossy"
2. Slightly luminous, but no sheen
3. No Knees, elbows, wrists, fingers, ears, or ankles
4. Rear views do not include "buns"
5. Walks with a "swagger"
6. Stomach is propotional to the rest of his body.
7. He is not portly.

4 Strange Tourist Attractions
1. The Hall of Mosses (WA)
2. Phillip Morris Cigarette Tours (VA)
3. The Soup Tureen Museum (NJ)
4. The Testicle Festival (MT)

7 Nicknames Given to President Grover Cleveland
1. Big Beefhead
2. The Buffalo Hangman
3. The Dumb Prophet
4. The Stuffed Prophet
5. The Pretender
6. His Accidency
7. Uncle Jumbo

Origins of 4 Native American tribal names:
1. *Apache*: the Zuni word for "enemy."
2. *Cherokee*: the Creek word for "people of different speech."
3. *Hopi*: from *hopituh*, or "peaceful ones"
4. *Sioux*: Chippewa name for a kind of snake.

State with the most pollution: Texas

5 Most-Read U.S. Newspapers
1. *Wall St. Journal*
2. *USA Today*
3. *L.A. Times*
4. *New York Times*
5. *Washington Post*

26 Things Elvis demanded be kept at Graceland at all times
Fresh ground beef, Hamburger buns, Case of Pepsi, Case of orange soda, Brownies, Milk, half & half, 6 cans of biscuits, Chocolate ice cream, Hot dogs, Sauerkraut, Potatoes, Onions, Bacon, Fresh fruit, Peanut butter, Banana pudding, Meat loaf, 3 packs each of Spearmint, Juicy Fruit, Doublemint gum, Cigarettes, Dristan, Super Anahist, Contac, Sucrets

TOILET TECH

Better living through bathroom technology.

YOU'RE CLEARED TO LAND

Inventor: Brooke Pattee of Lake Forest, California

Product: Toilet "landing lights"—a lighting system that illuminates the inside of your toilet bowl so you can see it in the dark.

How It Works: A transparent tube containing wiring and several lights is positioned beneath the upper rim of the toilet bowl. When you lift or lower the lid, the lights come on, bathing the inside of the bowl in light so that you can take care of business without blinding yourself in the middle of the night by turning on the bathroom light. An automatic timer turns the lights off after several minutes.

AS GOOD AS GOLD

Inventor: Japanese electronics giant Matsushita

Product: An electric toilet seat that uses gold dust to filter out unpleasant smells.

How It Works: When a person sits on the toilet seat, an electric fan begins blowing the air in the toilet bowl into a "deodorization device" containing the gold dust and zeolite; they act as a catalyst to oxidize and deodorize ammonia and other compounds. Another filter containing manganese removes compounds containing sulfur. Toilet seat air filters are popular in Japan, where "lavatories at home are often so small and airless that smells hang around for some time."

DIAPER ALARM

Inventor: Karel Dvorak of Toronto, Ontario

Product: A disposable diaper with a moisture sensor that sets off a flashing LED light when wetness is detected.

How It Works: A clothespin-like moisture sensor is clipped to the baby's diaper in such a way that it makes contact with the baby's skin. The sensor compares the electrical conductivity of the skin to that of a special layer of material inside the diaper. When the diaper becomes wet, the voltage changes and the LED light begins to flash, notifying mom that it's time for a new diaper.

THE TOILET THAT SHOPS

Inventor: Twyford, a toilet manufacturer in Cheshire, England

Product: The Versatile Interactive Pan (VIP), a toilet that analyzes your urine and stool samples for dietary deficiencies, compiles a shopping list of needed nutritional items, then e-mails your local supermarket to order the foods.

How It Works: "If, for example, a person is short on roughage one day," says Twyford spokesperson Terry Wooliscroft, "an order of beans or lentils will be sent from the VIP to the supermarket and delivered the same day." The toilet can also e-mail a doctor if it detects health problems. Added bonuses: The seat is voice activated and the toilet flushes automatically. About the only thing you can't do with the VIP is buy one—it's still in development. Twyford expects to have it ready for market by 2006.

BLAST PAD

Inventor: UltraTech Products of Houston, Texas

Product: The Flatulence Filter Seat Cushion—a foam seat cushion that doubles as a rear-end odor eater.

How It Works: The foam cushion contains a hidden "super-activated" carbon filter that absorbs unfortunate odors as soon as they are created. The filter is hidden inside the cushion's gray tweed fabric, so no one has to know it's there—for all anyone knows, it's just another seat cushion. The company also makes a smaller filter pad that you can wear inside your underpants, "for protection when you are not at your seat."

By Any Other Name: "Originally the seat cushion was named the TooT TrappeR. At the time, it seemed like the perfect name. In time, doctors became interested in the cushion, but felt that some would think it was a joke. For this reason, we changed the name to the Flatulence Filter Seat Cushion. This resulted in a more clinical-sounding name."

George H. W. Bush was the youngest Navy pilot of World War II. (He got shot down.)

WHAT'S THE NUMBER FOR 911?

People do some ridiculous things—even when they call 911.
Here are some more of our favorite transcripts of 911 calls,
from Leland Gregory's book, What's the Number for 911?

Dispatcher: "Nine-one-one, what's the nature of your emergency, please?"

Caller: "I'm trying to reach nine-eleven, but my phone doesn't have an eleven on it."

Dispatcher: "This is nine-eleven."

Caller: "I thought you just said it was nine-one-one."

Dispatcher: "Yes, ma'am. Nine-one-one and nine-eleven are the same thing."

Caller: "Honey, I may be old, but I'm not stupid."

Dispatcher: "Nine-one-one. Please state your emergency."

Caller: "Yeah, okay. Bill got hurt."

Dispatcher: "Who is Bill?"

Caller: "Just some dude I know. We were tossing the Nerf around, and the TV fell and cut up his leg...like."

Dispatcher: "We'll send someone right over."

Caller (to someone in the room): "Get the keg outta here, dude!"

Dispatcher: "Nine-one-one. What's the nature of your emergency?"

Caller: "My wife is pregnant, and her contractions are only two minutes apart!"

Dispatcher: "Is this her first child?"

Caller: "No, you idiot! This is her husband!"

Dispatcher: "Nine-one-one."

Caller: "Yeah, I'm having trouble breathing. I'm all out of breath. Damn...I think I'm going to pass out."

Dispatcher: "Sir, where are you calling from?"

Caller: "I'm at a pay phone. North and Foster. Damn..."

Dispatcher: "Sir, an ambulance is on the way. Are you an asthmatic?"

Caller: "No..."

Dispatcher: "What were you doing before you started having trouble breathing?"

Caller: "Running from the police."

Composer Irving Berlin is the only Academy Award presenter to give an Oscar to himself.

POLI-TALKS

*More proof that politicians don't
deserve much respect these days.*

"We are ready for any
unforeseen event that may or
may not occur."
—**Al Gore**

"Statistics show that teen
pregnancy drops off significantly after age 25."
—**Sen. Mary Anne
Tebedo (R-CO)**

"I can't believe that we are
going to let a majority of
people decide what's best for
this state."
—**Rep. John Travis
(D-LA)**

"What is the state of North
Carolina going to do about
its bludgeoning prison popu-
lation?"
—**Sen. Maggie
Tinsman (R-IA)**

"We don't want to open a
box of Pandoras."
—**Gov. Bruce King
(D-NM)**

"What right does Congress
have to go around making
laws just because they deem
it necessary?"
—**Marion Barry**

"She's a wonderful, wonderful person, and we're looking
to a happy and wonderful
night...uh, life."
—**Sen. Ted Kennedy,
about his then-fiancee**

"It's like an Alcatraz around
my neck."
—**Thomas Menino,
Boston mayor on
the shortage of
city parking**

"Our cabinet is always unanimous—except when we
disagree."
—**British Columbia
premier William
Vander Zalm**

"I don't know anyone here
that's been killed by a
handgun."
—**Rep. Avery
Alexander (R-LA)**

"What's a man got to do to
get in the top fifty?"
—**President Bill Clinton,
on a survey ranking the
Lewinsky scandal as the
53rd most significant
story of the century**

John Quincy Adams and Dwight D. Eisenhower were the only bald presidents (so far).

THE HISTORY OF FOOTBALL, PART V

Here's a sports trivia question for you: Which U.S. president threatened to ban college football, on the grounds that it was becoming too violent? Answer: Theodore Roosevelt. Here's the story of how football nearly pummeled itself into extinction.

BIG TIME

By the late 1880s, American football was beginning to spread from the original handful of eastern colleges to schools in other parts of the country. Notre Dame started its football program in 1887, and the University of Southern California followed a year later; Stanford and the University of California both launched programs in 1893. By 1897 teams were popping up all over the country.

Yale University remained the dominant force in American football—it lost only three games in the first 10 years of intercollegiate play. And because coach Walter Camp dominated Yale's program and had been so influential in shaping the modern game, his authority at the center of American football was unchallenged.

A VICTIM OF ITS OWN SUCCESS

But football was too much fun to remain the exclusive preserve of pampered "college boys." As the sport caught on in universities across the nation, athletic clubs in the surrounding communities began to form their own football leagues. So did church parishes, community groups, businesses, and small towns itching to earn big reputations. Regular play between such teams soon led to the same kinds of traditional rivalries and fierce grudge matches that by now were an entrenched part of the college game.

As the violence of these "semi-pro" leagues escalated beyond even that of college football, the sport returned ever closer to the anarchy of its medieval roots. In some areas of the country, Stephen Fox writes in *Big Leagues*, semi-pro football became little more than "a formalized excuse for beating up men from other communities."

Honeybees are not native to North America. They were introduced by explorers and colonists.

BAD NEWS

Twenty-one people died playing football during the 1904 season; another 23 would die the following year. Only a handful of those killed had been playing on college teams—the majority had been playing on semi-pro teams. But the college teams were still the organizing force behind football, and in the middle of the 1905 season, President Theodore Roosevelt, himself a football fan, summoned representatives from three of the major football powers—Harvard, Yale, and Princeton—to the White House and ordered them to clean up the sport. "Brutality and foul play," he told them, "should receive the same summary punishment given to a man who cheats at cards."

Roosevelt was no shrinking violet when it came to physical contests: The president broke his right arm while "stick fighting" and would eventually lose the sight in his left eye from a boxing injury. And he resumed stick fighting and boxing as soon as these injuries "healed." So if *he* was concerned about violence in football, there really was a problem.

NOTHING NEW

Harvard, Yale, and Princeton left the White House meeting promising to do better, but football didn't really change. And football's image was so tattered that some colleges were ready to ban the game with or without presidential support: Columbia abolished its football program in 1905 and did not reinstate it until 1915. Stanford and the University of California replaced their programs with rugby the same year. "The game of football," U.C.'s president Benjamin Wheeler declared, "must be made over or go."

For years, one of the biggest obstacles to cleaning up football had been Walter Camp himself. As chairman of the Intercollegiate Football Rules Committee, he had been able to fend off any fundamental changes to the game. Elliott Gorn writes in *A Brief History of American Sports:*

> Calls for "reform" of the game occasionally met with public approval, but they had little impact on the conduct of the game itself. Walter Camp saw no contradiction between honor and brutality. He defended—nearly always successfully—the game he loved against all efforts at significant reform; he remains one of the central figures whose efforts increased the game's violence.

Zap! The amount of energy coursing through your brain is

YALEGATE

Camp's iron grip on football loosened considerably beginning in 1905, following the publication of a number of articles in the *New York Evening Post*, and in *McClure's* and *Outlook* magazines detailing scandalous financial abuses in the Yale football program.

As amateur athletes, Yale players weren't supposed to receive compensation of any kind for playing football, a system that Camp enthusiastically endorsed...in public. "We do not make exceptions to the rules," he said, "hence our men are not eligible if they have received money or compensation for ball playing."

But what went on behind the scenes was another story entirely. As treasurer of the Yale Financial Union, Camp controlled the funds of all of Yale's major sports programs—not just football—and unknown to anyone, he had stashed more than $96,000 in a secret fund that he used to coddle his star players, putting them up in expensive dorms, paying their way through school (there were no football scholarships at the time), and even sending them on paid vacations, all of which he hid in the budget as "miscellaneous expenses."

And though as head of the Yale football program he served ostensibly as a part-time volunteer, Camp secretly paid himself a $5,000-a-year salary, while full-time Yale professors earned only $3,500 a year. He buried this expenditure under the heading "Maintenance of the field."

Yale's shady financial practices were no different from any other college at the time. Recruiting the country's best players and fielding championship teams year after year took a lot of money, and it had to come from somewhere. But the revelations about Yale came just as the pressure to clean up football violence was intensifying, and Camp, with his reputation as a "rock-ribbed standard bearer of Victorian honor in the midst of corruption" now seriously in question, was no longer able to block the reforms that others were determined to push through.

CHANGING OF THE GUARD

When Camp tried to resist Roosevelt's demand to clean up football, Chancellor Henry MacCracken of New York University decided he'd had enough. He organized a conference of 13 colleges *not* represented on Camp's tightly controlled rules committee, to discuss whether college football should be abolished altogether, or whether one last attempt at cleaning it up should be made.

The original group of 13 schools that met on December 9, 1905 expanded to 62 schools by the time they met a second time, on December 28. At this meeting the schools voted to form an organization called the Intercollegiate Athletic Association, which in 1910 changed its name to the National Collegiate Athletic Association (NCAA). The group also voted to create its own rules committee, headed by Captain Palmer Pierce of West Point, to push through the reforms that Camp had resisted for so long.

CAN'T WE ALL JUST GET ALONG?

Rather than compete against the old Intercollegiate Football Association, when the Intercollegiate Athletic Association met for the third time in January 1906, they agreed to merge, electing a reformer named E. K. Hall to serve as chair of the new joint rules committee. Camp was out as chairman—for good.

"Ever the good sportsman, Walter Camp stayed involved at the highest levels of football," Stephen Fox writes in *Big Leagues*. "But his reign had ended."

"Lavatory! Lavatory! Sis, boom, bah! Uncle John! Uncle John! Rah, rah, rah!" Now turn to page 480 for the final installment of The History of Football.

*   *   *

GET IN FORMATION

It was in about the 1880s that the current names of football positions were beginning to come into use.

• Because the "snapperback" stood at the center of the line of scrimmage, he became known simply as the "center."

• The forwards standing at either end of the line of scrimmage became known as "end men" and later as "ends."

• The back who played deepest became the "fullback," and the two backs who stood between the quarterback came to be known as "halfbacks."

In 1888 Yale football coach Walter Camp fell ill. His wife coached for the entire season.

FIRSTS

*More accounts of the very first appearance of
several things we take for granted. From
Book of Firsts, by Patrick Robertson.*

THE FIRST LIFE INSURANCE POLICY

Date: June 18, 1583

Background: The first recorded life insurance policy was taken out by London alderman Richard Martin, who paid a group of merchant underwriters a premium of £30 to insure the life of one William Gibbons for the sum of £383. The contract stipulated that this benefit should only be paid if the insured died within a year. Eleven months later Gibbons was gathered to the arms of his Maker. The underwriters then sought to evade payment by the dubious argument that he had not died within "the full twelve months accounting 28 days to each month." The case having been brought to court, it was ruled that "the month is to be accounted according to the Kalendar" and Martin received the money due to him.

THE FIRST ELECTRIC REFRIGERATOR

Date: 1913

Background: The first refrigerator for domestic use was the Domelre, an electrically powered machine manufactured in Chicago. It had a wooden cabinet with a compression-type refrigerating unit mounted in the top.

THE FIRST FILM ACTOR

Date: August 28, 1895

Background: The first motion picture to involve the use of actors was a brief costume drama titled *The Execution of Mary Queen of Scots*, which was shot by Alfred Clark in West Orange, New Jersey. The part of Mary was played by Mr. R. L. Thomas, secretary and treasurer of the Kinetoscope Co. After approaching the block and laying his head upon it, Thomas removed himself, the camera was stopped, and a dummy was substituted. The camera was then started again for the decapitation scene. This was also the first use of trick photography or special effects work in a film.

The Greek wine *retsina* is made with pine tree resin. So is turpentine.

THE FIRST LAUNDERETTE
Date: April 18, 1934
Background: The first laundrette was the Washateria, opened at Fort Worth, Texas, by J. F. Cantrell. It contained four electric washing machines that were charged for by the hour.

THE FIRST NUMBERING OF HOUSES
Date: 1463
Background: The first numbering of houses was introduced on the Pont Notre-Dame, Paris.

THE FIRST NYLON
Date: 1937
Background: The first nylon was developed and patented by the American chemical company E. I. du Pont de Nemours. The first commercially produced nylon product was toothbrush bristles, manufactured at du Pont's Arlington, New Jersey, plant in 1938. Nylon yarn was produced commercially for the first time in 1939, and made into stockings by various hosiery manufacturers. By mutual agreement, competing brands of nylon stockings were launched throughout the USA simultaneously on May 15, 1940.

THE FIRST INCOME TAX
Date: 1451
Background: The first income tax was the Catastro introduced in Florence, Italy, under Lorenzo de' Medici. It was later replaced by the Scala, an income tax levied on a progressive basis, but this degenerated into a convenient means of political blackmail and, on the overthrow of the Medicis in 1492, was repealed.

THE FIRE EXTINGUISHER
Date: 1734
Background: It was invented by German physician M. Fuches and consisted of glass balls filled with a saline solution designed to be hurled at blaze. Advertisements depicting a whole family lobbing these balls at a blazing inferno in their living room, with expressions of rapturous enjoyment on their faces, appeared in English journals up until World War I.

THE FOOD QUIZ

You shop for food, you cook it, you eat it....But how much do you really know about it? Take our food quiz and find out. Bon appétit!

1. Which is heavier: light cream or heavy cream?

a) Light cream

b) Heavy cream

c) Neither—all milk products, including cheese, are the same weight by volume. The only exception is Swiss cheese, which is lighter because it's filled with holes.

2. When a meal is served on an airline, how is it likely to differ from the same meal served on land?

a) It is likely to contain added sucrose, which has natural mellowing agents that reduce stress during long flights.

b) Entrees are likely to contain gelatin, which helps the food retain its natural shape in the pressurized cabin.

c) It probably contains more seasonings, but less salt. People taste food differently when flying, so extra seasoning is added. But they also dehydrate easily, so less salt is used.

3. In addition to adding their own flavor, how else do onions alter the taste of food?

a) They release a caffeinelike stimulant. The diner experiences a mild euphoria that enhances their enjoyment of the meal and perceives the food as being tastier than it actually is.

b) They release oils that coat the tongue, dulling the taste of everything except the onion.

c) They irritate tastebuds, making them more sensitive to taste.

4. How can you judge the quality of ice cream before you buy it?

a) Weigh it.

b) Twirl the container in midair. Well-balanced ice cream is of higher quality than ice cream that wobbles when thrown.

c) Squeeze it—ice cream, like fruit, isn't "ripe" until it's soft.

5. Botanically speaking, what is the difference between a fruit and a vegetable?

a) Color. Green or yellow means it's a vegetable. Red, blue, or purple means it's a fruit.

b) Seeds. If it has seeds, it's a fruit. If it doesn't, it's a vegetable.

c) Sugar content. A good rule of thumb is if it's sweet enough to be eaten for dessert, it's a fruit.

6. Apple seeds contain which of the following?

a) Cyanide

b) Lactose

c) LSD

7. When, if ever, is it safe to refreeze food?

a) It's never completely safe. Thawing and refreezing can "wake up" certain bacteria.

b) It's always safe, but texture and flavor may deteriorate.

c) Only when the food is refrozen within 90 minutes of thawing.

8. Most of the vitamins in a potato are located where?

a) In the skin

b) Near the skin

c) In the starch

9. Where does Mocha-Java coffee originally came from?

a) The Yemen port of Mocha. (*Java* means "coffee" in Yemeni.)

b) The Indonesian port of Java, where cacao beans are also grown.

c) The Yemen port of Mocha *and* the Indonesian port of Java.

10. In addition to adding flavor, how does a marinade change meat?

a) The cooked meat will be juicier.

b) The cooked meat will be drier.

c) The cooked meat will be better preserved. On average, it will remain fresh in the refrigerator three times as long as unmarinated cooked meat.

Answers on page 509.

NUDES & PRUDES

Even more proof that whether you're dressed
or naked, you can still be dumber than sin.

NUDE... The Florida Board of Medicine has indefinitely
suspended the medical license of physician William
Charles Leach after he examined at least three patients in
the nude or nearly nude. "He took off his lab coat and his shirt
and pants," one patient writes. "He then stood naked in front of
me and asked me to comment on his appearance." The suspension
has forced Dr. Leach to put on hold his plans for establishing the
first nude medical clinic in the state of Florida.

PRUDE... Finnish cellular phone maker Nokia and the Dutch
phone company KPN Telecom are protesting a decision by Tring,
an Amsterdam cell phone retailer, to give away a sex toy with
each cell phone purchase. "We've asked that it be stopped," says a
KPN spokeswoman. "It's not our style at all."

NUDE... Arne and Oeystein Tokvam, two elderly brothers living
in Oslo, Norway, got the show of a lifetime when a blonde-haired
woman they didn't know talked her way into their home and
began stripping off her clothing. The woman, who was in her 30s,
was soon joined by an older woman who also stripped naked and
began dancing around the brothers' home. "The older one was the
wildest of the two," Arne, 73, told a local newspaper. "We saw
everything."

After about 15 minutes, the mystery women put their clothes
on and left; that was when Oeystein, 80, discovered that the
brothers' safe was missing, and along with it $6,600 in cash and
two government checks for $1,700. "Never mind," says Arne. "It's
been a long time since we had that much fun."

PRUDE... Senegalese police detained two journalists for questioning after they published a photomontage that showed the head of
Prime Minister Mame Madior Boye, Senegal's first female prime
minister, pasted onto the body of a nude model. "We did not aim
to hurt the prime minister," a spokesperson for *Tract* newspaper
said following the arrests. "It was just meant as a joke."

It takes 4 hours to weave a hula skirt from 60 *ti* plants. The skirt will only last about 5 days.

GREAT BALLS OF FORE

In this article from National Post Business *magazine,
writer Ian Cruickshank slices open a golf ball
and takes a look at what makes it fly.*

IN THE BEGINNING

According to one popular theory, golf began about 1,000 years ago when Scottish shepherds inverted their crooks to knock rocks into rabbit holes. By the early 1600s, the balls had evolved into a combination of feathers and leather. A hatful of chicken feathers was boiled and then stuffed into a wet, three-piece leather covering. The feathers expanded, the leather contracted, and the resulting solid orb was then painted white.

The next ball revolution took place in 1845 with the development of the gutta-percha ball, made from sap imported from Malaysia. Later experimentation showed that the "gutty" flew farther and straighter when it was dented—hence the beginning of golf ball dimples. In the early 1900s, Cleveland businessman Coburn Haskell invented the modern ball, with a rubber core that was wound with elastics and then finished with a plastic cover.

BRANDS

Golfers are very loyal to their brand of balls, with nearly 70% of them returning to their favorite ball season after season. The main reason: golfers tend to worship the pros. They like to tee up the same type of ball used by players such as Tiger Woods or Mark O'Meara, who get paid millions of dollars to use a particular brand. All of the major manufacturers make a variety of brands, usually four to eight models, with some specializing in distance, some in spin and control, and others in a combination of distance, control and accuracy. If a ball is a commercial hit, the profit margin is substantial. Marketing costs, however, can be steep: a new ball introduction can cost up to $15 million in marketing costs.

DIMPLES

Dimples reduce drag at a ball's launch, and an indented ball will fly more than twice as far as a smooth ball. Although they all look very similar, different types of golf balls are full of subtle differ-

---

Tongue-tied: Crocodiles can't move their tongues.

ences. For example, the number, size and shape of the dimple patterns vary. They are arranged in patterns according to whether you are looking for distance or control. Bigger dimples mean less room for drag, which allows the ball to fly higher and spin more. The number of dimples ranges from about 350 to 400 per ball.

CONSTRUCTION

The basic golf ball follows the two-piece construction, which is generally a solid rubber core wrapped in a hard plastic cover. Balls with liquid cores (usually saline-based solutions) or cores that are wound in elastic are generally softer. Most good players are more concerned with control than distance, and these softer balls allow them to put more spin on the ball. Some of the newer balls have tungsten in the rubber core, which, according to manufacturers, makes the ball both hard for distance and soft for spin. Another trend in golf balls is a rubber core surrounded by a soft covering, which is then wrapped by a hard core, all of which is supposed to make the ball spin more. There is also new technology going into covers: titanium, which increases rigidity, making the ball snap back into its original form faster after contact with the club head.

TESTING

Golf balls must conform to standards set by the United States Golf Association and the Canadian Royal and Ancient Golf Club of St. Andrews. The maximum weight for a ball is 1.62 ounces. They must measure at least 1.68 inches in circumference but there is no limit to size. Each year, the USGA tests over 20,000 golf balls to ensure they conform to velocity and spin requirements. Reason: They don't want a manufacturer to juice up a ball with a smaller dimple pattern or a different core, which could allow the ball to fly much farther and render current golf courses obsolete.

The long-ball champ is Jason Zuback, an Alberta pharmacist, who recently won his fourth consecutive World Long Drive Championship (a combination of distance and accuracy) with a 376-yard blast—although his personal best is a Herculean 511-yarder.

*　　　*　　　*

"What is mind? No matter. What is matter? Never mind."
—**Thomas Hewitt Key**

PHOTOGRAPHY BEGINS TO GEL

Photography was a 19th-century technological wonder, and the early years of its development were incredibly productive. It turned another corner in 1878, with the introduction of the dry plate.

STILL WET AFTER ALL THESE YEARS

In the fifteen years since the invention of the daguerreotype in 1837, photography had made amazing progress. The collodion process and its descendants—ambrotypes, tintypes, and cartes-de-visite—were huge improvements, but they were still "wet-plate" processes.

Photographers had to apply fresh collodion to their glass photographic plates right before they took a picture, and then develop the plates immediately afterward, before the chemicals dried. That meant lugging all their chemicals and equipment, including a portable darkroom, wherever they went to take a picture. Every photo shoot was an expensive camping trip…which made photography off-limits to everyone except professionals and a handful of dedicated amateurs.

Someone either had to find a substitute for collodion or find a way to stop it from drying out so quickly, perhaps by mixing in substances that were slower to dry. They tried everything they could think of—honey, glycerine, raspberry syrup, beer—but nothing worked.

THE SMELL OF SUCCESS

Ironically, the person who finally stumbled onto the answer, English physician Richard Leach Maddox, wasn't even trying to solve the problem. Maddox didn't mind the inconvenience of the wet-plate process—he just hated the way it smelled. His photography studio was set up in a glasshouse, and when it heated up, the smell of the ether in the collodion was overpowering. He became determined to find a process that did not require ether.

In 1871 Maddox found one that showed a lot of promise: a silver-gelatin emulsion. He believed this was the key to a non-

---

He never got lost: T. D. Rockwell had his name and address tattooed on his body in…

smelling "dry-plate process," but the demands of his medical practice prevented him from spending the time needed to refine it. So, in a letter to the *British Journal of Photography*, Maddox invited others to pick up where he had left off.

Seven years later another Englishman, Charles Harper Bennett, refined the process and proved Maddox right. He discovered that he could "ripen" the gelatin emulsion by heating it to 90°F and holding it at that temperature for several days. Then, after washing the plate to remove excess chemical salts, Bennett discovered that he could create a "dry plate" that was *60 times* more sensitive to light than one made with the collodion or any other photographic process.

IN THE BLINK OF AN EYE

For decades, photographers had yearned to capture all that the human eye could see. Now, in a single stroke, Bennett had invented plates that worked *faster* than the human eye, allowing people to see things that it had never been possible to see before: horses in mid-gallop, birds flapping their wings in flight, children jumping rope, water droplets falling in mid-air. Before gelatin plates, all of these images had appeared as blurs—now they were crystal clear.

The invention of gelatin plates prompted new camera designs: bulky wooden tripod-mounted cameras were replaced by smaller units that photographers could easily hold in their hands. The new cameras were also more sophisticated: In the past people took pictures by removing the lens cap and replacing it a few seconds later, but gelatin plates were too sensitive for that. Precise exposure speeds, accurate to within a fraction of a second, were necessary. So camera makers added shutter systems that allowed for short and accurate exposure times. By 1900 it was possible to take exposures as short as 1/5000 of a second.

SCIENTIFIC METHOD

Just as important as the speed of the new gelatin plates was the fact that they remained photosensitive for months on end, which meant that they could be prepared well in advance of being used. Photographers no longer had to prepare plates themselves; they could buy them from the hundreds of small companies that sprang up to sell ready-made plates. They still had to develop the plates themselves, but at least now they could do it at their leisure.

Gelatin plates also helped bring standardization to the photography industry. In the past, each photographic plate was prepared from scratch moments before being put into use, so photosensitivity varied from plate to plate and from photographer to photographer. Not anymore: Now plates could be made under more controlled conditions, making their performance more predictable and reliable.

This mass production made it possible for two British scientists, Vero Charles Driffield and Ferdinand Hurter, to begin some of the first serious scientific studies of the chemistry and physics of photography. Through their research they calculated the optimum exposure time for photographic plates depending on lighting, temperature, and other factors, and they perfected the developing process to the point that people could develop exposures in absolute darkness, just by timing how long the exposures soaked in developing chemicals. As Driffield and Hurder unlocked photography's secrets, they helped to make it more accessible to ordinary people.

ONE MORE THING

The introduction of smaller, more sophisticated cameras and standardized, ready-made supplies simplified photography, but there were still a few hurdles that kept most people away.

For one thing, people still needed a darkroom or at least a *dark room*, because the gelatin plates had to be loaded into a camera in absolute darkness. The plates were so sensitive that exposing them to even a small amount of light caused them to fog over. And they were still made of glass, which was expensive, fragile, and heavy. Glass plates and plate holders added several pounds to the weight of a camera, which meant that no matter how small the cameras got, photography was still a costly and unwieldy affair.

But the most daunting problem of all was that most people still had to develop exposures themselves. If you wanted to *take* a picture, you had to *make* the picture. And if you weren't willing to do that, you were out of luck.

Then in 1880, George Eastman, a bookkeeper at the Rochester Savings Bank in Rochester, New York, decided to go into the gelatin-plate business.

To capture the rest of the story, turn to page 450.

The Earth spins 1,000 mph faster at the equator than at the poles.

MYTH-AMERICA

Some of the stories we recognize today as American myths were taught as history for many years. The truth might surprise you.

M YTH: Witches were burned at the stake during the Salem witch trials of 1692.

TRUTH: No witches were ever burned in Salem. A hundred fifty men and women were arrested under suspicion of witchcraft. In all, 19 people and two dogs were put to death as "witches and warlocks," all of them hanged except for one person, who was pressed to death by stones. Ten others were convicted, but not put to death. A few months later, the governor of Massachusetts dissolved the witch court. The judges didn't mind; they were running out of people to accuse.

MYTH: While writing *Walden*, Henry David Thoreau lived in isolation in the woods of Massachusetts.

TRUTH: Thoreau's two-year retreat to Walden Pond was like a little boy pretending that his backyard tree house is in the middle of the jungle. In truth, Thoreau built his famous cabin a scant two miles from his family's home and spent very little time in isolation. "It was not a lonely spot," wrote Walter Harding in *The Days of Henry Thoreau*. "Hardly a day went by that Thoreau did not visit the village or was visited at the pond." Thoreau was even known to return home on the weekends to raid the family cookie jar.

MYTH: The westward expansion of the 1800s offered American pioneers million of acres of fertile farmland.

TRUTH: The American frontier was not an organized democracy in which every "sodbuster" could own a piece of land with the promise of prosperity. The money of big corporations even then dominated the West. Although the federal government did in fact permit pioneers to stake large claims in the Great Plains, the arid climate and dry infertile soil rendered this land almost impossible for individuals to raise crops or maintain livestock on. To escape starvation, most pioneers were forced to sell their land to the corporations. In return, the corporations often offered the pioneers

All in the family: President Grant appointed 13 of his relatives to federal posts.

jobs as low-paid miners and farmhands. By the 1890s, almost 90% of the farmland west of the Mississippi River was owned by corporations.

MYTH: The American bald eagle, symbol of the United States, is a noble creature.

TRUTH: The American bald eagle, whom Benjamin Franklin referred to as "a bird of bad moral character," is an aggressive species that, according to news reports, has recently begun to terrorize people. Since they were removed from the endangered species list in the late 1990s, the birds have been using their large talons and sharp beaks to attack fishermen and picnickers. Eagles have also been known to snatch puppies from suburban backyards, terrifying residents.

MYTH: To escape Union capture, Confederate president Jefferson Davis fled Richmond disguised in his wife's dress.

TRUTH: Rather than admit defeat by surrendering to the Union army, Davis fled to Texas with the hope of reorganizing his troops. However, on May 10, 1865, he was apprehended in Georgia. Clad in a gray suit as he hastily greeted the Union troops, he accidentally grabbed his wife's cloak to protect him from the cold. Secretary of War Edwin M. Stanton presented the false story of Davis disguising himself in a dress to the *New York Herald*, which published it on May 16, 1865.

MYTH: "Jesse James was a man who killed many a man. / He robbed the Glendale train. / He stole from the rich and he gave to the poor. / He'd a hand and a heart and a brain."

TRUTH: Jesse Woodson James, who was born in Missouri in 1847, did indeed rob from the rich. Most of the money that he stole, however, he kept for himself. A child of slave-owning aristocrats, Jesse James made a name for himself as one of the Confederate marauders known as Quantrell's Raiders during the Civil War. His move to robbing banks after the war was inspired by a deep hatred of the Northern industry that was becoming widespread in the pastoral South. It is true that he killed many a man—most of them innocent bystanders.

Comedian Stan Laurel was married 8 times, but had only 4 wives.

MIRROR, MIRROR ON THE WALL

*Not that we're vain or anything, but we at the BRI find mirrors
endlessly fascinating. Here are some important facts about
the second-most important object in the bathroom.*

POOLS OF LIGHT

How do mirrors work? Generally speaking, by reflecting light. Most objects don't give off any light of their own. They can only be seen because light from other sources—the sun, a candle, a lightbulb—hits them and bounces off, hitting their eyes. Not all of the light bounces, though. Some is absorbed by the object and some is transmitted through the object. The part that does bounce back is the reflection. Flat shiny surfaces like water, metal, and mirrors reflect light well because very little of the light is absorbed or transmitted—most of it is reflected.

When light hits a mirror, it bounces off in the opposite direction, but at the exact same angle it came from. It appears as if the image is coming from behind the mirror, but it's not—what we see is a virtual image.

THE FIRST MIRRORS

For centuries, mankind's only mirrors were pools of water or polished metal. The first glass mirrors were made by Venetian craftsmen in the 1300s. Their method: They covered the back of a piece of glass with an amalgam of tin and mercury, rubbed flat and smooth. A piece of wool cloth would then be laid on top of the mercury and pressed with iron weights for more than a week. Then the excess mercury would be drained off. This method remained a carefully guarded secret, and for centuries Venice had a monopoly on mirrors.

In 1665 the chief minister to Louis XIV of France went to Italy and—at the risk of death—bribed 18 Venetian mirrorsmiths to move to France. Soon after their defection, the French passed a law making it illegal to import Venetian mirrors.

Three years later, a Frenchman named Louis Lucas beat the

The pouch on a pelican's beak can hold up to 2 gal. of water.

Venetians at their own game—he invented plate glass. Venetians only knew how to make blown glass, so each mirror started out as a bottle or cylinder which was slit open and flattened while still hot. The size of mirrors was therefore very limited.

But Lucas discovered how to pour molten glass onto an iron table where it could be flattened with an iron roller. Now mirrors could be made that were much larger. Soon France became famous for its mirrors. A very pleased Louis XIV purchased 700 mirrors and lined an entire hallway at the Palace of Versailles with them in a stunning display.

UPON FURTHER REFLECTION

In 1835 German chemist Justus von Liebig discovered a way to make a better mirror. He invented a process for using silver as a backing instead of tin and mercury. He flushed the glass with silver salts and then covered it with a solution of silver nitrate. After being heated and left undisturbed for an hour, a chemical reaction caused the metallic silver to separate and adhere to the glass. Then it was coated with shellac and painted with a black backing. And that's how mirrors were made for the next 150 years.

In mirror making today, silver or aluminum is vaporized, then sprayed onto glass. For finer mirrors—such as those used in telescopes—aluminum, chromium, or gold are heated in a vacuum tank. When they reach the critical temperature, they "flash" into vapor, filling the tank with metallic gas. A film is then deposited on whatever material is inside the tank.

MIRROR FACTS AND TRIVIA

• In the 1600s, the Dutch used to cover their mirrors with curtains when not in use, lest the reflectiveness be used up!

• In ancient China, reflective pieces of polished brass were placed over doorknobs so that evil spirits would scare themselves away.

• Ben Franklin mounted mirrors outside his second-story window so he could secretly see who was knocking at his door.

• The vanity license plate "3M TA3" was banned after someone looked at it in the mirror.

• A middle school in Oregon was faced with a unique problem: A number of girls were beginning to use lipstick and would apply it in the bathroom. That was fine, but for some reason, they would also press their lips to the mirrors, leaving dozens of little lip prints. Finally the principal called all the girls to the bathroom. She explained that the lip prints were a major problem for the custodian and asked the custodian to demonstrate how difficult it was to clean one of the mirrors. He proceeded to take out a long-handled brush, dip it into the nearest toilet, and scrub the mirror. After that, there were no lip prints on the mirrors.

• The word *mirror* comes from the Latin *mirari*, meaning "to wonder at." It's also the root word for *miracle* and *admire*.

• The world's largest mirrors (to date) sit inside the twin Keck Telescopes—the world's largest telescopes—at the W. M. Keck Observatory in Hawaii. Each mirror is made of 36 hexagonal segments which work together as a single piece. Diameter: ten meters (32 feet) across.

• In olden days some thought that the reflection of the body in a shiny surface or mirror was an expression of the spiritual self, and therefore if anything happened to disturb that reflection, injury would follow. This was the origin of the superstition that breaking a mirror would bring seven years of bad luck.

• Trade secret: Building managers install mirrors in lobbies because people complain less about waiting for slow elevators when they're occupied looking at themselves.

• In 1994 Russian astronauts orbiting in the Mir spacecraft tried using mirrors to reflect sunlight into northern areas of their country in an attempt to lengthen the short growing season. It didn't work.

• Ever wonder if the mirror in the dressing room is a real mirror or a two-way mirror? Here's as simple test: Place the tip of your fingernail against the reflective surface. If there's a gap between your fingernail and the image, it's a *genuine* mirror. But, if your fingernail *directly touches* the image, watch out—it very well could be a two-way mirror. Remember, though, that mirror technology is always changing, so no test is 100% foolproof.

*   *   *

Word Origin: Clock comes from the Latin *clocca* meaning "bell," since clock tower bells were rung on the hour. The same root gives us *cloak* which is shaped like a bell.

---

4 microns (millionths of a meter) thick. Spiders webs are as thin as 1 micron.

YOU'RE MY INSPIRATION

It's always fun to find out what—or who—inspired cultural (and pop cultural) milestones like these.

YELLOW JOURNALISM. In 1895 publisher William Randolph Hearst broke into the New York newspaper world by buying the *New York Journal* and copying feature-by-feature Joseph Pulitzer's New York *World*, then the nation's most popular paper. Hearst even hired away *World* cartoonist R. F. Outcault, who drew "The Yellow Kid" comic strip for the color comics section. Pulitzer retaliated by hiring another cartoonist to create a second "yellow" kid; the dueling strips attracted so much attention that the sensationalist style of journalism practiced by both papers became known as "yellow journalism."

MITSUBISHI LOGO. Today Mitsubishi is best known for its cars, but in the 1930s and '40s it was better known for its infamous Zero, the warplane that was used to launch the attack on Pearl Harbor. Although the company no longer produces airplanes, it still uses the same logo—*mitsu bishi*, or "three diamonds," arranged in the shape of an airplane propeller.

STATUE OF ST. MICHAEL. Located at Norway's Trondheim Cathedral, it is considered one of the greatest Gothic structures in all of Northern Europe. Sculptor Kristofer Leirdal, 85, created the statue for the 12th-century cathedral when it was being restored in 1969. He says he based the figure—that of a winged angel with a spear poised to slay a dragon—on singer Bob Dylan. "I saw him as a representative of American opposition to the Vietnam War," he recounted in 2001. "I thought it was appropriate to have a great poet on top of the tower."

SUBARU LOGO. In 1953 six Japanese companies merged to form one automobile company. They modeled their six-star logo after the Pleiades constellation, which also has six stars. In Japan the star cluster is known as *Subaru*.

Animal magnetism: Homing pigeons can't find their way home if a magnet is tied to their necks.

IT'S A WEIRD, WEIRD WORLD

Proof that truth really is stranger than fiction.

I'LL GET YOU, MY PRETTY

"High school student Brandi Blackbear has filed a federal lawsuit against the Broken Arrow, Oklahoma, school district. The suit claims Blackbear was unfairly suspended because the assistant principal believed her Wiccan 'curse' actually caused a teacher to become ill. 'I, for one,' said the Oklahoma director of the American Civil Liberties Union, 'would like to see the evidence that a 15-year-old girl made a grown man sick by casting a magic spell.'"
—*Bizarre News*

LIFE IN THE FAST LANE

WALTHAM ABBEY, Essex—"A senior citizen was involved in a low speed chase after he decided to go for a cruise in his electric wheelchair along the M25, Britain's busiest motorway. According to Police Inspector Keith Fitzjohn, the man, whose name was not disclosed, was intercepted and taken home after being 'lectured on the folly of driving an electric wheelchair on the M25.'"
—*Funny Times*

MONK-ING AROUND

BANGKOK—"Two Buddhist monks are suspected of ignoring their vows by drinking in a bar 62 miles north of Bangkok. According to police, bar employees said the monks—disguised in wigs and hats—had been there several times, drinking and singing karaoke. Buddhist monks are supposed to shave their heads and live simple lives devoid of materialism, forswearing wordly pleasures such as alcohol, sex and, apparently, karaoke."
—**Associated Press**

A CASE OF COWLICK

PEREIRA, Colombia—"A Colombian hairdresser says he has found a way to lick baldness—literally. His offbeat scalp treatment involves a special tonic and massage—with a cow's tongue. 'I feel more manly, more attractive to women,' says customer Henry Gomez. 'My friends even say "What are you doing? You have more hair. You look younger."'"

—CNN *Fringe*

TRICK AND TREAT

"Home-invading robbers tied up a Westminster, California, family on Halloween night, 2000, and loaded up their valuables, diligently pausing several times to pass out candy to trick-or-treaters."

—*News of the Weird*

THE CRYING GAME

BANGKOK—"Kesaraporn Duangsawan captured the hearts of the judges and walked away with 6,000 baht (about $135) as first runner-up in a Thai beauty contest. When pageant organizers discovered the beauty queen was a man, the disgraced 22-year-old admitted his fraud and handed back the prize money, but asked to keep the Miss Media runner-up sash 'as a memento.'"

—Reuters

TOOTH IS STRANGER THAN FICTION

"Singing hymns and praying for peace and luck, thousands of Buddhists greeted a holy tooth, believed to have belonged to Buddha, when it arrived in Taiwan. Monks in saffron robes escorted the tooth, encased in a miniature golden pagoda, off a flight from India. Dozens of women prostrated themselves. Others knelt, clasping their hands in front to express their reverence. Buddhists say the tooth brings blessings and keeps them from disaster."

—Wacky *News*

A FAREWELL TO ARMS

"Police in Manchester, England, stunned Louis Makin, 27, when they went to his home and asked if they could throw away his arm. Makin had the arm amputated two years ago after being attacked by thugs. It had then been frozen to be used as evidence, and police needed permission to destroy it. 'I didn't know they still had it,' said Makin."

—"The Edge," *The Oregonian*

Stop your wine-ing. You need four tons of grapes to make one ton of raisins.

GOING POSTAL

Sending a letter through the mail seems so simple—put a stamp on it and drop it in a mailbox—that it's difficult to imagine that it took centuries for postal service to evolve into the form we recognize today. Here's a look at how it happened.

THE ROMAN EMPIRE

When the Roman republic was founded in 509 B.C., it was little more than a city-state. But after centuries of conquest, it grew into an empire that included large parts North Africa, most of Western Europe, and the entire Mediterranean.

Maintaining control over such a large area required that the central government in Rome be in regular contact with its representatives in every corner of the empire. This required a good system of roads and, just as importantly, a reliable and speedy postal system. Rome had both.

The emperor Augustus (27 B.C.–14 A.D.) is credited with establishing the imperial postal service, the *cursus publicus*, which consisted of relays, or *posts*, of runners stationed at intervals of 5 to 12 miles apart along the empire's military roads. Later, boats were employed to carry mail from port to port across the Mediterranean Sea, and the runners were replaced by horse-drawn carriages. At the system's peak, a message could travel as far as 170 miles in 24 hours, a speed unsurpassed in Europe until the 19th century.

THERE'S A CATCH

There was, however, one major difference between the Roman postal system and our modern one: the *cursus publicus* was for official government communications only. If private citizens wanted to send a message to another part of the empire, they had to hire a courier to deliver it in person.

The collapse of the Roman Empire in 476 A.D. marked the end of centralized authority in Europe and split the continent into numerous kingdoms who waged war not only against each other, but also against their own subjects as they strived to establish authority. Parts of the *cursus publicus* lasted for more than 400 years after the Roman Empire collapsed, but in the centuries that followed, travel and trade across Europe declined, and so did literacy, which became the almost exclusive preserve of clerks and the clergy. By the time the last vestiges of the Roman system disappeared in Western Europe in the 9th century, it didn't even matter—there wasn't much demand for a public postal system since few people could read or write.

A NEW ERA

But things began to change in the 11th century. With the founding of numerous universities, monasteries, and cathedrals across Europe, correspondence began to increase somewhat, prompting many institutions to set up their own private corps of foot-messengers. Few of these services carried private mail, though, because the level of literacy was still low.

It wasn't until after Johannes Gutenberg invented the movable-type printing press in about 1450 that literacy rates began rising to the point where letter carrying could become a profitable business. Local messenger services began popping up in towns and cities all over Europe. Some of these expanded into regional and nationwide services—the largest founded in 1290 by an Italian named Amadeo Tasso.

Tasso introduced courier service to one Italian city after another. After he died, his descendants continued to add new routes...*lots* of new routes. His family married into another prominent courier family, the Della Torres, and as the years passed, their combined business continued to expand. By the late 1500s, the family business, now known by the Germanicized name Thurn and Taxis, employed more than 20,000 couriers and delivered mail quickly, reliably, and *very* profitably, all over Europe.

By now a number of the royal houses of Europe, not comfortable with the idea of entrusting government communications to private courier services, began setting up their own national postal systems. In 1477 King Louis XI of France established the French Royal Service with 230 mounted couriers; England's Henry VIII followed in 1516.

COMMON CARRIER

Neither of these systems attempted to provide service to the entire country, and neither accepted private mail...at first. But by 1600 it

mail to more than 500 different addresses along their route each day.

had dawned on the French government that charging private citizens to carry their mail would help offset the cost of operating the system, so it began accepting private mail for the first time. In 1627 a schedule of regular fees and timetables was put in place; eight years later, the English set up a similar postal service for the general public, completely independent from the one used by the government.

As these and other government-run mail services expanded, they began to restrict the activities of privately owned enterprises like Thurn and Taxis, forbidding them to compete in areas served by the national post. Thurn and Taxis managed to hang on until 1867, when, after 577 years in business, it sold its last remaining postal lines to the Prussian government. The era of large-scale, privately owned postal systems was over: by 1875, virtually every postal service in the world was a government monopoly.

THE NEW WORLD

Initially, there were no post offices in the New World. When a ship pulled into port, it dropped bags of mail at a nearby tavern or coffeehouse, where the European colonists would go to pick it up. Most such places also had a bag for outgoing mail—for a penny you could drop a letter in the bag, which an outgoing ship would deliver to a similar tavern or coffeehouse on the other side of the Atlantic.

It took a while for regular mail service to get established in the colonies. This was due in large part to the fact that initially individual colonies didn't trust one another...and the need for communication between residents in neighboring colonies was minimal. It was much more common for colonists to send letters home to Europe.

Then, in 1737, a struggling 31-year-old printer named Benjamin Franklin became the postmaster of Philadelphia. Franklin distinguished himself in the position, and in 1753 was appointed one of two joint postmasters general for the colonies. In the two decades that followed, Franklin did much to improve and expand the colonial postal service. He reorganized virtually the entire system, personally inspecting post offices, conducting surveys, and laying out newer, shorter routes. During these years, postal riders traveling between New York and Philadelphia began carrying mail at night as well as during the day, cutting the delivery time in half.

A field bee flies 50,000 miles to collect enough nectar to produce a pound of honey.

By the time the British fired him for pro-Revolutionary sympathies in 1774, Franklin had established regular, scheduled mail service from Maine to Florida and into Canada, and had also significantly improved mail service to England. (Ironically, although Franklin is better known as the first U.S. Postmaster General, he served for little more than a year before leaving the job to become ambassador to France.)

PROGRESS

One of the hardest things about running the postal service in the new republic was keeping up with the rapid growth of the country. If anything, the U.S. Post Office grew faster than the country it served. As late as 1789, there were only 75 post offices in the entire country. Over the next 40 years, the number grew to more than 8,000, and by 1901 there were 76,945.

As the U.S. Post Office grew, the industrial revolution was vastly increasing the speed at which mail could be transported across the country. Mail that had once been transported on foot and by horseback along narrow dirt trails came to be delivered first by stagecoach, then by canal boat and steamboat, and then beginning in the 1830s, by railroad.

HURRY UP AND WAIT

Transporting mail quickly and broadening the range of services offered was one thing; figuring out how to *sort* mail more quickly proved to be a much greater challenge. At the turn of the 20th century, the U.S. mail was still sorted almost entirely by hand, just as it had been nearly 200 years before. Tentative steps toward automating the sorting process were made in the late 1920s, but the Great Depression and World War II put off real modernization for another 15–20 years.

The first automated mail-sorting equipment was finally put in place in the 1950s, and in 1963 the Postal Service introduced the ZIP Code (ZIP for "Zoning Improvement Plan") to further speed mail processing. But these improvements barely kept pace with the steadily increasing volumes of mail, especially business mail, which by 1963 made up 80% of the total. In 1966 the Chicago Post Office literally ground to a halt under tons of mail it could not process quickly enough.

Cost of mailing a letter more than 400 miles in 1816: 25¢.

A large part of the problem was that the U.S. Post Office had grown into a huge, inefficient, money-losing government agency subject to the whims and politics of Congress. In the late 1960s, a federal commission recommended reconstituting the U.S. Post Office as a nonprofit corporation wholly owned by the government but managed by an independent board of directors, and in August 1970, President Nixon signed the Postal Reorganization Act into law. On July 1, 1971, the old U.S. Post Office became the U.S. Postal Service.

BRAVE NEW WORLD

This reorganization effectively removed Congressional pressure to maintain low stamp prices—and along with it, taxpayer subsidies. The price of stamps began to climb, both to cover the full costs of delivering the mail and also to finance continuing modernization and automation. In 1971 a first-class stamp cost 8¢; the price rose to 13¢ in 1975, to 20¢ in 1981, 29¢ in 1991, and 34¢ in 2001.

Besides the increase in the price of stamps, another way the U.S. Postal Service attempted to cover its costs without taxpayer support was to change stamp subjects to make them more appealing to collectors.

"That's how Tweety Bird and Sylvester have come to displace George Washington and Abe Lincoln," says Michael Laurence, publisher of a stamp-collecting newspaper in Ohio. "It didn't take the Post Office long to realize that revenue from stamps retained and not used was money in the bank."

Perhaps the best example of this was the 1993 Elvis stamp—an estimated 38.5 million of the 500 million Elvis stamps sold were never used to send a letter, the highest unused percentage of any stamp ever issued by the U.S. Postal Service.

WE'RE NUMBER ONE

Today, the U.S. Postal Service delivers mail to more than 134 million addresses around the country, and provides service to a larger geographical area than any other postal service on Earth. It delivers more than 200 billion pieces of mail every year, which makes up more than 46% of the world's card and letter mail volume. Who's number two? Japan, which handles less than 7%.

Squares: Stamp collecting is the most popular hobby in the world.

WHO WANTS TO MARRY A MILLIONAIRE?

Trying to cash in on the success of Who Wants to Be a Millionaire?, *the we'll-try-anything Fox Network came up with this concept for a TV show, easily one of TV's darkest hours. (Two hours, actually.)*

THE CONCEPT

Quite possibly the most degrading and humiliating moment in network television history—for contestants and viewers—*Who Wants to Marry a Millionaire* was exactly what the show's title suggested: a chance to marry a millionaire live on TV. Fifty eligible females vied to win the hand of a mystery millionaire, who had supposedly been chosen from a pool of more than 100 millionaire bachelors—all of whom presumably would have been willing to marry a "nobody," only moments after meeting them for the first time, on national TV.

The mysterious future husband would remain hidden behind a screen, quizzing his potential mates-for-life as they strutted across the stage in swimsuits, wedding gowns, and other attire. Then, after nearly two hours of edge-of-your-seat suspense, he would step out, reveal his true identity, and marry his chosen bride on the spot. The show was kind of like a high-stakes "till-death-us-do-part" *Dating Game*…only with better prizes: The bride got a $35,000 engagement ring, a free Caribbean cruise honeymoon, and an Isuzu Trooper. Estimated value: $100,000. The husband didn't get quite as much, but it didn't matter—after all, he was a millionaire.

THE VERY SPECIAL DAY

Religious leaders condemned the show for undermining the institution of marriage, but Fox went ahead with it anyway…and on Valentine's Day 2000, more than 23 million people tuned in to watch real estate developer Rick Rockwell, 42, step out from behind the screen to choose Darva Conger, 34, a Gulf War veteran and emergency room nurse, as his bride.

THE MORNING AFTER

The Rockwell-Conger union wasn't exactly love at first sight: many viewers found their first kiss almost too creepy to bear, and things got worse after that. They slept in separate rooms during their "honeymoon" cruise, and within a week of returning to port, Conger was in Las Vegas seeking a quickie annulment.

By then, Rockwell's Prince Charming image was taking quite a beating. A website called *The Smoking Gun* revealed that in 1991 a judge had issued a restraining order against Rockwell after his ex-fiancée accused him of hitting and threatening to kill her. (Rockwell denied hitting her.)

That was just the beginning—it turned out that Rockwell wasn't a millionaire real estate developer after all; he was a stand-up comedian and occasional motivational speaker with a lot less than the $2 million in assets he was supposed to have to qualify for the show. The *Vancouver Province* newspaper quoted real estate agents who described him as a "flake" and a "loser whose only investment property is a low-end condo that leaks."

As for Conger, it turns out that she wasn't what she claimed to be, either. She wasn't a Gulf War veteran—she spent the entire war stationed at Scott Air Force Base in Illinois. "You can't call yourself a Gulf War veteran if you've never been to the Gulf," retired army colonel Daniel Smith explained to reporters.

CASHING IN... AND CASHING OUT

A judge annulled the marriage on April 5, 2000; by that time, Conger and Rockwell both were well on their way to making the most—financially, at least—of their brush with fame. Conger, who donated her $35,000 engagement ring to charity, signed a deal to pose in *Playboy* for an estimated $500,000. She later launched her own website, *www.darvashouse.com*. As for Rick Rockwell, his once-sleepy comedy show suddenly sold out all over the country.

About the only people involved who didn't cash in were the folks at Fox—as soon as the network learned of Rockwell's restraining order, it cancelled its scheduled rebroadcast of the show and later announced it was abandoning its entire lineup of upcoming "exploitative reality specials," including *Plastic Surgery Nightmares*, *Busted on the Job 5*, and *The World's Biggest Bitches*.

"They're gone," a spokesperson told reporters. "They're over."

THEY WENT THATAWAY

*A few more stories about the final days
of the famous, from our files.*

BENEDICT ARNOLD
Claim to Fame: Revolutionary War general and turncoat
whose name became synonymous with treason

How He Died: In exile, suffering from asthma, dropsy, and gout.

Postmortem: Described as "the very genius of war" by his men,
General Arnold helped turn the tide of the war in favor of the
Americans at the second battle of Saratoga in 1777.

But Arnold became bitter at having been passed up for a promotion and for other perceived slights, and in 1779 switched his
allegiance to the British. He conspired to surrender West Point to
them in exchange for £20,000, but failed when his British accom-
plice, Major John André, was captured.

André was hanged as a spy, but Arnold managed to escape, and
he later led a raid against American soldiers in his own home state
of Connecticut before fleeing to England. There, "inactive, ostra-
cized, and ailing," he lived with his wife and children until his
death in June 1801 at the age of 60.

According to one account of Arnold's last days, shortly before
he died he asked to be dressed in his Revolutionary uniform. "Let
me die in my old uniform," he wheezed through his asthma, "God
forgive me for ever putting on any other."

TYRONE POWER

Claim to Fame: Swashbuckling Hollywood actor best known for
his action-adventure films

How He Died: From a heart attack caused by a sword fight.

Postmortem: In 1958 he was filming *Solomon and Sheba* on
location in Madrid, Spain. One scene called for Power (playing
Solomon) and actor George Sanders (playing Solomon's brother)
to fight a duel on a staircase using 15-pound swords. Because

---

In 1986, 183 Adams were christened in the state of Oregon...but not a single Eve.

Sanders was a pathetic swordfighter, Power's scenes had to be filmed twice—close-ups with Sanders, and wide shots with a double who knew how to use a sword. It doubled his workload. After eight takes of one shot, Power was so exhausted that he walked off the set, refusing to film a ninth take. "I've had it," he told the director.

He began trembling uncontrollably and had to be helped back to his trailer. His makeup man made him some tea, but Power was unable to lift his arms to drink it. When no one could find the studio's doctor, Power was bundled into a car and driven to a nearby U.S. airbase for treatment. But he never made it—he had a heart attack in the car and was dead before he ever reached the hospital. Note: *Solomon and Sheba*, refilmed with Yul Brynner playing Solomon, was released in 1959.

LUDWIG VAN BEETHOVEN

Claim to Fame: German composer

How He Died: Possibly by lead poisoning

Postmortem: Beethoven's last years were filled with excruciating pain: He suffered from abdominal pains, bad digestion, headaches, diarrhea, rheumatism, fever, irritability, and depression. He never knew the cause of his myriad maladies, despite having consulted with numerous doctors. On March 26, 1827, he died as he had lived for so many years: in agony. He was 57.

Snipping a lock of hair from the recently deceased was a popular custom in the 19th century. Fortunately for us, Beethoven had a lot of fans...and a lot of hair. Admirers snipped him nearly bald, and several confirmed samples of his hair survive to this day. A few strands were recently subjected to an X-ray fluorescence spectroscopy, which revealed lead concentrations of more than 100 times the level considered normal. It was enough lead to account for nearly all of Beethoven's symptoms, including his deafness. During his lifetime no one knew that lead was toxic—it was used in paint and in pottery, and was even added to wine to remove any bitterness. Beethoven could have poisoned himself with lead in any number of ways.

"If he had a favorite pewter mug that he drank from all his life, that alone could clearly be the culprit," says Russell Martin, author of *Beethoven's Hair*.

THE BIRTH
OF SCOTCHGARD

*We mentioned the accidental discovery of Scotchgard in an
earlier* Bathroom Reader, *but we've wanted to include
a longer version for years. Here's the story.*

SLICK DISCOVERY

After graduating from college in 1952, Patsy Sherman took a part-time job as a chemist with 3M. One day, while working on a new kind of synthetic rubber, an accident occurred: a bottle of a synthetic latex compound fell on the floor, splattering her assistant's tennis shoes with a milky, saplike substance.

They tried to wipe it off with soap, water, alcohol, and other solvents, but nothing worked—everything they tried just rolled off. Then she noticed that although the compound didn't alter the look or feel of the canvas shoe, as the shoe got dirtier, the spots where the chemical had landed remained white and clean.

Sherman found that fabric dipped in the compound prevented anything from penetrating it. The compound seemed to surround each fiber with a chemical shield that was impervious to water, oil, and dirt. It took three years to refine it, but when she was done she had invented a revolutionary new product that made fabrics stain-proof. 3M named it Scotchgard.

Eventually, dozens of Scotchgard products were developed for use on raincoats, carpets, upholstery, clothing, paper packaging, and even motion-picture film. It was one of 3M's most profitable products ever and funded their growth into a global industry.

Update: Scientists recently discovered that Scotchgard molecules pervade the world environment and are present in the bodies of most Americans. It's not necessarily a dangerous contamination, but because the molecules are inert, they will never deteriorate. 3M has been unable to find a more environmentally friendly formula, so in the year 2000, they announced they were phasing out the product. That's bad news for the La-Z-Boy company: 90% of their fabrics were once treated with Scotchgard.

The World's Largest Office Chair is in Anniston, Alabama. It's 33 feet tall.

FAMOUS FOR 15 MINUTES

Here's more proof that Andy Warhol was right when he said that "in the future, everyone will be famous for 15 minutes."

THE STAR: Danny Almonte, 12-year-old pitcher for the Rolando Paulino All-Stars Little League team in the Bronx

THE HEADLINE: *Little League Champ Pitches Perfect Game; Too Bad He's Not as Little as His Parents Say He Is*

WHAT HAPPENED: Alamonte became an instant celebrity after he pitched a no-hitter in the opening game of the Little League World Series, the first since 1957. His major league heroes Randy Johnson and Ken Griffey, Jr. called to congratulate him, and New York mayor Rudolph Giuliani gave the entire team the key to the city.

But there was trouble brewing: For months, Alamonte had been dogged by rumors that he was actually 14, not 12, which would have made him ineligible to play in Little League. Two rival teams even hired private investigators to look into the rumors, but it wasn't until *Sports Illustrated* obtained a birth certificate that showed Danny was born on April 7, 1987, not April 7, 1989 as his parents claimed, that things started to unravel. Dominican government officials confirmed the authenticity of the certificate, just as investigators in the U.S. discovered that 14-year-old Danny not only wasn't enrolled in school as his father claimed—a violation of the law—but that he and his father were in the country illegally, on expired tourist visas.

THE AFTERMATH: Danny's father was banned for life from any association with Little League; so was team founder Rolando Paulino. The All-Stars were stripped of their third-place title in the Little League World Series, and all of their records—including Alamonte's no-hitter—were expunged from the Little League record book. About the only thing the team didn't lose was its key to the city of New York—Mayor Giuliani said he wouldn't ask for it back, explaining that "it would only add to the hurt and the pain that the innocent children of this team are experiencing."

Your kidneys, weighing about 5 oz. each, process about 425 gallons of blood a day.

THE STAR: Ilanit Levy, the Israeli contestant in the 2001 Miss Universe pageant

THE HEADLINE: *Beauty Queen Takes Flak for Wearing Flak Jacket*

WHAT HAPPENED: Citing a desire to "reflect the current tension in the Middle East," Miss Israel made news all over the world by incorporating body armor into the formal wear she wore during the pageant: She modeled a diamond-encrusted blue flak jacket over a camouflage evening gown. "It's very Israeli," she explained to reporters. "We have to show ourselves the way we really are."

THE AFTERMATH: The armored look won Levy plenty of headlines , but it didn't win her the Miss Universe crown. She made it all the way to the finals before being eliminated in the swimsuit contest and losing to Miss Puerto Rico.

THE STAR: Samuel Feldman, a 37-year-old Pennsylvania advertising executive

THE HEADLINE: *Adman Avoids Squeezing the Charmin—but Squeezes Just About Everything Else*

WHAT HAPPENED: In 1997 local media outlets in suburban Bucks County, Pennsylvania, began reporting a rash of "assaults" on baked goods in supermarkets and bakeries. Somebody was squeezing, crumbling, and poking thousands of dollars' worth of baked merchandise, damaging it to the point that it was no longer salable. The reign of bakery terror went on for two years before Samuel Feldman was identified as the culprit, thanks to security cameras that caught him in the act on seven different occasions. Dubbed the "Cookie Crumbler" by local reporters, Feldman went on trial in November 2000, charged with destroying $800 worth of cookies and more than $7,000 worth of bread, including 175 bags of bagels, 227 bags of dinner rolls, and 3,087 loaves of bread.

Feldman's wife, Sharon, came to his defense at the trial. "Freshness is important," she told the jury, hoping to convince them that her husband only wanted what was best for his family and was a little too picky in how he went about it. She almost succeeded: Jurors actually tried to acquit Feldman on the bread charge, but the judge overruled them, finding him guilty and telling Feldman that his conduct was "not just odd, it was criminal."

Puff Daddy: Studies show that a nonsmoking bartender inhales

THE AFTERMATH: Feldman was sentenced to 180 days of probation, was ordered to pay $1,000 in restitution, and was advised to seek psychological counseling.

THE STARS: Princess Meriam Al Khalifa of Bahrain and Lance Corporal Jason Johnson of the U.S. Marines

THE HEADLINE: *Love-Struck Couple Ignites Royal Headache for U.S. State Department, Bahrain Royal Family*

WHAT HAPPENED: In January 1999, Johnson met his future wife by chance in a shopping mall while stationed in Bahrain. The two soon fell in love, but Princess Meriam's family forbade her to date Johnson and even put her under police surveillance when they suspected she was seeing him anyway. She was, and when her family found out, they ordered her to end the relationship.

Rather than obey, the couple eloped—on November 2, 1999, Johnson snuck Princess Meriam out of Bahrain using a fake military ID and brought her to the United States, where they were later married in a Las Vegas wedding chapel.

There were just two problems: the princess had entered the country using the same fake ID she had used to sneak out of Bahrain; and her father is the second cousin of the ruling Emir of Bahrain. That made her case an international incident. As her relatives in Bahrain used diplomatic channels to demand her return, American politicians began lining up on Princess Meriam's side, calling on the U.S. Immigration and Naturalization service to allow her to remain in the United States. Their story made headlines all over the world, and a Hollywood studio began production of a TV movie based on it even before knowing how it would end.

THE AFTERMATH: If the INS moved to deport Princess Meriam, she was prepared to request asylum on the grounds that if she returned home she faced persecution for marrying a non-Muslim. Neither Bahrain nor the United States wanted a public trial, and in the end her family dropped their demand that she be returned to Bahrain. The INS issued her a green card, which allows her to remain in the U.S. permanently. As for Lance Corporal Johnson, he was reduced in rank to private for helping his fiancée leave Bahrain without permission, and given an early honorable discharge. The couple now lives in Las Vegas.

---

the equivalent of 36 cigarettes during an 8-hour shift.

FAMILY FEUD

You can't always get along with everyone in your family…
but these guys just out and out declared war on each other.

HAFT VS. HAFT VS. HAFT

The Contestants: Herbert Haft, who bought his first drugstore in 1955; his wife, Gloria; their daughter Linda; and their sons Robert and Ronald.

The Feud: Over the years Herbert Haft built his single drugstore into a huge regional chain called Dart Drugs. He also built up the Trak Auto chain of auto parts stores and Consolidated Properties Inc., the family's real estate division, all of which were part of the Dart Group conglomerate.

In the 1970s, he invited his sons into the business. Robert signed on in 1977 and founded Crown Books. He became famous as the chain's spokesman, telling TV viewers, "If paid full price, you didn't buy it at Crown Books." By 1993 the Dart Group was worth more than $500 million…but it wouldn't be for long.

In June 1993, *The Wall Street Journal* published an article that speculated that Robert Haft was the child most likely to take over as head of the family business when Herbert retired. The article infuriated Herbert—he saw it as his "business obituary"—and he responded by firing Robert, Linda, and even Gloria from the company. He and Ronald tried to run the Dart Group together but were soon at each others' throats. In September 1994, four outside directors seized control of the Dart Group in an attempt to save it from the feuding Hafts.

They were too late—by the time the smoke cleared, Dart Group was no more. Consolidated Properties Inc. filed for bankruptcy in 1995, and Crown Books went under in 1998. (Herbert and Gloria's marriage was another casualty—they divorced in 1994 after 45 years of marriage.)

And the Winner Is: Nobody. As of February 2000, Herbert and Robert were still duking it out, this time with dot.com drugstores. Robert founded Vitamins.com; Herbert runs HealthQuick.com. Says Herbert, "I wish Robert well."

Of the 80,000 known species of plants, only 50 are cultivated regularly.

BEHIND THE HITS

Ever wonder what inspired some of your favorite songs?
Here are a few more inside stories about popular tunes.

The Artist: Beck
The Song: "Loser"
The Story: One day, Beck was fooling around at producer Karl Stephenson's house. Beck started playing slide guitar, and Stephenson began recording. As Stephenson added a Public Enemy–style beat and a sample from Dr. John's "I Walk on Gilded Splinters," Beck attempted to freestyle rap—something he had never done before. Frustrated at his inability to rap, Beck began criticizing his own performance: "*Soy un perdedor*" ("I'm a loser" in Spanish). Beck wanted to scrap it, but Stephenson thought it was catchy. Stephenson was right—"Loser" made Beck a star.

The Artist: David Bowie
The Song: "Fame"
The Story: In 1975, as Bowie and his band were playing around in the studio with a riff that guitarist Carlos Alomar had come up with, former Beatle John Lennon dropped in. When they played the riff for Lennon, he immediately picked up a guitar, walked to the corner of the room and started playing along and muttering to himself, "Aim…aim!" When he said, "Fame!" the song started to come together. Bowie ran off to write some lyrics while the band worked out the music. Bowie gave writing credit to Lennon, saying: "It wouldn't have happened if John hadn't been there."

The Artist: The Byrds
The Song: "The Ballad of Easy Rider"
The Story: In an effort to convince Bob Dylan to write the theme song for *Easy Rider*, Peter Fonda gave him a private screening of the movie. Dylan didn't like the movie and wouldn't write the song. But he scribbled the words "The river flows, it flows to the sea, wherever the river flows, that's where I want to be" on a napkin and told Fonda: "Give this to McGuinn," referring to Roger McGuinn of the Byrds. Fonda gave McGuinn the napkin, and McGuinn immediately finished the song. But when Dylan learned

---

Brrrr: The Antarctic flea spends 9 months of the year frozen (but alive) under the ice.

that he had gotten songwriting credit, he called McGuinn and chewed him out, saying he didn't want to be associated with it in any way. Dylan co-wrote the song, but McGuinn got all the credit.

The Artist: Aerosmith
The Song: "Walk This Way"
The Story: Guitarist Joe Perry and bassist Tom Hamilton were exhausted from rehearsing the new riff they had written, so they took a break to see a movie—*Young Frankenstein*. Says Hamilton, "There's that part in the movie where Igor says 'Walk this way,' and the other guy walks the same way with the hump and everything. We thought it was the funniest thing we'd ever seen." After the movie, they told singer Steven Tyler that the name of the song had to be "Walk This Way." Tyler rushed out and scribbled the lyrics to the song on the walls of the studio's stairway, and the band recorded the song right then.

The Artist: The Crystals
The Song: "He's a Rebel"
The Story: Phil Spector wanted to record "He's a Rebel," but the publisher told him it was taken—another producer, Snuff Garrett was preparing to record it with singer Vikki Carr. Spector ran out in a panic and dragged vocalist Darlene Love and a bunch of musicians into the studio to cut the song. That evening, Garrett was preparing to record the song when his studio guitarist walked in. He glanced at the music and exclaimed, "Hey, man, I just played this!" Garrett asked "Where?" "In Studio C," the guitarist replied. By the time Garrett got to the studio to see what was going on, Spector had already put the finishing touches on his version—the version that became the hit.

The Artist: The Rolling Stones
The Song: "Jumpin' Jack Flash"
The Story: One rainy winter morning, Mick Jagger and Keith Richards were in Richards's living room when Jagger suddenly jumped up, frightened by a stomping noise. Richards explained, "Oh, that's just Jack, the gardener. That's jumpin' Jack." The two laughed and Richards began fooling around on the guitar, singing, "Jumpin' Jack." Inspired by the lightning, Jagger added "Flash!"

About 45% of all prescription drugs contain ingredients originating in the rainforest.

MYTH-SPOKEN

Some of the best-known quotes in history weren't said by the people they're attributed to...and some weren't even said at all!

Line: "If you can't stand the heat, get out of the kitchen."
Supposedly Said By: Harry Truman
Actually: Although Truman decided to take credit for this saying in his autobiography, he didn't coin the phrase. He was actually quoting his good friend and chief military aide, Major General Harry Vaughan.

Line: "Say it ain't so, Joe."
Supposedly Said By: A little boy to "Shoeless" Joe Jackson
Actually: Baseball legend has it that when White Sox left fielder "Shoeless" Joe appeared to testify before the Grand Jury about his part in fixing the 1919 World Series, a heartbroken little boy gazed up at his hero and pleaded: "Say it ain't so, Joe." It never happened. The line was made up by a journalist.

Line: "What's good for General Motors is good for the country."
Supposedly Said By: Charles Wilson, former GM president and U.S. secretary of defense
Actually: Wilson was misunderstood and misquoted. He really said: "For years I thought what was good for our country was good for General Motors—and vice versa." Wilson was trying to say that GM wanted to look out for the American people and not just make a profit, but over time it has been corrupted to mean the reverse.

Line: "I disapprove of what you say, but I will defend to the death your right to say it."
Supposedly Said By: Voltaire, French philosopher and author
Actually: This saying first appeared over 100 years after Voltaire died. Using the pen name S. G. Tallentyre in her 1906 book *The Friends of Voltaire*, writer E. Beatrice Hall created this aphorism to paraphrase a section in one of Voltaire's essays.

With enough training, an elephant can throw a baseball faster than a human can.

NUDE LAWSUITS

As The Peoples Court's Doug Llewellyn might say,
"If you're naked and angry, don't take matters into
your own hands. Take 'em to court."

THE PLAINTIFF: Two Philadelphia Eagles cheerleaders, identified in court papers as Jane Doe #1 and Jane Doe #2
THE DEFENDANTS: Twenty-three NFL teams who played games in Philadelphia between 1986 and 2000
THE LAWSUIT: The cheerleaders claim that for 15 years, visiting teams spied on Eagles cheerleaders in their dressing room by peeking through cracks in walls and doorways and even drilling holes in walls.

"These players viewed the Eagles cheerleaders in various stages of undress, including in complete nudity, when preparing for showering," the lawsuit alleges. "It was common knowledge among virtually the entire National Football League, while at the same time a carefully guarded secret, known only to the players and team employees." The women seek $150,000 from each team for "invasion of privacy, trespass, and intentional infliction of emotional distress."
THE VERDICT: Pending.

THE PLAINTIFF: Nicole Ferry, formerly an art major at the University of Southern Florida
THE DEFENDANT: The University of Southern Florida
THE LAWSUIT: In September 1999, Ferry attended a lecture on controversial art; one of the examples shown to the class was a suggestive photograph of a nude male posterior being embraced by female hands. Attending the lecture was optional—students were warned in advance that controversial art is controversial, and were told that they were free to skip class if they wanted to. Ferry attended the lecture anyway, was offended, and later filed a lawsuit against the school, alleging "sexual harassment."
THE VERDICT: USF settled the case for $25,000, but school officials insist the settlement is not an admission of wrongdoing. "For us as an institution, not to present that type of work would be something far more worthy of a lawsuit," said a spokesperson.

Central Africa has the largest variety of animals dangerous to man. Ireland has the smallest.

DUMB CROOKS

More proof that crime doesn't pay.

GONE TO POT

INDIANA—"An Indiana farmer was the victim of a cruel prank when he received a phone call from the 'authorities,' busting him for growing marijuana in his backyard. During the conversation, the man was told that if he brought the plant, roots and all to the station, charges would not be pressed. Believing the call to be real, he cut down the eight-foot plant and carried it into the lobby of the sheriff's office. He was then placed into custody for suspected felony cultivation by surprised officers."

—*Bizarre News*

BLESSINGS FROM ABOVE

"A Tampa, Florida, burglar who decided to rob a 24-hour convenience store didn't know the store was open 24 hours. He cut a hole in the roof, then fell through and onto the coffee pot just as a police officer was buying some coffee."

—"The Edge," *The Oregonian*

LET'S MAKE A DEAL

"Kidnappers who abducted Gildo dos Santos near his factory in a suburb of São Paulo, Brazil, demanded $690,000 in ransom, but Santos escaped. The next day, Santos got a phone call asking for $11,500 to defray the cost of the abduction. After negotiating a discount of 50%, Santos called police, who were waiting when Luiz Carlos Valerio showed up to collect payment."

—*Dumb Crooks*

"HE WAS REALLY HANDSOME..."

"A Kwik-Fill gas station attendant in Syracuse, New York, stole $300 from the till, then tried to cover it up by calling police and reporting that the station had been robbed. His plan was foiled, however, when police asked him to describe the robber and he gave them a perfect description of himself."

—*Syracuse Post-Standard*

Most dangerous animal in Ireland: the bumblebee.

BAD TIMING

"Sherman Lee Parks of Arkansas escaped from jail on the day he was scheduled to be released. He was re-arrested and is now back in jail."

—FHM *Magazine*

EGO TRIP

"Andrew T. Burhop of Des Moines, Iowa, was arrested after robbing a bank in Muscatine. Police didn't have much trouble finding the culprit, since Burhop's getaway car had a vanity license plate, which read 'Burhop.'"

—*Des Moines Register*

PAINT IT BLACK

"Constable Duncan Dixon, from Naskup, British Columbia, was called to a mischief in progress. A young male was witnessed spray-painting the roof of a gazebo.

"'When I arrived, the witnesses pointed him out,' says Dixon, but the alleged perpetrator denied it.

"'I looked at his hands, which were covered in gold spray paint. I noted he had the cap to a spray paint can in his pocket.'

"'He continued to insist that he wasn't responsible. I also noticed his friends' shoes were painted with, of course, gold paint. This wasn't the biggest nail in the coffin of the young man: he had painted his name on the gazebo roof—first and last names.'"

—*The Valley Voice*

ACCIDENTAL IDIOT

"James Brian Kuenn, 40, on trial in Largo, Florida, for murder, said the victim's death was accidental and that he was so embarrassed at the accident that he 'made it look like murder to throw police off.' Must have worked. He was convicted."

—**Universal Press Syndicate**

NO FORE-THOUGHT

"Robbery suspect Denis Jesper, 20, was arrested at a Miami country club, where he had been hiding from police in a ficus tree next to the golf course. He revealed himself by calling out to a golfer who hit into the rough, 'Hey, hey, your ball is over there.'"

—*Wacky News*

Half of the members of the Rodeo Cowboys Assoc. have never worked on a ranch.

WEIRD CANADA

*Canada: land of beautiful mountains, clear lakes, bustling cities...
and some really weird news reports. Here are some of the
oddest entries from BRI member, Therese Morin.*

HOW MUCH FOR NOT ROBBING SOMEONE?

Over the 2000 holiday season, officials in Edmonton, Alberta, tried to encourage motorists to obey the rules of the road by having police officers in unmarked cars find and reward the safest drivers in town. Traffic officers tailed drivers for as long as half an hour to determine if they were truly law-abiding, then pulled the puzzled motorists over and offered them a free steak dinner for two at "Tom Goodchild's Moose Factory."

TOKEN OF OUR APPRECIATION

Over a period of 13 years, Edmonton transit worker Salim Kara patiently built a fortune of $2.3 million (Canadian) by stealing coins from fare machines using a rod with a magnetized tip. No one suspected the 44-year-old delinquent until he purchased an $800,000 house on a yearly salary of $38,000. He was sentenced to four years in prison in 1996.

OUTHOUSE NEWS

•In Tiverton, a tiny island community in Nova Scotia, "Outhouse" is the most common last name.

• In Quesnel, B.C., it's still a legal requirement to have an outdoor out house, at least 20 feet (6 metres) from your house, but not more than 100 feet (30 metres). It has to be "fly tight", too.

BETTER BY THE BAGFUL

Back in the 1980s the citizens of Desmond, Ontario needed to raise money to renovate their school. A raffle? A rummage sale? No, "Manurefest." They filled 600 bags with manure and sold them for $3 each. Some were sheep manure (sold as "Ewedunnit"), some were cow manure, and some were a guinea fowl-hen blend. "Some of it," says spokesman Henk Reininck, "was vintage—eight years old. And it don't smell at all." Manurefest has become an annual event. Next to the manure, they now sell baked goods.

In 1971 it rained in Chile's Atacama Desert...for the first time since the 16th century.

FLYING CAKES

Every January, residents of the small community of Manitou Springs, Saskatchewan get together to see who can fling their Christmas fruitcake the farthest. In the Great Fruitcake Toss, there are no rules; contestants can use catapults, slingshots, and even specially designed guns, but most prefer the "Olympic-style" discus throwing method.

WATCH WHERE YOU'RE GOING

It should be obvious to everyone, but in Ontario it's illegal for motorized vehicles to have a television on the dashboard or the front seat.

RUB-A-DUB-DUB

The Yukon isn't just the capital of the Klondike Gold Rush, it's also the capital of Bathtub Racing. They've been doing it since 1992. Every August, "tubbers" race 5 by 3-ft regulation size bathtubs 480 miles from Whitehorse down the Yukon River to Dawson City. There's another bathtub race in Nanaimo, B.C. The Loyal Nanaimo Bathtub Society has been holding a 36-mile race every July since 1967.

HOLE-Y COW!

Canada has more doughnut shops per capita than any other country on earth—one for every 9,000 of its 30 million residents.

LOONEY LAWS

• It is legal for women to go topless in public in Ontario.

• In Oak Bay, British Columbia garbage crews don't have to pick up your thrash if it "oozes."

• It's against the law to have a toilet room smaller than 1 square meter (10 square feet) in Halifax, Nova Scotia.

STICKS AND STONES

In 1991, a GM assembly line foreman in Ontario, reprimanded a worker for having bad body odor. The worker complained to the Workers Compensation Tribunal about loss of appetite, lack of sleep, and sexual dysfunctions brought on by the foreman's insensitive remarks. The Tribunal awarded him $3,000 for "job stress."

What do turtles and honeybees have in common? They're both deaf.

CLASSIC HOAXES

One last classic hoax for you to enjoy.

THE SIR FRANCIS DRAKE ASSOCIATION
Background: In 1913 thousands of people with the last name Drake received a letter from the "Sir Francis Drake Association," an organization founded for the purpose of settling the estate of the legendary British buccaneer who had died 300 years earlier. The letter claimed that the estate was still tied up in probate court, and that since Drake's death in 1596 the value had grown to an estimated $22 billion. Any Drake descendant who wanted a share of the estate was welcome—all they had to do was contribute toward the $2,500-a-week "legal expenses" needed to pursue the case. When the estate was settled, each contributor would be entitled to a proportional share. There was no time to waste—the fight was underway and any Drake descendant who hesitated risked being cut out entirely.

Exposed: The Sir Francis Drake Association was the work of Iowa farmer-turned-conman Oscar Merrill Hartzell. But he didn't invent the hoax—the first of hundreds of similar swindles took place within months of Drake's death in 1596. Hartzell got the idea for his version after his mother was conned out of several thousand dollars in another Drake estate scam. When he tracked down the crooks who had swindled her and realized how much money they were making, Hartzell decided that rather than call the police, he would keep quiet…and launch his own scam. Using the money he'd recovered for his mother, Hartzell promptly sent out letters to more than 20,000 Drakes. Thousands took the bait. Hartzell eventually expanded the scam to target people who weren't even named Drake.

Final Note: By the time the feds caught up with him 20 years later, Hartzell had swindled an estimated 70,000 people out of more than $2 million. Rather than admit they'd been duped, many of the victims donated an additional $350,000 toward his legal defense. Hartzell was convicted of mail fraud and sentenced to 10 years in federal prison; a few years later he was transferred to a mental institution, where he died in 1943.

IT'S A BUST

In 1971, Wallace Reyburn wrote a book called Bust-Up: The Uplifting Tale of Otto Titzling and the Development of the Bra. *Is there any truth in Reyburn's story? None whatsoever, cross our hearts. But it is so entertaining that we can't restrain ourselves from retelling it (for the real story of the bra, turn to page 167.)*

THE MYTH OF TITZLING

Otto Titzling was the son of a bridge builder, born in Hamburg, Germany, in 1884. The family emigrated to America when Otto was three. While his brothers followed their father into the bridge-building business, Otto was obsessed with women's underwear and preferred to use his knowledge of load capacity to design new lingerie products.

The story goes that Titzling got his start in 1912 after befriending a heavily-endowed opera singer named Swanhilda Olafsen. "I get tired after hauling these things around all day," she complained, so Otto came to her rescue with a new invention—the "chest halter." When other similarly endowed women began requesting chest halters for themselves, Otto set up shop with a partner, a salesman named Hans Delving.

Obviously a marketing genius, Delving came up with the memorable slogan for padded bras: "What God has forgotten, we stuff with cotton." And it was Delving who suggested they market a line of panties with the slogan, "Not the Best Thing in the World But the Next Thing to It."

GOOD SPORTS

Together the two men came up with many innovations in breast support. After Swedish Olympic runner Lois Lung kicked herself in the breast while going over a hurdle, injuring herself and costing her the gold medal, Otto invented an inflatable bra designed for female athletes. (When the company received a letter of complaint from a woman who said her bra had been punctured by her boyfriend while pinning on a corsage, Delving suggested sending her a letter of condolence along with a copy of *Gone With the Wind*.)

The buck stops here: the average American gives less than 1% of their total income to charity.

Next they unveiled a model with a change purse built into the cleavage. Delving suggested a front-fastening model that was dubbed the "Sesame" because it opened so easily. This model fell flat because it looked strange hanging on the laundry line, which women considered to be bad advertising for their assets. Titzling also came up with a special chest halter specifically designed for trapeze artists who spent a lot of time hanging upside down.

BUSTED DREAMS

According to Reyburn, things were going along swell until Titzling came up against an unscrupulous dress designer named Philippe de Brassière. The Depression was in full swing, so nobody was buying de Brassière's dresses—he decided he needed an item that ladies would buy even if they were broke. He stole Titzling's idea, added some lace, and began presenting the product as his own. Titzling sued, but it was a hard-fought case because he had never patented his invention. After a lengthy and expensive trial, Titzling won only token damages. Broke and dispirited, he was unable to keep the business afloat and died a few years later. Hans Delving died in combat in World War II, and Philippe de Brassière went down in history, Reyburn declares, lending his name to the product he stole.

*   *   *

ROYAL TRENDSETTER

When Princess Victoria, eldest daughter of Queen Victoria, wed Prince Frederick William of Prussia, she picked out music of her two favorite composers. One was the "Bridal Chorus" from Richard Wagner's opera "Lohengrin," and the other was the "Wedding March" from Mendelssohn's "A Midsummer Night's Dream."

Copy cat brides in England chose the same music, thus starting a tradition that has spread across the globe. Wagner's music is commonly known as, "Here comes the bride, all dressed in white..." and the bride and groom exit the church to the familiar strains of Mendelssohn: "DUM! DUM! da DUM dum dum dum DA da da DUM dum DUM!"

The upstroke of a bird's wing moves it forward, the downstroke only keeps it airborn.

SEEING DOUBLE

The bare bear asked the dear deer, "What do you call two words that sound alike but are spelled differently?" Of course, a deer can't speak bear, but if it could it would have said, "A homophone." The phrases below describe some of our favorite homophones. Can you figure out what they're trying to say?

1. Bad-smelling chicken

2. Candy-coated hotel room

3. Moby Dick's cry

4. Revenue on little nails

5. Bullwinkle's chocolate delight

6. Rabbit fur

7. Funny bone

8. No Shakespeare allowed

9. A bumpy way to go

10. Counting your smells, sights, tastes, sounds, and feelings

11. The scared guy hid low

12. They talked about gross stuff

13. Almost speechless Mr. Ed.

14. Promised lyric poem

15. Letterhead and envelopes going nowhere

16. Spirit of a fish

17. Worried wigwams

Answers

1. Foul fowl; 2. Sweet suite; 3. Whale wail; 4. Tacks tax; 5. Moose mousse; 6. Hare hair; 7. Humorous humerus; 8. Barred bard; 9. Coarse course; 10. Senses census; 11. Coward cowered; 12. Discussed disgust; 13. Hoarse horse; 14. Owed ode; 15. Stationary stationery; 16. Sole soul; 17. Tense tents

---

James Madison was the first U.S. president to wear long pants.

CELEBRITY GOSSIP

*Here's the BRI's cheesy tabloid section—a
bunch of gossip about famous people.*

MARTHA STEWART

Twenty-three-year-old landscraper Matthew Munnich filed a lawsuit against Martha Stewart, claiming that the design magnate had attacked him with her car. Reportedly, as Munnich and his crew worked on property next door to Stewart's New York estate, she pulled up in a dark Suburban and asked if they had put up a fence. When Munnich replied, "No," Stewart grew angry and began yelling things like "F***ing liar!" and "You and your f***ing illegal aliens are no good!" Looking directly at Munnich, Stewart then backed her Suburban into him, briefly pinning him against an electronic security box before tearing off. Stewart denies everything.

BURT REYNOLDS

Burt Reynolds spends more on his toupees than most people make in a year. In late 1996, he filed for bankruptcy. Among his $4.5 million in liabilities was a $12,200 bill from Edward Katz Hair Design—his custom hairpiece designer.

JANE FONDA

In 1970 the actress, activist, and fitness guru was arrested for kicking a police officer when he found her with a large amount of pills. All charges were dropped when it was discovered that the pills Fonda was carrying were vitamins.

WILLIAM SHATNER

William Shatner once starred in a movie filmed entirely in the failed "universal language," Esperanto.

JERRY SEINFELD

When Seinfeld went onstage for his first-ever stand-up performance, he was paralyzed by stage fright and forgot his entire routine. He ran off the stage in a panic, mumbling a few lines to the crowd: "The beach. Driving. Shopping. Parents."

Your liver—the largest organ in your body—processes about a quart of blood a minute.

WILLIAM'S WISDOM

Observations from William O. Douglas, one of America's greatest Supreme Court justices (1939–1975), and a defender of free speech.

"The right to be let alone is indeed the beginning of all freedom."

"It was against a background poignant with memories of evil procedures that our Constitution was drawn."

"As nightfall does not come at once, neither does oppression. In both instances, there is a twilight when everything remains seemingly unchanged. And it is in such twilight that we all must be most aware of change in the air—however slight—lest we become unwitting victims of the darkness."

"An arrest is not justified by what the subsequent search discloses."

"The framers of the Constitution knew human nature as well as we do. They had lived in dangerous days; they knew the suffocating influence of orthodoxy and standardized thought. They weighed the compulsions for restrained speech and thought against the abuses of liberty. They chose liberty."

"Those who won our independence believed…liberty to be the secret of happiness and courage to be the secret of liberty."

"Restriction of free thought and free speech is the most dangerous of all subversions. It is the one un-American act that could most easily defeat us."

"Whatever the reason, words mean what they say."

"What a man thinks is of no concern to government."

"A requirement that literature or art conform to some norm prescribed by an official smacks of an ideology foreign to our system."

"Words uttered under coercion are proof of loyalty to nothing but self-interest."

"Common sense often makes good law."

"When a man knows how to live dangerously, he is not afraid to die. When he is not afraid to die, he is, strangely, free to live."

Floods cause more death and destruction in the U.S. than any other natural disaster.

THE ORIGIN OF SOAP OPERAS, PART II

Part II of our story on the creation of a truly American form of storytelling…and soap peddling. (See page 277 for Part I.)

TV OR NOT TV?

In 1949 Procter & Gamble formed an entire corporate division to "produce, or acquire, and produce, radio, television and motion picture shows, programs, and other forms of entertainment." And by the early 1950s, they were producing more content than any of the major Hollywood studios. TV airwaves were filled with Procter & Gamble–produced shows, including *Truth or Consequences*, *This Is Your Life*, Westerns, sitcoms, adventure shows, variety shows, and children's shows.

But not a single TV soap opera.

TV shows cost so much more to make than radio shows that Procter & Gamble preferred to focus on programs that would be broadcast in the evening, when viewing audiences were largest. Furthermore they wondered whether women would stop doing their housework long enough to sit down and watch a televised soap. And even if they did, some executives worried, was it right for the company to encourage them to do so? "It was almost a decadent implication that we were taking housewives away from their work and families," said P&G executive Ed Trach.

MAKING THE SWITCH

Finally, in 1956 Procter & Gamble filmed an experimental pilot for a TV version of *Ma Perkins*. They quickly realized that making the transition from radio to TV would be even more difficult than they had imagined. After 15 years of listening to *Ma Perkins* on the radio, listeners had formed their own ideas of what she should look like. The TV version couldn't help but seem inauthentic and disappointing; sure enough, it flopped.

So they decided to create a TV soap from scratch. This, too, proved to be a challenge—*The First Hundred Years*, P&G's first original TV soap, lasted only nine months.

P&G's next effort, *Search for Tomorrow*, debuted in September 1951. By the end of its first year on the air it had five million regular viewers. (And once it found an audience, it kept it: At the time the show finally went off the air in December 1986, it was the longest running daily show in the history of American network television.)

THE TELEVISION ERA BEGINS

Once *Search for Tomorrow* convinced P&G that TV soaps could work, they created a TV version of its radio soap "The Guiding Light," which ran on both radio and TV until 1956. It was another huge hit, so they added still more soaps to the daytime lineup. By the mid-1950s, they had more than a dozen TV soaps on the air.

Then Irna Phillips, creator of "The Guiding Light" (and the person credited with introducing organ music and the amnesia storyline to soaps) suggested that P&G switch from the traditional 15-minute length to a 30-minute format. She figured that one 30-minute soap would be cheaper to produce than two 15-minute soaps, each with their own sets and staff.

P&G balked. Would viewers sit still for one half-hour soap when they could change channels and get two of the 15-minute soaps they were used to? Company execs resisted the idea for more than two years before they finally caved in and allowed Phillips to create *As the World Turns*, and commissioned another soap called *The Edge of Night* from another producer, both to be 30 minutes long.

The two shows premiered on the same day in 1956 and by 1957 were the two highest rated soaps on television. That was all it took—every single soap opera on the air switched to the half-hour format. And as soap fans—and advertisers—made the switch to TV, the era of radio soaps came to an end. The last of the radio soaps went off the air on November 25, 1960.

FROM FANTASY...

Story lines had changed a great deal over 25 years. Depression-era listeners had preferred escapist themes that allowed them to forget their troubles. "Our Gal Sunday," for example, was about an orphan girl from a Colorado mining town who marries "England's richest, most handsome lord, Lord Henry Brinthrope," and "Mary

Worth the wait? In 1986, in the very last scene of "Search for Tomorrow," after

Noble: Backstage Wife" was about a common Iowa girl who marries a movie star. Other soaps showcased the lives of men and women with interesting careers: ministers, doctors and nurses, and glamorous movie actresses.

...TO FEELING THEIR PAIN

For whatever reason, housewives of the 1950s were much more interested in commiserating with characters than they were in escaping with them or watching them in their careers. Fantasy-themed soap operas steadily lost viewers to soaps featuring people battling terrible illnesses, coming to terms with miserable childhoods, and going on trial for murders they did and did not commit. *The Secret Storm*, one of the most popular early TV soaps, focused almost entirely on the suffering of the Ames family after Mrs. Ames dies in a car accident in the very first episode.

LOVE IN THE AFTERNOON

But the most obvious change over the years was the Great Unmentionable—S-E-X. The earliest radio soaps had featured romance, but no sex. In her 27 years on the radio, Helen Trent, the fictional heroine of the show "The Romance of Helen Trent" never consummated a single romance. From 1933 until she went off the air in 1960, her intimate life consisted of an occasional quick kiss and once in a while a sigh or two.

The subject of adultery, when it first appeared in radio soaps in the 1940s, was limited to married women suspecting that their husbands were cheating (invariably, they weren't). Even divorce remained a taboo subject until the late 1940s; soap opera writers could only end marriages by killing one of the characters off.

By the early 1950s, most soaps had a lone, unmarried "bad girl" character who had affairs. But these encounters were never depicted onscreen, only hinted at with kisses, knowing glances, and the occasional dance with the offending male character. Once an affair was established in this way, it could be discussed, but *never* shown, and the "bad girl" was always punished for her transgressions in the end.

MARRIAGE PROBLEMS

Another barrier fell in 1956, when a story line on *As the World Turns* called for an unhappily married character to divorce his wife and marry his mistress. Procter & Gamble forced the show's producers to kill the story line before it got too far, but there was no turning back.

The next love triangle came in 1957, when a male character on *Search for Tomorrow* fell in love with his wife's sister. The tale was made deliberately short in case viewers complained, but they didn't—and the theme of morally weak husbands lured into sin by immoral temptresses became a daytime staple. By the late 1960s, such love triangles often resulted in illegitimate children; the paternity secrets and child custody disputes that followed could keep a story line going for years.

SOAP GLUT

By March 1970, there were 20 soaps on the air—10 full hours every afternoon; and with the soap audience spread so thin over so many shows, ratings began to sag. In the cutthroat battle for viewers, two new themes began to emerge as audience pleasers.

The first was "young love"—romance and affairs between central characters who were younger than 35, the average age of soap opera viewers. The second was "relevancy"—soaps that dealt realistically with controversial issues of the day, such as drug abuse, abortion, interracial relationships, and the Vietnam War. (*One Life to Live* spent five months on a story line involving Pap tests, and another eight months on one involving venereal disease.)

GENERATION GAP

Unlike its competitors, Procter & Gamble stuck to its official policy of avoiding controversial subjects. Big mistake: Racier soaps like *General Hospital* and *All My Children* won the lion's share of high school and college-age women (and not a few men) who discovered soaps in the 1970s; meanwhile, P&G's traditional audience—housewives—was shrinking as increasing numbers of women entered the workforce.

Eventually Procter & Gamble spiced up its soaps, but only succeeded in alienating traditional viewers without attracting new ones. By the 1980s, many of its longest running soaps were in trouble: *The Edge of Night* was cancelled in 1984, and *Search for Tomorrow* went off the air two years later.

The highest temperature ever reached in Britain was 98.2°F on August 9, 1911, in Surrey.

SOAPS ON THE ROPES?

By the 1980s, much of the action and excitement in the soap opera world had moved from daytime television to primetime. The trend started in 1978 when *Dallas* premiered on CBS. The first successful primetime serial since *Peyton Place* (1964–1969), *Dallas* inspired a host of imitators, including *Dynasty*, *Knots Landing*, *Falcon Crest*, *The Colbys*, and *Flamingo Road*.

Between 1995 and 1999, the daytime soap opera audience shrank by more than a third; this time because of a real-life soap opera—the O. J. Simpson murder trial.

The case, which unfolded live on TV for more than a year, had as many heroes and villains, twists and turns as any soap opera could dream of having, and yet it was real. Millions of soap opera fans abandoned their shows to follow the Simpson trial and the numerous legal shows and talk shows that followed in its wake. How could a fictional drama hope to compete?

Just as importantly, networks and cable channels discovered that true-crime shows and tabloid talk shows could be produced for a fraction of the cost of a soap opera, and could thus earn huge profits even when they didn't attract as many viewers.

YOU BE THE JUDGE

Today, "lapsed" soap opera fans—people who used to watch soaps but no longer do—outnumber fans who still watch the shows. Networks and soap opera producers are working hard to get them back: ABC launched a 24-hour all-soap cable channel so that people who can't watch soaps during the day can tune in and watch them in the evenings or over the weekend. *All My Children* and other soaps let viewers decide the outcome of story lines by voting on possible outcomes over the Internet. *Days of Our Lives* let viewers vote to determine the paternity of a character's baby. And *Passions* even let fans decide whether a character should live or die. (Viewers chose death.)

Will any of these measures work? Will soap operas pull out of their current slump and be restored to their former glory? Or will they continue a slow slide into oblivion? The answer is as unpredictable as the soaps themselves. All you can do is "tune in tomorrow..."

A giraffe can run faster than a horse and can go longer without water than a camel.

OFF YOUR ROCKER

We'll bet that you didn't know that your favorite singers could talk, too. Here are some of the profound things they have to say.

"I get a lot of influences from electric shavers."
—**Iggy Pop**

"We can fly, you know. We just don't know how to think the right thoughts and levitate ourselves off the ground."
—**Michael Jackson**

"A performer to me is like a racehorse, except that I don't eat hay."
—**Neil Young**

"If women didn't like criminals, there would be no crime."
—**Ice-T**

"My attitude, in purely intellectual terms, was 'screw you.'"
—**Neil Diamond**

"I totally appreciate being able to buy, say, this thousand-dollar cashmere blanket...because if I couldn't, I would hate to have to go back to regular blankets."
—**Stevie Nicks**

"Folk singing is just a bunch of fat people."
—**Bob Dylan**

"The ocean scares me."
—**Brian Wilson**

"A lot of Michael's success has been timing and luck. It could just have easily have been me."
—**Jermaine Jackson**

"I think the highest and lowest points are the important ones. All the points in between, are, well, in between."
—**Jim Morrison**

"You can write a book on each of my thoughts."
—**Vanilla Ice**

"I'd like to get a beer-holder on my guitar like they have on boats."
—**James Hetfield**

"Hair is the first thing. And teeth is the second. Hair and teeth. A man got those two things he's got it all."
—**James Brown**

UNCLE JOHN'S STALL OF FAME

You'd be amazed at the number of articles BRI members send in about the creative ways people get involved with bathrooms, toilets, toilet paper, etc. So we've created Uncle John's "Stall of Fame" to honor them.

Honoree: Thomas Suica of Monaca, Pennsylvania

Notable Achievement: Beating the system... with toilets

True Story: In November 2000, the Sky Bank announced it was building a branch on a vacant lot next to Suica's home. Suica, a plumber, didn't like the idea of a bank moving in next door—so he fought back by installing 10 "decorative" toilets on the roof of his garage. About every month or so after that, he rearranged them to create scenes commemorating the changing seasons. (His Christmas display: Santa's sleigh being pulled by 10 toilet reindeer.)

When the borough of Monaca fined Suica $135 and cited him for creating "unsanitary and unsafe conditions" on his roof, Suica fought back in court... and won: Judge Thomas Mannix threw out the citation, finding that the borough "had not proved the toilets, which Suica bought new, were unsanitary."

Update: Sky Bank eventually abandoned its plans to build a bank next to Suica's house. So is he taking his toilets down? Not a chance—Suica "says he will continue his protest, because he does not trust the bank."

Honoree: Joseph Taviani of Bath, Pennsylvania

Notable Achievement: Decorating his rental properties in a fashion worthy of a town named Bath

True Story: What is it about Pennsylvanians? In July 2001, Taviani planted toilets on the lawns in front of three rental properties he owns in Bath. Two were stolen immediately; one, at last report, is still there. Why toilets? "When you think of Bath, you think of a bathroom," Taviani explains. "Tubs were too big."

Honoree: Alberoni, a "low-born, clever opportunist" who worked for the bishop of Parma, Italy, in the late 1700s

Notable Achievement: Promoting himself using bathroom diplomacy

True Story: One of the French king's most obnoxious underlings was the Duc de Vendôme; he was notorious for conducting business while seated on the pot and "offering visitors a view of his backside as he got up to wipe himself." Most people had to put up with this rude treatment, but the bishop of Parma refused and sent Alberoni as his potty-proxy.

Where others saw only a French moon, Alberoni saw opportunity. "Upon seeing this spectacle," Barbara Kelatsas writes in *Inside the Pastilles of the Marquis de Sade*, "Alberoni exclaimed, 'O! culo de angelo!' and rushed to embrace the ducal posterior. This worshipful attitude, and his ability to make good cheese soups, enabled him to attach himself to the Duc de Vendôme and make his fortune."

Honoree: Irene Smith, a member of the St. Louis Board of Aldermen in Missouri

Notable Achievement: Taking care of business…while taking care of business

True Story: In July 2001, Smith and three other lawmakers were staging a filibuster over a redistricting plan that they felt would hurt their constituents. Smith had to go to the bathroom, but the president of the board told her that if she left the room for any reason, she would lose the floor and her filibuster would end. Rather than abandon her cause, Smith held out for 40 minutes; then, when she couldn't put off nature's call any longer, "her aides surrounded her with a sheet, tablecloth, and quilt while she appeared to use a trash can to relieve herself," according to one account. "What I did behind that tablecloth was my business," she explained afterward.

No word on whether Smith won her redistricting fight, but she certainly won the day—the Board of Aldermen adjourned without voting on the controversial plan…but not without condemning Smith. "The people in Missouri must think we're a bunch of morons," Mayor Francis Slay told reporters.

IT'S A WEIRD, WEIRD WORLD

More proof that truth really is stranger than fiction.

WHY DIDN'T WE THINK OF THAT?

"A Denver woman has filed for divorce after finding out her husband of seven years had been faking being deaf and mute. In recently-filed court papers, Bill Drimland admitted to the ruse to escape what he called 'incessant nagging' from his wife."

—*Bizarre News*

OH, DEER

"A Pennsylvania couple woke up to find a strange intruder in their home. A deer had run into the house and into the bathroom, somehow managing to turn on the water and knock over a bottle of bubble bath. He then submerged himself in the frothy water. The Becks called state the Game Warden, who arrived with tranquilizers. 'The guy said: "There's nothing wrong. He's just in there taking a bubble bath,"' said Beck. The animal was subdued, removed from the house and released back into the wild."

—*Ananova.com*

YOU ANIMAL!

"Many Nigerians hold to the belief that people can be turned into animals and vice versa. Over the last two years, Nigerian newspapers have covered many such incidents, including the turning of two children into dogs, the turning of a vulture into a man, and the turning of a schoolboy into a yam."

—*Discovery News*

ROBBIN' HOOD

"In Australia, a man named Rob Banks, who was convicted of robbing banks, has been given a new trial because the judge said the jury may have been swayed by his name. This time he will be tried under an alias."

—"The Edge," *The Oregonian*

It would take 27,000 spider webs to produce a single pound of spider silk.

BRIDGE OVER DUBLIN WATER

"Irish hospital worker Willie Nugent decided he would raise money for charity by swimming across a river in downtown Dublin. There was only one problem: Nugent can't swim. So instead he crawled across a bridge, in movements 'resembling a breast stroke.'"

—Universal Press Syndicate

MINTY FRESH

"A farmer in India has been charged with manslaughter after allegedly killing a police officer with his rancid breath. While attempting to arrest Raji Bhattachara of Bhopal, the officer smelled the curry on the farmer's breath and died from an asthma attack."

—Maxim magazine

THAT'LL LEARN YA

"After being charged £20 for a £10 overdraft, 30-year-old Michael Howard of Leeds legally changed his name to "Yorkshire Bank are Fascist Bastards." The bank has now asked him to close his account. Mr. Bastards has asked them to repay his 69-pence balance by check made out in his new name."

—Manchester Guardian

VEGETABLY INCORRECT

"Kathy Szarko, the artist who created the 6-foot-tall Mr. Potato Head as a symbol for Rhode Island's tourism campaign, was upset after it was removed...for being racist because it was brown. 'He's a potato,' she said. 'That's why he's brown.'"

—Universal Press Syndicate

PISTOL PACKIN' PADRES

"Last week it became legal for Kentucky ministers to pack heat inside a house of worship, as long as they have a concealed weapons permit. Not all religious officials agree with the change. 'A friend of mine said it, and I'm going to repeat it,' said the Rev. Nancy Jo Kemper, 'Jesus would puke.'"

—Wacky News

Can't confirm or deny. The CIA once called an assassination team the "Health Alteration Committee"

IF YOU...

Life, as a series of possibilities.

IF YOU...
are brushing your hair, it's best to stop after about the 25th stroke. That's the right number for the best distribution of your hair's natural oils. Much more brushing than that can cause damage.

IF YOU...
have hair growing out of your armpit, you've got *hirci*. That's the fancy word for armpit hair.

IF YOU...
are stuck in the grip of a crocodile's jaw, jam your thumbs in its eyeballs. (Good luck.)

IF YOU...
get a "mustache" from drinking grape or cherry juice, you can quickly wipe it off with a bit of toothpaste dabbed on a washcloth.

IF YOU...
are an average American, your butt is 15 inches long.

IF YOU...
sneeze your most powerful sneeze, it'll come flying out of your face at a little more than 100 mph.

IF YOU...
have to choose between total lack of sleep or food for the next 10 days, go with lack of food. You'll die from total lack of sleep sooner (in about 10 days) than from starvation (a few weeks).

IF YOU...
are the electrician in charge of the lighting on a movie or TV set, you're a "gaffer." If you're an assistant to the gaffer, you're known as the "best boy."

IF YOU...
weigh 120 pounds on Earth, you'd weigh about 20 pounds on the moon.

IF YOU...
listen to a cricket chirp, you can figure out the temperature. Count the number of chirps per 15 seconds and add 40. That'll give you the temperature (Fahrenheit).

IF YOU...
are trying to find a tiny object on the floor, put a bare light at floor level. The light will cause the object to cast a shadow, making it easier to spot.

A freshly hatched crocodile is 3 times longer than the egg from which it emerged.

"YOU PRESS THE BUTTON, WE DO THE REST"

In this installment of our history of photography, we tell you about the man who is to photography what Colonel Sanders is to fried chicken: George Eastman, founder of Eastman Kodak.

CAMERAMAN

On November 13, 1877, a 23-year-old bank clerk named George Eastman walked into a camera store in Rochester, New York, and paid $49.58 for a camera and some equipment. Eastman bought only the essentials, but in those days "the essentials" included a tripod, glass plates, a plate holder, containers of photographic chemicals, and more than a dozen other items, including a tent to serve as a darkroom.

Eastman took his camera with him on a trip to Mackinac Island in Lake Huron, where he photographed some of the local sights. But as fascinated as he was by photography, he loathed the amount of equipment that was required. "It seemed," he said, "that one ought to be able to carry less than a pack-horse load."

MADE IN ENGLAND

Eastman began to experiment to see if he could simplify the process. He bought a subscription to the *British Journal of Photography*, and by chance his first issue was the one reporting Charles Harper Bennett's perfection of the gelatin dry-plate process. The article prompted him to abandon the collodion "wet process" and start making his own gelatin plates.

"The English article started me in the right direction," he wrote. "At first I wanted to make photography simpler merely for my own convenience, but soon I thought of the possibilities of commercial production."

Like most other commercial plate makers, Eastman started out making them one at a time. He heated chemicals in an old teakettle, poured them over glass plates, then smoothed out the emulsion with a rod. It was a cumbersome, time-consuming process, and that made precoated plates expensive. Eventually, Eastman

---

The 1953 film *The Moon Is Blue* was condemned by the Roman Catholic Legion invented a machine to coat gelatin plates automatically, then, in April 1880, started manufacturing them to sell to local photographers and photo supply stores.

ON A ROLL

The Eastman Dry-Plate Company grew rapidly on the strength of gelatin plate sales, but that didn't stop Eastman from introducing a product in 1884 that he believed would make glass plates obsolete: it was a roll of photosensitive paper, or "film," that could be used *instead* of glass plates. Eastman sold this film in a box that could be attached to existing cameras, in place of the box that held the glass plates.

Using glass plates, photographers could take at most a few shots before having to reload the camera, which usually required a darkroom; with Eastman's roll film there was enough paper for 50. Added bonus: Roll film wasn't heavy. "It weighs two and three-quarters pounds," Eastman explained. "A corresponding amount of glass plates and holders would weigh fifty pounds."

A TOUGH SELL

Eastman's new film seemed such an obvious improvement over glass plates that he believed it would take the photographic world by storm. He was wrong: Professional photographers had too much money invested in glass-plate technology. Besides, glass plates made negatives as large as 20 by 24 inches, which captured an incredible amount of detail and produced beautiful photographs. Eastman's film couldn't duplicate the quality.

At first Eastman tried to adjust his product line to accommodate the needs of professional photographers, but he soon realized that this was exactly the opposite of what he should be doing. And that was when he changed photography forever.

"When we started out with our scheme of film photography," he recalled in 1913, "we expected that everybody who used glass plates would take up films, but we found that in order to make a large business we would have to reach the general public."

JUST PLAIN FOLKS

Eastman was one of the first people to understand that the number of people who wanted to take pictures was potentially much larger than the number of those who were interested in developing their own film. He realized that if he was the first person to patent a complete ans simple camera "system" that anyone could use, he would have that market all to himself.

In 1888, Eastman patented what he described as a "little roll holder breast camera," so called because the user held it against their chest to take a picture. But what would he call it? He wanted the name of his camera to begin and end with the letter K—he thought it a "strong and incisive" letter—and to be easy to pronounce in any language. He made up a word: Kodak.

CLICK

Just as Eastman intended, his camera was easy to use: The photographer simply pulled a string to set the shutter, pointed the camera at the subject, pushed a button to take the picture, then turned a key to advance the film. The user didn't even have to focus: the lens was designed so that anything more than six feet away was always in focus. Price: $25—a lot of money in those days, but half what Eastman had paid for his first camera equipment 11 years earlier.

But the most important selling point of this new system was that Eastman offered to develop and print all of the pictures taken with Kodak cameras—something no camera maker had ever offered before. He sold the Kodaks loaded with enough film for 100 pictures, and when these were used up the owner could, for $10, mail the entire camera back to Rochester. The company would remove the film, process and print the pictures, and return them to the owner along with the camera, freshly loaded with enough film for 100 more pictures.

"You press the button," the company's slogan went, "We do the rest."

PICTURE PERFECT

The Kodak camera went on sale in June 1888. It was followed by an improved model, the Kodak No. 2, in 1889. By September of that year, Eastman had sold more than 5,000 cameras in the U.S. and was developing an average of 7,000 photographs a day.

Eastman quickly came to understand that the real money in the photography business wasn't in selling cameras—each customer needed only one—it was in selling and processing film. This gave him an incentive to lower the cost of his cameras, so that more people could afford to buy the film. In 1895 he introduced a Pocket Kodak camera, which at $5 was Kodak's first truly affordable camera. Then in 1900 he introduced the Brownie, which sold for $1. Eastman sold more than 100,000 Brownies in the first year.

KODAK MOMENTS

Most photographers had approached photography as an art form, but Eastman worried that if his customers did the same thing, they might get bored with their new hobby and find something else to do. He believed that if he could convince the public to use their cameras to document birthdays, summer vacations, and other special moments of their lives—once a family purchased a camera they would never go without one again.

Accordingly, Kodak's advertisements featured parents photographing their children, and children photographing each other. The Kodak Girl, one of the most popular advertising icons of the early 20th century, was shown taking her camera everywhere: to the mountains and the beach, on yachts, and on bicycle rides in the country.

"Don't let another week-end slip by without a Kodak," the magazine ads cooed. "Take a Kodak with you." And millions of people did.

PATENTS PENDING

Eastman believed that the best way to stay ahead of the competition was to constantly improve his products, and to protect his improvements with patents, which would guarantee sole ownership of those markets. In 1886 he became one of the first American businessmen to hire a full-time research scientist, Henry Reichenbach.

One of Reichenbach's first triumphs was a roll film that used a solution of guncotton or *nitrocellulose*—the same substance that served as the basis for the collodion process—as a base, instead of paper. The first rolls went on sale in August 1889; when it did, film as we know it was born and the word *snapshot* entered the language.

BROUGHT TO YOU BY THE LETTER K

True to form, Eastman patented the chemistry and every step of the manufacturing process so that Kodak would have the roll film market all to itself; then, when the profits started rolling in, he used the money for more research and more patents—so that the company would continue to dominate the industry it had played such a huge part in creating.

In 1891 Kodak marketed its first "daylight-loading" camera, which allowed the user to reload film into a camera without a darkroom. In 1896, just a year after the discovery of X-rays, Eastman began manufacturing plates and paper for X-ray photographs; that same year, Kodak began selling the first motion picture film. Film for "talkies"—motion pictures with sound—followed in 1929.

These advancements continued long after Eastman's death in 1932. In 1936 Kodak brought Kodachrome Film to market, the world's first amateur color slide film; they introduced color print film in 1942. Instamatic cameras, which used easy-to-load film cartridges instead of rolls, came out in 1963; the company sold more than 50 million Instamatics in the next seven years alone. Super-8 home movie cameras hit the market in 1965, and Kodak dominated that market too.

KING OF THE HILL

Decades of continuous innovation have turned Kodak into a household word, synonymous with photography itself. When astronaut John Glenn became the first American to orbit Earth in 1962, a Kodak camera in the space capsule recorded the event. When Neil Armstrong walked on the moon seven years later, he had a Kodak with him.

Eastman accomplished what he had set out to accomplish—he brought photography to the masses. Now, with the advent of digital technology, film photography may soon disappear, like the disposable cameras Kodak makes today. But that doesn't take away from the miracle of what the pioneers of photography achieved—capturing actual images from the air and preserving them for all time, an amazing feat that once seemed as impossible as catching lightning in a bottle.

*   *   *

Random Fact: King James IV banned golf from Scotland in 1491 for the simple reason that, it "looketh like a silly game."

Find a worm in your apple? Don't worry—it means the apple has no pesticides.

FAMILY FEUDS

*Is blood thicker than water? Not when there's money
and power involved. Here are two feuds from
the BRI files that prove the point.*

MURRY WILSON VS. THE BEACH BOYS
The Contestants: Murry Wilson, father of three of the
Beach Boys—Dennis, Brian, and Carl Wilson—and the
uncle of Mike Love. He was also the band's first manager... and
according to his three sons, he was also an abusive tyrant.

The Feud: Murry managed the band for the first three years of its
existence, from 1962 until 1964. By then the Wilsons and the
Loves had had enough of his explosive temper, and they fired him
while working on the tracks for "I Get Around."

At first Murry refused to accept that his sons were even capable
of firing him. Then, convinced that he was the one responsible for
their success, he retaliated by forming a new group, the Sun Rays,
and set out to "teach those ungrateful little bastards a lesson."

And the Winner Is: The Beach Boys—although for a short time
it seemed that the Sun Rays might actually make it big. Their
third single, "I Live for the Sun," actually made it onto the pop
charts, but that was the best they ever did. "After several more
singles," Dennis Wilson writes, "they faded into the background."

From Beyond the Grave: Before he died in 1973, Murry Wilson
reconciled with his son, Brian...they even wrote a song together
in 1969, called "Break Away." But behind Brian's back, Murry had
sold Brian's publishing company, Sea of Tunes, which he controlled. Murry got $700,000; Brian got nothing. Brian sued, and
won $10 million, but never got the publishing rights back. The
final winner: Murry Wilson.

CHARLES AND J. FRANK DURYEA

The Contestants: Charles and his brother J. Frank, two bicycle
makers living in Springfield, Massachusetts, in the 1880s.

The Feud: The Duryea brothers are generally credited with building the first working automobile in the United States. After read-

---

The Wok began as a Bronze Age Mongolian helmet that doubled as a cooking pan.

ing a description of German automaker Karl Benz's car in an 1889 issue of *Scientific American*, they set out to make a car of their own; on September 1, 1893, they drove their car 600 feet down the streets of Springfield.

One question still haunts the Duryea family today: Which of the brothers deserves the most credit for inventing the car? Not long after they started building it—and before they had one that actually worked—Charles went back to his bicycle business in Peoria, Illinois, and did not return for more than a year. By the time he got back, J. Frank had solved all of the technical problems by himself, without any help from Charles.

Unfortunately, for all his talent as a mechanic, J. Frank neglected to make sure he received credit for his contributions. He let Charles file the patent for their engine…and Charles listed himself as the only inventor. For the rest of his life he took full credit for the Duryea automobile, dismissing J. Frank as "simply a mechanic" he'd hired to execute his designs. The resulting feud shortened the life of their auto company, too: The brothers only managed to make 13 cars before they closed up shop and went their separate ways.

And the Winner Is: Nobody, not even after all these years. Charles and Frank's descendants are still fighting over which brother is the true inventor of the first American car.

* * *

A CLASSIC HOAX

The Amazing Fasting Girl

Background: In the 1870s, a Welsh teenager named Sarah Jacobs became famous for her ability to fast for months on end. Her parents put her on exhibit, claiming she'd gone more than two years without eating a single piece of food.

Exposed: Concerned that the exhibit was a fraud, Welsh officials decided to test the Jacob family's claims by putting young Sarah in the care of a professional nurse, who would verify whether the girl ate anything or not. When she died from starvation nine days later, her parents were arrested and went to prison for fraud.

A groaner: What do you call Santa's helpers? Subordinate clauses.

AUNT LENNA'S PUZZLER

One day we made the mistake of saying, "We're bored."
Auntie Lenna handed us this and said, "It's easy! Just
count the triangles. There are more than 50 and
less than 100." Answer on page 513.

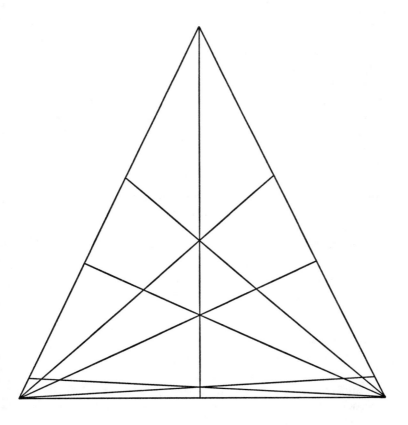

Number of fireflies it would take to generate the visible brightness of the sun: 14.3 billion.

SWAN SONGS

Why are we so intrigued by death? Because it's a part
of life....And besides, we've all got to go sometime.
So why not enjoy a chuckle while we're here?

DEATH AND TAXES

In late 1997, homeowner Eugene Bearringer stopped paying taxes on his home in Toledo, Ohio. Repeated attempts to contact Bearringer and his out-of-state relatives were futile, so in November 2000, county officials foreclosed on the property and sold it at auction—sight unseen—to William Houttekier of Temperance, Michigan. The following week, Houttekier went to Toledo to tour his new home...and found Bearringer's skeletal remains on the living room floor, where they had laid undiscovered and undisturbed for more than two years—about the same length of time that he'd gone without paying his property taxes. Bearringer, an asthmatic, had apparently died from natural causes.

County Auditor Larry Kaczala explained that the foreclosure and auction went according to standard procedure—without anyone from the county ever stepping foot on the premises. "The government would have no right to go onto that property," he explained, "because we don't own it. We just sell it for the back taxes."

"I always wondered what happened to that dude," a neighbor told reporters. "It got awful quiet over there."

LAST STOP

In September 2001, the city of Calcutta, India, announced that it would begin playing calming classical music in each of the city's 17 subway stations "to discourage passengers from trying to commit suicide." Since 1984 fifty-nine passengers have tried to kill themselves by jumping onto the tracks in front of trains; twenty-six of the attempts succeeded. The campaign also includes posters with slogans like "I don't like to die in this beautiful world."

"Hopefully, people contemplating suicide will listen to our music and see our posters and get diverted from killing themselves at the stations," says subway system spokesman S. C. Banerjee.

Northern southpaws: Polar bears are left-handed.

THE
EXTENDED
SITTING
SECTION

A Special Section
of Longer Pieces

Over the years, we've had
numerous requests from BRI members
to include a batch of long articles—
for those leg-numbing experiences.
Well, the BRI aims to please...
So here's another great way
to pass the uh...time.

FOOD OF THE GODS

You probably didn't give it much thought the last time you chomped down on a Hershey's, but the history of chocolate is as rich and as satisfying as the taste of chocolate itself.

SO CLOSE...AND YET SO FAR

On May 9, 1502, Christopher Columbus set sail on his fourth—and what turned out to be last—trip from Spain to the New World. He was searching for a direct water route to Asia, plus whatever riches he could find along the way.

In August 1502, he landed at Guanaja Island, 30 miles off the coast of modern-day Honduras. He spied an enormous dugout canoe in the waters nearby and ordered his men to seize it.

The vessel turned out to be a Mayan trading canoe, probably from somewhere on the Yucatán Peninsula, and it was loaded with a full cargo of trading goods—colorful clothing, wooden swords, flint knives, copper hatchets, small copper bells, and other items. As Columbus's son Ferdinand recounted years later, the Mayans who had been in the canoe were also carrying a cargo of "almonds." Very *valuable* almonds, it turned out. Ferdinand wrote:

> The natives seemed to hold these almonds at a great price, for when they were brought on board ship together with their goods, I observed that when any of these almonds fell, they all stooped to pick it up, as if an eye had fallen from their head.

MOVING ON

But Columbus wasn't interested in almonds—he was looking for gold and other riches. "As there was nothing of importance in those Guanaja Islands," Ferdinand Columbus later wrote, "he did not tarry there."

Columbus and his men traveled as far south as modern-day Panama before returning home to Spain, where he died in 1506. He never did find his passage to Asia, and although he was the first European to come in contact with the cacao beans he mistook for almonds, he died without ever tasting chocolate.

ORIGINS

The cacao plant is native to Central America. There is evidence that the Maya established cacao plantations as early as 600 A.D., after harvesting and trading the wild cacao beans for hundreds of years. They used cacao beans to make *chocol haa*, or "hot water," a frothy chocolate beverage flavored with vanilla, hot chili powder, and other spices, including *achiotl*, a spice similar to allspice that left the drinker's mouth, lips, and facial hair bright red, "as if they had been drinking blood." But only Maya royalty were allowed to drink *chocol haa*; everyone else had to settle for *balche*, a fermented beverage made from honey and bark. Cacao beans were so valuable that by 1000 A.D. they were being used as currency, which is why Columbus's captives treated them with such reverence.

The Aztecs acquired a taste for cacao from their contact with the Maya, and by 1200 A.D. they were collecting tributes of cacao from the tribes they dominated, including the Maya. The Aztecs believed that cacao was a gift of the feathered serpent god Quetzalcoatl, who repeatedly brought a cacao tree to Earth on a ray of sunlight and taught early people how to make *cacahuatl*, or "bitter water," the chocolate beverage that they believed gave them universal wisdom and knowledge.

FROM ON HIGH

The Aztecs made *cacahuatl* in much the same way the Maya made *chocol haa*: they ground cacao beans into a powder, stirred it into water, and then gave it a froth by lifting the beverage high in the air and pouring it into a second container on the ground. But unlike the Maya, the Aztecs preferred their *cacahuatl* cold; this was the beverage that the Spanish conquistador Hernán Cortés was served by the Aztec emperor Montezuma in an elaborate ceremony in 1519, when he became one of the first Europeans, if not the very first, to taste chocolate.

There was certainly nothing like *cacahuatl* in the Old World, and it took a while for Europeans arriving in the New World to acquire a taste for it. "Chocolate…is a crazy thing valued in that country [Mexico]," Jesuit missionary and historian José de Acosta wrote in 1590. "It disgusts those who are not used to it, for it has a foam on top, or a scumlike bubbling."

"It seemed more a drink for pigs, than a drink for humanity," agreed the Italian historian Girolamo Benzoni, one of the first people to describe the experience to readers in Europe:

> I was in [Mexico] for more than a year, and never wanted to taste it, and whenever I passed a settlement, some Indian would offer me a drink of it, and would be amazed when I would not accept. But then, as there was a shortage of wine, so as not to be always drinking water, I did like the others. The taste is somewhat bitter, it satisfies and refreshes the body, but does not inebriate, and it is the best and most expensive merchandise, according to the Indians of that country.

CHANGING TASTES

With time the Spaniards developed a taste for *cacahuatl* which, like the Maya, they preferred hot, flavored with cinnamon and vanilla and sweetened with cane sugar, which was unknown to the Aztecs. And rather than froth their *cacahuatl* by pouring it from a high container into a low one as the Aztecs had, the Spaniards used a wooden swizzle stick or beater called a *molinillo*. Frothing it with a beater became the standard means of preparing chocolate for the next 200 years.

YOU WON'T HEAR THIS ON THE HERSHEY TOUR

By the late 1500s, the Spaniards had abandoned the Aztec name *cacahuatl*—"bitter water"—and coined a new word, *chocolatl*, possibly a combination of the Maya word for "hot," *chocol*, and adding it to the Aztec word for "water," *atl*.

Why would they do this? Their chocolate was sweetened, not bitter and they drank it hot like the Mayans did. But some historians speculate that there may have been another reason: just as the Spaniards were initially disgusted by the bitter taste and frothy brown appearance of *cacahuatl*, they may have also been disgusted by its name.

In many Romance languages, including 16th-century Spanish, the sound *caca* has scatological connotations. "It is hard to believe that the Spaniards were not thoroughly uncomfortable with a noun beginning with *caca* to describe a thick, dark-brown drink which they had begun to appreciate," anthropologists Sophie and Michael Coe write in *The True History of Chocolate*. The Spaniards "desperately needed some other word, and we would not be at all surprised if it was the learned friars who came up with *chocolatl* and *chocolate*."

CURE-ALL

No one knows for sure when chocolate first arrived in Europe. Cortés may have brought some back to Spain with him on his trips in 1519 or 1528. The first *recorded* appearance of chocolate in Europe was in 1544, when some Dominican friars took a delegation of Mayans to visit Prince Philip of Spain. Nobody knows if the prince tried the chocolate, and if so, what he thought of it. In any event, it took a few years for the new taste to catch on in Spain.

By the time the first commercial shipments of cacao beans began arriving in Spain from plantations in Central and South America in 1585, the exotic beverage was appreciated mostly for its "medicinal" value. "This drink is the healthiest thing, and the greatest sustenance of anything you could drink in the world," one chocolate advocate wrote in the 1550s, "because he who drinks a cup of this liquid, no matter how far he walks, can go a whole day without eating anything else."

EUROPEAN TOUR

In 1655 England seized the Caribbean island of Jamaica from Spain, including a number of thriving cacao plantations. Up to that point chocolate was practically unheard of outside of Spain. Then, in 1657, London's first chocolate café opened, advertising "an excellent West India drink, called Chocolat." Similar cafés soon opened up in the Netherlands, France, Belgium, Germany, Switzerland, Austria, and Italy. Hot chocolate quickly established itself as the drink of choice of the European aristocracy (no one else could afford it); by 1690 chocolate was so popular in England that the British Parliament passed a law forbidding the selling of it without a license, giving King William and Queen Mary a financial stake in the booming trade.

SOMETHING TO CHEW ON

In the late 1600s, chocolate began appearing as a flavoring in food. In France you could buy chocolate biscuits and pastilles; in Spain, chocolate rolls and cakes. In Italy, you could order chocolate soup, chocolate liver, and chocolate pasta—including chocolate lasagna. And in 1727, an Englishman named Nicholas Sanders became the first person, as far as historians can tell, to make a hot chocolate drink using milk instead of water.

Myth-conception: No matter what anyone tells you, elephants are *not* afraid of mice.

But you still couldn't find a chocolate *bar*—not in Europe, not anywhere in the world. Nobody knew how to make chocolate in solid form in the 17th century—chocolate preparation had hardly advanced at all since the time of Cortés. The beans were ground, usually by hand, and then shaped into wafers or cakes that were dissolved in hot water to make drinking chocolate, which if you wanted, you could pour into your food. That was about it.

A PRESSING MATTER

Things began to change when, in 1828, a Dutch chemist named Coenraad Johannes Van Houten invented a hydraulic press that could remove fatty cocoa butter from the ground cacao beans, leaving behind a solid "cake" that could then be ground into a fine powder—what we know as *cocoa powder*. Then he treated it with alkaline salts to prevent it from separating when added to hot water.

Drinking chocolate was changed forever. As anthropologists Sophie and Michael Coe write in *The True History of Chocolate*,

> In the year 1828, the age-old, thick and foamy drink was dethroned by easily prepared, more easily digestible cocoa. Van Houten's invention of the defatting and alkalizing processes made possible the large-scale manufacture of cheap chocolate for the masses, in both powdered and solid form.

PASSING THE BAR

The next great change came in 1847, when an English chocolate maker named Francis Fry figured out a way to combine cocoa powder and sugar with melted cocoa butter (instead of the usual warm water) to create a chocolate paste that could be pressed into molds and formed into solid shapes. It was the world's first eating chocolate, which the firm sold under the sophisticated-sounding French name *Chocolat Délicieux à Manger*, ("Delicious Chocolate for Eating").

Then in 1867, a Swiss chemist named Henri Nestlé discovered how to make powdered milk through evaporation. In 1879, after several years of collaborating with Nestlé, Swiss chocolate maker Daniel Peter finally figured out how to add Nestlé's powdered milk to his chocolate, creating the world's first milk chocolate.

That same year, another Swiss chocolate maker, Rudolphe Lindt, invented a process he called "conching." Until then, chocolate was much coarser and grittier than it is today, kind of like gran-

---

The acid in your stomach is strong enough to dissolve razorblades.

ulated sugar. Lindt's conching process crushed chocolate paste beneath huge granite rollers for more than 72 hours, at which point the particles became so tiny and smooth that the resulting chocolate literally melts in your mouth—the first chocolate to do that. Lindt's invention so vastly improved the texture of chocolate that conching quickly became a universal process and coarse, gritty chocolate became a thing of the past.

CHOCOLATE FOR THE MASSES

The Industrial Revolution helped to make chocolate more affordable than ever. Now it was possible to grind massive quantities of cacao beans with steam-powered grinders and using hydraulic presses to separate cocoa butter from cocoa powder was much more efficient than making chocolate by hand... and the cost savings were passed on to the consumer.

The invention of chocolate that could be eaten created a huge demand for cocoa butter, which caused the price to go through the roof, and made chocolate bars expensive. Anyone could afford to *drink* chocolate, but if you wanted to eat it, you had to be wealthy.

Then in 1893, Milton Snavely Hershey, owner of the world's largest caramel factory, visited the World's Columbian Exposition in Chicago and saw a demonstration of chocolate-making machinery given by Lehmann and Company, a German chocolate maker. Hershey was so impressed by what he saw that when the exhibition closed he bought the machinery and began making chocolate-coated caramels. "Caramels are only a fad," he told anyone who would listen, "chocolate is a permanent thing."

In 1900 he sold his caramel company so that he could focus exclusively on chocolate, and he went about manufacturing it the same way that he'd become the king of caramel—he built the largest chocolate factory on the face of the earth.

Hershey then applied the principles of mass production to the manufacture of chocolate—he built his factory on 1,200 acres of Pennsylvania dairyland, and then bought up thousands more acres—until he owned enough dairy farms to supply his factory with fresh milk. He built an entire town, Hershey, Pennsylvania, to give his workers someplace to live, as well as another—Hershey, Cuba—near his sugar mill in the Caribbean.

Hershey manufactured his chocolate bars and Hershey's

The movie *Grease* was released in Venezuela under the name *Vaselina*.

kisses on such an enormous scale—as much as 100,000 pounds of chocolate a day—that he was able to realize huge cost savings, which he passed on to the consumer. He priced his Hershey bars at just a nickel a piece, and they sold at that price until 1969. And rather than settle for selling his chocolate regionally, as other American chocolate companies did at the time, he set his sights on selling his products throughout the United States. He also expanded his sales beyond the traditional outlets of candy stores and drugstores, selling chocolate bars at newsstands, in grocery stores, at bus stations, even in restaurants. Soon, his candy bars were everywhere.

KID STUFF

Hershey didn't think of his products as candy. In fact, he forbade his employees from referring to chocolate as candy. He claimed there was more energy in an ounce of chocolate than there was in a pound of meat. Chocolate wasn't "merely a sweet," he said, it was nutritious food.

Regardless of what Hershey thought, most people considered chocolate candy, more for kids than grown-ups. That began to change during World War I, when the government sent candy and chocolate to soldiers in battle. Why? It was cheap, it didn't spoil, and its high sugar content provided a quick energy boost. American soldiers consumed huge quantities of chocolate during the war, and when the war was over they continued to indulge their habit.

During World War II, virtually the nation's entire candy output was diverted into the war effort. American soldiers brought Hershey bars with them wherever they went; in many places they became a form of currency. The U.S. Air Force was the largest purchaser of M&M's during the war; it bought them by the ton for bomber pilots flying long missions over North Africa and the Pacific. The Army was the #2 customer; it issued M&M's to soldiers in tropical regions where ordinary chocolate melted too easily.

During WWII, the average G.I. consumed 50 pounds of candy and chocolate a year, three times what he had eaten before the war. And he brought his appetite for chocolate home with him. It wasn't just for kids anymore; it was the food that had kept the fighting man strong. The two world wars helped to establish what Hershey had been saying for more than 40 years—that chocolate is for everyone.

No surprise—Brightest city, when seen from space: Las Vegas, Nevada.

THE BIRTH OF BIG-TIME SPORTING EVENTS

Ever wonder how they come up with all those tournament championship events that fill the weekend TV schedule? Well, like everything else, they all had a beginning. Here are a few of the biggest.

THE MASTERS

In the 1920s, the world of golf was dominated by a lawyer from Georgia named Bobby Jones. Jones retired from the golf circuit in 1930 at the age of 28, having hit the peak of his career when he won not only the U.S. and British Opens but also the U.S. and British Amateurs, all in the same year. This feat, known as the Grand Slam, has never been repeated.

Throughout his career, Jones maintained amateur status—he never earned a penny playing golf. Then he retired from the game to spend more time with his family and build his law practice. He went on to write golf books and articles, design better clubs, and make instructional movies. But more than anything else, he wanted to design the world's finest golf course near his hometown of Atlanta—a private course where he could play without being mobbed by fans.

Of Course

Jones teamed up with New York banker Clifford Roberts and began to look for property. They wanted land that had a stream, contours, and beauty. As soon as they laid eyes on Fruitlands Nursery, they knew they had found what they were looking for.

Fruitlands was the first commercial nursery in the south, started by a horticulturist named P. J. Berckman. It was a 365-acre farm with trees, flowers, and shrubs imported from all over the world. When Berckman's son, Prosper, died in 1910, the business closed and his heirs began to look for a buyer. The purchase price—at the outset of the Depression—was $70,000. Jones and Roberts bought it.

Work on the golf course began in 1931 and progressed slowly. Each of the holes was named after one of the shrubs or trees that

---

Number of states that celebrate "National Admit You're Happy Day": 19.

grew there: Pink Dogwood, Juniper, Firethorn, and so on. Jones hit thousands of test shots as the course was in being made. He wanted three approaches to each hole: the safe route, the hard route, and the crazy route. It was finally finished in 1933.

The course was so beautiful that the USGA approached Jones with the idea of holding a tournament there, but he declined, feeling that if there were to be a tournament on his course, he should host it. So that's what he did. He held his first tournament in 1934, calling it the Augusta National Invitation Tournament. People came from 38 states to watch golfers compete for a $1,500 purse, and every hotel room in the town of Augusta, population 60,000, was full.

Call Me Master

Roberts wanted to call it "The Masters," but Jones thought that sounded presumptuous. Everyone called it The Masters anyway, so in 1939, Jones relented and the title was officially changed. The Masters remains the only major golf tournament to return to the same site every year.

Bobby Jones played in the first 12 tournaments, but never won. His best finish was a tie for 13th place, which was at the very first tournament. He never even broke par, but continued to participate because his name was a big draw. He died in 1971 at the age of 69.

THE AMERICA'S CUP

Most people think the America's Cup is American. But it isn't... or at least it didn't start out that way. In 1851 Prince Albert hosted the Great London Exhibition in order to pay tribute to the technological advances of the day. In conjunction with the event, Queen Victoria invited all nations of the world to participate in a 53-mile yacht race around the Isle of Wight. The prize was a trophy made of 134 ounces of pure silver.

Over a dozen British vessels entered the race...and one American boat, called the *America*. Owner John Cox Stevens was certain he was going to win. And he did—by a wide margin.

The trophy, then called the One Hundred Guinea Cup was awarded to Stevens and his crew. He considered having it melted down and cast into medals, but instead donated it to the New York Yacht Club in 1857, with the stipulation that it be awarded to win-

---

According to New York's Center for the Strange, 70% of witches are registered Republican.

ners of an international boat race. The trophy and the race were named after the boat, and the America's Cup was born.

The Streak

The race is held approximately once every three years. Americans sailing under the New York Yacht Club flag have won the trophy 25 times in a row over 126 years—the longest winning streak in sports. It wasn't until 1983 that an Australian entry took the trophy away from the United States.

The *America* sailed in 51 subsequent races under various owners, but only entered one America's Cup event, where it placed 4th out of 15. In 1921 it was sold to the U.S. Navy and placed in storage in Annapolis, where it suffered years of neglect and decay. In 1942 the roof of the storage shed collapsed under heavy snow, crushing the famous boat. Some of the original wood was salvaged from the ship and used to create a replica, which is now on display at the Naval Academy museum.

WIMBLEDON

Believe it or not, croquet was once considered a serious sport. The All England Croquet Club was founded in 1868, but by 1875 was suffering from a drop in membership because more people were playing a new sport: lawn tennis. So to increase revenue, they removed a croquet lawn and installed a tennis court. Then they changed their name to the All England Lawn Tennis and Croquet Club.

That same year, the club needed to purchase a new roller to care for the lawns, and it was expensive. To raise money, they decided to hold a tournament. An ad placed in the *Times* solicited entries, and *The Field* magazine was persuaded to donate a trophy. Twenty-two people entered the first tournament—men only—and 200 people paid a shilling apiece to watch, more than enough to cover the cost of the lawn roller.

Tennis, Anyone?

The club decided to hold a tournament every year, and every year it grew bigger. Named after the section of London where it was held, Wimbledon quickly became the most important championship event in the world of tennis. By 1884 women were allowed to compete; men's doubles were added that year as well. Mixed doubles were added in 1913.

May Sutten of the U.S. became the first non-Brit to win, claiming the title in both 1905 and 1907; since then, only two players from Great Britain have won. In 1922 Wimbledon moved to a new site and built a stadium big enough to seat 14,000 with standing room for thousands more. In 1932 the two-week event drew 200,000 fans, despite the worldwide economic depression. During World War II, the grounds were used for military purposes. After the war, when air travel became feasible, international participation soared. However, Wimbledon was open only to amateur players.

Change Brings Change

In 1967 the BBC sponsored a tennis tournament for professional players to publicize its move from black-and-white to color broadcasting. The organizers of Wimbledon watched as many of their champions appeared on national TV, attracting media attention and winning huge purses. The following year, Wimbledon was opened to all players—amateur and professional. Today there are 34 courts located on 42 acres. Attendance approaches half a million, and the prize money given out each year tops $12 million.

THE KENTUCKY DERBY

Edward Smith Stanley, 12th Earl of Derby, was good friends with Sir Charles Bunbury. Both enjoyed breeding horses. Together they founded a new horse race in 1780, a one-mile test of three-year-old thoroughbreds near Derby's country estate in Epsom, England. But before the first race could be held, it had to be named. Which founder should the race be named after—Bunbury or Derby? They flipped a coin...and that's how the word *derby* came to mean a horse race.

In Kentucky, horses flourished on bluegrass pastures that grew from Russian seed brought by immigrants. Because of this, the state became one of the most important thoroughbred breeding centers in the United States, and horse racing became a popular pastime. In 1832 the town fathers of Louisville, Kentucky, bought land from a local family, the Churchills, and built a racetrack.

But the track was too far from town to attract crowds and had to compete against other area tracks that were much more popular. Racing floundered there until the arrival of Meriwether Lewis

Clark, Jr. "Lutie" Clark was the grandson of explorer William Clark and a member of the same Churchill family on whose property Louisville's racetrack was located.

After a trip to Europe in 1873, where he studied the layout of the Epsom Downs Derby, Lutie was full of ideas of how to improve racing in Louisville and how to eliminate bookmaking by using the French *pari-mutuel* wagering machines. (Pari-mutuel betting is a system where the winners divide the total amount bet, in proportion to the amount they wagered individually. The odds change according to what people wager, and there is less chance of manipulation than with other systems.)

And...They're Off!

With financial backing from his family, Clark leased 80 acres from his Churchill uncles, oversaw construction of a new grandstand and track, sold stock in the venture, and organized the betting. The track—dubbed the Louisville Jockey Club Course—opened on May 17, 1875. Although there were far more important races being run in Kentucky that day, the success of the new track was assured when a horse named Aristides set a new world record for the mile-and-a-half run. The crowd went wild. The Kentucky Derby was born.

In spite of his success, Lutie Clark's quick temper and irascible nature made him quite unpopular. His wife and children left him, and the Churchill family cut him out of the will, leaving him only a few acres of property and a job as overseer of the racetrack. People stopped calling it the Louisville Jockey Club and started calling it Churchill Downs as an insult, to remind Clark who held the purse strings. He committed suicide in 1899.

Back from the Brink

By 1902 the Derby was on the verge of bankruptcy. Then Matt Winn became the manager. Winn had a gift for publicity and promotion, which he used to rebuild the legacy. He hired John Philip Sousa's band to entertain. He had two airplanes shipped in for races—and they made the first recorded flights in the state of Kentucky. During World War I, he pledged 10% of track profits to the Red Cross. During the potato shortage of 1918, he turned the entire infield into a huge potato patch. During World War II, he invited the Army to use the infield for public demonstrations of the new Sherman tanks. He even invited the State Fair to hold the

---

Crazy? Nearly 60% of adults say they would like to walk without shoes in New York City.

event in the grounds.

Winn improved the grandstand seating and built a clubhouse. He courted the press. He courted radio broadcasters. He courted movie stars. Business increased, public opinion changed, and revenues skyrocketed. Because of Matt Winn, the Kentucky Derby became an international event. He ran it until his death in 1949.

Today, the Kentucky Derby is one of the world's best-known races. It's been run every May since 1875. Over 100,000 people come to view the race, and millions more watch it on TV.

THE INDY 500

Around the turn of the 20th century, automobiles were a new and wondrous invention. And Detroit was emerging as the car capital of the world.

Carl Fisher was a businessman in Indianapolis. He made a fortune selling Prest-O-Lite acetylene-powered headlights. In 1909 he sold his business to Union Carbide for millions...just before the invention of car batteries made Prest-O-Lites obsolete.

Fisher wanted to build something with his money, and he decided that what Indianapolis needed was a racetrack for automobiles. In those days, roads were little more than trails and it was difficult to find a place where a driver could really "open 'er up." A racetrack would also give car manufacturers a place to test their new models and pit them against each other. It would put Indianapolis on the map.

Full Speed Ahead

Fisher set up a consortium, elected himself president, and bought 328 acres of countryside for $72,000. He hired an army of 400 workers who moved, on average, 1,500 square yards of dirt every 10 hours to build the two-and-a-half-mile track.

The track itself was made of crushed stone covered by 300,000 gallons of asphalt oil. Turns were banked to handle speeds up to 70 mph. The track was lighted, naturally, with Prest-O-Lite gas. But the best part was that here, the spectators could watch an entire race from start to finish. Fisher called it the Indianapolis Motor Speedway.

The first race on the new track was held August 19–21, 1909. Ten thousand people showed up. On the first day, there was a crash when a tire flew off due to loose lug nuts. The two men in the car were killed. On the second day, everything went well, but the third day, on the final race, a tire blew out and the car spun out of control and crashed into the crowd. The mechanic and two spectators were killed. The race continued, but then another car skidded out of control because the road surface was crumbling under the onslaught. The car slammed into a bridge, injuring the driver. Officials stepped in and stopped the race.

Papers Blast Fisher's Folly

Editorial headlines across the nation blared "Slaughter as a Spectacle" and "Commercial Murder." Protests were mounted. Petitions were circulated. Prohibitions were called for. The Indianapolis Motor Speedway became known as "Fisher's Folly."

But Fisher was not a man to give up easily. First he installed guardrails. Then he decided that the gravel-and-asphalt surface was to blame. He replaced it with bricks—3,200,000 of them—and the Indianapolis Motor Speedway became known as the Brickyard. Still, with other racetracks being built in cities like Chicago and Atlanta, business began to fall off. To promote his Speedway, Fisher announced that in 1911, the best American cars would go up against the best European cars for a purse of $25,000. The race would be 500 miles long and was called the Indianapolis Motor Speedway 500-Mile International Sweepstakes. The Indy 500 was born.

What Comes Around Goes Around

The Indy 500 has been run almost every year since 1911, closed only during the two world wars. It's now the oldest auto race in the world, and the Speedway is the largest spectator-sport facility in the world, with over 250,000 permanent seats. The purse is now around $9 million. In 2000, the Indy 500 placed first among televised motorsports events and generated over $100 million in sponsorship exposure. Besides the Indianapolis 500, the Speedway also hosts the Brickyard 400 and the United States Grand Prix.

Carl Fisher died in Miami in 1939 at the age of 65, but his dream lives on.

"Without music, life would be a mistake." —**Nietzsche**

PALM PILOT

Now that you've got a few minutes to yourself, why not try your hand at predicting the future? Reading palms is like checking your horoscope—even if you don't believe in it, it can be fun to see what your hands are "telling" you

GIVE THEM A HAND

No one knows for sure where palm reading originated. It's know to have existed since ancient time in China, the Middle East, India (where Gypsy fortune-telling is believed to have started), and Greece.

The Greek physician Hypocrites used palmistry to diagnose illness, and the Roman emperor Julius Caesar is said to have used it to judge the character of his men. In the Middle Ages, witch hunters studied the palms of suspects for spots of pigment—a sure sign, they believed, that the person was in league with the Devil Ironically, a few centuries later, the Pope banned palm reading on the grounds that it, too, was a form of devil worship. Palmistry made a comeback during the Renaissance, and in the 17th century, unsuccessful attempts were made to develop scientific explanations for its basic principles.

By studying a person's hands, you can surmise quite a bit about their health, hygiene, and nervous habits and possibly even pick up clues about their occupation—someone who works with their hands outdoors will have rougher hands than someone who works at a desk job.

But a real belief in palm reading—or any other form of fortune-telling for that matter—requires a leap of faith. You can either believe it not. It's up to you.

HANDS-ON TRAINING

Here are a few pointers you can use to read palms like the pros:

• **Timing is everything.** Read hands at least two hours after the subject has eaten, and when the hands are at normal room temperature. If you read the hands when they're too hot or too cold, the reading may be inaccurate. According to Eastern tradition, the best time to read hands is at dawn.

Termites are not related to ants. They are a member of the cockroach family.

- **Use good lighting.** Rule of thumb: If you can't see 'em, you can't read 'em.

- **Read both hands.** Palmists believe that the changes a person goes through in life are recorded in the dominant hand—for right-handed people, that means the right hand; for lefties it's the left hand. The hand that's not dominant gives a better picture of what they were like at the beginning of their life.

GENERAL APPEARANCE OF THE HANDS
The study of the shape of hands is known as chirognomy.

- **Square-shaped hands.** These people have strong powers of reasoning, but they're offset by a lack of idealism. They're stubborn, but they're also patient and have a strong respect for the law.

- **Round-shaped hands.** People with round, or "conic" hands are said to be creative, but also impulsive and impatient. They're open to new things but bore easily.

- **Large hands.** People with big hands are analytical, perhaps even too much so—they can spend so much time on every tiny detail of their lives that they lose sight of the big picture.

- **Small hands.** People with small hands are thought to be the opposite of those with large hands: they grasp the big picture immediately but pay little or no attention to detail.

- **Long, skinny hands.** These people are cautious—they carefully consider all options before deciding on a course of action.

- **Hairy hands.** If a man, it means he's capable of change. If a woman, it means she's capable of extreme cruelty. If a man's hands are are completely hairless, he's a coward. If woman's hands are, she's feminine.

THE PALMS
- **Wide, open palms.** Both tolerant and generous.
- **Narrow palms.** Unkind, lacking sympathy for others.
- **Soft palms.** Lazy.
- **Firm palms.** Active, straightforward.
- **Thick, chubby palms.** Self-centered.
- **Hollow palms.** Lacking courage and character.

Price of a writing pen containing Abe Lincoln's "genetic essence": $1,650.

- **Lined palms.** The more lines, the more sensitive the person.

FINGERS 'N' PALMS

- **Long palm, short fingers.** Impulsive—the smaller the hand, the more impulsive they are likely to be.
- **Long palm, long fingers.** Strong attention to detail.
- **Short palm, long fingers.** Too strong an attention to detail; obsessive.
- **Short palm, short fingers.** Impulsive *and* obsessive.

READING BETWEEN THE LINES

Studying the lines of the hand or palm is known as chiromancy.

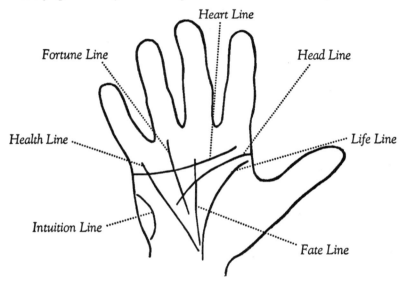

The Life Line: This line crosses the palm diagonally across from the base of the thumb.

- A long, broad life line with few other lines crossing it is an indicator that the person is likely to live a long life. If it's short, narrow, and crossed by many lines, the person is likely to be sickly, and their life may be shortened because of it.

- Lines that cross the life line are indicators of past, present, or future troubles, and if the cross occurs at the very end of the life line, it means they will die a sudden death.

• A double life line is an indicator of tremendous strength, but if the life line ends in a fork, it means the person will lose much of that strength in later years.

The Fate Line: This line starts at the wrist and runs up the center of the palm toward the middle finger.

• Not everyone has a fate line. If a person doesn't, it means that their life is likely to be uneventful. If they do have one and it's long and broad, they will have an interesting life and are likely to move up in the world. But if there are lots of crosses along the line, they will face many obstacles on the road to success.

• A fate line that starts on the life line indicates that they have strong family support for the goals they're working to achieve.

• If the fate line divides into two or more branches, the person will have at least one major career or life change. Lines that branch down and away from the fate line mean they will experience setbacks.

• If a person has lines that branch up and away from the fate line, they are likely to enjoy success in multiple areas of life. If it's wavy, they are indecisive and are unlikely to accomplish very much that is substantial.

The Heart Line: This line starts below the pinkie and crosses the palm horizontally.

• The heart line measures your potential for love and affection. A long, broad heart line means the person is very loving and idealistic; a short, narrow heart line indicates that they are selfish, and devoid of passion, and may even have a criminal mind.

• A heart line with many branches means that they will make a lot of friends in life, but if any of the branches cross the life line, some of the person's close friends will die.

• If a person has no heart line at all, they are a bitter, manipulative person who takes advantage of others—a person without a heart line, according to some palmists, is a person without a heart.

The Head Line: This horizontal line begins above the thumb, running horizontally across the palm.

• This line is supposed to be an indicator of intelligence: if it is well formed and conspicuous, the person has strong powers of concentra-

---

Whenever actress Joan Crawford remarried, she replaced all the toilet seats in her house.

tion…but if it intersects with the life line, they are insecure.

• A long line means a person can concentrate well; a shorter line means they tend to focus only on subjects that interest them. A short, straight head line means they have a lot of common sense.

• If the person has two parallel head lines, that means they put as much energy into personal pursuits as they put into their career. And if the head line forks into two or more lines, it means they are capable of using their intelligence diplomatically—in other words, they're a good liar.

• If the head line connects to the fate line, they're prone to bad luck.

The Fortune Line (Sun Line): This line runs vertically from the wrist to the ring finger.

• A person's fortune in life will be as clear and prominent as the fortune lines on the palms of their hands. If the line is prominent and well developed, they will never have to worry about money, and may even achieve great wealth.

• If they have more than one fortune line, they will have more than one source of wealth. A broken fortune line means that they will make and lose as many fortunes as there are breaks in the line. If the line remains strong, they will regain their lost wealth.

• If the fortune line runs alongside the life line, that means the person will inherit a large fortune from a relative…but if the fortune line crosses their life line, that means their relatives will take advantage of them and waste their money.

• If the fortune line starts near the head line, that means a person will only achieve great wealth after a lifetime of saving and hard work. If the fortune line is crossed in places by smaller lines, that means they will face obstacles as they build their fortune.

The Health Line (Mercury Line): This line starts below the thumb and runs diagonally across the palm toward the pinkie.

• This line works differently from the other lines—the harder it is to see, the healthier and stronger one is likely to be. If it's long and prominent, one's health is likely to be problematic.

• If the health line is crooked, a person will likely experience many different kinds of health problems throughout their life.

• A broken health line means digestive problems; red lines crossing the health line mean frequent fevers; many little lines crossing it mean frequent headaches.

The Intuition Line: This line starts below the pinkie, arcs down and inward toward the palm, and then back out again, ending above the wrist.

• If someone says they're not an intuitive person, don't even bother looking for this line—only intuitive people have it.

• A person has to have an intuition line on each hand to be deeply intuitive—if they do, they may even be psychic.

• If only one palm has an intuition line, they are not making good use of their potential at the present.

THE FINGERS

• **Fingers in general.** Short fingers indicate that the person is impulsive, has trouble concentrating, and may be hyperactive. Fingers that bulge at each finger joint are said to mean that the person pays great attention to detail and may be overly critical.

• **Thumb.** A person with short thumbs is stubborn; a person with long thumbs has a strong sense of purpose. Straight thumbs indicate generosity; crooked thumbs indicate selfishness. If your thumbs are hairy but the rest of your fingers aren't, you're a genius. (If all of your fingers are hairy, you're bad-tempered.)

• **Index finger.** A short index finger means the person is irresponsible; if it's long, they're domineering. If the finger is straight, the person is of good character. If it is crooked, the person has little or no self-respect.

• **Middle finger.** A long middle finger means the person is very cautious; if it's short they're always in a hurry. (If the person is gesturing with their middle finger, they're aggressive and rude.)

• **Ring finger.** If the ring finger is long, the person is greedy and materialistic. If it's short, they're prone to gambling.

• **Pinky finger.** If the finger is long, the person will do well in life; if it's short, they will have a difficult time making ends meet. A straight pinky finger indicates the person takes advantage of opportunities that come their way; a crooked pinky means the person lacks vision and will probably let those opportunities slip away.

The human brain can hold 5 times as much information as is in the *Encyclopedia Brittanica*.

THE HISTORY OF FOOTBALL, PART VI

Here's a football trivia question: After football was invented in 1880, how much time passed before somebody figured out how to throw a spiral pass? Answer: 25 years. Hard to believe, but true. Here's the story.

CLEANING UP THEIR ACT

When the Intercollegiate Athletic Association met in January 1906, it instituted a number of reforms that they hoped would change the way football was played:

• The reforms cut the length of the game from 70 minutes to 60, dividing the game into two 30-minute halves; and they made it illegal for one player to hurdle over another.

• They required a minimum of six men on the offensive line of scrimmage, which made it difficult to use mass formations like the flying wedge.

• They created a "neutral zone" on the line of scrimmage: Instead of the line of scrimmage being drawn through the *center* of the ball, players now lined up along *either side* of the ball, and were not allowed to step into the neutral zone in between until the ball went into play. This was intended to reduce the bare-knuckled brawling that routinely broke out when opposing players lined up toe-to-toe; sometimes it took as long as 20 minutes to pull fighting players apart and resume the game.

• They raised the number of yards needed for a first down from 5 to 10.

LOOKING FORWARD

But the most important change of all: In 1906 the Association legalized the forward pass, largely on the suggestion of Georgia Institute of Technology coach John Heisman.

Heisman had witnessed his first forward pass while watching the North Carolina Tar Heels play against the Georgia Tech Bulldogs in 1895. The score was tied, 0–0, late in the game, and the

---

Bad omen: In 1916 Cumberland College's quarterback was knocked unconscious in the first pl

Tar Heels were losing ground. On the next down, the Carolina fullback ran behind his scrimmage line hoping to find a place to punt. No luck—there was no room to punt, so he just hurled the ball downfield in desperation; one of his teammates happened to catch it and ran 70 yards for a touchdown, winning the game.

The move was illegal, and the Bulldogs' legendary coach Pop Warner demanded that the touchdown be tossed out. But the referee let football's first touchdown pass stand—because he hadn't actually seen it.

I'LL PASS

As concerns over increasing football violence mounted in the decade that followed, Heisman saw the forward pass as a means of cleaning up the game. He figured that if players could throw the ball over and past mass formations, defending players would have no choice but to spread themselves out across the football field, and mass plays would become obsolete. But he didn't get his way until 1906, when Yale's Walter Camp was finally shoved aside.

At first the forward pass was restricted: If a quarterback wanted to throw a pass, he had to move at least five yards to the left or right of center before throwing. To make officiating easier, football fields were marked with lengthwise stripes five yards apart, changing their appearance from a gridiron to a checkerboard.

If the ball hit the ground or was touched by an interior lineman before it was caught, possession of the ball went to the other team. If the receiver touched the ball but was not able to catch it, it became a free ball. All the defending team had to do to get possession was knock the receiver down or shove him out of the way so that he couldn't catch a forward pass.

TOSS-UP

Making matters worse was the fact that nobody really knew how to throw a football. Some players threw it sidearm; others threw it underhand like a softball or even with both hands, like a medicine ball. Whichever way they were thrown, underhand passes were inaccurate, and the odds of successfully catching them were slim.

Few football coaches thought forward passes were worth the risk, least of all the established football powers in the Northeast. Mass plays had always worked in the past, and they saw no need to

against Georgia Tech. They went on to lose, 222–0, the worst defeat in football history.

fix something that wasn't broken, no matter what the reformers thought. As a result, it was the less-established football programs in the Midwest and West—with little or nothing to lose—who were the first to become proficient in the use of the forward pass.

FARM TEAM

One of the first such schools was St. Louis University. In the summer of 1906, coach Eddie Cochems took his team out into the countryside near Lake Beulah, Wisconsin, where they experimented with the move for more than two months.

Back then footballs were nicknamed "blimps"—they were chubbier than they are today—and Cochems had to figure out how best to hold and throw the ball. He instructed his players to grab the ball near the two lacings closest to the end, where it was narrowest, and to throw it overhand with a twist, as if they were pitching a fastball, so that the ball would rotate on its long axis.

Within an hour his players were throwing perfect spirals 40 yards downfield, and in the season that followed, St. Louis won every game it played, scoring a total of 402 points against opponents and yielding only 11. But the Eastern football powers did not take the teams of the West seriously, and continued playing football as they always had.

MORE TO COME

Football was growing rapidly, and so were the number of injuries and deaths. In 1909, 33 people died playing football, and 246 more were seriously injured. The NCAA pushed through another round of reforms in 1910:

• They outlawed aiding the ball carrier by pushing or pulling him down the field, and also banned "interlocked interference"—teammates grabbing onto one another to execute mass plays.

• They increased the number of players on the offensive line of scrimmage from six to seven, further discouraging mass plays.

• Flying tackles were banned, and defensive players were forbidden to interfere with the receiver, other than to catch or block the ball.

• Halves were split into 15-minute quarters, giving tired players a little more time to rest. And for the first time, players who were withdrawn from the game were allowed to return. In the past players who were taken out had to stay out; as a result, tired players tended to stay in the game rather than take a break, which increased the number of injuries.

• Most importantly, the NCAA lifted some of the restrictions on the forward pass. Now the passer was allowed to throw the ball anytime he was at least 5 yards behind the line of scrimmage (that restriction wasn't removed until 1945), though it was illegal to throw a pass farther than 20 yards. The requirement that he move at least 5 yards left or right of center was removed, and the checkerboard playing field reverted back to the traditional grid-iron.

• It was about this time that "head harnesses"—stiff leather caps with ear flaps—began to come into use, as did the first shoulder pads.

ONE MORE ROUND

Two years later, in 1912, the NCAA made some of the last major changes to football. They set the field size at 100 yards long by 53⅓ yards wide, moved the kickoff from midfield to the 40-yard line, and created the fourth down.

They also lifted most of the remaining restrictions on forward passes, removing the 20-yard limit and establishing 10-yard "end zones" at either end of the field. For the first time, catching a pass thrown over the goal line counted as a touchdown instead of as a "touchback" that awarded possession of the ball to the defending team on their 20-yard line.

PASS PERFECT

The major football powers remained suspicious of the forward pass even with all of the restrictions removed. That changed in 1913, when Notre Dame coach Jesse Harper wrote a letter to the Army team asking them if they had an opening in their schedule "and if so, would they give us a game." There was an opening on November 1, 1913, so Army invited Notre Dame to come and play at West Point.

Notre Dame's quarterback, Charley Dorais, and left end, Knute Rockne, had spent much of their summer vacation practicing forward passes on the beaches of Lake Erie. "Perfection came to us only through daily, tedious practice," Rockne wrote in 1930.

Notre Dame played three games before meeting Army, racking up 169 points—all from forward passing—and giving up only seven

As of the end of the fall 2000 season, they've won 113 games in a row over 10 years.

to its opponents. But not many people noticed because the school wasn't a major football power at the time.

No one—least of all the Army team—was prepared for the events at West Point that first day of November. "We went out to play Army like crusaders, believing we represented not only our own school but the whole aspiring Middle West," Rockne remembered. "The Cadet body and most of the other spectators seemed to regard the engagement as a quiet, friendly work-out for the Army."

SNEAK ATTACK

Notre Dame began the first quarter playing a fairly conventional game; its defensive line held against Army, forcing them to kick. When Notre Dame got the ball, Dorais's first attempts at throwing short passes failed; then he told his teammates, "Let's open things up."

The next pass was successful; Dorais only threw it 11 yards, but it so startled Army that they held a huddle to discuss it. Following one particularly rough scrimmage, Rockne started limping as if he'd been hurt, and continued limping through the next three plays, as Notre Dame advanced steadily down to the Army 25-yard line. The normally boisterous crowd was silent as it took in the Midwesterners' new kind of game.

"After that third play," he remembered, "the Army halfback covering me figured I wasn't worth watching. Even as a decoy, he figured I was harmless." On the next play, Dorais signaled that he would throw the next pass to Rockne. Football was about to change forever:

> I started limping down the field, and the Army halfback covering me almost yawned in my face, he was that bored. I put on full speed and left him standing there flat-footed. I raced across the Army goal line as Dorais whipped the ball, and the grandstands roared at the completion of a 40-yard pass. Everybody seemed astonished. There had been no hurdling, no tackling, no plunging, no crushing of fiber and sinew. At the moment when I touched the ball, life for me was complete.

A WHOLE NEW BALL GAME

Notre Dame went on to complete 14 out of 17 passes, gaining 243 yards and scoring five touchdowns in the process, beating Army 35–13. The potential of the forward pass was laid out for everyone to see: A team that few people had heard of had come roaring out of the Midwest to humble a major Eastern football power, master of the old-style game, on their own home field.

"Goliath," Tom Perrin writes in *Football: A College History*, "learned again what a missile can do in the hands of David."

With the arrival of the forward pass, all the major elements of modern football were in place. Very little has changed in the game since then, except for the advent of pro football and the NFL...but that's another story, perhaps for the next Bathroom Reader.

* * *

...THE GOOD OLD DAYS

"There was no bad blood between [Yale and Princeton], but...in the very first scrimmage it became apparent that the practice of turning one cheek when the other is smitten is not to be entertained for a moment. As the game progressed, this fact became more potent. The eye of the umpire was the only thing they feared, and when his attention was diverted the surreptitious punches, gouges, and kicks were frequent and damaging....The favorite methods of damaging an opponent were to stamp on his feet, to kick his shins, to give him a dainty upper cut, and to gouge his face in tackling."

—*The New York Times*, **describing the national championship game between Yale and Princeton in 1888**

LET'S PLAY MAYA BALL

"Among the Maya the ball game was related to fertility, the sun, warfare, and sacrifice by decapitation. A high-ranking captive might be forced to play a game in which he might lose his head. Courts were often built against staircases. In some well-documented instances, the loser in the game was taken to the top, bound up to form a ball, and rolled down the stairs to his death."

—*The Aztecs, Maya, and Their Predecessors*, **by Muriel Porter Weaver**

CASTLE GRANDE

Was it the world's most expensive private residence...or the world's biggest white elephant? Luckily, California's Hearst Castle is open for public tours. Pay it a visit and see for yourself.

OTHER PEOPLE'S MONEY
In 1894 William Randolph Hearst, age 31, a member of one of California's wealthiest families and the publisher of the *San Francisco Examiner*, commissioned an architect to build a mansion on a large tract of land in Pleasanton, California.

Somehow, he never got around to telling the owner—his mother—he was building himself a house on her property. When she found out, she took it and kept it for herself. There wasn't much William could do about it—his mother, the widow of U.S. Senator George Hearst, controlled the family's entire $20 million fortune. William hadn't inherited a penny of his father's estate and had nothing in his own name, not even the *Examiner*. His mother owned that, too.

Twenty-five years later, Hearst, now 56, wanted to build a hilltop house on the 60,000-acre ranch his mother owned in San Simeon, a small coastal whaling town halfway between San Francisco and Los Angeles. Hearst was fond of camping with his family and an entourage of as many as 50 guests and servants at the site, but wanted something "a little more comfortable."

A SLIGHT CHANGE IN PLANS

By now Hearst was well on his way to becoming one of the most powerful publishers in the country...but his mother still controlled the family fortune. He must have learned something from his 1894 experience, because he told his mother about the plan for San Simeon *before* he started construction, and he limited himself to a single tiny "Jappo-Swisso bungalow." Mrs. Hearst agreed to let him build, but insisted on keeping the property in her name because, she explained, "I'm afraid he might get carried away." She had good reason to worry.

Just a few months later, in April 1919, Hearst's mother died of influenza. William, her only son, inherited everything...and began rethinking his simple bungalow. He told architect Julia Morgan that he wanted something a little bigger.

"I don't think it was a month before we were going on a grand scale," Morgan's employee Walter Steilberg remembered. The bungalow quickly evolved into a large house...then a mansion... and finally one *enormous* mansion called Casa Grande, surrounded by three smaller "cottages"—Casa del Sol, Casa del Mar, and Casa del Monte—giving the hilltop retreat the appearance of an entire Mediterranean hill town.

Hearst called it *La Cuesta Encantata*, "The Enchanted Hill." To the public, it would become known as Hearst Castle.

AN UPHILL BATTLE

That was the plan, but as Julia Morgan explained to Hearst, bringing the large project to completion would not be easy or cheap. For one thing, there was no paved road and the rocky, barren spot where Hearst wanted to build was 1,600 feet up, which meant there was no easy way to get construction materials to the site. And with no topsoil, there was no way to plant the trees and gardens Hearst wanted, either. Furthermore, San Simeon was in the middle of nowhere, which meant that skilled workers would have to be brought in from hundreds of miles away and housed and fed on site.

None of this mattered to Hearst. He'd loved San Simeon since childhood, and for the first time in his life he had the money to build his dream house. Nothing was going to get in his way. The dirt trail up the hill was paved; the pier in the town of San Simeon was enlarged to allow steamships to unload construction materials; dormitories were constructed for the workers; and tons of topsoil were hauled up to the site, enough to bury 50 acres of land under four feet of dirt. Construction began in 1919...and was still underway more than 30 years later when Hearst died in August 1951

SALE OF THE CENTURY

While Morgan was working on the building plans, Hearst was ha.d at work indulging what his mother had once described as his "mania for antiquities"—he spent millions of dollars acquiring entire train-loads of antiques to furnish and decorate the 165 rooms—including 56 bedrooms and 19 sitting rooms—and the 61 bathrooms that made up his estate. His timing was perfect: cash-strapped European governments were instituting income and estate taxes to finance rebuilding in the aftermath of World War I. Once-wealthy families found themselves having to auction off artwork, antiques, and even entire castles, monasteries, and country estates to raise cash to pay their taxes. Hearst was their biggest customer.

RECYCLED MATERIALS

Hearst was especially fond of acquiring "architectural fragments"—floors, doorways, windows, mantles, chimneys, etc.—that could be carted off to San Simeon and set into the concrete walls of his estate. For more than 20 years, he compulsively bought just about everything that caught his eye and shipped it across the Atlantic to warehouses in the Bronx; from there most of it was sent by rail to warehouses in San Simeon.

Hearst peppered Julia Morgan with suggestions on which artifacts should go where, and none of these treasures were too sacred to be "improved" if need be. If something was too small, Morgan had it enlarged; if it was too big, she had chopped it down to size. "So far we have received from Hearst, to incorporate into the new buildings, some 12 or 13 railroad cars of antiques," Morgan wrote in 1920:

> They comprise vast quantities of tables, beds, armoires, secretaries, all kinds of cabinets, church statuary, columns, door frames, carved doors in all stages of repair and disrepair, over-altars, reliquaries, lanterns, iron grille doors, window grilles, votive candlesticks, torchères, all kinds of chairs in quantity, door trims, wooden carved ceilings....I don't see myself where we are ever going to use half suitably, but I find that the idea is to try things out and if they are not satisfactory, discard them for the next thing that comes that promises better.

THE COLLECTOR

Not all of this booty ended up at Hearst Castle—Hearst owned a castle in Wales, a beachfront mansion in Santa Monica, a 50,000-acre estate near Mt. Shasta in the northern part of California, and more. But he bought more antiques, artworks, and architectural fragments than even these buildings could hold; to this day thousands of his purchases sit in their original packing crates in Hearst Corporation warehouses around the country.

If you're an average adult, you'll eat 2,000 pounds of food this year.

COMPANY'S COMING

By the mid-1920s, enough of the construction had been completed at San Simeon to allow Hearst to begin entertaining guests as diverse as Winston Churchill, Charlie Chaplin, Calvin Coolidge, and George Bernard Shaw. He provided them with plenty to do: hiking, trout fishing, horseback riding, and tennis; there was also a billiard room, library, movie theater, and indoor and outdoor swimming pools. If guests wanted to play golf, there was even an airplane standing by to fly them to the nearest course. If they wanted to look at elephants, giraffes, or other exotic animals, that wasn't a problem either: Hearst's estate was also home to the largest privately owned zoo in the world.

A FEW SMALL PROBLEMS

When guests arrived at the estate, they quickly discovered that for all its grandeur, it wasn't very comfortable. Some guest rooms gave up so much space to antiques and art that there wasn't any room left for closets. The buildings could also be quite drafty, and the chimneys smoked terribly.

Hearst's peculiar quirks as host added to the discomfort. He didn't believe in serving his guests breakfast in bed, or even bringing them coffee. There were no kitchens in the guest houses, so anyone who wanted something to eat had to get dressed and come to Casa Grande.

The cocktail hour before dinner was another oddity. It could last as long as two hours or more, but Hearst served only one cocktail to each guest (two if you arrived early, drank quickly, and got lucky). Anyone caught smuggling their own liquor into San Simeon soon found their bags packed and set next to the car that was waiting to take them away.

Rationing his booze may have come back to haunt Hearst in ways he could never have imagined: one of his most ungrateful guests was a hard-drinking writer named Herman Mankiewicz, who went on to co-write the screenplay for *Citizen Kane*, a film about a "fictional" newspaper baron who lives in an enormous castle called Xanadu, an obvious blast at Hearst (see page 355).

Hearst was one of the wealthiest men in the country, but the Great Depression finally caught up with him in 1936; he found himself more than $100 million in debt at a time when newspaper circulation and advertising revenues were sharply off. At 74, he lost control of his business empire and was forced to sell off real estate, newspapers, and half of his art collection. He managed to hang on to San Simeon, but only by agreeing to halt construction and paying "rent" to his creditors until his financial situation improved.

HE'S BA-A-ACK

Hearst finally regained control in 1945 when he was 82, and immediately resumed construction at San Simeon. But Hearst's health was deteriorating, and in 1947 he was forced to move to Los Angeles to be closer to his doctors. He never returned to his castle, and died in August 1951 at the age of 88.

The Hearst Corporation directors were not nearly as infatuated with San Simeon as Hearst had been—they wanted to get rid of it. But nobody would buy it, because nobody could afford it.

The company offered it to the University of California free of charge...but the university refused to accept the "gift" unless it was accompanied by a huge endowment to cover operating costs. Finally in 1958, the corporation donated the buildings and the surrounding land to the State of California, which now operates it as a tourist attraction.

THE BIG QUESTION: HOW MUCH DID IT COST?

William Randolph Hearst spent so much money so quickly over so many years that it's difficult to calculate just how much he spent building and furnishing San Simeon. *The Guinness Book of World Records* estimates that he spent as much as $30 million (or $277 million in 2001 dollars). By contrast, Microsoft founder Bill Gates's mansion cost only $60 million.

That makes Hearst Castle easily the most expensive private residence ever built...and it's still unfinished.

*   *   *

"I do not seek, I find."
—Picasso

Survey says: most adults believe we will make "first contact" with alien life by the year 2100.

MYTH-ADVENTURE: THE TRUE STORY OF CAPTAIN KIDD

*Here at the BRI, we're huge fans of Richard Zacks' books.
They're great bathroom reading. He has a new book coming out:*
The Pirate Hunter—The True Story of Captain Kidd. *Here's
a teaser from his masterpiece,* An Underground Education

WORKIN' FOR THE MAN

While the popular image of buccaneers is peg-legged,
eye-patched rascals, the ultimate anti-authority free
agents, roving the seas, plundering ships, raping women, and brawling, the reality is much worse. They did all that *and* worked for the
government.

Prior to 1856, it was standard operating procedure for western
nations either to commission privateers directly or to wink at the
actions of freelance pirates, so long as those thieves were preying
on the commerce of other nations. Piracy was often state-supported
economic terrorism. Captain Kidd, for example, was no Joan of Arc,
but he was no "Captain Kidd," either.

MEET CAPTAIN KIDD

William Kidd (c. 1645–1701) was a plain-speaking, high-tempered
Scotsman who had made his fortune as captain and ship owner,
trading goods in the colonies. In 1696, the 51-year-old Kidd was
a prosperous New York businessman, comfortably settled with his
wife and family. That year, Kidd and his friend Robert Livingston
connived with the newly appointed governor of New England,
Richard Coote, Earl of Bellamont, the King of England's cousin,
to receive an unusual privateering commission.

In times of war, wealthy investors routinely funded privateering
vessels to attack the enemy's merchant ships and divvy the plunder.
This was an English naval tradition dating back to Sir Frances Drake.
But what was extraordinary about this commission was that it also
entitled Kidd to attack pirate ships of all nationalities and keep their

Johanne Relleke of Rhodesia was stung by bees 2,443 times on January 28, 1962. He survived.

booty—no questions asked. It was an amazing financial opportunity.

SMART INVESTMENT

Kidd's royal commission—secured by Bellamont—did, in fact,

> give and grant full Power and Authority to Captain William Kidd, Commander of the ship Adventure Galley...to apprehend, seize and take into Custody the said Thomas Too, John Ireland, Tho Wake, and William Maze, and all other Pirates, Free-booters and Sea-Rovers, of what Nation whatsoever, whom he should find or meet with, upon the said Coasts or Seas of America, or in any other Seas or Parts, with their Ships and Vessels, and all such Merchandize, Money, Goods, and Wares as should be found on board of them.

The mission began as an attempt by Britain to crack down on four colonial pirates, but was cunningly expanded so that Kidd would have maximum leeway to capture "prizes"—non-English ships.

In addition to Livingston and Lord Richard, four of the most powerful men in England secretly invested the £6,000 it would cost to outfit the ship. The prospect of profits from this legal larceny was dizzying. If Kidd captured two large ships, the backers could easily receive a hundredfold return on that investment in a year. In the official contract with Kidd, four obscure merchants were listed as the investors, but they were shills. The real backers were John Somers, Lord Chancellor of England; Sir Robert Wadpole, Earl of Orford, First Lord of the Admiralty; and two secretaries of state, the Earl of Romney and the Duke of Shrewsbury. The king was to receive 10% of the booty as well, "chiefly to show that he was a partner in the undertaking," according to *The Real Captain Kidd—A Vindication*, by Sir Cornelius Dalton. Kidd and Livingston stood to receive 7.5% each, while if the haul totaled more than £100,000, Kidd was to be allowed to keep the ship.

SHAKY START

The mission got off to a bad start in March 1696; Kidd and a London merchant handpicked 100-plus English sailors for the *Adventure Galley*, but before they departed the coast, a British man-of-war seized the bulk of his crew. Now, Kidd sailed to New York to round up a new crew, but his articles allowed him to offer the crew shares of only a quarter of the spoils (instead of the usual half) and there

Tombstones were originally put over graves so that the dead could not escape.

would be no regular wages; the voyage would be strictly "no pur-chase, no pay," or in sailor slang, "no prey, no pay."

Kidd was forced to sign the piratical scum of the New York wharf, out-of-work scallywags. Once out of the harbor, he had no luck whatsoever at finding pirate ships, and headed to the Indian Ocean. He was fired upon, but when he captured the vessel, it turned out to be a Dutch ship. His crew—led by gunner William Moore—voted to take her as a prize anyhow, but Kidd, pistols in hand, changed their mind. Kidd then spied a merchant ship and swung into action. Employing a standard battle tactic, he flew French colors to trick his adversary and lured the giant *Quedagh Merchant* to come alongside. When an officer of that ship boarded, holding French papers of clear passage, Kidd hoisted the British flag and declared the ship captured. Although the *Quedagh Merchant* was clearly an Arme-nian ship with a crew of Moors and a few Christians aboard, the officer presented French papers, which made it a legitimate prize, given the state of war at the time between England and France. And it was a rich prize. The *Quedagh Merchant* was packed with fine cloths, silks, and jewels, worth per-haps as much as £400,000.

MUTINY!

Kidd who had taken another ship traveling with French papers, hauled his prizes back to Ste.-Marie, in Madagascar. His articles stated that he must take the captured ships back to Boston (or to London, if armed British escort appeared) so that an Admiralty Court could rule on whether they were legitimate captures and could document the spoils.

In Madagascar stood the *Moca Frigate*, a former merchant ship turned pirate by a man named Robert Culliford. When Kidd (with his mounted cannon) hit port, his pirates abandoned ship. Kidd had proposed that they capture the *Moca* as well, but instead, his men swore they'd shoot him if he tried. Ninety-seven of them mutinied over to Culliford and promptly attacked Kidd.

Receiving no wages with Kidd, the most the men could hope for was a share of one-quarter of the spoils, *if* an admiralty court ruled in their favor in Boston; with Culliford, they might split up everything, and right away. Here's how Kidd described what hap-pened next:

The said Deserters came on board, and carried away Guns, Powder, Shot, small Arms, Sails, Anchors, Cables, Surgeon's Chests, and what else they pleased; and threatened several times to murder the Narrator [i.e., Kidd]. Their Wickedness was so great, after they had plundered and ransacked sufficiently, [they] went Four Miles off to one Edward Weiche's House, which his the Narrator's chest was lodged, and broke it open; and took out Ten Ounces of Gold, 40 Pound of Plate, 370 Pieces of Eight, the Narrator's Journal, and a great many Papers that belonged to him, and the People of New York that fitted them out.

OUT OF LUCK

Kidd was left with 13 sailors; his original ship was leaking badly (requiring 8-man shifts to bail her out); and his prize was far too big to sail with his reduced crew. The date was early in 1699.

Kidd was two years past his contracted return date, and no doubt his powerful backers were getting nervous. And now the East India Company reported in London that "they had received some information...that Kidd had committed several acts of piracy, particularly in seizing a Moorish ship called the *Quedagh Merchant*."

The vastly profitable East India Company had no desire to enrage the great mogul of India by allowing British pirates to prey upon Moorish ships, especially since the great mogul, a now-forgotten potentate, then controlled an enormous empire and could expel the Brits.

With a single order, Kidd was officially declared a pirate.

BAD TRIP

Captain Kidd spent six long months in Madagascar trying to round up a crew, then headed for Boston. When Kidd and his skeleton crew finally reached Anguilla in the West Indies and found out they were wanted for piracy, they were dumbfounded. Once again the crew started deserting. Kidd no longer had sailors enough to sail his prize to Boston, so he traded for a smaller ship complete with crew and moved an undisclosed portion of the remaining booty aboard. (How much booty has intrigued treasure hunters ever since.)

Kidd could have stayed in the Caribbean a very wealthy man. At least £10,000 of treasure remained and possibly as much as £40,000 or even more. Instead he sailed north. In New York Harbor, he handed over the two French passes (which would clear him of the piracy charges) to an old friend to deliver to his backer, New England governor Coote, who was then in Boston.

SAVED?

Coote (as you remember, cousin to the king of England) sent the postmaster of Boston out to Block Island to give a message to Kidd. The note declared the governor was sympathetic to Kidd's version of the events and then concluded:

> I make no manner of doubt but to obtain the King's pardon for you, and for those few men you have left who I understand have been faithful to you, and refused as well as you to dishonour the Commission you have from England....I assure you on my Word and Honour I will perform nicely what I have promised.

Kidd, who was joined on ship by his wife and family, responded with great relief to the news that the governor would take up his cause; and he guessed aloud that the East India Company must have heard of acts of piracy committed by Captain Robert Culliford, using the mutinied members of Kidd's former crew. But, on July 1, 1699, when Kidd and his few remaining crew members sailed into Boston Harbor, Governor Coote promptly had them arrested.

England dispatched a Navy ship to ferry Kidd back to justice. The House of Commons sniffed a scandal and demanded that Kidd not be tried until it was back in session. Unfortunately for Kidd, that meant spending a year in Newgate Prison.

ON TRIAL

On March 6, 1701, the House of Commons began to examine Kidd's papers. Included among them, as clearly stated in the Parliament papers, were Two French Passes from the ships Kidd had captured. Nonetheless, Kidd was ordered to stand trial in Admiralty Court—and it was specifically stated that his papers should be delivered there for his trial. The court then stunned Kidd by charging him not with piracy but with the murder of William Moore, the ship's gunner.

Testimony from paid informants painted the following picture of the crime. While the ship was anchored off the coast of Africa, after more than a year without taking a single prize, Kidd called Moore a "lousy dog." Moore replied: "If I be so, you have made me

---

Lightning bolts are only about two inches wide.

one." Kidd, in a rage, swung an iron-hooped bucket, which caught Moore flush in the temple. Moore died the next day.

BETRAYED

Kidd claimed that he never meant to kill Moore, and that threat of mutiny had been strong at the time. Testifying for the Crown were two of Kidd's crew who had mutinied, signed up with Culliford, and gone out on later pirate voyages; they were offered pardons in exchange for turning Crown's evidence.

After one especially absurd statement, Kidd complained: "It signifies nothing to ask any questions. These rogues will swear to anything." Then later, he asked: "Have you not been promised your life to swear away mine?"

The judge intervened: "He is not bound to answer that question. He is very fit to be made as evidence for the Crown."

It took the jury an hour to bring in a guilty verdict.

As for the piracy charges, the judge, Lord Chief Baron, shaped the trial so that it all hinged on whether or not Captain Kidd received French passes from the captured ships, which apparently never found their way to the Admiralty Court. The lord chief summed up:

> And as to the French passes there is nothing of that appears by any proof; and for aught I can see, none saw them but himself, if there ever were any. "Four respected British officers testified to Kidd's valor during the French war in the Caribbean and one noted that Kidd had fought off a mutiny to prevent his ship from going 'a-pirating.'"

But Kidd was convicted of piracy. When sentenced to death, he told the court: "My lord, it is a very hard sentence. For my part, I am the innocentest person of them all, only I have been sworn against by perjured persons."

THE END?

In prison, Kidd refused to confess to the chaplain and refused repeated requests to cast blame on the ministers that backed his mission. (Perhaps he was still hoping for a pardon.) On May 24, 1701, Captain William Kidd was brought to Execution Dock at Wapping. The noose about his neck, he kicked out unto eternity and the rope broke. Kidd would have to be re-hoisted up the ladder and turned off a second time. In the little waiting period, he told the chaplain at the gallows that his greatest sorrow was leaving his wife and children in New York without getting a chance to say good-bye.

The next day in Parliament, Lord Chancellor Somers admitted he had had a secret share in Kidd's voyage but claimed there was nothing illegal in that. In fact, he pointed out that "owners of the said ship had lost their expenses and had not received any benefit from the grant."

The East India Company soon after reported to the great mogul of India that the "evil pirate" Captain Kidd had been hanged. Britain's inroads in India eventually led to conquering the entire subcontinent.

Robert Culliford, the pirate captain of the *Moca Frigate*, applied for pardon and, with a lawyer at his side, was granted amnesty by the Admiralty Court.

Kidd's hard-earned estate was forfeited after his hanging, taken from his wife and children. Queen Anne used the money to found the Greenwich Hospital.

The British Admiralty dangled Captain Kidd's dead body—encased in pine resin and bound by leather straps—for years from a specially constructed gallows over the Thames River to serve as a warning to other pirates.

*   *   *

BLAH BLAH BLAH (BLAH)

Bla, blablah bla "blabla." Blah bla, bla blah bla. Bla blabla.

Blah bla bla blah bla? Bla bla bla, Bla Blablablah, bla blah bla bla bla. Blá blabla. Blah bla-blabla blah. Bla—bla *blabla*—bla. Blabla blabla; bla blah, bla bla bla'a bla. Bla "bläbla." Blah bla-blabla bla. Blabla Blabla Blå bla blah?

Blah blablah bla.

"Blah blabla," bla Blablablah, "Bla blah bla blabla...blah bla, 'bla bla bla.'" Blabláh bla—bla blabla blá bla—bla blahbla bla. Blabla Blablablah blah bla bla-blâbla. Bla bla, bla blabla, bla bláh bla. Bla bla: *blabla* bla. Bla Blablablah, "Bla bla bla bla, bla bla'a blablah. Blah BLA BLA BLA!"

JOIN THE PARTY

Pop quiz: What does the U.S. Constitution say about political parties? Answer: Nothing—there were no political parties immediately after the American Revolution, and the Founding Fathers hoped there never would be. So how did the political parties come to be? Here's how.

PARTY POOPERS

For all the diversity of opinion among the Founding Fathers in the 1770s, there was one thing that virtually everyone agreed upon: political parties were a *very* bad idea.

In his farewell address as president, George Washington referred to political parties as "the worst enemy" of democratic governments, "potent engines by which cunning, ambitious and unprincipled men will...subvert the power of the people." Alexander Hamilton equated political parties with "ambition, avarice, and personal animosity." And Thomas Jefferson could hardly agree more: "If I could go to heaven but with a party," he wrote, "I would not go there at all."

ENGLISH LESSONS

The Founding Fathers' abhorrence of political parties was in response to the partisan politics that characterized England's House of Commons. The Commons was supposed to serve as a check on the power of the monarch, but successive kings had been able to use their vast wealth, power, and control of public offices to create a party of royalists. Thus, it had been reduced to members fighting among themselves instead of working together to advance the common good.

This was what the Founding Fathers were trying to avoid in the United States: warring factions that would pursue selfish interests at the expense of the nation.

But what exactly *was* the national interest? And if the Founding Fathers couldn't agree on what the national interest was, who among them got to decide? These fundamental questions caused the first factions to form in American political life.

Grover Cleveland got more popular votes in the 1888 presidential election,

FIRST FEUD: THE ARTICLES OF CONFEDERATION

Bringing the original 13 colonies together to form the United States had not been easy. The Founding Fathers drafted the first U.S. Constitution, the Articles of Confederation, in 1777, but it was flawed. The Americans had just won independence from one central government—England—and they were reluctant to surrender the power of the individual states to a new central government, so they intentionally made that government weak.

But it soon became obvious that the federal government established by the Articles of Confederation was too weak to be effective at all. The most glaring problem was that it had no power to tax the states, which meant that it had no means of raising money to pay for an army to protect its territories from encroachment by Britain and Spain. In 1787 a constitutional convention was held in Philadelphia to draw up an entirely new document.

It was during the debates over the creation and ratification of the new constitution that some of the first and most significant political divisions in American history began to emerge. Those who supported the idea of strengthening the federal government by weakening the states were known as "Federalists," and those who opposed the new constitution became known as the "Anti-Federalists."

The Federalists won the first round: 9 of the 13 states ratified the U.S. Constitution, and Congress set March 4, 1789 as the date it would go into effect. Elections for Congress and the presidency were held in late 1788. George Washington ran unopposed and was elected president.

TROUBLE IN THE CABINET

Washington saw the presidency as an office aloof from partisan divisions and hoped his administration would govern the same way. But by 1792, Washington's cabinet had split into factions over the financial policies of Alexander Hamilton, the secretary of the treasury.

Perhaps because he was born in the British West Indies and thus did not identify strongly with the interests of any particular state, Hamilton was the foremost Federalist of his age. He strongly believed in using the power of the federal government to develop the American economy. In 1790 he proposed having the government assume the remaining unpaid Revolutionary War debts of the states and the Continental Congress. This would help establish the creditworthiness of the new nation, albeit by enriching the speculators who bought up the war debt when most people thought it would never be repaid. Hamilton's plan also meant that states that had already paid off their war debt would now be asked to help pay off the debts of states that hadn't, which added to the controversy.

Secretary of State Thomas Jefferson supported the new Constitution but had Anti-Federalist leanings. He grudgingly agreed to support Hamilton's plan, on one condition: Hamilton had to support Jefferson's plan to locate the new capital city on the banks of the Potomac River. Hamilton agreed.

Hamilton got his debt plan, and Jefferson got Washington, D.C. (Jefferson later regretted the deal, calling it one of the greatest mistakes of his life.)

A BATTLE ROYAL

Then in December 1790, Hamilton proposed having Congress charter a Bank of the United States as a means to regulate U.S. currency. This time Jefferson thought Hamilton had gone too far. He vehemently opposed the idea, arguing that a national bank would benefit the commercial North more than the agricultural South (Jefferson was a Southerner), and would further enrich the wealthy while doing little to help common people.

Hamilton's financial policies, Jefferson said, were intended to create "an influence of his [Treasury] department over the members of the legislature," creating a "corrupt squadron" of congressmen and senators who would work "to get rid of the limitations imposed by the Constitution [and] prepare the way for a change, from the present republican form of government, to that of a monarchy, of which the English constitution is to be a model."

SPLITTING UP

Like Jefferson, Hamilton deplored political parties. But he and his supporters were also adamant about chartering a national bank and strengthening the powers of the Federal government. Faced with the determined opposition of Jefferson and his allies, they began to organize what became known as the Federalist Party.

Jefferson also began to organize. In May 1791, he and fellow

Columbus traveled at an average speed of 2.8 mph on his first voyage across the sea.

Virginian James Madison made a trip to New York to meet with State Chancellor Robert Livingston, New York governor George Clinton, and U.S. Senator Aaron Burr.

"The meetings among the New York and Virginia leaders, however informal, were among the most fateful in American history," A. James Reichley writes in *The Life of the Parties*. "The first links were formed in an alliance that was to last, in one form or another, for almost 150 years and that was to be a major shaping force in national politics from the administration of Jefferson to that of Franklin Roosevelt."

Jefferson, Madison, and the others saw themselves as defenders of the new republic against Hamilton and the "monarchical Federalists." The party they formed became known as the Democratic-Republicans, or Republicans for short. Historians consider them the first opposition party in U.S. history, as well as the direct antecedent of the modern Democratic Party.

ONE SETBACK AFTER ANOTHER

The Democratic-Republicans lost their battle: Hamilton pushed his bank legislation through Congress, and President Washington signed it into law. They lost another major battle in 1792, when Governor Clinton ran against John Adams for vice president and lost. A third defeat came in 1796 when Washington declined to run for a third term as president: Jefferson ran for president against Vice President Adams...and lost by only three electoral votes.

THE ALIEN AND SEDITION ACTS

In 1793 France—which was in the throes of its own revolution—declared war against England, giving the Federalists and Democratic-Republicans something new to disagree about. The Jeffersonian Republicans sided with republican France, and the Federalists sided with England; neither side thought the United States should get involved in the war. Partisan emotions intensified in 1796, when the French began an undeclared war on American shipping as part of their war against England and refused to receive President Adam's minister to France.

Angered by the insults, the Federalists began preparing for what they thought was an imminent war with France. They tripled the size of the army, authorized the creation of the U.S. Navy (the Continental Navy had been disbanded in 1784), and then in the face of the unanimous opposition of the Democratic-Republicans in Congress, passed what became known as the Alien and Sedition Acts.

The Alien Acts said that aliens (who were assumed to have Democratic-Republican leanings) had to live in the United States for 14 years—up from 5—before they would be eligible to vote. The acts also permitted the detention of citizens of enemy nations and increased the president's power to deport "dangerous" aliens. The Sedition Act outlawed all associations whose purpose was "to oppose any measure or measures of the government of the United States," and imposed stiff punishments for writing, printing, or saying anything against the U.S. government.

READING BETWEEN THE LINES

By the time the Alien and Sedition Acts expired or were repealed four years later, only one alien had been deported and only 10 people were convicted of sedition, including a New Jersey man who was fined $100 for publicly "wishing that a wad from the presidential saluting cannon might 'hit Adams in the ass.' "

But no one knew that back in 1798. To Jefferson and his supporters, it was obvious that the Alien Acts, and especially the Sedition Act, were targeted at them. Republicans could now be fined or jailed for speaking out against the Adams administration, and if they weren't U.S. citizens, they could even be deported.

The fact that the Sedition Act expired following the 1800 presidential election seemed to prove their suspicions that the law was intended to curb Anti-Federalist dissent. While the acts were in force, Adams and the Federalists were legally protected from Democratic-Republican criticism, but if they happened to lose the election of 1800, the expiration of the Sedition Act would leave them free to criticize the Democratic-Republicans.

There was more: The Democratic-Republicans also feared that Adams, having tripled the size of the Army, would begin using it against his political opponents. As if to confirm their fears, in 1799 Adams called out Federal troops to put down an anti-tax rebellion led by Pennsylvania farmers opposed to taxes levied for the anticipated war with France.

Tough guy: When Martin Van Buren was vice president,

The Democratic-Republicans were convinced that if the Federalists remained in power, democracy's days were numbered, so they began mounting their strongest effort yet to capture the White House and the Congress.

A TOUGH CALL

John Adams had mixed feelings about running for reelection. He hated living in Washington, D.C., and he hated being president. The president "has a very hard, laborious, and unhappy life," he warned his son John Quincy Adams. "No man who ever held the office of president would congratulate a friend on obtaining it." And now that he was completely toothless, he was incapable of making public speeches in support of his candidacy for re-election.

The only reason Adams ran at all was because he was determined to prevent Jefferson from getting the job. Adams liked Jefferson personally, but he saw himself and Jefferson as "the North and South poles of the American Revolution." He strongly disagreed with Jefferson's views on government and the Constitution, and feared that Jefferson would drag the country into a European war to defend France.

CHANGE OF FORTUNE

The Democratic-Republicans, who believed that freedom was on the line, had no such reluctance—although Jefferson, announcing that he would "stand" for election rather than "run" for it, remained at his Monticello estate during the campaign. The party fought a hard campaign for him.

On election day, Adams carried New England, and Jefferson won most of the South. New York proved to be the swing state, which helped Jefferson, because his running mate was Aaron Burr. As founder and head of the Tammany political machine in New York, Burr was able to deliver the state to Jefferson, allowing him to win the presidency with 73 electoral votes to Adams's 65. The Democratic-Republicans also won control of both houses of Congress.

FEDERALIST FAREWELL

The Federalists had accomplished much in the years following the Revolution: they had succeeded in drafting the U.S. Constitution, which strengthened the power of the Federal government; they had enacted economic programs that strengthened credit and helped the economy grow.

But by 1800 their best days were behind them. "Federalism, as a political movement, was a declining force around the turn of the century," historian Paul Johnson writes in *A History of the American People*, "precisely because it was a party of the elite, without popular roots, at a time when democracy was spreading fast among the states. Adams was the last of the Federalist presidents, and he could not get himself re-elected."

THE LAST STRAW

It got worse for the Federalists. They vehemently opposed the War of 1812, and in the fall of 1814, when things seemed to be going very badly for the United States, Federalist delegates from New England met secretly in Hartford, Connecticut, to draft a series of resolutions listing their grievances with the Federal government, which a negotiating committee would then bring to Washington, D.C. Some of the delegates to the secret convention had even discussed seceding from the Union.

Bad timing: By the time the negotiating committee arrived in Washington to protest the war, it was not only over, it had actually ended on a *positive* note, thanks to Andrew Jackson's victory in the Battle of New Orleans.

When the rest of the country learned that the Federalists had been holding secret meetings to contemplate splitting off from the rest of the country, the party's image took a pounding. "Republican orators and publicists branded the Hartford convention an act of subversion during wartime," A. James Reichley writes, "ending what was left of Federalism as a political force."

But the die was cast. In spite of themeslves, the Founding Fathers had created what they most feared...political factions. The era of the two-party system in the United States had begun.

*   *   *

"Under democracy one party always devotes its chief energies to trying to prove that the other party is unfit to rule—and both commonly succeed and are right."

—H. L. Mencken

The
Back Side

You're not done yet:

Here are the answers
to the quizzes found on pages
61, 151, 223, 295, 361, and 395...

...And info about how to be a part
of the Bathroom Readers' Institute

BRI BRAINTEASERS
(Answers from page 223)

1. One hour. Windup clocks don't have A.M./P.M. settings.

2. He could, but he would be pretty uncomfortable being buried alive.

3. The match.

4. They've got different partners.

5. A 50-cent piece and a nickel. (Only one of them is not a nickel.)

6. The Earth is always under you, so you are eating *over* dirt?

7. His new computer/word processor is a pencil.

8. Nine.

9. He's the town minister.

10. One hour.

11. One. If he combines all of his haystacks, they all become one big stack.

*   *   *

TEST YOUR EGG I.Q.
(Answers from page 61)

1—c) Egg shells are porous—as an egg ages, moisture escapes and is replaced by outside air, causing it to become more buoyant over time. Fresh eggs contain the least air and sit right at the bottom of the glass; older eggs are lighter and tend to "stand" at the bottom. Rotten eggs contain so much air that they float right to the top.

2—c) Also known as "chalazae cords," these strands connect the yolk to the ends of the eggshell; the resulting "tug-of-war" helps to reduce movement and keep the yolk centered inside the egg.

24% of commuters say that when stuck in traffic, they think "deep thoughts."

3—b) Grade A and AA are the Food and Drug Administration's two highest egg classifications. They have nothing to do with the size, freshness, or vitamin content of the egg—they indicate the quality of the egg white and yolk. Grade AA eggs, slightly higher in quality, have the plumpest yolks and the thickest whites.

4—b) There's a pocket of air in the larger end of the egg and it's the most likely source of contamination from foreign bacteria. Storing the egg with the tapered end pointing down causes the yolk—which is more perishable than the white—to settle toward the tapered end, as far away from the air pocket as possible. When the egg is stored with the tapered end up, the yolk can settle right on top of the pocket, potentially speeding the rate at which the egg will spoil.

5—a) Raw eggs wobble because the white and yolk are still fluid and move around inside the egg when you spin it. Cooked eggs are at least partially solidified and have a much smoother spin.

* * *

THE RIDDLER
(Answers from page 151)

1. Wet.
2. Hi Bud.
3. A telephone.
4. Holds up the other one.
5. A dead bird.
6. Post office.
7. A glove.
8. None. It was Noah who brought them, not Moses.
9. A hole.
10. Noise.
11. A river.
12. The outside.
13. The letter T.
14. Nine.
15. A date.
16. Mash them.
17. A scale.
18. Silence.
19. Night and day.

The Earth weighs an estimated 100,000 tons more than it did one year ago today.

THE FOOD QUIZ
(Answers from page 395)

1—a) Light cream is heavier. "Heavy" and "light" refer to the fat content, not the weight. Heavy cream contains a higher percentage of milk fat (36%) than light cream (15%–18%), but since fat is lighter than water—the other major component of cream—increasing the percentage of fat reduces the percentage of water, lowering the overall weight.

2—c) The air in a jet plane in flight is lower in pressure and less humid than what most people are used to, which affects the way food tastes. The low pressure impairs the passengers' sense of taste by reducing the volatility of the molecules that give food its odor and taste. Low humidity causes people to become dehydrated, especially if they've been drinking alcohol or coffee—both are diuretics that cause your body to eliminate water. So it's not unusual for an airline to add extra seasoning, with the exception of salt, which would further increase the body's need for water.

3—c) The oils that irritate your eyes when you chop an onion have the same effect on your tastebuds and your sense of smell: they irritate your taste and smell receptors slightly, and in this "raw" state the receptors are more sensitive than they would be otherwise.

4—a) Air is whipped into ice cream as part of the manufacturing process, and it's not uncommon for manufacturers of cheaper brands to whip extra air into their ice cream, reducing the amount of actual ice cream in the container and lowering its weight. So if you want to try a new brand of ice cream but aren't sure how good it is, compare its weight to the same size container of a brand you're familiar with. If the unfamiliar brand weighs as much or more, it's likely to be similar or even better in quality.

5—b) Botanists consider only the "ovary" of a plant—the part that contains the seeds—to be the fruit; so technically speaking, pumpkins, tomatoes, cucumbers, peas, and even corn are all considered fruit. Any other part of a plant that is edible—the leaf, root, stem, and so on—is considered a vegetable.

6—a) It's true—apple seeds contain trace amounts of cyanide, as do apricot and peach seeds. But the amount of cyanide in a single apple seed is so small that it would take hundreds of seeds to amount to a lethal dose. And even if you ate that many seeds you'd probably survive unharmed, because the husk of an apple seed is so hard it's indigestible, even if it's been cooked. The apple seeds—and the cyanide they contain—would pass through your body completely intact.

7—b) Many people incorrectly believe that freezing food more than once makes it unsafe to eat. This myth dates back to the late 1920s, when frozen food pioneer Clarence Birdseye stamped the words "DO NOT FREEZE" on his packages of frozen foods. He feared that if people mishandled his products by repeatedly thawing and refreezing them, they'd blame the resulting poor quality on his company, which might harm sales. Some people mistakenly interpreted Birdseye's warning to mean that refreezing food is dangerous.

8—b) The most vitamin-rich part of the potato is the pulp just beneath the skin. When you peel a potato, you invariably remove some of the pulp in the process; that's why it's a good idea to cook potatoes with the skins on whenever possible.

9—c) Coffee beans from the port of Mocha in southwestern Yemen had lots of acid but not much flavor; beans from the port of Java in Indonesia had lots of flavor but not much acid. A well-rounded cup of coffee requires both acid *and* flavor, and it eventually occurred to people that blending the two types of beans would result in a better-tasting cup of coffee than was possible with Mocha or Java beans alone.

10—b) Marinades usually contain acids that tenderize meat. But in the process of tenderizing, they also degrade its ability to retain moisture, which makes the meat drier when cooked. So why bother marinating meat in the first place? It's a tradeoff—the tenderness and the flavor obtained by marinating the meat more than makes up for the loss of moisture…at least according to people who like marinades.

*   *   *

THE NAME GAME
(Answers from page 361)

1. GEORGE. "Farmer" from the Greek *georgos* "earth worker," which was derived from the elements *ge*, "earth," and *ergon*, "work."

2. AMY. "Beloved" from Old French *aimée*.

3. MICHAEL. From the Hebrew name *Mikha'el*, meaning "who is like God."

4. BARBARA. "Foreign" from the Greek *barbaros*.

5. DANIEL. "God is my judge" from the Hebrew name *Daniyel*.

6. EDWARD. "Rich guard" from the Old English *ead*, "rich, blessed," and *weard*, "guard."

7. AMANDA. "Lovable" from Latin *amanda*. This name was created in the 17th century by the playwright Colley Cibber.

8. HENRY. "Home ruler" from the Germanic *Heimerich*, which came from the elements *heim*, "home," and *ric*, "power" or "ruler."

9. JOEL. "YAHWEH is God," from the Hebrew name *Yoel*. Joel was a minor prophet in the Old Testament. YAHWEH is the name of the Hebrew God, represented in Hebrew by the "four letters" *Yod He Waw He*, and written in Roman script as *YHWH*. Because it was considered blasphemous to utter the name of God it was only written and never spoken, so the original pronunciation was lost.

10. SUSAN. From the Hebrew word *shoshan*, meaning "lily." In modern Hebrew, it also means "rose."

11. LINDA. "Beautiful" from the Spanish *Linda*

12. MELISSA. "Bee" from the Greek.

13. ANN. "Grace" from the French and German forms of *Hannah*.

14. ROBERT. "Bright fame" from Germanic *hrod*, "fame," and *beraht*, "bright."

Why does one Taiwan company make dinner plates out of wheat? So people can eat them.

15. STEPHEN. "Crown" from the Greek *stephanos*.

16. JOHN. English form of *Johannes*, the Latin form of the Greek name *Ioannes*, itself derived from the Hebrew name *Yochanan*, meaning "YAHWEH is gracious."

*   *   *

POLITICALLY CORRECT QUIZ
(Answers from page 295)

1—c) Demaret is the mother of David Vetter, a boy who suffered from a disease called "severe combined immunodeficiency" and died in 1984 at the age of 12. "The notion of making a comedy about a life-threatening disease is, in and of itself, a travesty," she writes. "It dishonors the memory of my son David and is an insult to families and children who are born with his disease and died from it."

Counters a Disney spokesman, "The bubble is a setup for a road-trip comedy. It doesn't make fun of immune deficiencies."

2—b) Public servants who gossip face reprimands, sensitivity training, and even dismissal if they refuse to stop. Council member Alcebiades Pereira da Silva says he drafted the law to stop incoming administrations from using gossip to persecute workers from previous administrations.

3—b) "It's a common mistake," says High Priest Kevin Carlyon. "Even the TV series *Bewitched* showed broomsticks being ridden backwards, but this is not correct."

4—a) They want to outlaw the cramped "gestation crates" used to house pregnant pigs. According to Floridians for Humane Farms, "Pigs confined in gestation crates experience chronic stress, frustration, depression, and other psychological disorders."

5—a) Willand also told students that Pocahontas "did handsprings in the nude." But the poster and the Pocahontas trivia "weren't meant to be offensive, they were just meant to perk attention." The school forbade Willand from using "phraseology which does not manifest a clear concern for student sensibilities." He's suing, alleging that the reprimand was "unjust."

6—b) "The website should be corrected," says Mangal Prabhat Lodha, a state legislator who says the cat's name is an insult. "We are not asking for a renaming. We just want mention of the cat to be removed from the website."

7—c) The group wants to replace "all thy sons" with "all of us" or "all our hearts." Protestor Frances Wright explains, "Parents of children in Canada don't call their girl children 'sons.'"

8—a) After studying corked and capped wines over a period of 24 months, the Institute found that metal screwcaps do a better job of helping white wine retain its sulfur dioxide, which protects against oxidation. "Up to this point, in retaining freshness and overall aroma, a screwcap has performed better," says a spokes-man. The Institute plans to continue the study over 10 years.

* * *

AUNT LENNA'S QUIZ
(Answers from page 457)

Uh-oh. Aunt Lenna refuses to tell us the answer. She says if we want to know we have to consult "Madame Bathroomia." But while we were waiting for Madame to return our call, we counted 82. How many did you count?

Uncle John's
Bathroom Reader series

Uncle John's **Supremely Satisfying** Bathroom Reader,
copyright © 2001, $16.95

Uncle John's **All-Purpose Extra Strength** Bathroom Reader,
copyright © 2000, $16.95

Uncle John's **Absolutely Absorbing** Bathroom Reader,
copyright © 1999, $16.95

Uncle John's **Great Big** Bathroom Reader,
copyright © 1998, $16.95

Uncle John's **Giant 10th Anniversary** Bathroom Reader,
copyright © 1997, $16.95

Uncle John's **Ultimate** Bathroom Reader (#8),
copyright © 1996, $12.95

The **Best of** Uncle John's Bathroom Reader,
our favorites from BRs #1–#7,
copyright © 1995, $16.95

Uncle John's **Legendary Lost** Bathroom Reader,
BRs #5, #6, & #7 together,
copyright © 1999, $18.95

U.S. shipping & handling rates:
• 1 book: $3.50 • 2–3 books: $4.50
• 4–5 books: $5.50 • 6–9 books: $1.00 per book

—— Contact Info ——

Bathroom Readers' Press
P.O. Box 1117, Ashland, OR 97520
Phone: 541-488-4642 Fax: 541-482-6159
brorders@mind.net / www.bathroomreader.com

Advanced Global Distib. (U.S.): 800-284-3580 / Fax: 800-499-3822
Raincoast Books (Canada): custserv@raincoast.com

VISIT THE BRI WEBSITE!

www.bathroomreader.com

• Visit the "Throne Room"—a great place to read!

• Receive our irregular newsletters via e-mail!

• Submit your favorite articles and facts!

• Suggest ideas for future editions!

• Order additional BRI books!

• Become a BRI member!

Go with the Flow!

THE LAST PAGE

FELLOW BATHROOM READERS:
The fight for good bathroom reading should never be taken loosely—we must sit firmly for what we believe in, even while the rest of the world is taking pot shots at us.

We've proven we're not simply a flush-in-the-pan.

So we invite you to take the plunge: Sit Down and Be Counted! by joining the Bathroom Readers' Institute. Send a self-addressed, stamped envelope to: BRI, P.O. Box 1117, Ashland, Oregon 97520. Or contact us through our website at *www.bathroomreader.com.* You'll receive your attractive free membership card and a copy of the BRI newsletter (sent out irregularly via e-mail), receive discounts when ordering directly through the BRI, and earn a permanent spot on the BRI honor roll!

ભ   ભ   ભ

UNCLE JOHN'S NEXT BATHROOM READER IS IN THE WORKS!

Don't fret—there's more good reading on the way. In fact, there are a few ways you can contribute to the next volume:

• Is there a subject you'd like to see us research? Write to us or contact us through our website (*www.bathroomreader.com*) and let us know. We aim to please.

• Have you seen or read an article you'd recommend as quintessential bathroom reading? Or is there a passage in a book or website that you want to share with us and other BRI members? Tell us how to find it. If you're the first to suggest it and we publish it in the next volume, there's a free book in it for you.

Well, we're out of space, and when you've gotta go, you've gotta go. Hope to hear from you soon. Meanwhile, remember:

Go with the flow!